THE CARTOON INTRODUCTION TO ECONOMICS

VOLUME ONE: MICROECONOMICS

THE CARTOON INTRODUCTION TO ECONOMICS

VOLUME ONE: MICROECONOMICS

BY **GRADY KLEIN** AND **YORAM BAUMAN, Ph.D.**
THE WORLD'S FIRST AND ONLY **STAND-UP ECONOMIST**

A NOVEL GRAPHIC FROM HILL AND WANG
A DIVISION OF FARRAR, STRAUS AND GIROUX
NEW YORK

HILL AND WANG
A DIVISION OF FARRAR, STRAUS AND GIROUX
18 WEST 18TH STREET, NEW YORK 10011

PRINTED IN THE UNITED STATES OF AMERICA
FIRST EDITION, 2010

LIBRARY OF CONGRESS CATALOGING-IN-PUBLICATION DATA

KLEIN, GRADY.
    THE CARTOON INTRODUCTION TO ECONOMICS / BY GRADY KLEIN AND
YORAM BAUMAN. — 1ST ED.
        V. : CM.
    CONTENTS: VOL. 1. MICROECONOMICS.
    ISBN: 978-0-8090-9481-3 (PBK. : ALK. PAPER)
1. MICROECONOMICS. I. BAUMAN, YORAM. II. TITLE.

HB172. K67 2009
338.5—DC22

2009015727

WWW.FSGBOOKS.COM

16

FOR ANNE AND LIAM AND BENJAMIN
—GK

FOR JOEL AND BETTY,
AND IN MEMORY OF HOLLY AND HELEN
—YB

CONTENTS

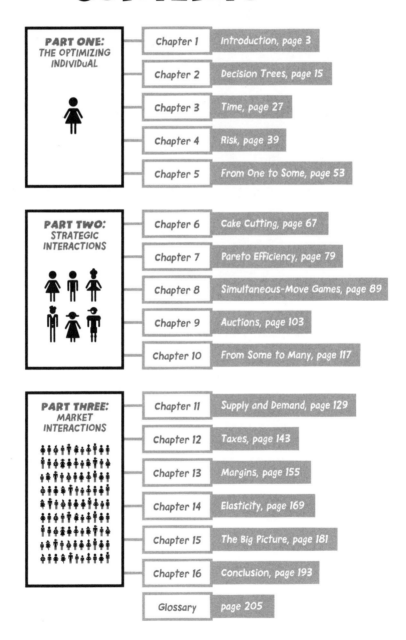

PART ONE
THE OPTIMIZING INDIVIDUAL

CHAPTER 1
INTRODUCTION

THIS BOOK IS ABOUT ONE **VERY IMPORTANT** TYPE OF PERSON...

...A PERSON WE ECONOMISTS CALL **THE OPTIMIZING INDIVIDUAL!**

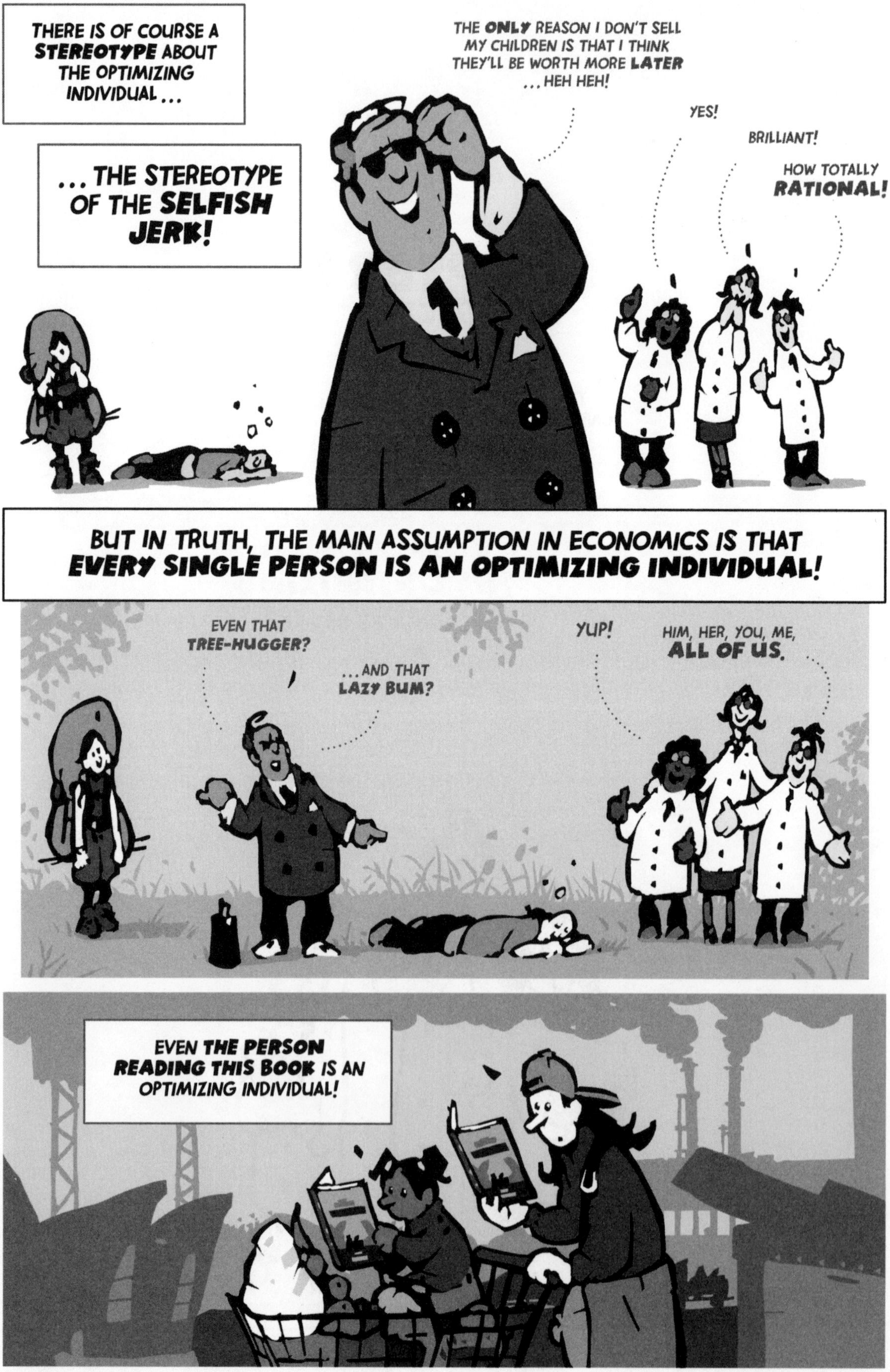
THERE IS OF COURSE A STEREOTYPE ABOUT THE OPTIMIZING INDIVIDUAL ...
... THE STEREOTYPE OF THE SELFISH JERK!
THE ONLY REASON I DON'T SELL MY CHILDREN IS THAT I THINK THEY'LL BE WORTH MORE LATER ... HEH HEH!
YES!
BRILLIANT!
HOW TOTALLY RATIONAL!
BUT IN TRUTH, THE MAIN ASSUMPTION IN ECONOMICS IS THAT EVERY SINGLE PERSON IS AN OPTIMIZING INDIVIDUAL!
EVEN THAT TREE-HUGGER?
... AND THAT LAZY BUM?
YUP!
HIM, HER, YOU, ME, ALL OF US.
EVEN THE PERSON READING THIS BOOK IS AN OPTIMIZING INDIVIDUAL!

IN THE EYES OF ECONOMISTS, **ALL** OPTIMIZING INDIVIDUALS ARE **CREATED EQUAL.**

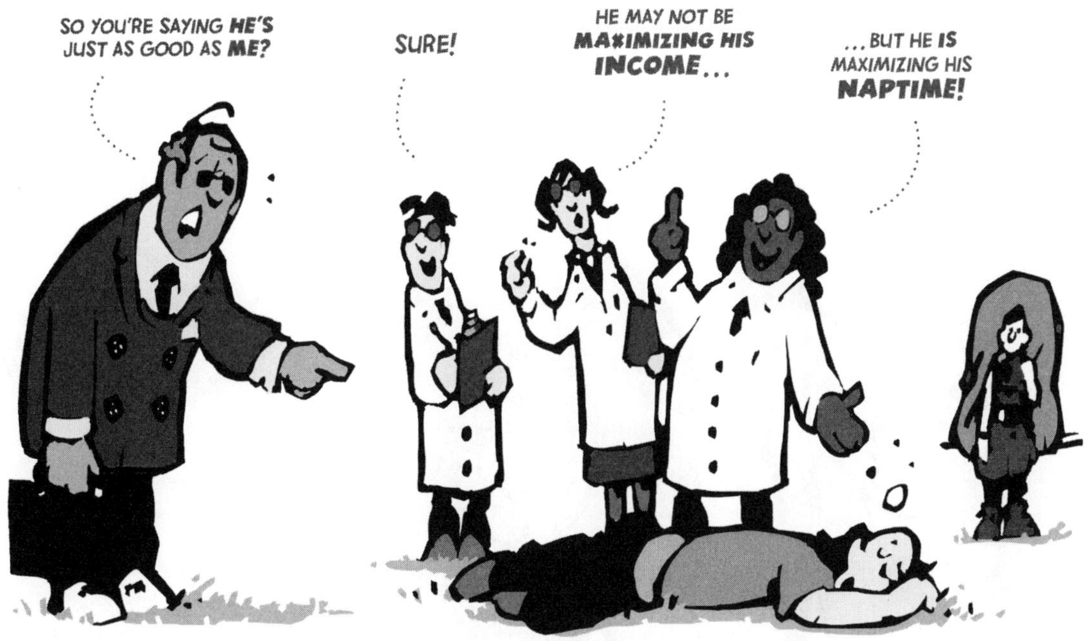
SO YOU'RE SAYING **HE'S** JUST AS GOOD AS **ME?**
SURE!
HE MAY NOT BE **MAXIMIZING HIS INCOME**...
...BUT HE **IS** MAXIMIZING HIS **NAPTIME!**

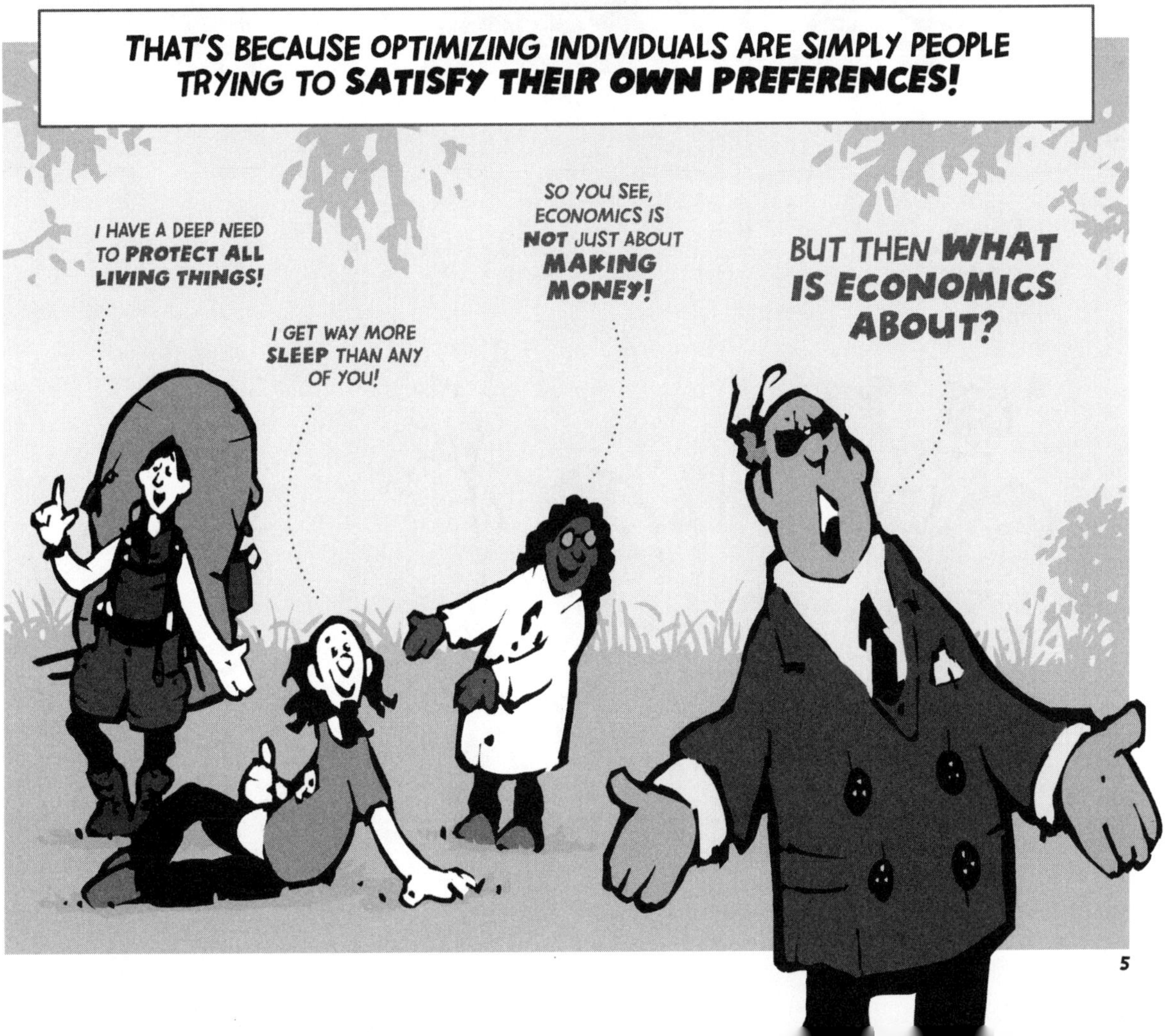
THAT'S BECAUSE OPTIMIZING INDIVIDUALS ARE SIMPLY PEOPLE TRYING TO **SATISFY THEIR OWN PREFERENCES!**
I HAVE A DEEP NEED TO **PROTECT ALL LIVING THINGS!**
I GET WAY MORE **SLEEP** THAN ANY OF YOU!
SO YOU SEE, ECONOMICS IS **NOT** JUST ABOUT **MAKING MONEY!**
BUT THEN **WHAT IS ECONOMICS ABOUT?**

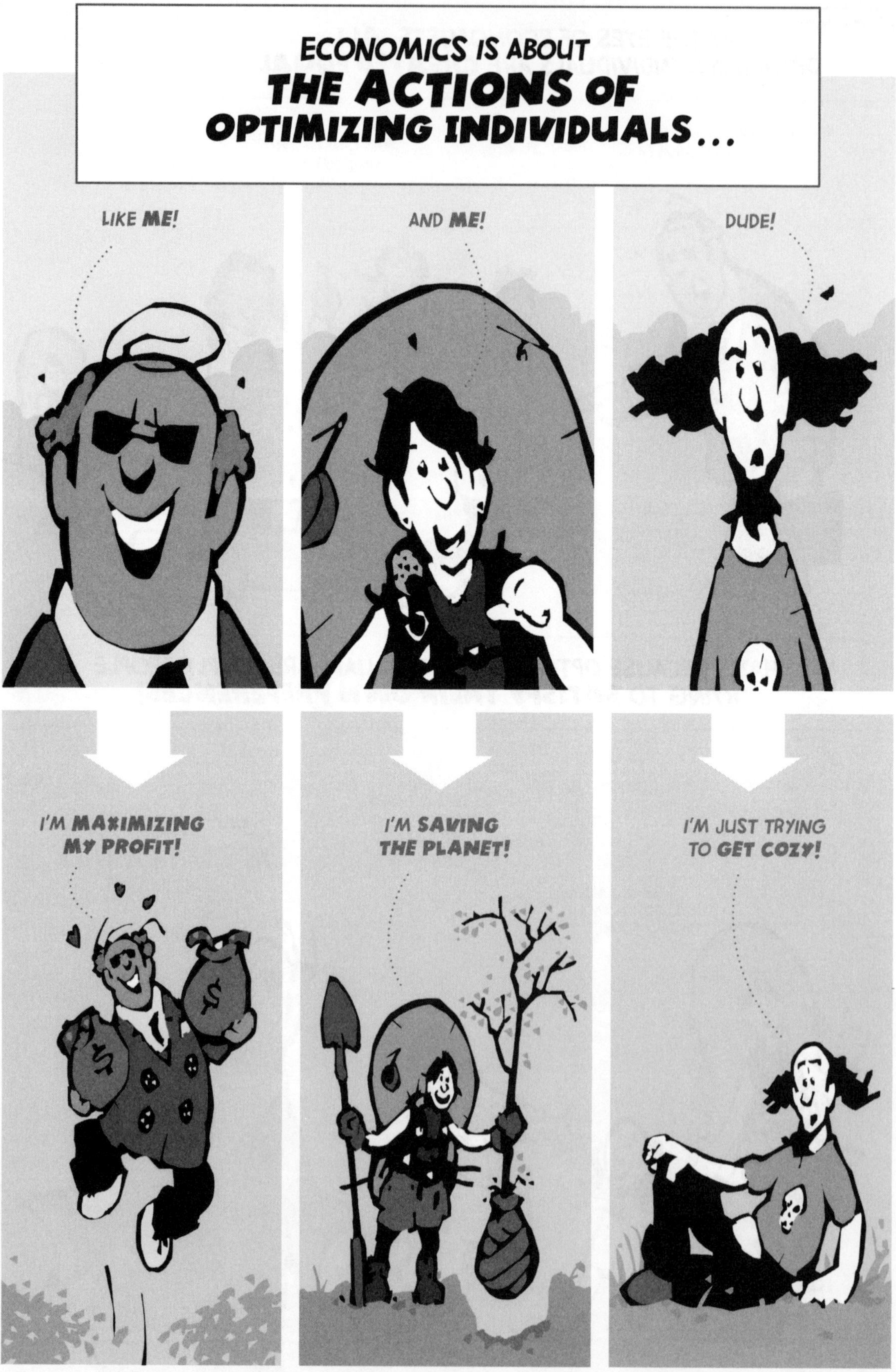
ECONOMICS IS ABOUT THE ACTIONS OF OPTIMIZING INDIVIDUALS...
LIKE ME!
AND ME!
DUDE!
I'M MAXIMIZING MY PROFIT!
I'M SAVING THE PLANET!
I'M JUST TRYING TO GET COZY!

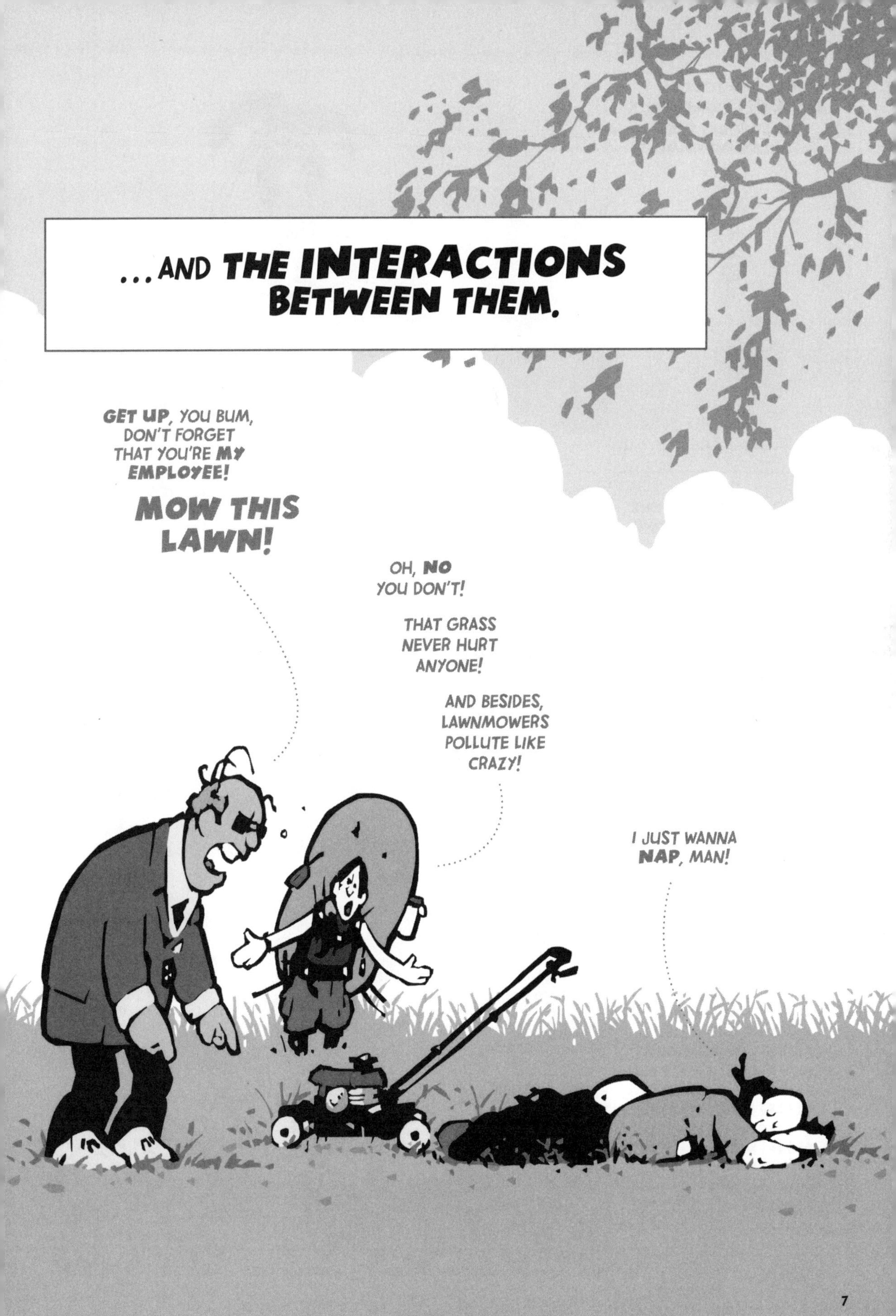
...AND THE INTERACTIONS BETWEEN THEM.
GET UP, YOU BUM, DON'T FORGET THAT YOU'RE MY EMPLOYEE!
MOW THIS LAWN!
OH, NO YOU DON'T!
THAT GRASS NEVER HURT ANYONE!
AND BESIDES, LAWNMOWERS POLLUTE LIKE CRAZY!
I JUST WANNA NAP, MAN!

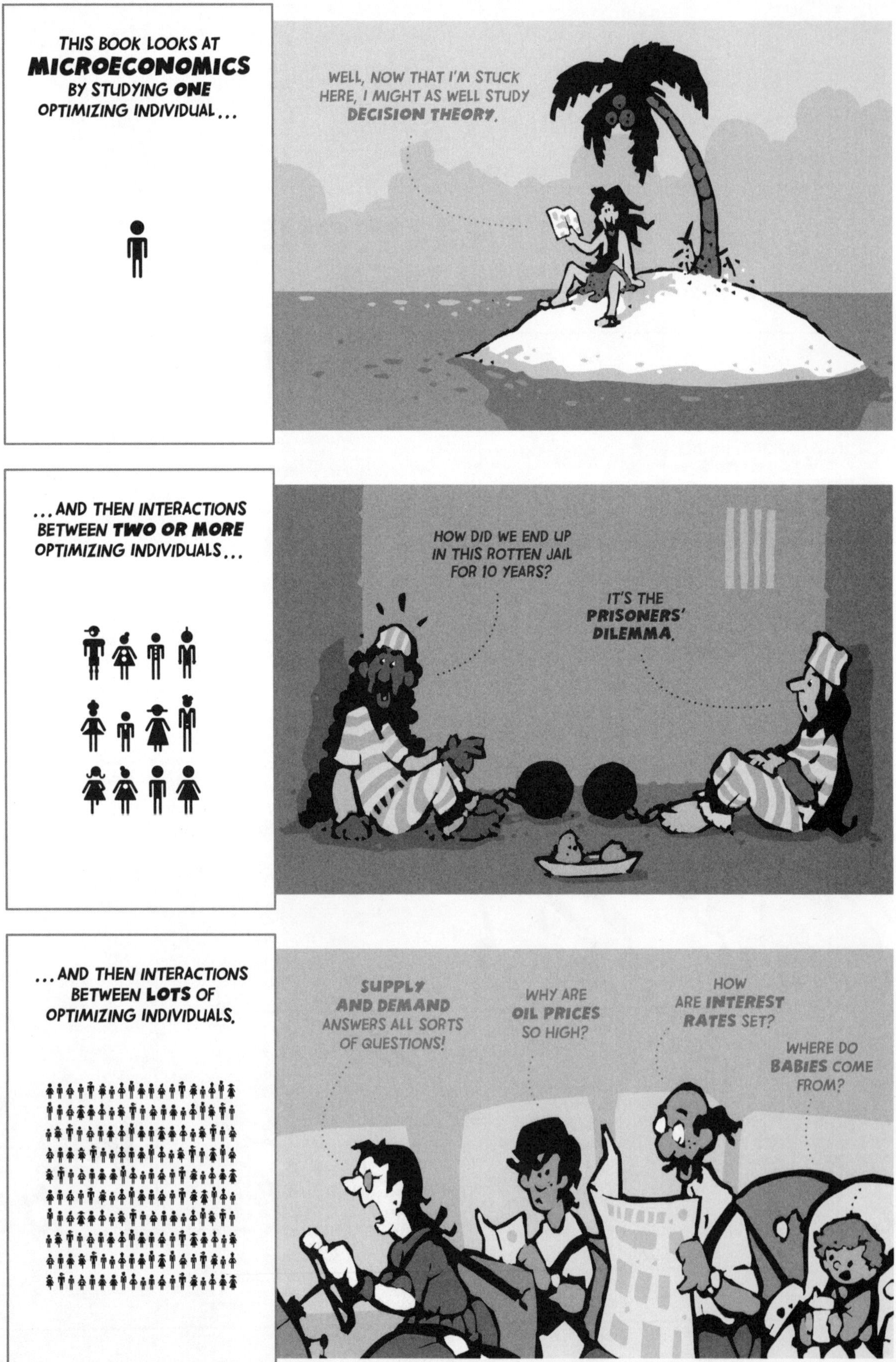
THIS BOOK LOOKS AT **MICROECONOMICS** BY STUDYING **ONE** OPTIMIZING INDIVIDUAL...
WELL, NOW THAT I'M STUCK HERE, I MIGHT AS WELL STUDY **DECISION THEORY**.
...AND THEN INTERACTIONS BETWEEN **TWO OR MORE** OPTIMIZING INDIVIDUALS...
HOW DID WE END UP IN THIS ROTTEN JAIL FOR 10 YEARS?
IT'S THE **PRISONERS' DILEMMA**.
...AND THEN INTERACTIONS BETWEEN **LOTS** OF OPTIMIZING INDIVIDUALS.
SUPPLY AND DEMAND ANSWERS ALL SORTS OF QUESTIONS!
WHY ARE **OIL PRICES** SO HIGH?
HOW ARE **INTEREST RATES** SET?
WHERE DO **BABIES** COME FROM?

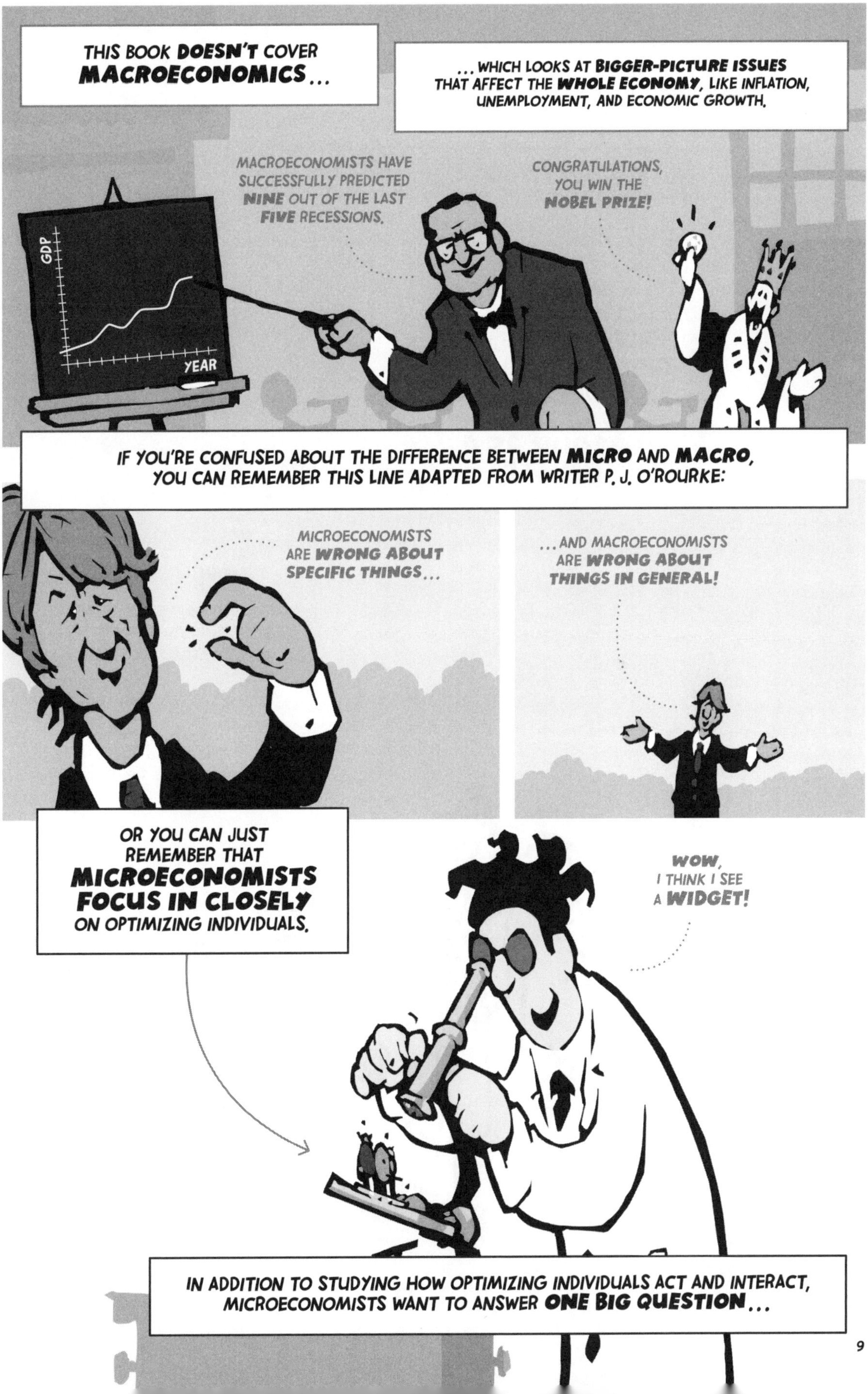
THIS BOOK DOESN'T COVER MACROECONOMICS...
...WHICH LOOKS AT BIGGER-PICTURE ISSUES THAT AFFECT THE WHOLE ECONOMY, LIKE INFLATION, UNEMPLOYMENT, AND ECONOMIC GROWTH.
GDP
YEAR
MACROECONOMISTS HAVE SUCCESSFULLY PREDICTED NINE OUT OF THE LAST FIVE RECESSIONS.
CONGRATULATIONS, YOU WIN THE NOBEL PRIZE!
IF YOU'RE CONFUSED ABOUT THE DIFFERENCE BETWEEN MICRO AND MACRO, YOU CAN REMEMBER THIS LINE ADAPTED FROM WRITER P. J. O'ROURKE:
MICROECONOMISTS ARE WRONG ABOUT SPECIFIC THINGS...
...AND MACROECONOMISTS ARE WRONG ABOUT THINGS IN GENERAL!
OR YOU CAN JUST REMEMBER THAT MICROECONOMISTS FOCUS IN CLOSELY ON OPTIMIZING INDIVIDUALS.
WOW, I THINK I SEE A WIDGET!
IN ADDITION TO STUDYING HOW OPTIMIZING INDIVIDUALS ACT AND INTERACT, MICROECONOMISTS WANT TO ANSWER ONE BIG QUESTION...

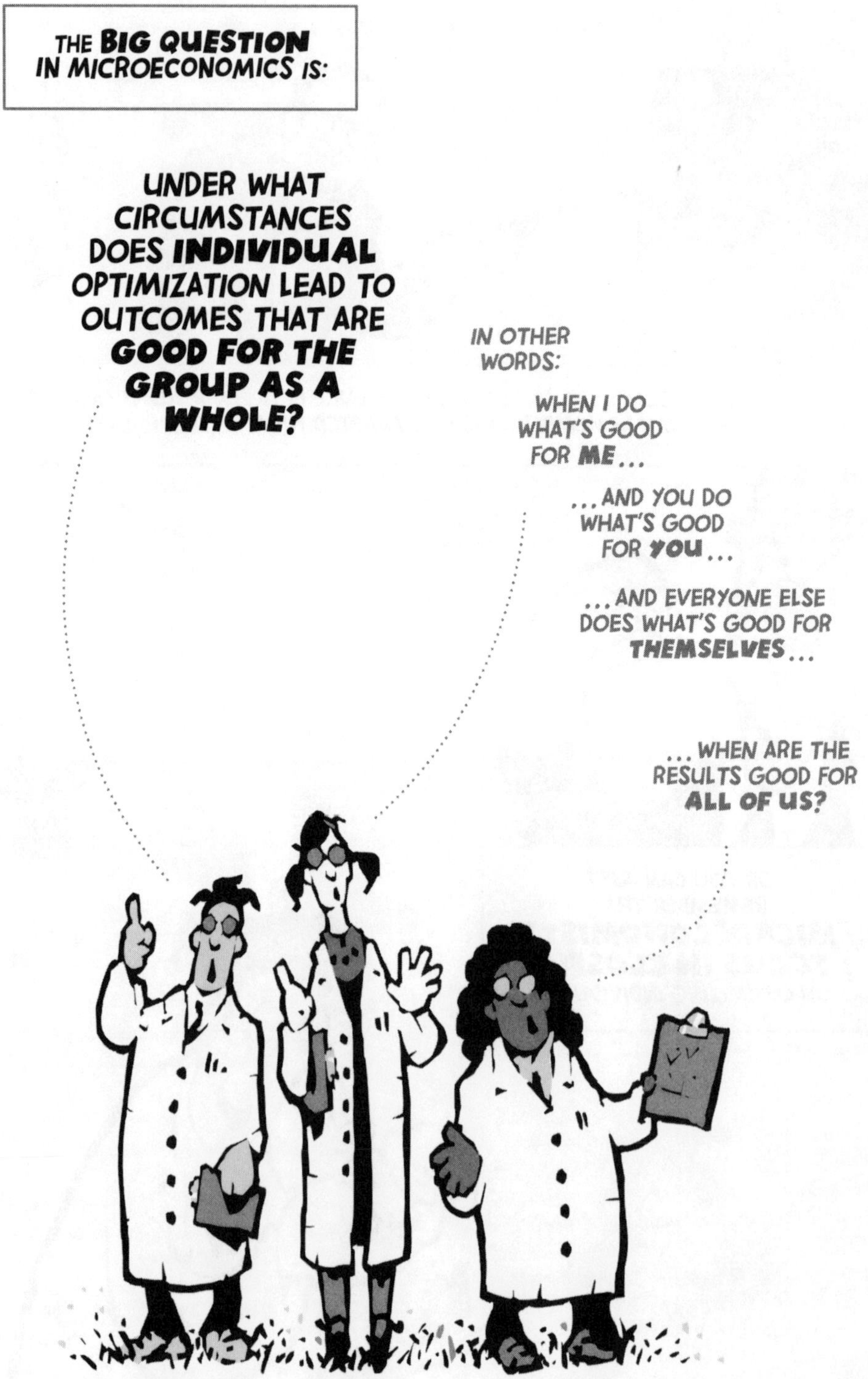
THE BIG QUESTION IN MICROECONOMICS IS:
UNDER WHAT CIRCUMSTANCES DOES INDIVIDUAL OPTIMIZATION LEAD TO OUTCOMES THAT ARE GOOD FOR THE GROUP AS A WHOLE?
IN OTHER WORDS:
WHEN I DO WHAT'S GOOD FOR ME...
...AND YOU DO WHAT'S GOOD FOR YOU...
...AND EVERYONE ELSE DOES WHAT'S GOOD FOR THEMSELVES...
...WHEN ARE THE RESULTS GOOD FOR ALL OF US?

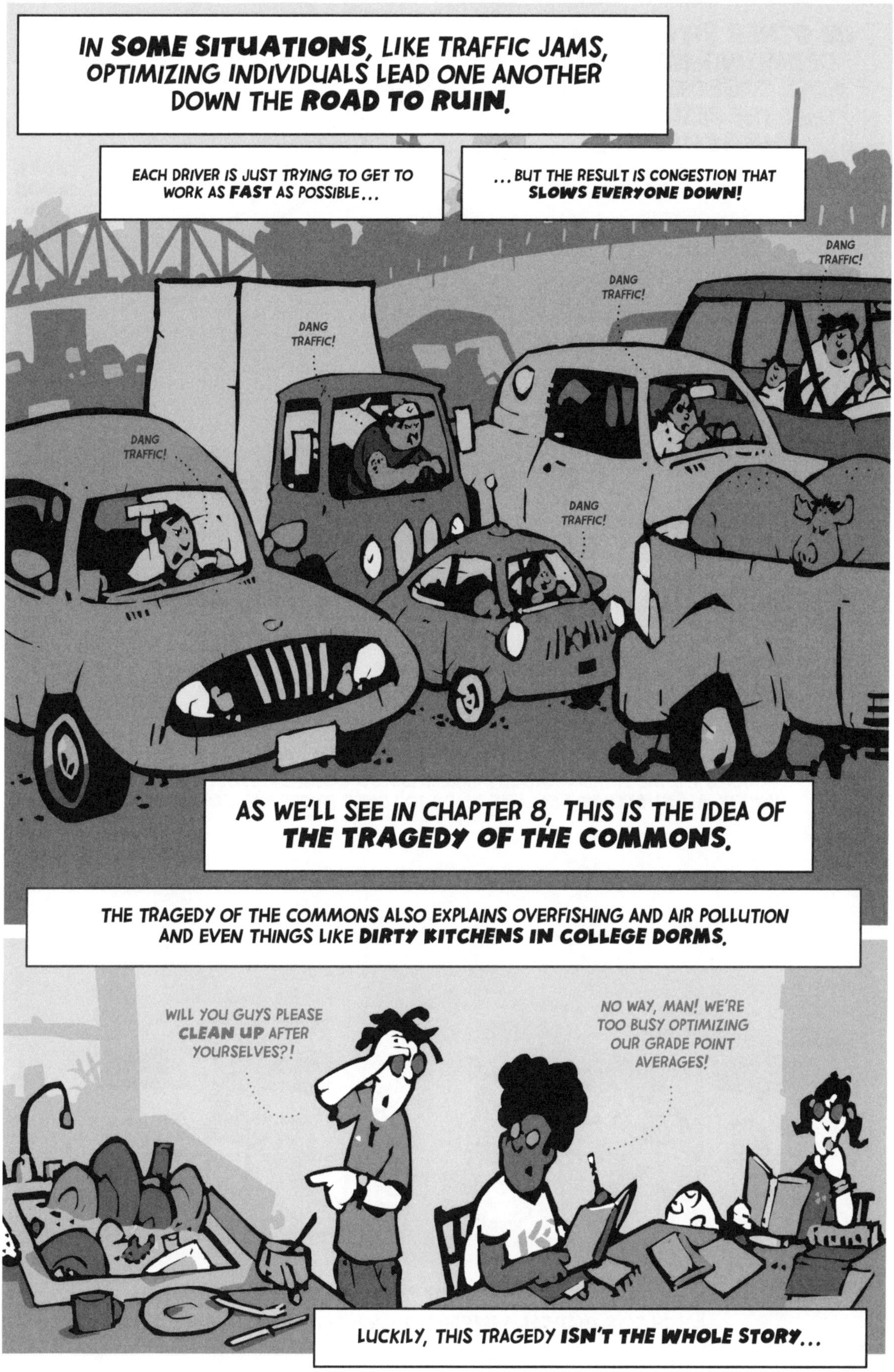
IN SOME SITUATIONS, LIKE TRAFFIC JAMS, OPTIMIZING INDIVIDUALS LEAD ONE ANOTHER DOWN THE ROAD TO RUIN.
EACH DRIVER IS JUST TRYING TO GET TO WORK AS FAST AS POSSIBLE...
...BUT THE RESULT IS CONGESTION THAT SLOWS EVERYONE DOWN!
DANG TRAFFIC!
DANG TRAFFIC!
DANG TRAFFIC!
DANG TRAFFIC!
DANG TRAFFIC!
AS WE'LL SEE IN CHAPTER 8, THIS IS THE IDEA OF THE TRAGEDY OF THE COMMONS.
THE TRAGEDY OF THE COMMONS ALSO EXPLAINS OVERFISHING AND AIR POLLUTION AND EVEN THINGS LIKE DIRTY KITCHENS IN COLLEGE DORMS.
WILL YOU GUYS PLEASE CLEAN UP AFTER YOURSELVES?!
NO WAY, MAN! WE'RE TOO BUSY OPTIMIZING OUR GRADE POINT AVERAGES!
LUCKILY, THIS TRAGEDY ISN'T THE WHOLE STORY...

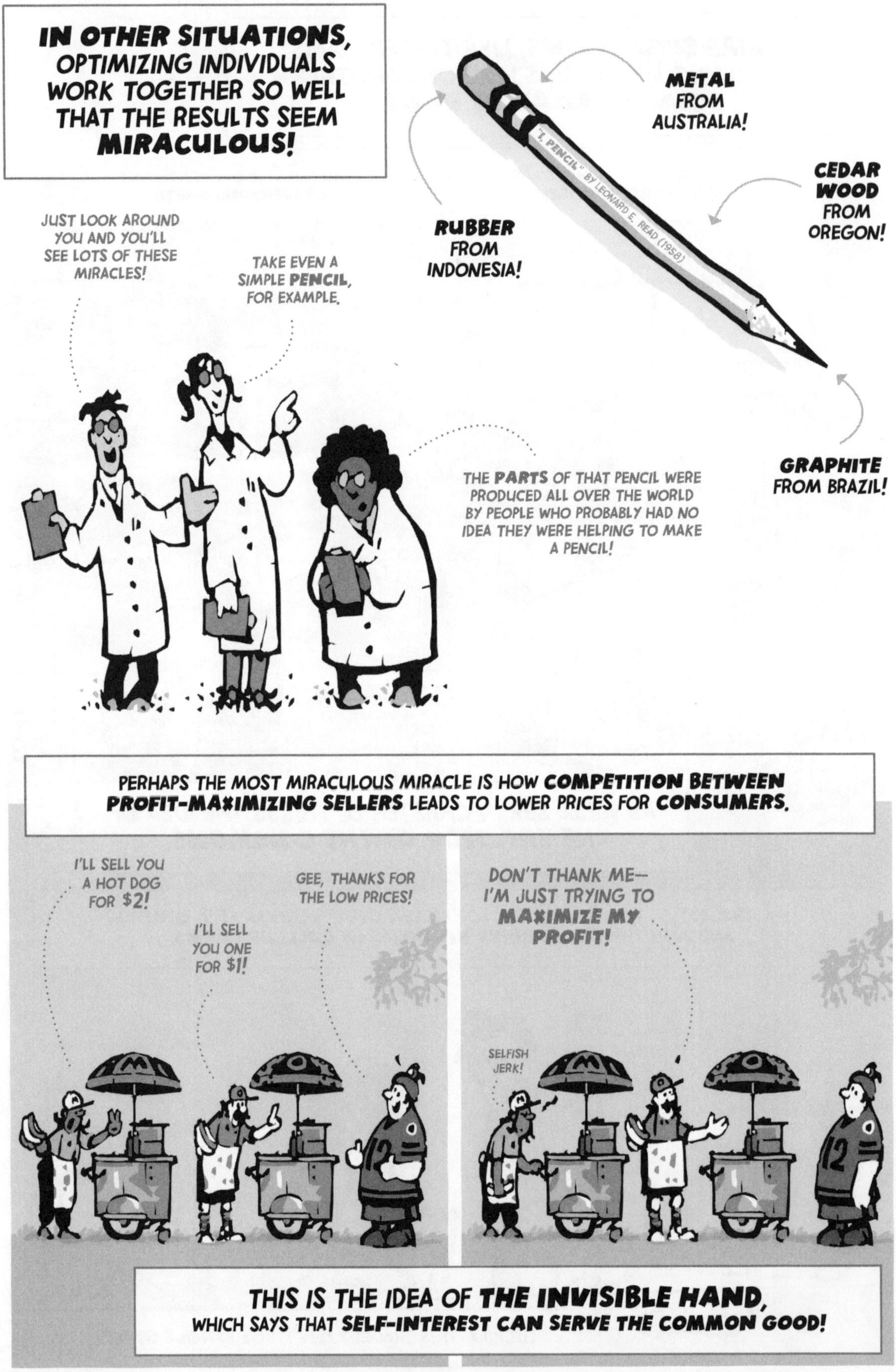
IN OTHER SITUATIONS, OPTIMIZING INDIVIDUALS WORK TOGETHER SO WELL THAT THE RESULTS SEEM MIRACULOUS!
JUST LOOK AROUND YOU AND YOU'LL SEE LOTS OF THESE MIRACLES!
TAKE EVEN A SIMPLE PENCIL, FOR EXAMPLE.
"I, PENCIL" BY LEONARD E. READ (1958)
METAL FROM AUSTRALIA!
CEDAR WOOD FROM OREGON!
RUBBER FROM INDONESIA!
GRAPHITE FROM BRAZIL!
THE PARTS OF THAT PENCIL WERE PRODUCED ALL OVER THE WORLD BY PEOPLE WHO PROBABLY HAD NO IDEA THEY WERE HELPING TO MAKE A PENCIL!
PERHAPS THE MOST MIRACULOUS MIRACLE IS HOW COMPETITION BETWEEN PROFIT-MAXIMIZING SELLERS LEADS TO LOWER PRICES FOR CONSUMERS.
I'LL SELL YOU A HOT DOG FOR $2!
I'LL SELL YOU ONE FOR $1!
GEE, THANKS FOR THE LOW PRICES!
SELFISH JERK!
DON'T THANK ME— I'M JUST TRYING TO MAXIMIZE MY PROFIT!
THIS IS THE IDEA OF THE INVISIBLE HAND, WHICH SAYS THAT SELF-INTEREST CAN SERVE THE COMMON GOOD!

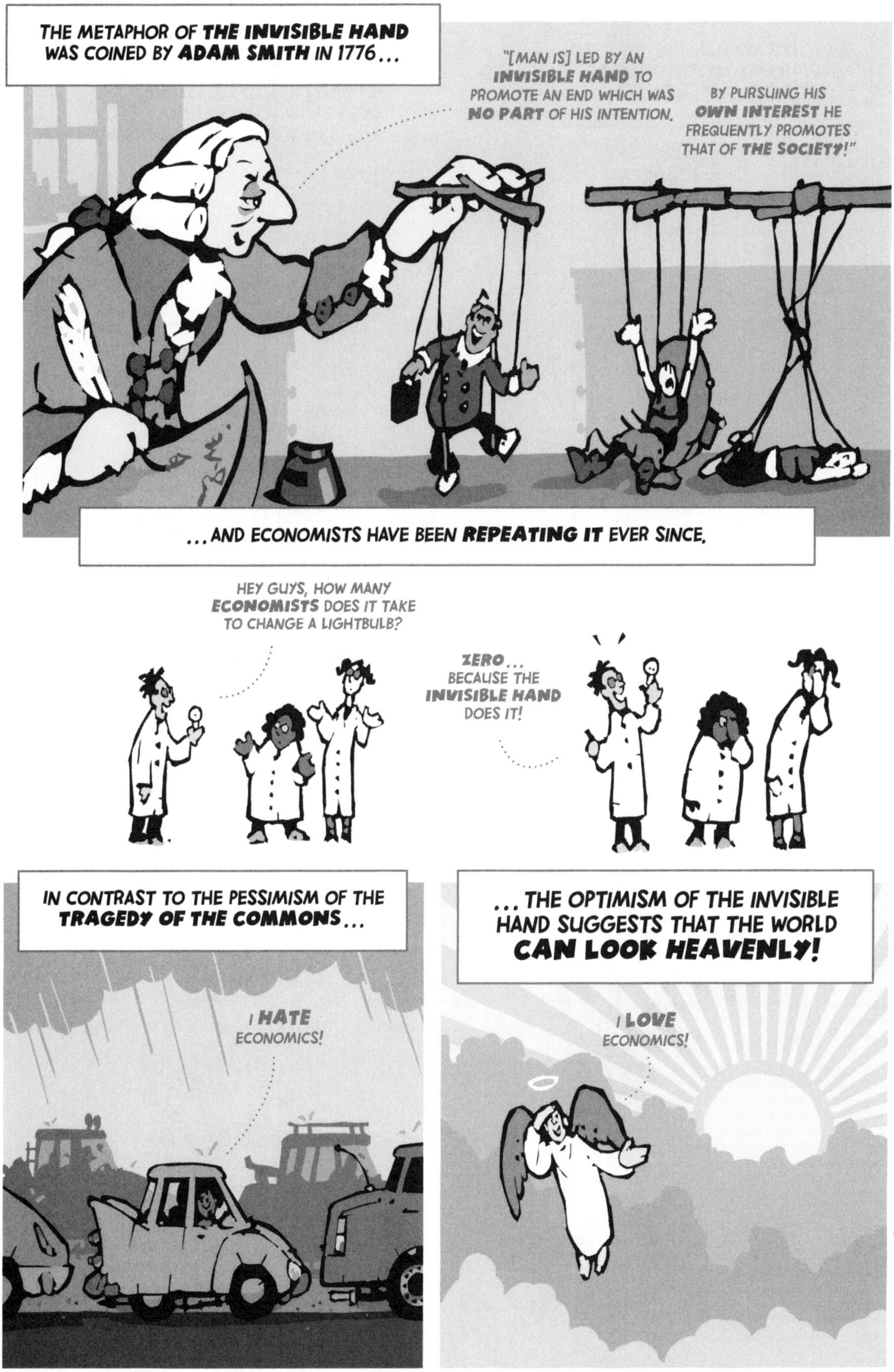

THE METAPHOR OF **THE INVISIBLE HAND** WAS COINED BY **ADAM SMITH** IN 1776...
"[MAN IS] LED BY AN **INVISIBLE HAND** TO PROMOTE AN END WHICH WAS **NO PART** OF HIS INTENTION.
BY PURSUING HIS **OWN INTEREST** HE FREQUENTLY PROMOTES THAT OF **THE SOCIETY**!"
...AND ECONOMISTS HAVE BEEN **REPEATING IT** EVER SINCE.
HEY GUYS, HOW MANY **ECONOMISTS** DOES IT TAKE TO CHANGE A LIGHTBULB?
ZERO... BECAUSE THE **INVISIBLE HAND** DOES IT!
IN CONTRAST TO THE PESSIMISM OF THE **TRAGEDY OF THE COMMONS**...
I **HATE** ECONOMICS!
...THE OPTIMISM OF THE INVISIBLE HAND SUGGESTS THAT THE WORLD **CAN LOOK HEAVENLY!**
I **LOVE** ECONOMICS!

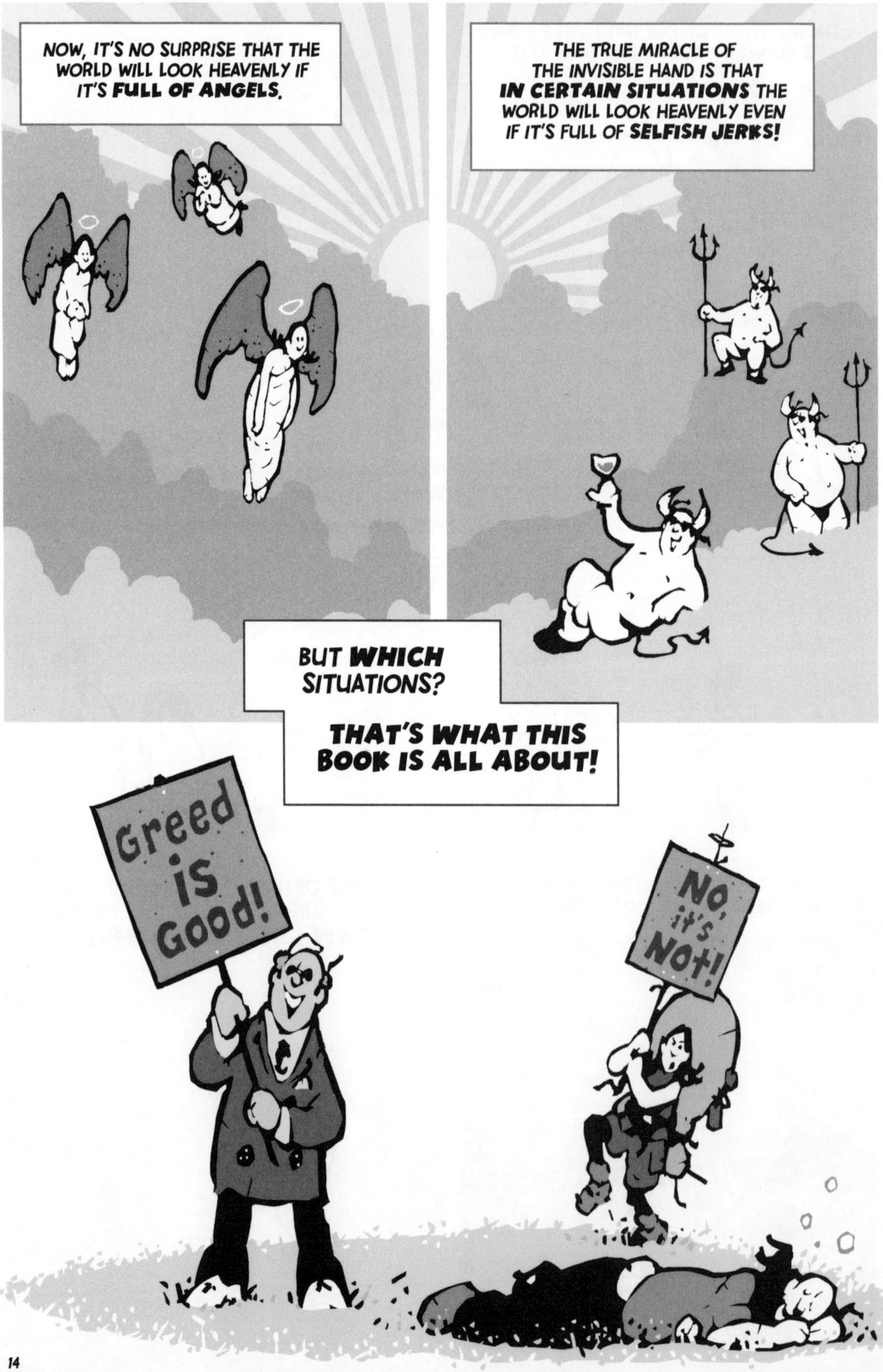
NOW, IT'S NO SURPRISE THAT THE WORLD WILL LOOK HEAVENLY IF IT'S **FULL OF ANGELS.**
THE TRUE MIRACLE OF THE INVISIBLE HAND IS THAT **IN CERTAIN SITUATIONS** THE WORLD WILL LOOK HEAVENLY EVEN IF IT'S FULL OF **SELFISH JERKS!**
BUT **WHICH** SITUATIONS?
THAT'S WHAT THIS BOOK IS ALL ABOUT!
Greed is Good!
No, it's Not!

CHAPTER 2
DECISION TREES

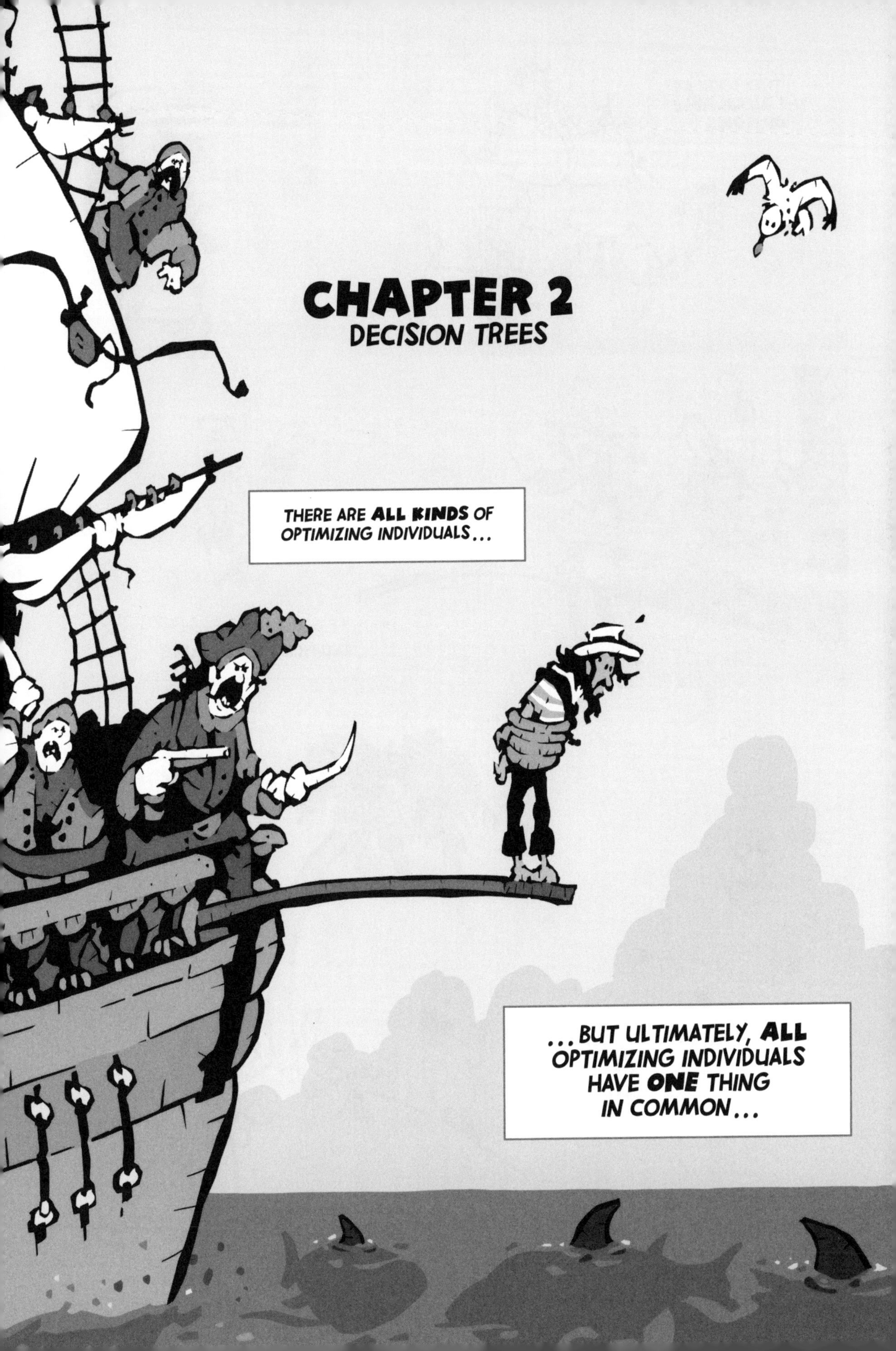
THERE ARE **ALL KINDS** OF OPTIMIZING INDIVIDUALS…
…BUT ULTIMATELY, **ALL** OPTIMIZING INDIVIDUALS HAVE **ONE** THING IN COMMON…

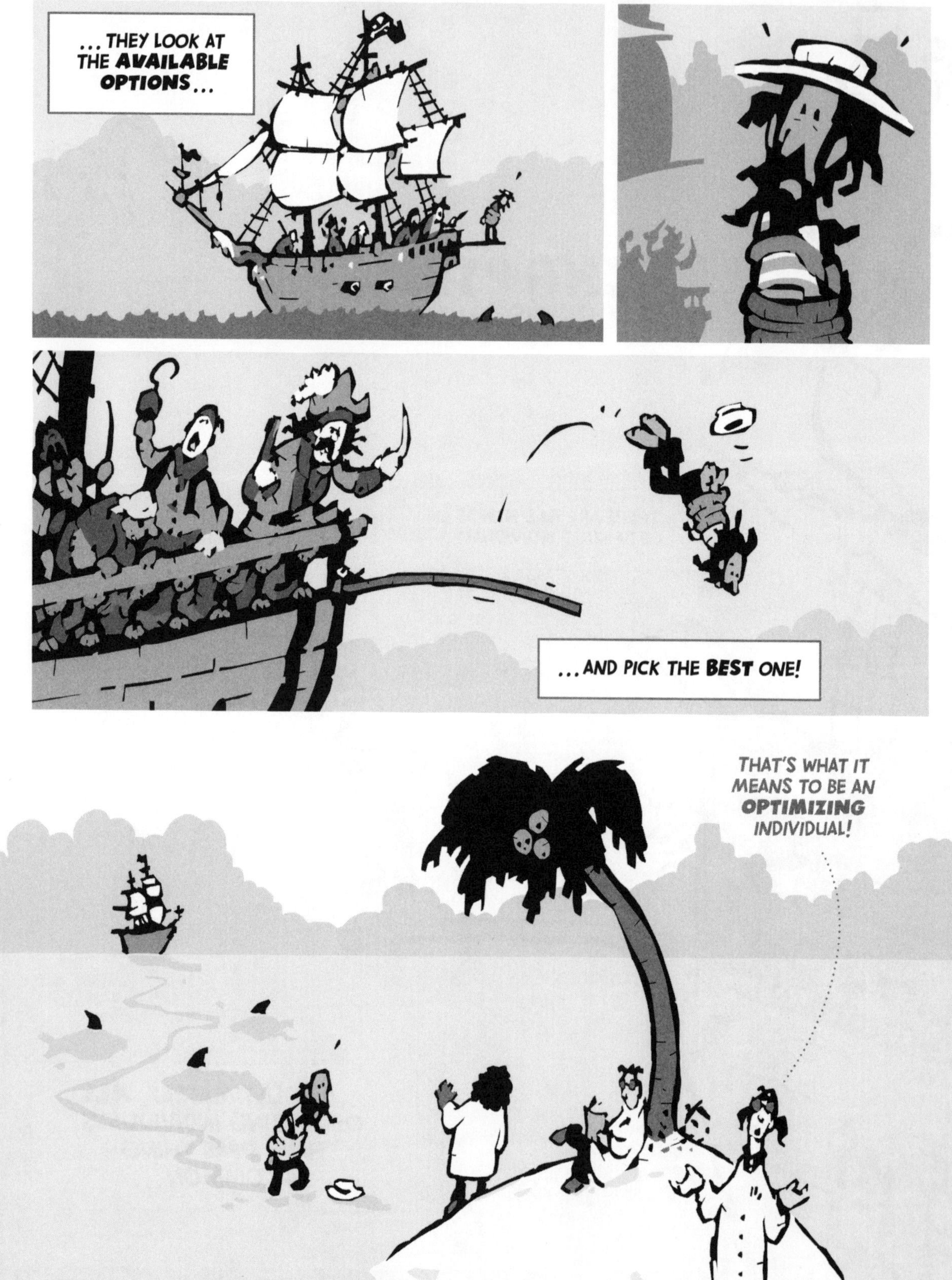

...THEY LOOK AT THE AVAILABLE OPTIONS...
...AND PICK THE BEST ONE!
THAT'S WHAT IT MEANS TO BE AN OPTIMIZING INDIVIDUAL!

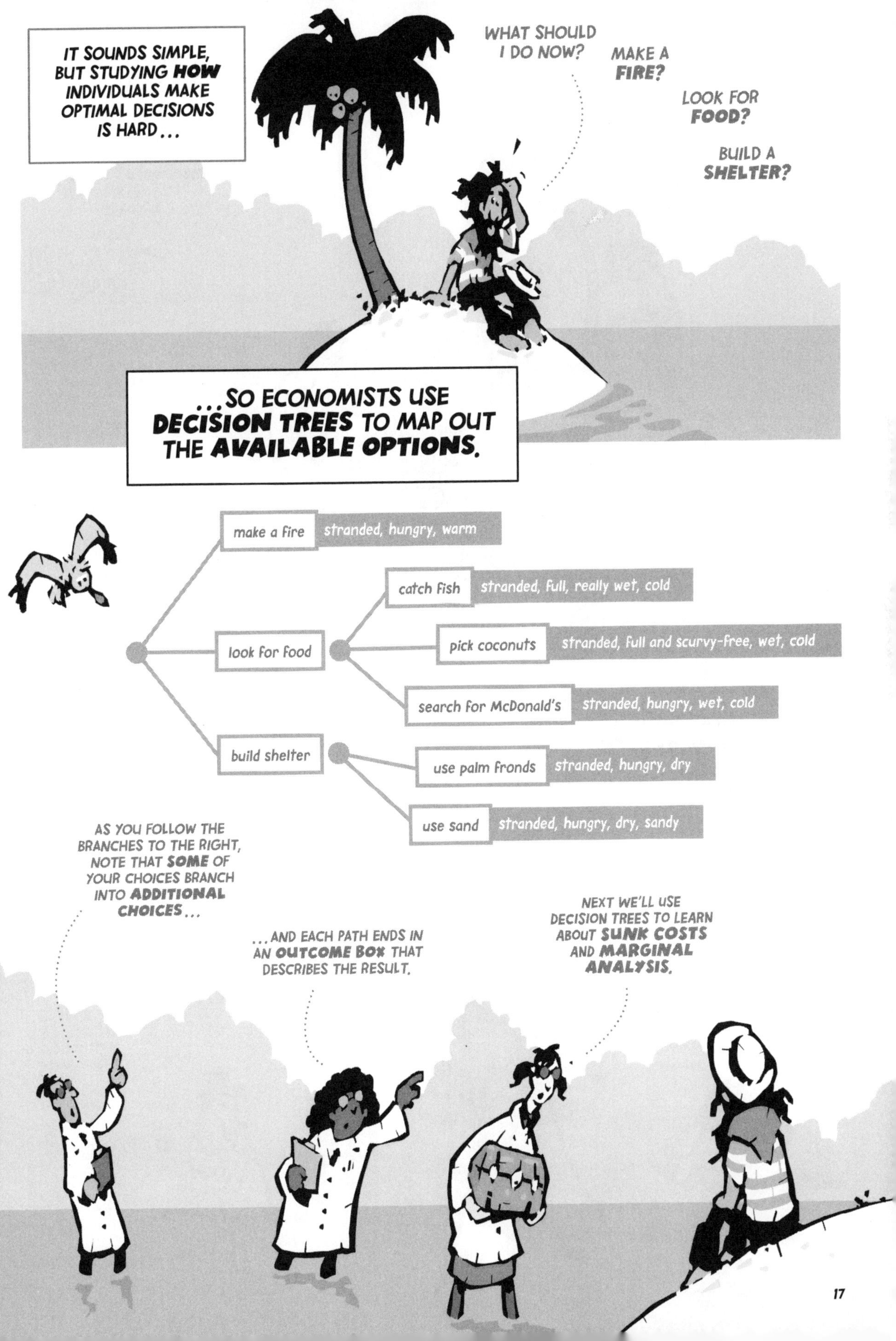
IT SOUNDS SIMPLE, BUT STUDYING HOW INDIVIDUALS MAKE OPTIMAL DECISIONS IS HARD...
WHAT SHOULD I DO NOW?
MAKE A FIRE?
LOOK FOR FOOD?
BUILD A SHELTER?
...SO ECONOMISTS USE DECISION TREES TO MAP OUT THE AVAILABLE OPTIONS.
make a fire
stranded, hungry, warm
look for food
catch fish
stranded, full, really wet, cold
pick coconuts
stranded, full and scurvy-free, wet, cold
search for McDonald's
stranded, hungry, wet, cold
build shelter
use palm fronds
stranded, hungry, dry
use sand
stranded, hungry, dry, sandy
AS YOU FOLLOW THE BRANCHES TO THE RIGHT, NOTE THAT SOME OF YOUR CHOICES BRANCH INTO ADDITIONAL CHOICES...
...AND EACH PATH ENDS IN AN OUTCOME BOX THAT DESCRIBES THE RESULT.
NEXT WE'LL USE DECISION TREES TO LEARN ABOUT SUNK COSTS AND MARGINAL ANALYSIS.

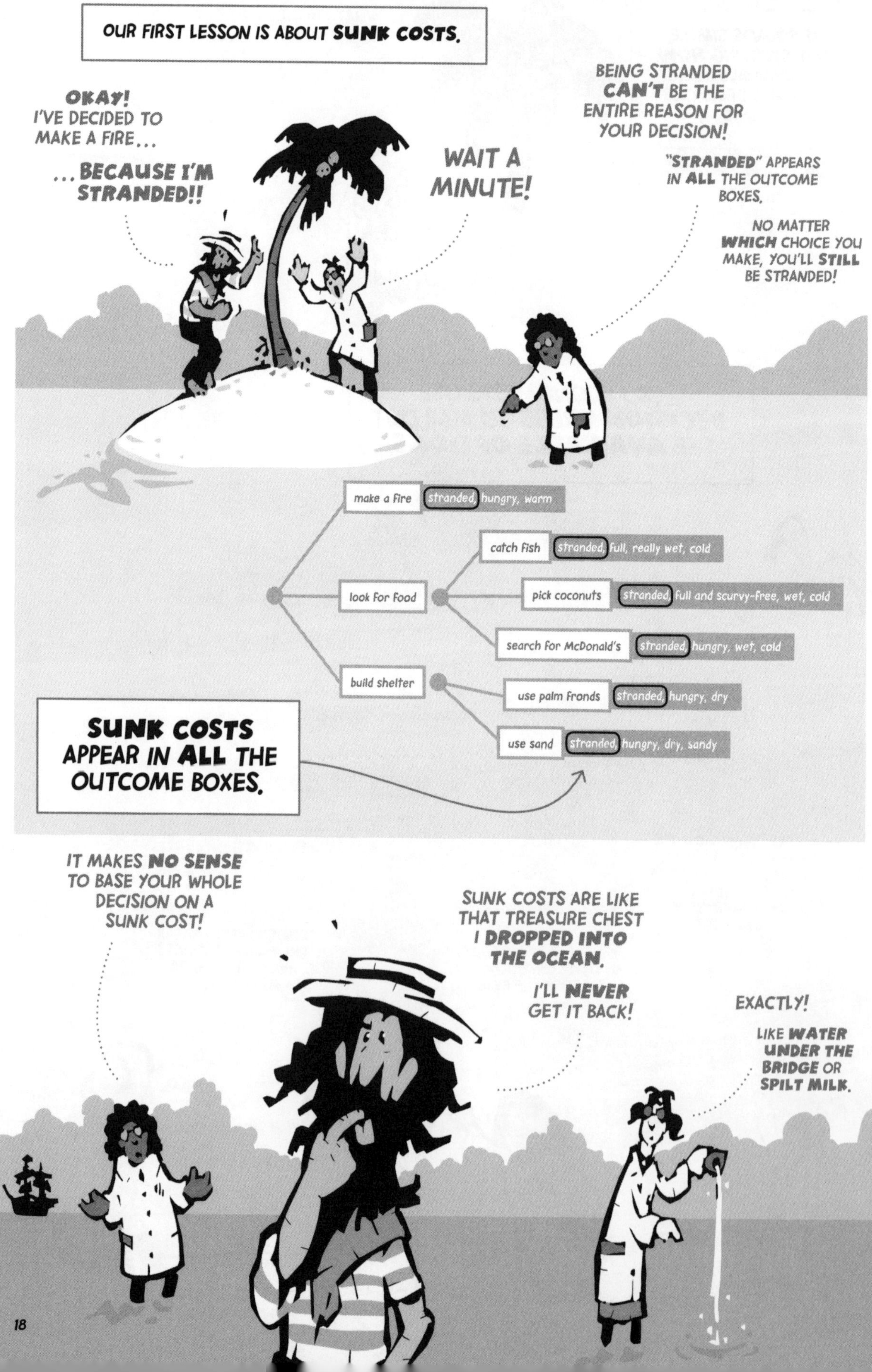

OUR FIRST LESSON IS ABOUT **SUNK COSTS.**
OKAY! I'VE DECIDED TO MAKE A FIRE...
...**BECAUSE I'M STRANDED!!**
WAIT A MINUTE!
BEING STRANDED **CAN'T** BE THE ENTIRE REASON FOR YOUR DECISION!
"**STRANDED**" APPEARS IN **ALL** THE OUTCOME BOXES.
NO MATTER **WHICH** CHOICE YOU MAKE, YOU'LL **STILL** BE STRANDED!
make a fire
stranded, hungry, warm
look for food
catch fish
stranded, full, really wet, cold
pick coconuts
stranded, full and scurvy-free, wet, cold
search for McDonald's
stranded, hungry, wet, cold
build shelter
use palm fronds
stranded, hungry, dry
use sand
stranded, hungry, dry, sandy
SUNK COSTS APPEAR IN **ALL** THE OUTCOME BOXES.
IT MAKES **NO SENSE** TO BASE YOUR WHOLE DECISION ON A SUNK COST!
SUNK COSTS ARE LIKE THAT TREASURE CHEST I **DROPPED INTO THE OCEAN.**
I'LL **NEVER** GET IT BACK!
EXACTLY!
LIKE **WATER UNDER THE BRIDGE** OR **SPILT MILK.**

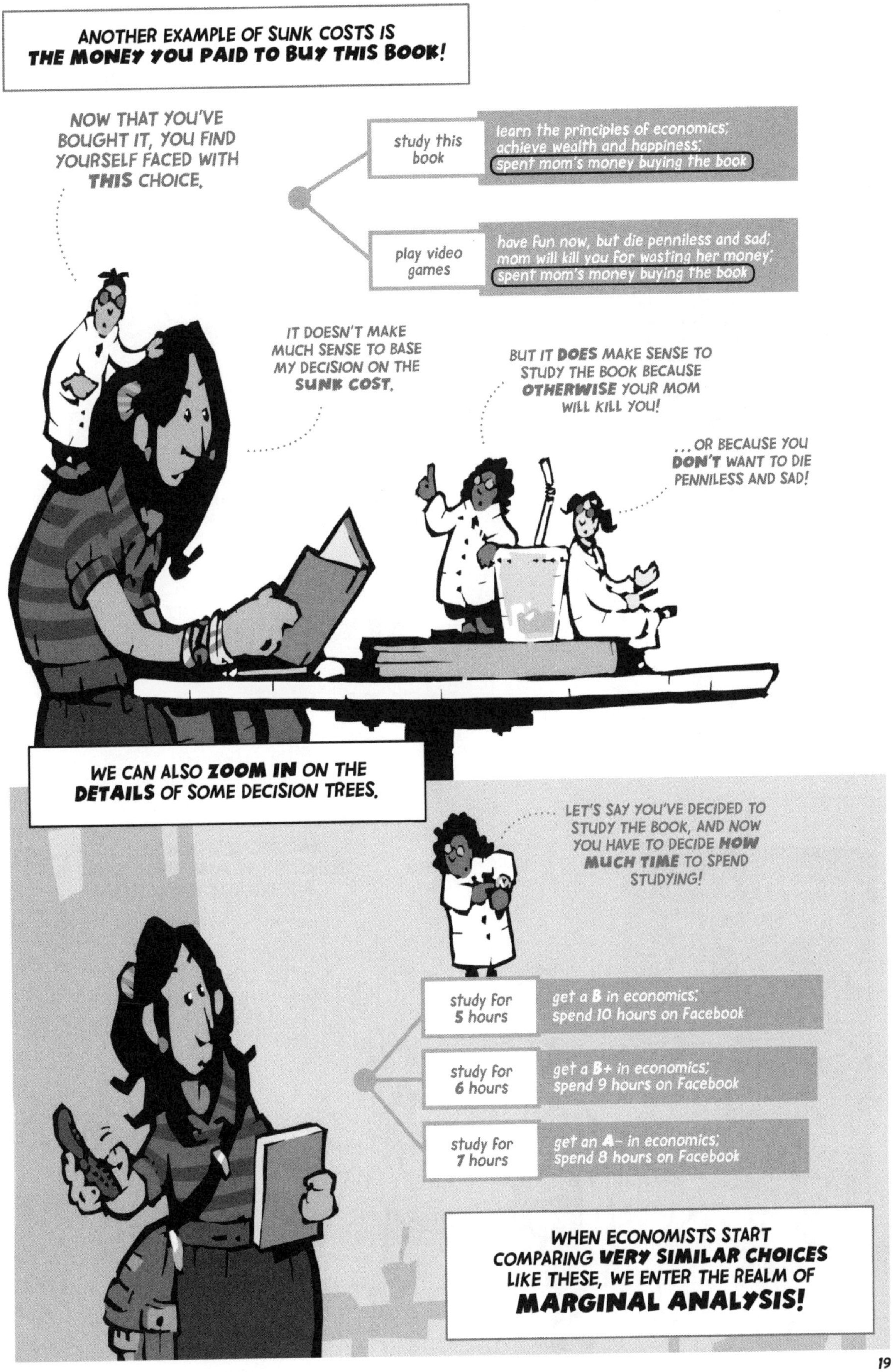

ANOTHER EXAMPLE OF SUNK COSTS IS **THE MONEY YOU PAID TO BUY THIS BOOK!**
NOW THAT YOU'VE BOUGHT IT, YOU FIND YOURSELF FACED WITH **THIS** CHOICE.
study this book
learn the principles of economics; achieve wealth and happiness; spent mom's money buying the book
play video games
have fun now, but die penniless and sad; mom will kill you for wasting her money; spent mom's money buying the book
IT DOESN'T MAKE MUCH SENSE TO BASE MY DECISION ON THE **SUNK COST.**
BUT IT **DOES** MAKE SENSE TO STUDY THE BOOK BECAUSE **OTHERWISE** YOUR MOM WILL KILL YOU!
...OR BECAUSE YOU **DON'T** WANT TO DIE PENNILESS AND SAD!
WE CAN ALSO **ZOOM IN** ON THE **DETAILS** OF SOME DECISION TREES.
LET'S SAY YOU'VE DECIDED TO STUDY THE BOOK, AND NOW YOU HAVE TO DECIDE **HOW MUCH TIME** TO SPEND STUDYING!
study for 5 hours
get a **B** in economics; spend 10 hours on Facebook
study for 6 hours
get a **B+** in economics; spend 9 hours on Facebook
study for 7 hours
get an **A–** in economics; spend 8 hours on Facebook
WHEN ECONOMISTS START COMPARING **VERY SIMILAR CHOICES** LIKE THESE, WE ENTER THE REALM OF **MARGINAL ANALYSIS!**

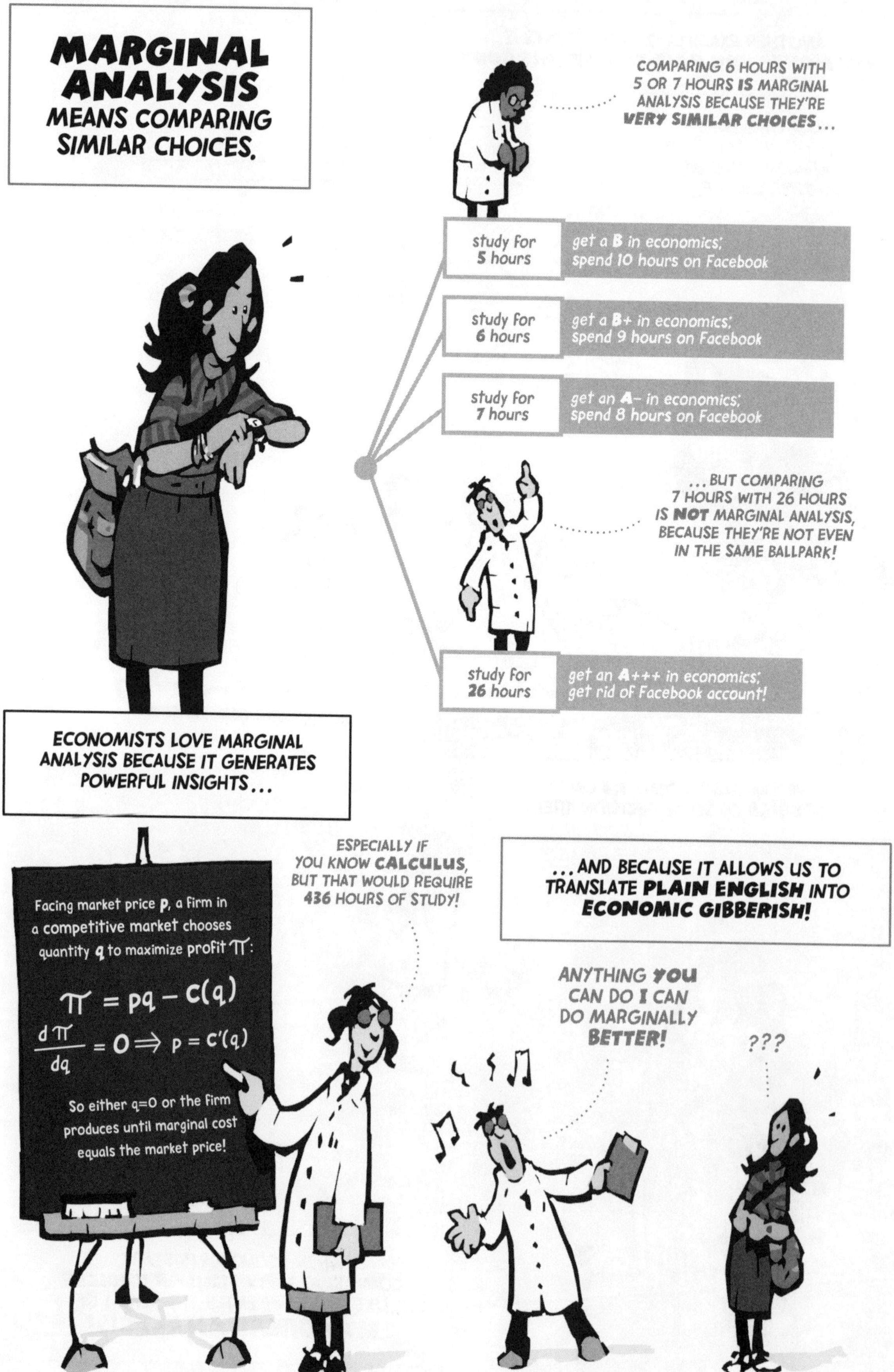

MARGINAL ANALYSIS
MEANS COMPARING SIMILAR CHOICES.

COMPARING 6 HOURS WITH 5 OR 7 HOURS **IS** MARGINAL ANALYSIS BECAUSE THEY'RE **VERY SIMILAR CHOICES**...

study for **5** hours	get a **B** in economics; spend 10 hours on Facebook
study for **6** hours	get a **B+** in economics; spend 9 hours on Facebook
study for **7** hours	get an **A–** in economics; spend 8 hours on Facebook

...BUT COMPARING 7 HOURS WITH 26 HOURS IS **NOT** MARGINAL ANALYSIS, BECAUSE THEY'RE NOT EVEN IN THE SAME BALLPARK!

| study for **26** hours | get an **A+++** in economics; get rid of Facebook account! |

ECONOMISTS LOVE MARGINAL ANALYSIS BECAUSE IT GENERATES POWERFUL INSIGHTS...

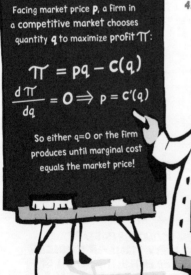

ESPECIALLY IF YOU KNOW **CALCULUS**, BUT THAT WOULD REQUIRE 436 HOURS OF STUDY!

Facing market price **p**, a firm in a competitive market chooses quantity **q** to maximize profit **π**:

$$\pi = pq - c(q)$$

$$\frac{d\pi}{dq} = 0 \Rightarrow p = c'(q)$$

So either q=0 or the firm produces until marginal cost equals the market price!

...AND BECAUSE IT ALLOWS US TO TRANSLATE **PLAIN ENGLISH** INTO **ECONOMIC GIBBERISH**!

ANYTHING **YOU** CAN DO I CAN DO MARGINALLY **BETTER**!

???

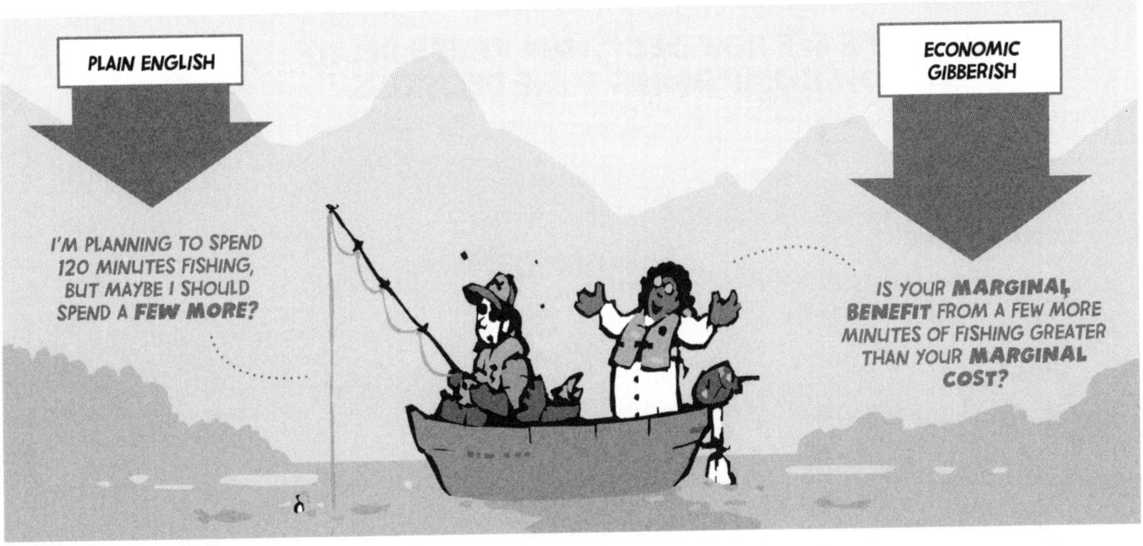
PLAIN ENGLISH
I'M PLANNING TO SPEND 120 MINUTES FISHING, BUT MAYBE I SHOULD SPEND A **FEW MORE?**
ECONOMIC GIBBERISH
IS YOUR **MARGINAL BENEFIT** FROM A FEW MORE MINUTES OF FISHING GREATER THAN YOUR **MARGINAL COST?**

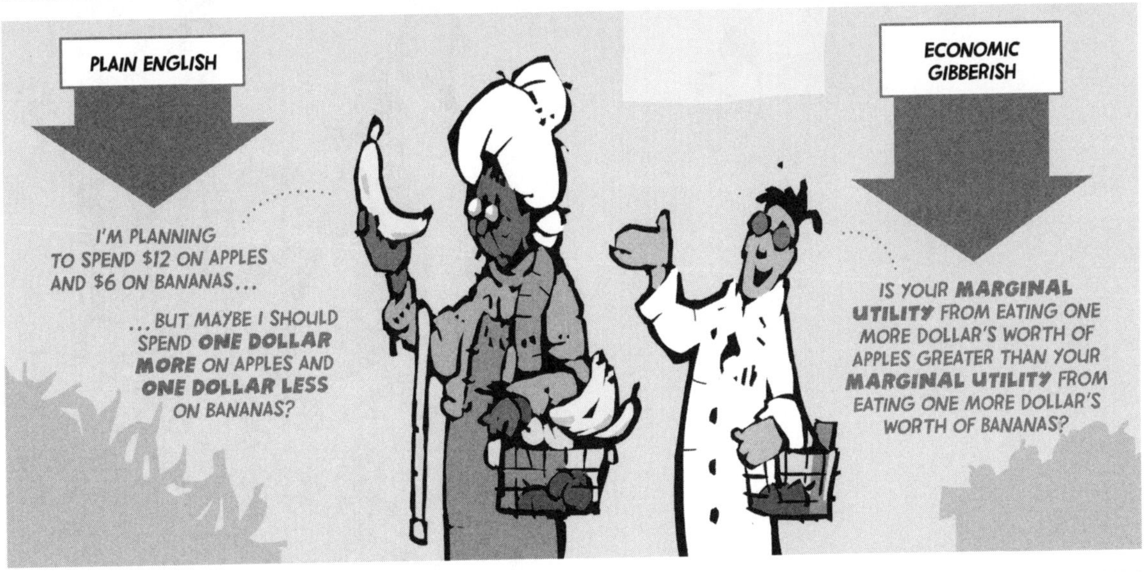
PLAIN ENGLISH
I'M PLANNING TO SPEND $12 ON APPLES AND $6 ON BANANAS...
...BUT MAYBE I SHOULD SPEND **ONE DOLLAR MORE** ON APPLES AND **ONE DOLLAR LESS** ON BANANAS?
ECONOMIC GIBBERISH
IS YOUR **MARGINAL UTILITY** FROM EATING ONE MORE DOLLAR'S WORTH OF APPLES GREATER THAN YOUR **MARGINAL UTILITY** FROM EATING ONE MORE DOLLAR'S WORTH OF BANANAS?

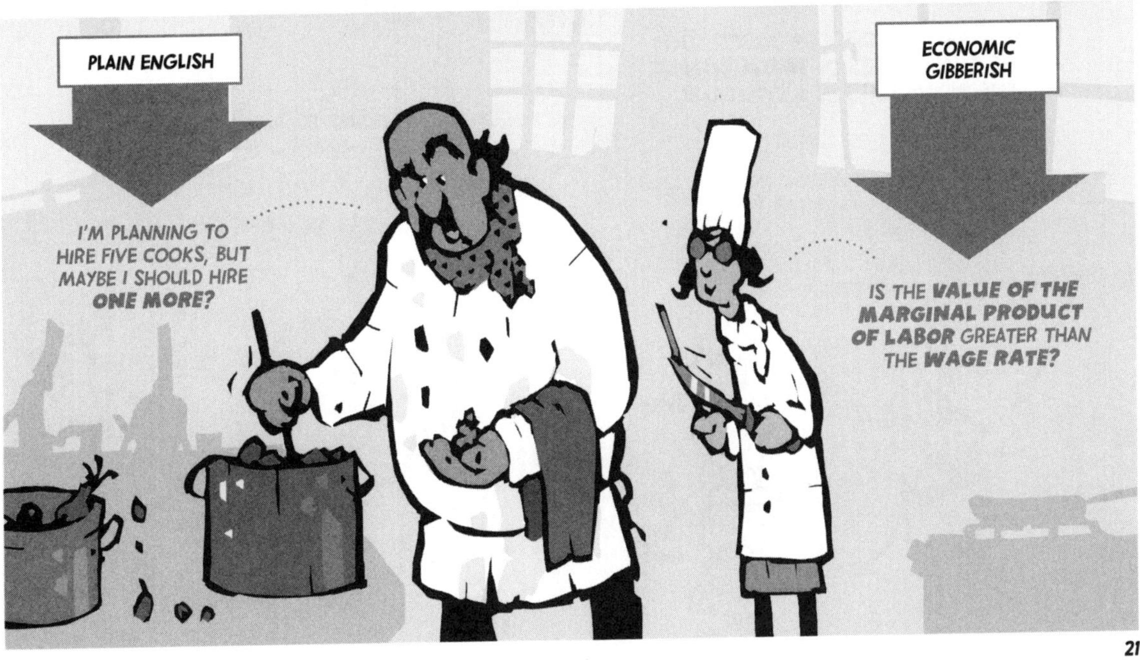
PLAIN ENGLISH
I'M PLANNING TO HIRE FIVE COOKS, BUT MAYBE I SHOULD HIRE **ONE MORE?**
ECONOMIC GIBBERISH
IS THE **VALUE OF THE MARGINAL PRODUCT OF LABOR** GREATER THAN THE **WAGE RATE?**

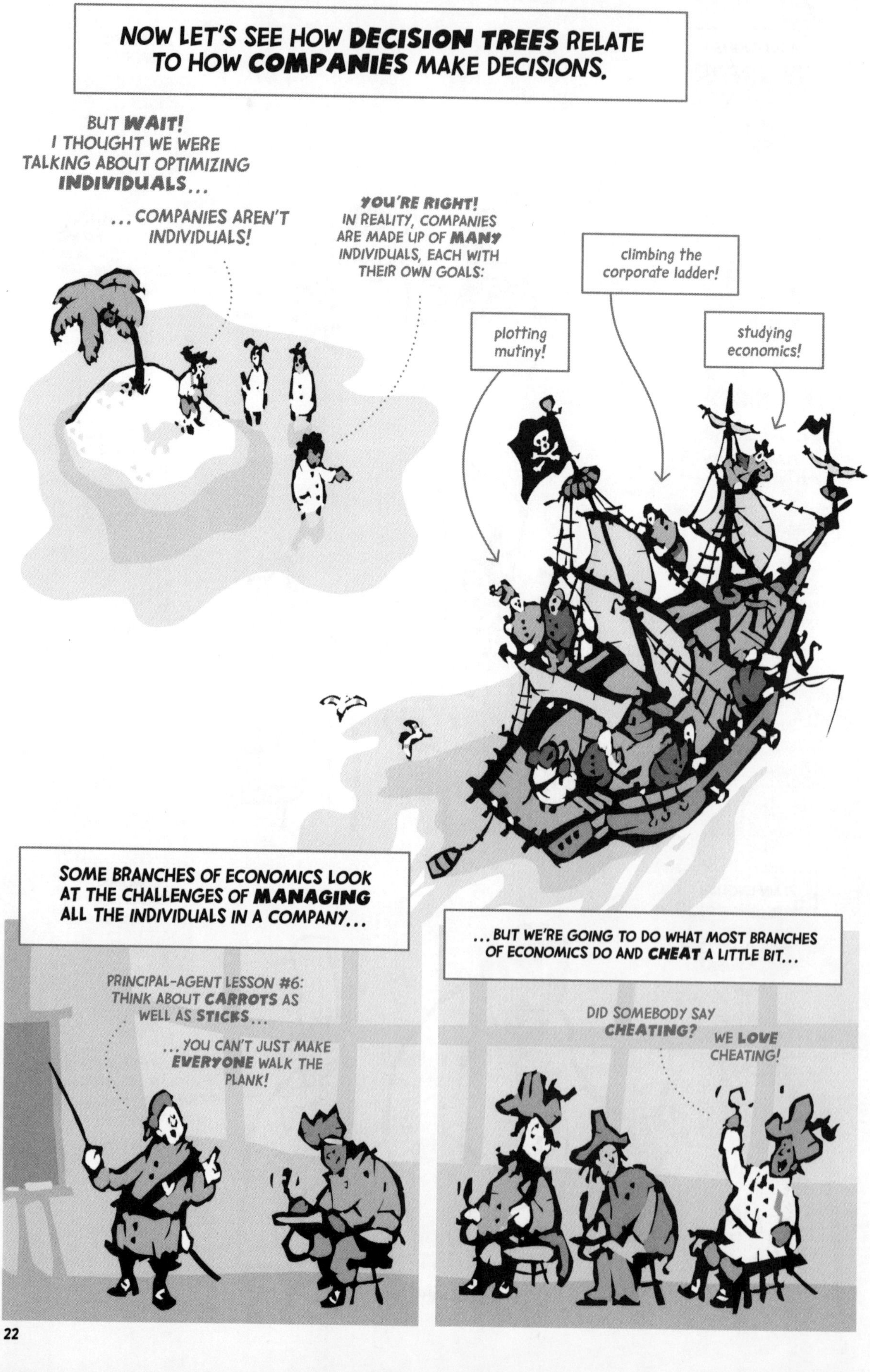
NOW LET'S SEE HOW DECISION TREES RELATE TO HOW COMPANIES MAKE DECISIONS.
BUT WAIT! I THOUGHT WE WERE TALKING ABOUT OPTIMIZING INDIVIDUALS...
...COMPANIES AREN'T INDIVIDUALS!
YOU'RE RIGHT! IN REALITY, COMPANIES ARE MADE UP OF MANY INDIVIDUALS, EACH WITH THEIR OWN GOALS:
climbing the corporate ladder!
plotting mutiny!
studying economics!
SOME BRANCHES OF ECONOMICS LOOK AT THE CHALLENGES OF MANAGING ALL THE INDIVIDUALS IN A COMPANY...
PRINCIPAL-AGENT LESSON #6: THINK ABOUT CARROTS AS WELL AS STICKS...
...YOU CAN'T JUST MAKE EVERYONE WALK THE PLANK!
...BUT WE'RE GOING TO DO WHAT MOST BRANCHES OF ECONOMICS DO AND CHEAT A LITTLE BIT...
DID SOMEBODY SAY CHEATING?
WE LOVE CHEATING!

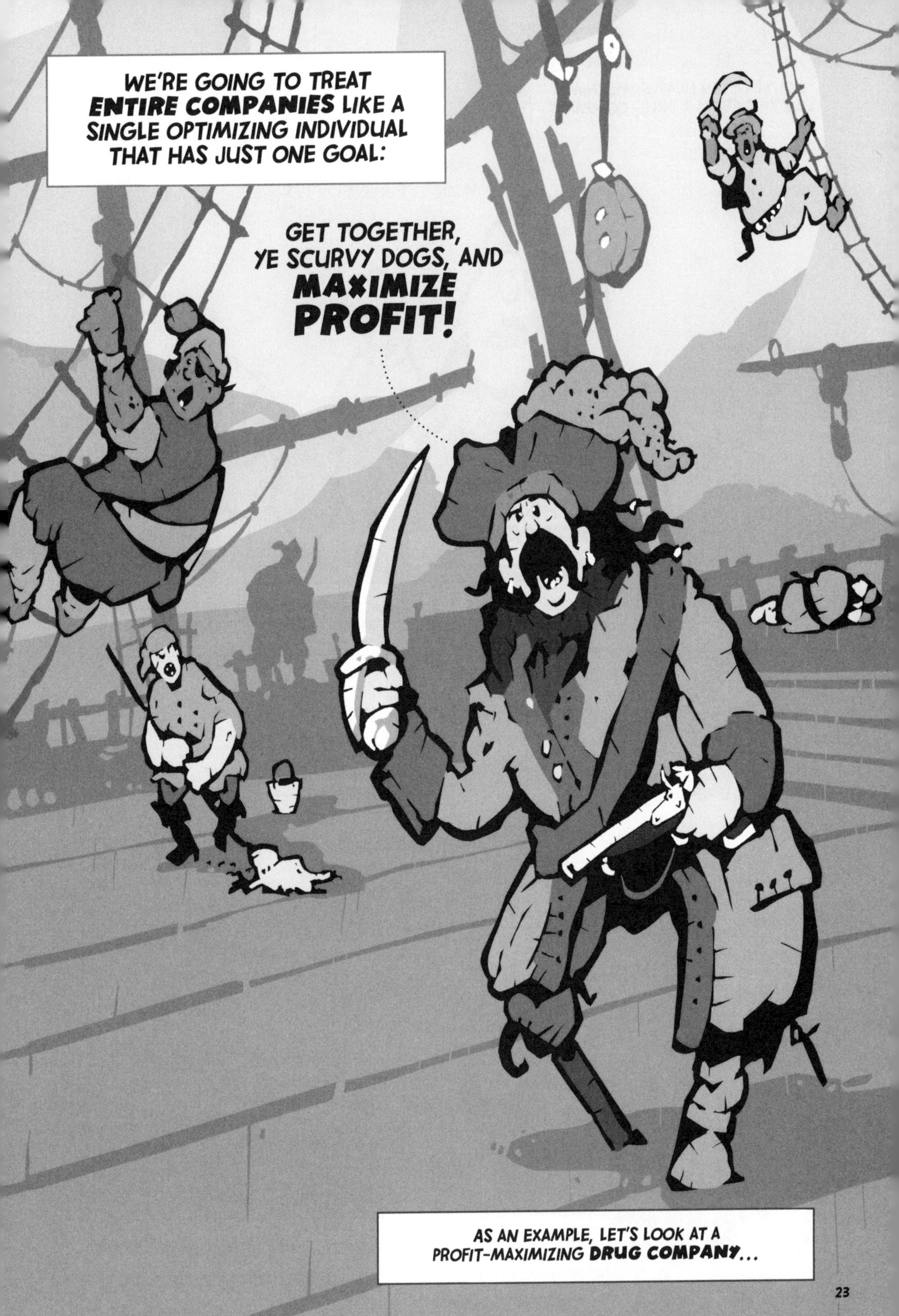
WE'RE GOING TO TREAT **ENTIRE COMPANIES** LIKE A SINGLE OPTIMIZING INDIVIDUAL THAT HAS JUST ONE GOAL:
GET TOGETHER, YE SCURVY DOGS, AND **MAXIMIZE PROFIT!**
AS AN EXAMPLE, LET'S LOOK AT A PROFIT-MAXIMIZING **DRUG COMPANY**...

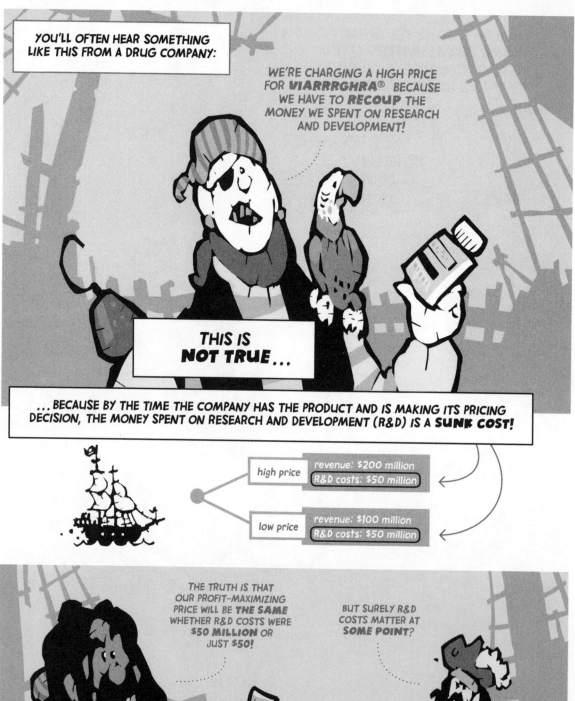

YOU'LL OFTEN HEAR SOMETHING LIKE THIS FROM A DRUG COMPANY:

WE'RE CHARGING A HIGH PRICE FOR **VIARRRGHRA**® BECAUSE WE HAVE TO **RECOUP** THE MONEY WE SPENT ON RESEARCH AND DEVELOPMENT!

THIS IS **NOT TRUE**...

...BECAUSE BY THE TIME THE COMPANY HAS THE PRODUCT AND IS MAKING ITS PRICING DECISION, THE MONEY SPENT ON RESEARCH AND DEVELOPMENT (R&D) IS A **SUNK COST!**

high price — revenue: $200 million / R&D costs: $50 million

low price — revenue: $100 million / R&D costs: $50 million

THE TRUTH IS THAT OUR PROFIT-MAXIMIZING PRICE WILL BE **THE SAME** WHETHER R&D COSTS WERE **$50 MILLION** OR JUST $50!

BUT SURELY R&D COSTS MATTER AT **SOME POINT**?

YES, THEY **DO**: SUNK COSTS MATTER **BEFORE** THEY ARE SUNK.

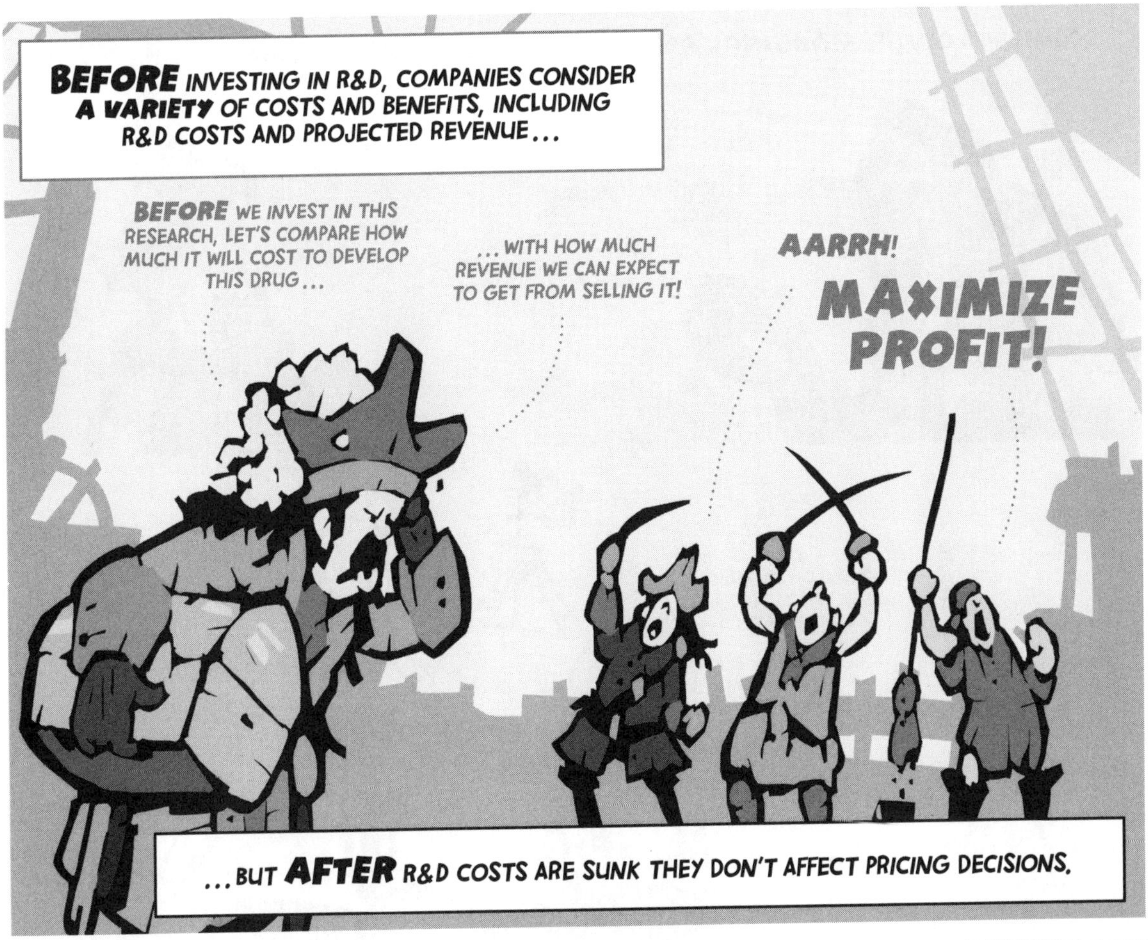
BEFORE INVESTING IN R&D, COMPANIES CONSIDER A VARIETY OF COSTS AND BENEFITS, INCLUDING R&D COSTS AND PROJECTED REVENUE...
BEFORE WE INVEST IN THIS RESEARCH, LET'S COMPARE HOW MUCH IT WILL COST TO DEVELOP THIS DRUG...
...WITH HOW MUCH REVENUE WE CAN EXPECT TO GET FROM SELLING IT!
AARRH!
MAXIMIZE PROFIT!
...BUT AFTER R&D COSTS ARE SUNK THEY DON'T AFFECT PRICING DECISIONS.

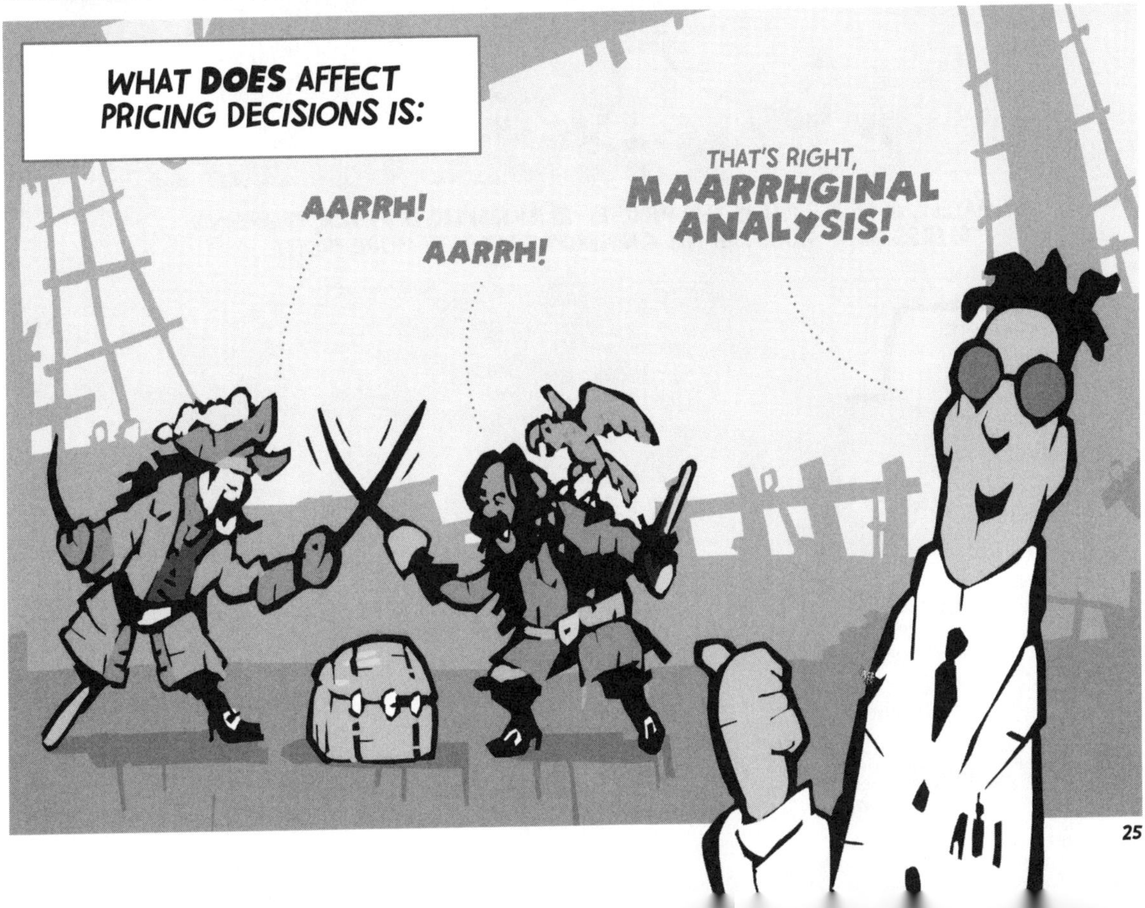
WHAT DOES AFFECT PRICING DECISIONS IS:
AARRH!
AARRH!
THAT'S RIGHT, MAARRHGINAL ANALYSIS!

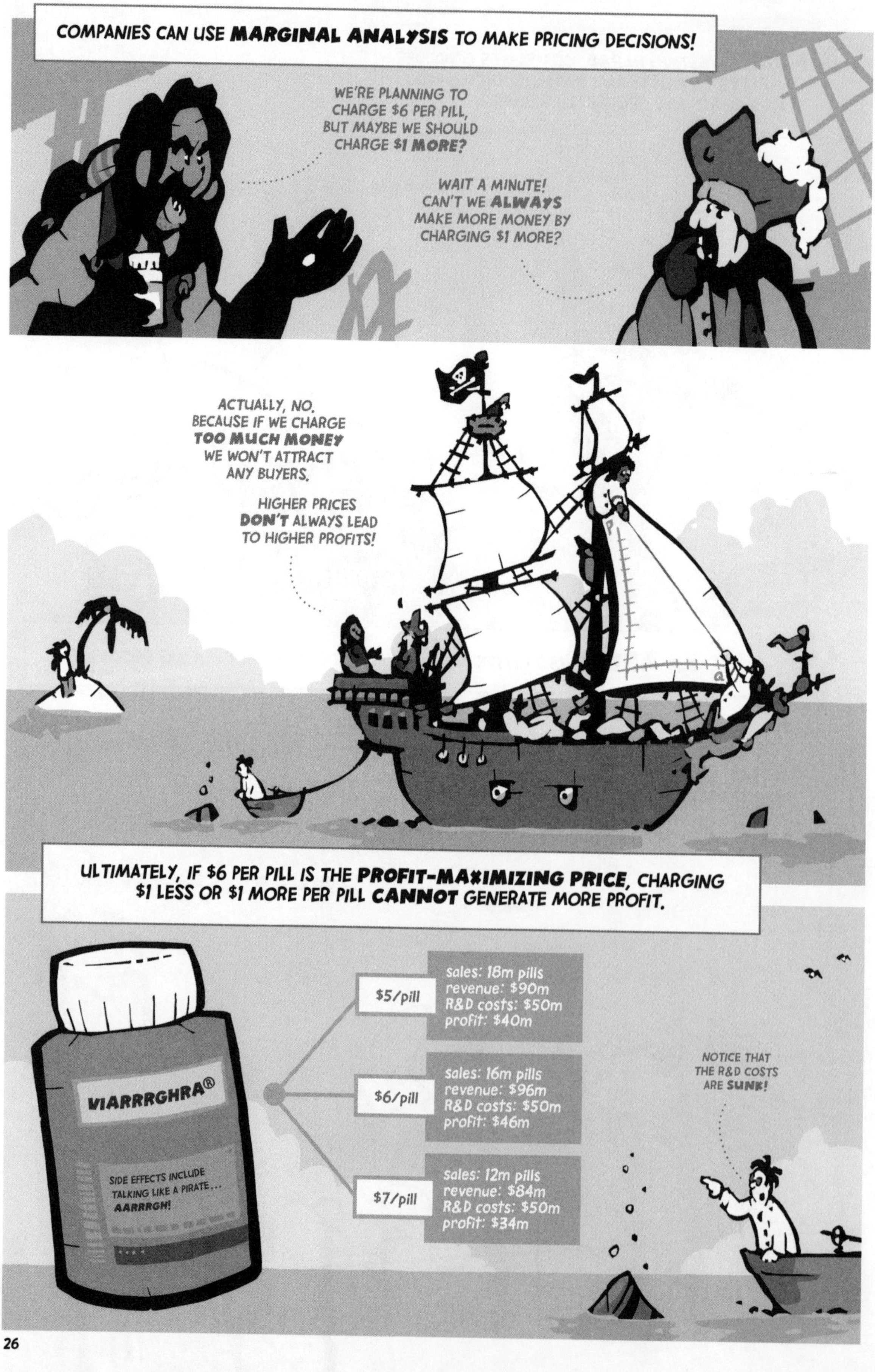

COMPANIES CAN USE **MARGINAL ANALYSIS** TO MAKE PRICING DECISIONS!
WE'RE PLANNING TO CHARGE $6 PER PILL, BUT MAYBE WE SHOULD CHARGE **$1 MORE?**
WAIT A MINUTE! CAN'T WE **ALWAYS** MAKE MORE MONEY BY CHARGING $1 MORE?
ACTUALLY, NO. BECAUSE IF WE CHARGE **TOO MUCH MONEY** WE WON'T ATTRACT ANY BUYERS.
HIGHER PRICES **DON'T** ALWAYS LEAD TO HIGHER PROFITS!
ULTIMATELY, IF $6 PER PILL IS THE **PROFIT-MAXIMIZING PRICE**, CHARGING $1 LESS OR $1 MORE PER PILL **CANNOT** GENERATE MORE PROFIT.
VIARRRGHRA®
SIDE EFFECTS INCLUDE TALKING LIKE A PIRATE... AARRRGH!
$5/pill
sales: 18m pills
revenue: $90m
R&D costs: $50m
profit: $40m
$6/pill
sales: 16m pills
revenue: $96m
R&D costs: $50m
profit: $46m
$7/pill
sales: 12m pills
revenue: $84m
R&D costs: $50m
profit: $34m
NOTICE THAT THE R&D COSTS ARE **SUNK!**

CHAPTER 3
TIME

BUT ENOUGH ABOUT COMPANIES, LET'S GET BACK TO **THE OPTIMIZING INDIVIDUAL.**

I WON THE **LOTTERY!**

$20 MILLION!

DON'T FORGET TO READ THE **FINE PRINT**...

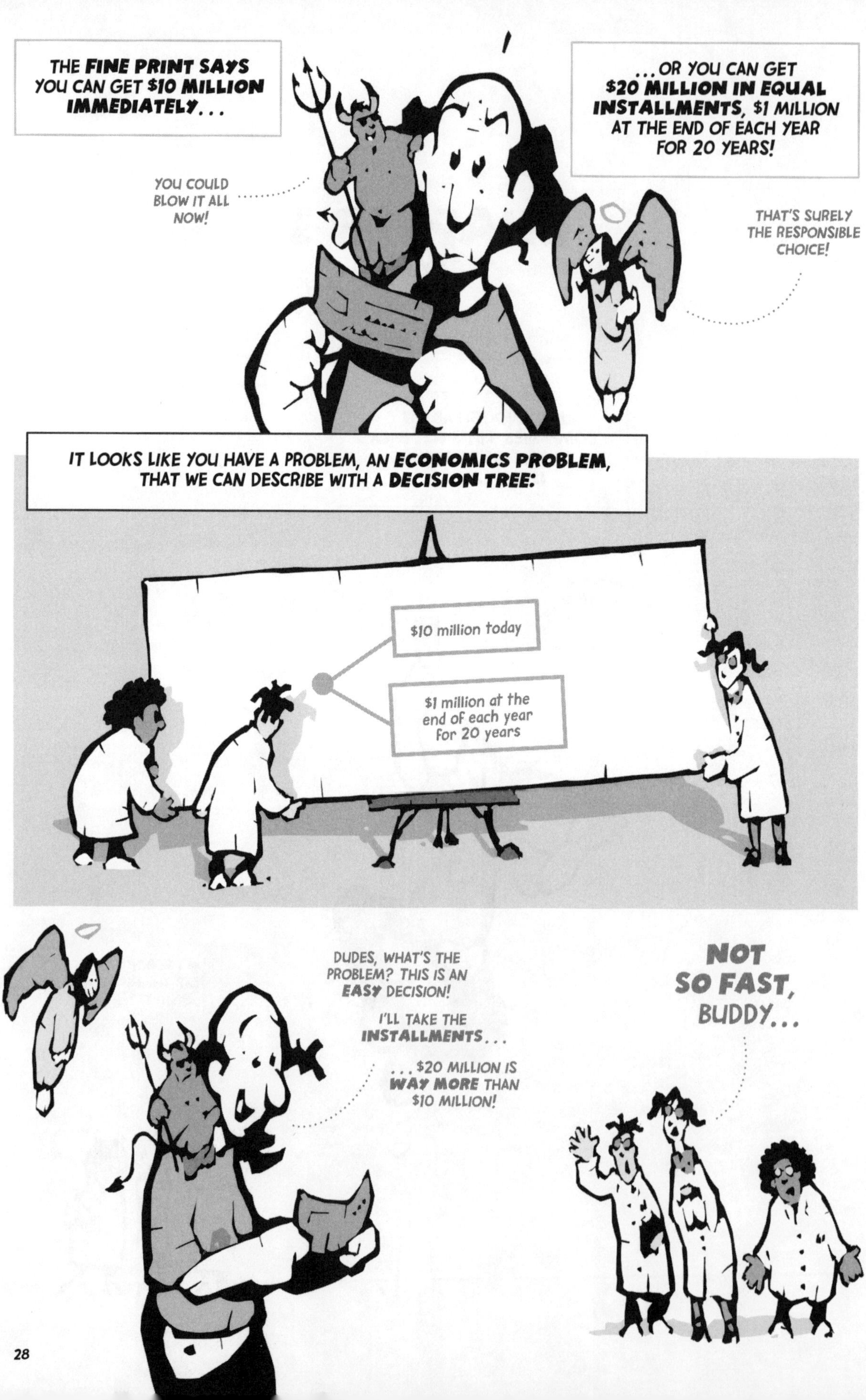
THE FINE PRINT SAYS YOU CAN GET $10 MILLION IMMEDIATELY...
...OR YOU CAN GET $20 MILLION IN EQUAL INSTALLMENTS, $1 MILLION AT THE END OF EACH YEAR FOR 20 YEARS!
YOU COULD BLOW IT ALL NOW!
THAT'S SURELY THE RESPONSIBLE CHOICE!
IT LOOKS LIKE YOU HAVE A PROBLEM, AN ECONOMICS PROBLEM, THAT WE CAN DESCRIBE WITH A DECISION TREE:
$10 million today
$1 million at the end of each year for 20 years
DUDES, WHAT'S THE PROBLEM? THIS IS AN EASY DECISION!
I'LL TAKE THE INSTALLMENTS...
...$20 MILLION IS WAY MORE THAN $10 MILLION!
NOT SO FAST, BUDDY...

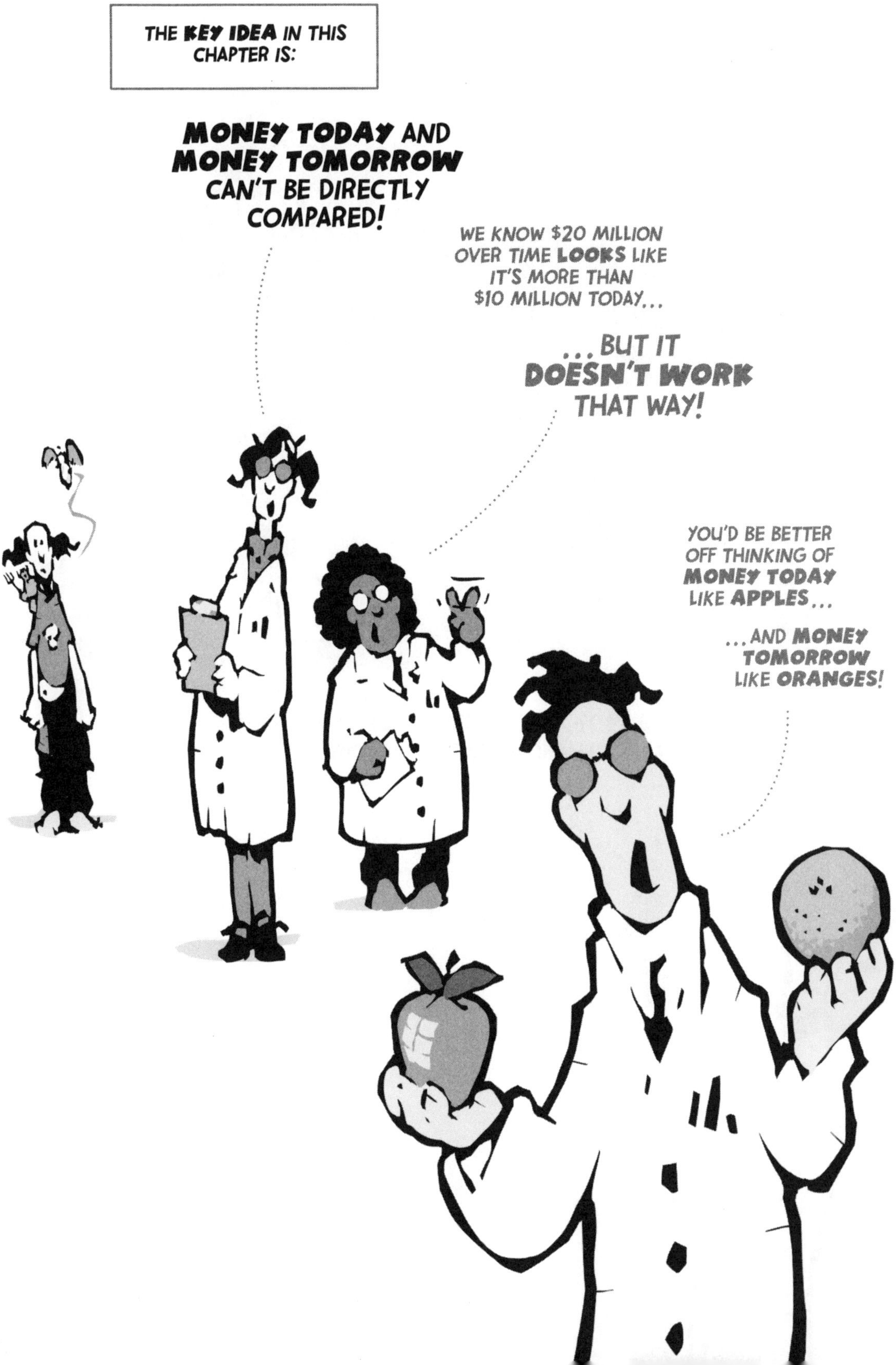
THE KEY IDEA IN THIS CHAPTER IS:
MONEY TODAY AND MONEY TOMORROW CAN'T BE DIRECTLY COMPARED!
WE KNOW $20 MILLION OVER TIME LOOKS LIKE IT'S MORE THAN $10 MILLION TODAY...
...BUT IT DOESN'T WORK THAT WAY!
YOU'D BE BETTER OFF THINKING OF MONEY TODAY LIKE APPLES...
...AND MONEY TOMORROW LIKE ORANGES!

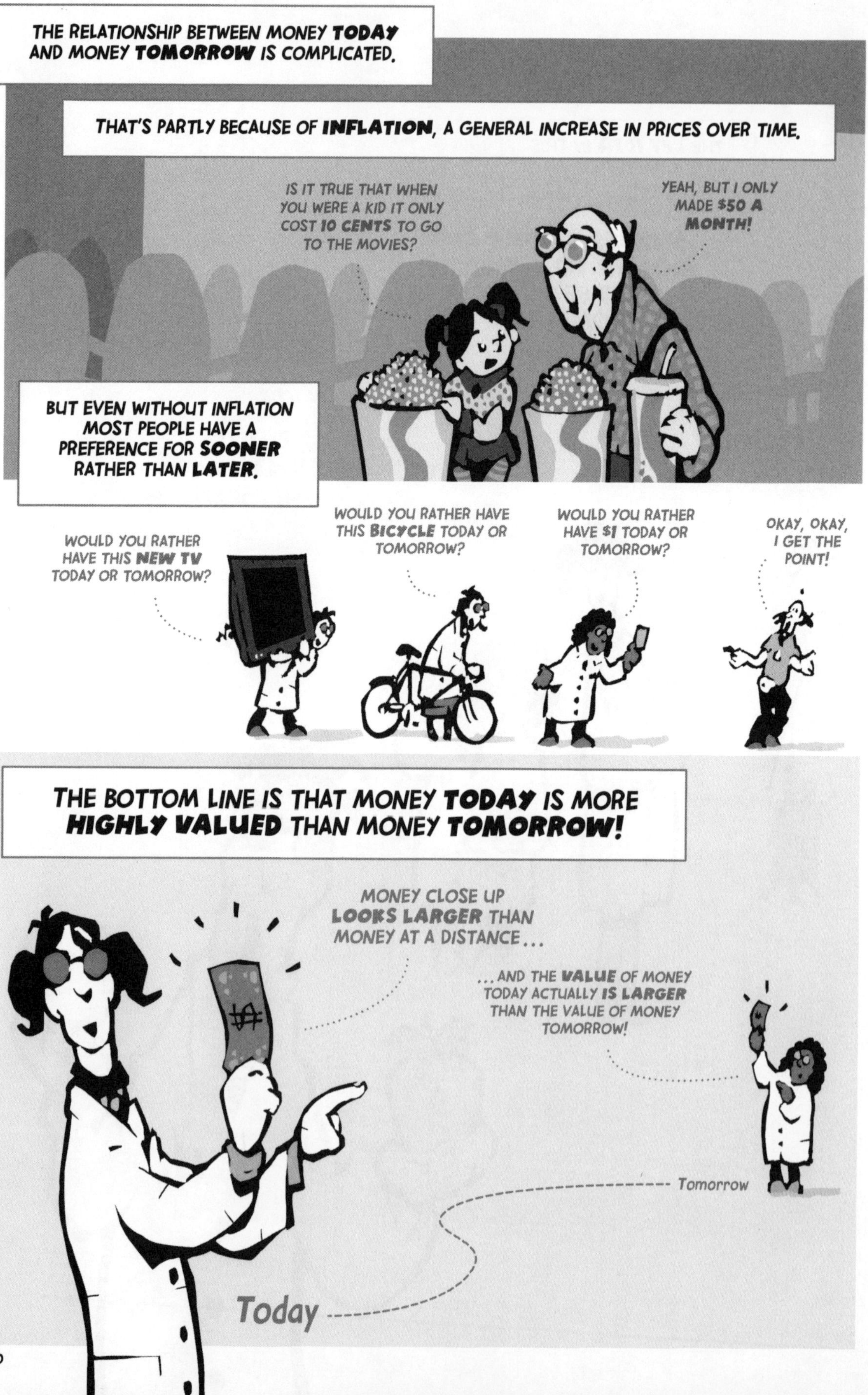
THE RELATIONSHIP BETWEEN MONEY TODAY AND MONEY TOMORROW IS COMPLICATED.
THAT'S PARTLY BECAUSE OF INFLATION, A GENERAL INCREASE IN PRICES OVER TIME.
IS IT TRUE THAT WHEN YOU WERE A KID IT ONLY COST 10 CENTS TO GO TO THE MOVIES?
YEAH, BUT I ONLY MADE $50 A MONTH!
BUT EVEN WITHOUT INFLATION MOST PEOPLE HAVE A PREFERENCE FOR SOONER RATHER THAN LATER.
WOULD YOU RATHER HAVE THIS NEW TV TODAY OR TOMORROW?
WOULD YOU RATHER HAVE THIS BICYCLE TODAY OR TOMORROW?
WOULD YOU RATHER HAVE $1 TODAY OR TOMORROW?
OKAY, OKAY, I GET THE POINT!
THE BOTTOM LINE IS THAT MONEY TODAY IS MORE HIGHLY VALUED THAN MONEY TOMORROW!
MONEY CLOSE UP LOOKS LARGER THAN MONEY AT A DISTANCE...
...AND THE VALUE OF MONEY TODAY ACTUALLY IS LARGER THAN THE VALUE OF MONEY TOMORROW!
Tomorrow
Today

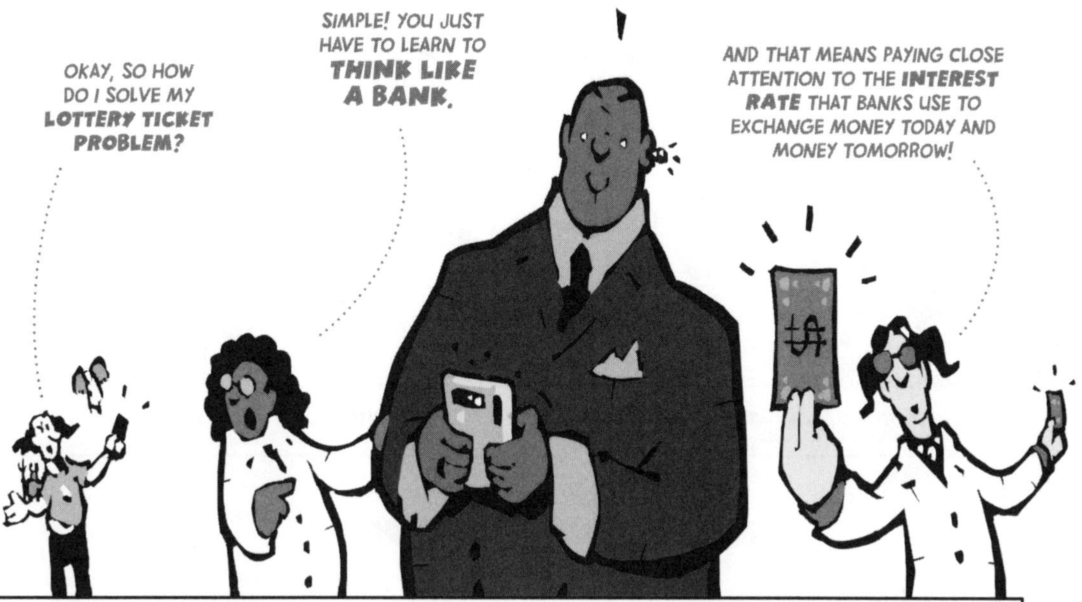
OKAY, SO HOW DO I SOLVE MY LOTTERY TICKET PROBLEM?
SIMPLE! YOU JUST HAVE TO LEARN TO THINK LIKE A BANK.
AND THAT MEANS PAYING CLOSE ATTENTION TO THE INTEREST RATE THAT BANKS USE TO EXCHANGE MONEY TODAY AND MONEY TOMORROW!

THE **INTEREST RATE** ALLOWS US TO TURN MONEY TODAY INTO MONEY TOMORROW, AND VICE VERSA.

IF YOU PUT MONEY IN A BANK TODAY,
THE INTEREST RATE DETERMINES HOW MUCH MONEY YOU'LL **HAVE IN THE FUTURE.**

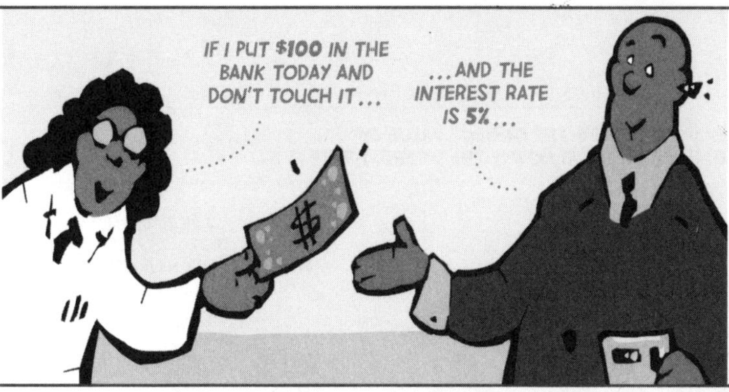
IF I PUT $100 IN THE BANK TODAY AND DON'T TOUCH IT...
...AND THE INTEREST RATE IS 5%...

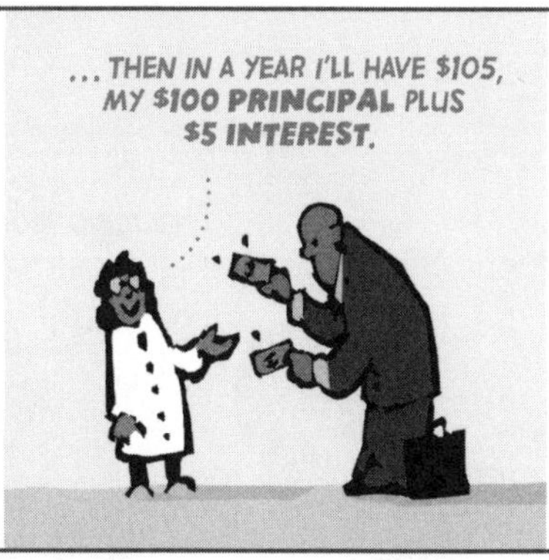
...THEN IN A YEAR I'LL HAVE $105, MY $100 PRINCIPAL PLUS $5 INTEREST.

AND **IF YOU BORROW MONEY FROM A BANK TODAY,**
THE INTEREST RATE DETERMINES HOW MUCH MONEY YOU'LL **OWE THEM IN THE FUTURE.**

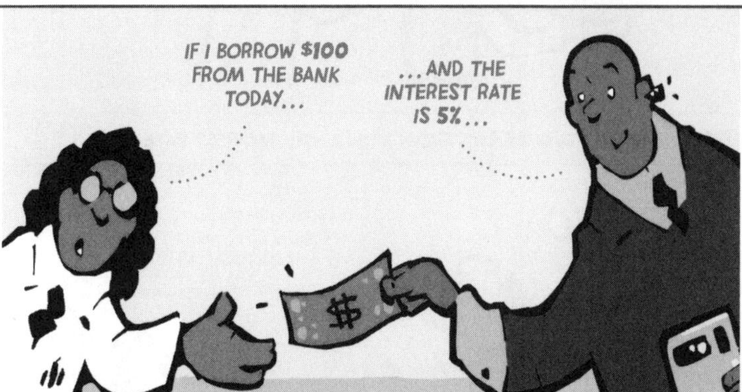
IF I BORROW $100 FROM THE BANK TODAY...
...AND THE INTEREST RATE IS 5%...

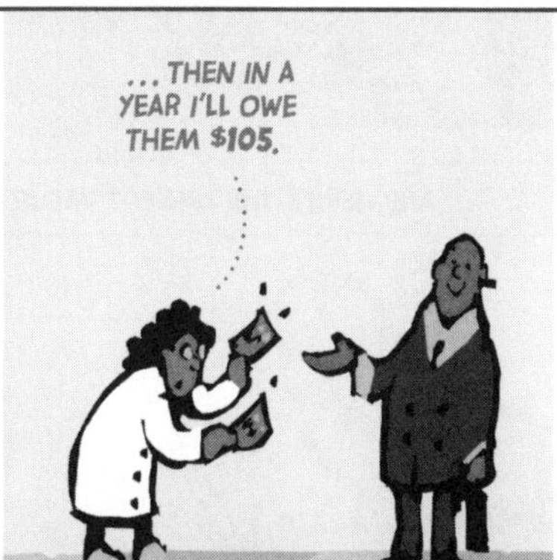
...THEN IN A YEAR I'LL OWE THEM $105.

IN ECONOMICS LINGO, THIS MEANS THAT $100 IS THE **PRESENT VALUE** OF GETTING $105 IN ONE YEAR IF THE INTEREST RATE IS 5%.

PRESENT VALUE IS THE VALUE **TODAY** OF ONE OR MORE **FUTURE** PAYMENTS.

IT ALLOWS US TO **TRANSLATE MONEY TOMORROW INTO MONEY TODAY.**

YOU CAN TURN A ONE-TIME PAYMENT OF MONEY TOMORROW INTO MONEY TODAY BY USING:

THE **FORMULA** FOR **THE PRESENT VALUE OF A LUMP SUM**

PV is the present value

x is the amount of money to be received in the future (at the end of **n** years)

$$PV = \frac{x}{(1+r)^n}$$

r is the interest rate (r=0.05 for a 5% interest rate)

If you like math, you can find more details at **www.cartooneconomics.com**. If you don't like math, we promise this chapter is as hard as it gets!

FOR EXAMPLE, HERE'S THE PRESENT VALUE OF GETTING $100 **ONE YEAR** FROM NOW IF THE INTEREST RATE IS 5%:

$$\frac{100}{(1+.05)^1} = \$95.24$$

IF YOU PUT **$95.24** IN THE BANK NOW AT 5% INTEREST, IN ONE YEAR YOU'LL HAVE **$100**!

AND HERE'S THE PRESENT VALUE OF GETTING $100 **TWO YEARS** FROM NOW IF THE INTEREST RATE IS 5%:

$$\frac{100}{(1+.05)^2} = \$90.70$$

IF YOU PUT **$90.70** IN THE BANK NOW AT 5% INTEREST, IN TWO YEARS YOU'LL HAVE **$100**!

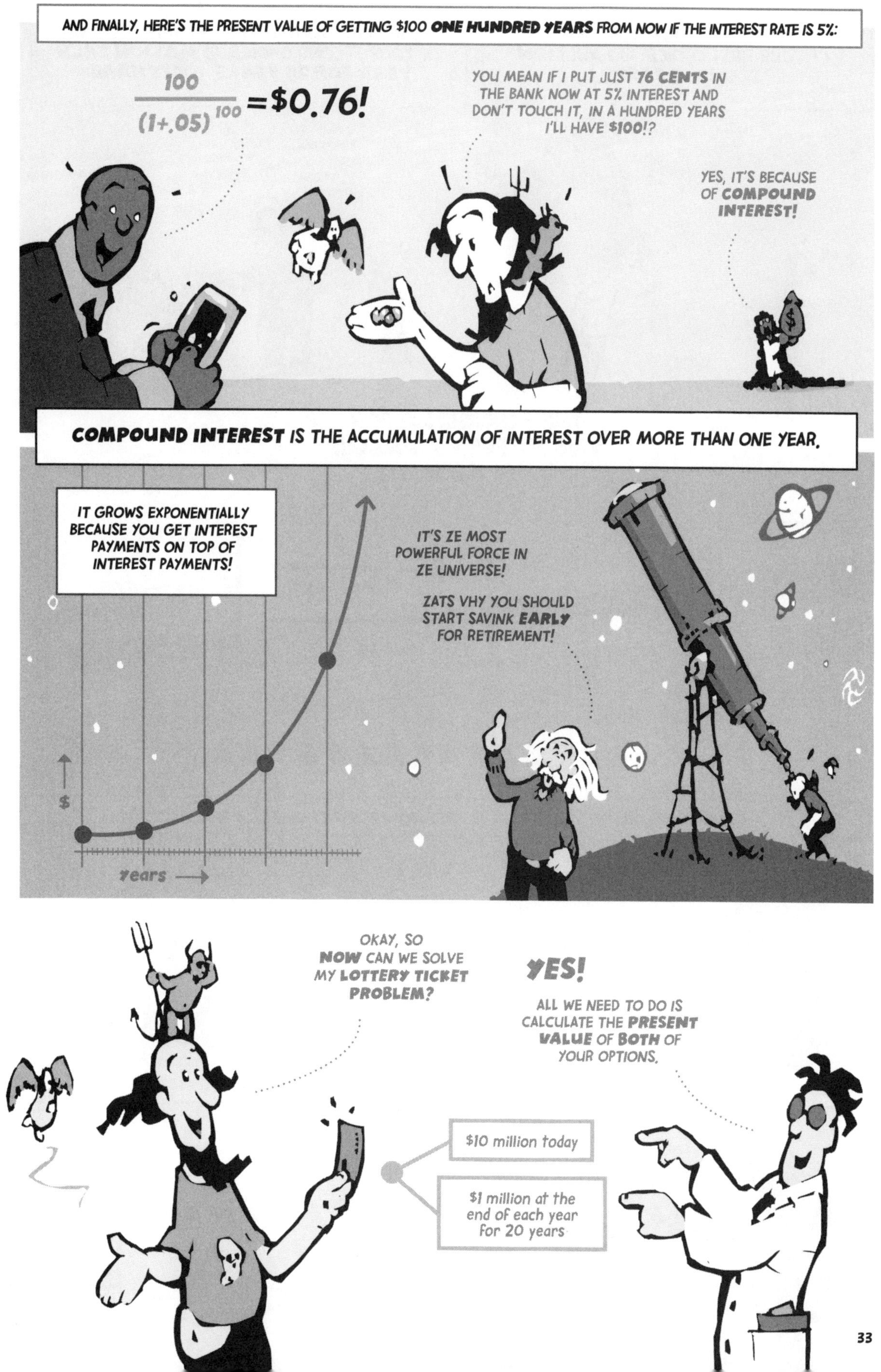
AND FINALLY, HERE'S THE PRESENT VALUE OF GETTING $100 ONE HUNDRED YEARS FROM NOW IF THE INTEREST RATE IS 5%:
$\frac{100}{(1+.05)^{100}}$ =$0.76!
YOU MEAN IF I PUT JUST 76 CENTS IN THE BANK NOW AT 5% INTEREST AND DON'T TOUCH IT, IN A HUNDRED YEARS I'LL HAVE $100!?
YES, IT'S BECAUSE OF COMPOUND INTEREST!
COMPOUND INTEREST IS THE ACCUMULATION OF INTEREST OVER MORE THAN ONE YEAR.
IT GROWS EXPONENTIALLY BECAUSE YOU GET INTEREST PAYMENTS ON TOP OF INTEREST PAYMENTS!
$
years
IT'S ZE MOST POWERFUL FORCE IN ZE UNIVERSE!
ZATS VHY YOU SHOULD START SAVINK EARLY FOR RETIREMENT!
OKAY, SO NOW CAN WE SOLVE MY LOTTERY TICKET PROBLEM?
YES!
ALL WE NEED TO DO IS CALCULATE THE PRESENT VALUE OF BOTH OF YOUR OPTIONS.
$10 million today
$1 million at the end of each year for 20 years

CALCULATING THE **PRESENT VALUE** OF YOUR FIRST CHOICE, **$10 MILLION TODAY**, IS **EASY**...

IS THE POPE CATHOLIC?

...IT'S $10 **MILLION!**

... BUT CALCULATING THE **PRESENT VALUE** OF YOUR SECOND CHOICE, **$1 MILLION EACH YEAR FOR 20 YEARS**, LOOKS **HARD**:

THIS OPTION INVOLVES 20 PAYMENTS OVER 20 YEARS, SO WE'LL NEED TO ADD UP 20 SEPARATE LUMP-SUM CALCULATIONS!

OR WE CAN JUST USE ...

THE **FORMULA** FOR **THE PRESENT VALUE OF AN ANNUITY**

AN **ANNUITY** JUST MEANS YOU GET A FIXED AMOUNT OF MONEY ON AN **ANNUAL** BASIS FOR SOME NUMBER OF YEARS.

x is the amount to be received at the end of **each year** for **n** years

$$PV = x \left[\frac{1 - \frac{1}{(1+r)^n}}{r} \right]$$

r is the interest rate (r=0.05 for a 5% interest rate)

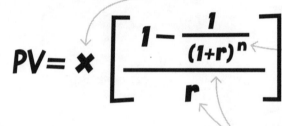

SO HERE'S THE PRESENT VALUE OF THE LOTTERY ANNUITY **IF THE INTEREST RATE IS 5%:**

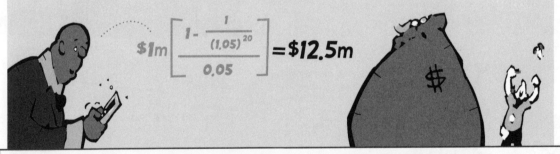

$$\$1m \left[\frac{1 - \frac{1}{(1.05)^{20}}}{0.05} \right] = \$12.5m$$

AND HERE'S THE PRESENT VALUE OF THE LOTTERY ANNUITY **IF THE INTEREST RATE IS 10%:**

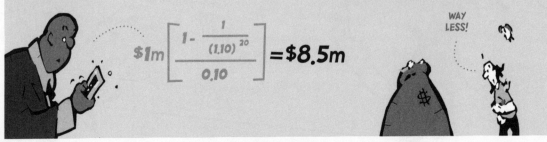

$$\$1m \left[\frac{1 - \frac{1}{(1.10)^{20}}}{0.10} \right] = \$8.5m$$

WAY LESS!

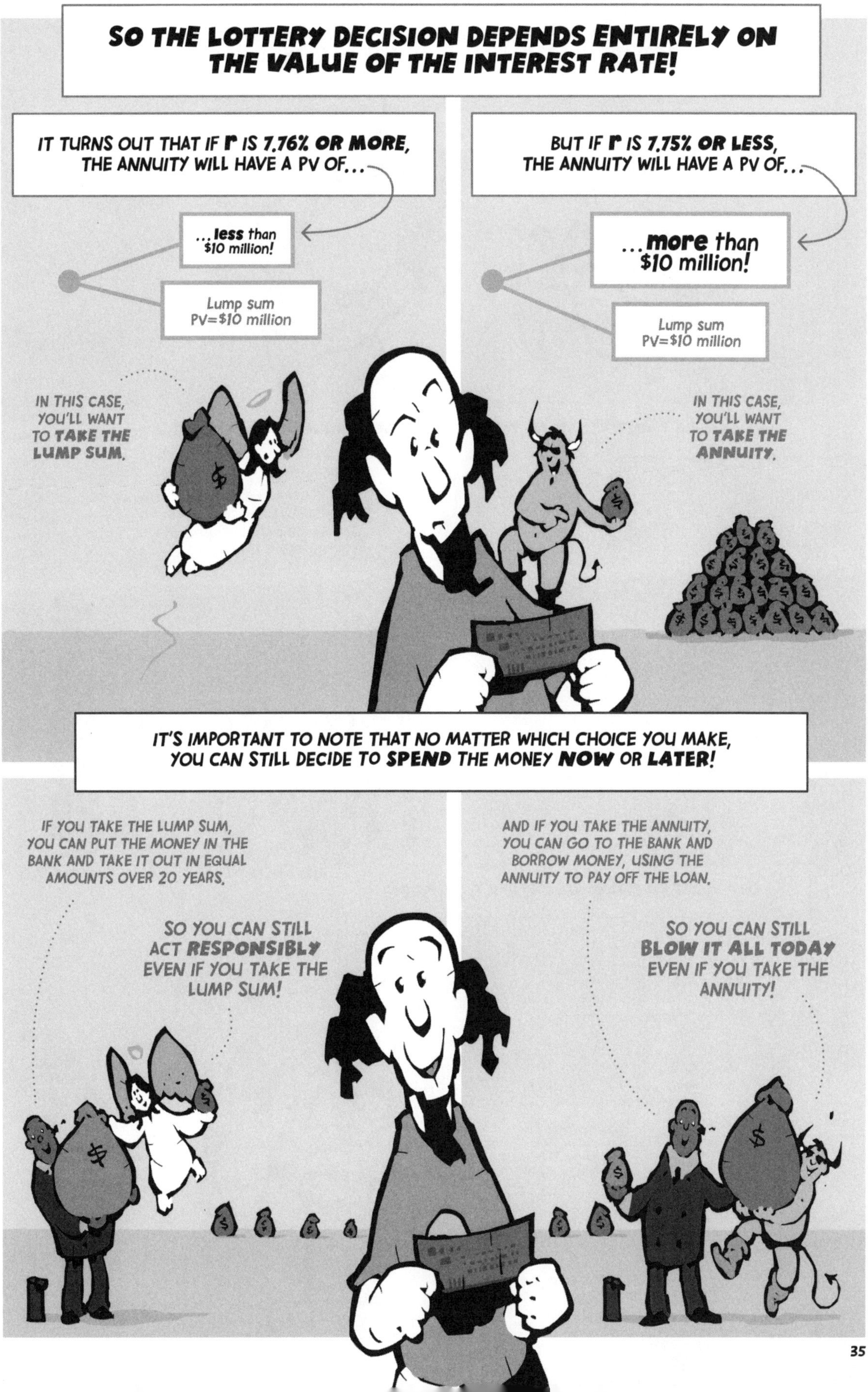
SO THE LOTTERY DECISION DEPENDS ENTIRELY ON THE VALUE OF THE INTEREST RATE!
IT TURNS OUT THAT IF r IS 7.76% OR MORE, THE ANNUITY WILL HAVE A PV OF...
...less than $10 million!
Lump sum PV=$10 million
BUT IF r IS 7.75% OR LESS, THE ANNUITY WILL HAVE A PV OF...
...more than $10 million!
Lump sum PV=$10 million
IN THIS CASE, YOU'LL WANT TO TAKE THE LUMP SUM.
IN THIS CASE, YOU'LL WANT TO TAKE THE ANNUITY.
IT'S IMPORTANT TO NOTE THAT NO MATTER WHICH CHOICE YOU MAKE, YOU CAN STILL DECIDE TO SPEND THE MONEY NOW OR LATER!
IF YOU TAKE THE LUMP SUM, YOU CAN PUT THE MONEY IN THE BANK AND TAKE IT OUT IN EQUAL AMOUNTS OVER 20 YEARS.
SO YOU CAN STILL ACT RESPONSIBLY EVEN IF YOU TAKE THE LUMP SUM!
AND IF YOU TAKE THE ANNUITY, YOU CAN GO TO THE BANK AND BORROW MONEY, USING THE ANNUITY TO PAY OFF THE LOAN.
SO YOU CAN STILL BLOW IT ALL TODAY EVEN IF YOU TAKE THE ANNUITY!

LIKE THE LOTTERY CHOICE, **ALL** DECISIONS INVOLVING TIME AND MONEY DEPEND ON THE VALUE OF THE INTEREST RATE.

r REALLY IS ALMIGHTY!

THAT'S **ONE THING** WE CAN AGREE ON.

FOR EXAMPLE, r MATTERS *IF YOU'RE* **THINKING OF STARTING A SMALL BUSINESS:**

THE LOWER THE INTEREST RATE, THE MORE ATTRACTIVE IT IS TO BORROW MONEY AND GIVE IT A TRY!

| give it a try | borrow $100,000 now, and then earn $60,000 a year for the next 30 years |
| keep your day job | earn $50,000 a year for the next 30 years |

OR IF YOU'RE **THINKING OF BUYING A NEW CAR:**

THE LOWER THE INTEREST RATE, THE MORE ATTRACTIVE IT IS TO BUY THE HYBRID!

| buy Toyota Prius hybrid | spend $30,000 now, plus $2,000 for gas each year for the next 10 years |
| buy Toyota Corolla | spend $20,000 now, plus $3,000 for gas each year for the next 10 years |

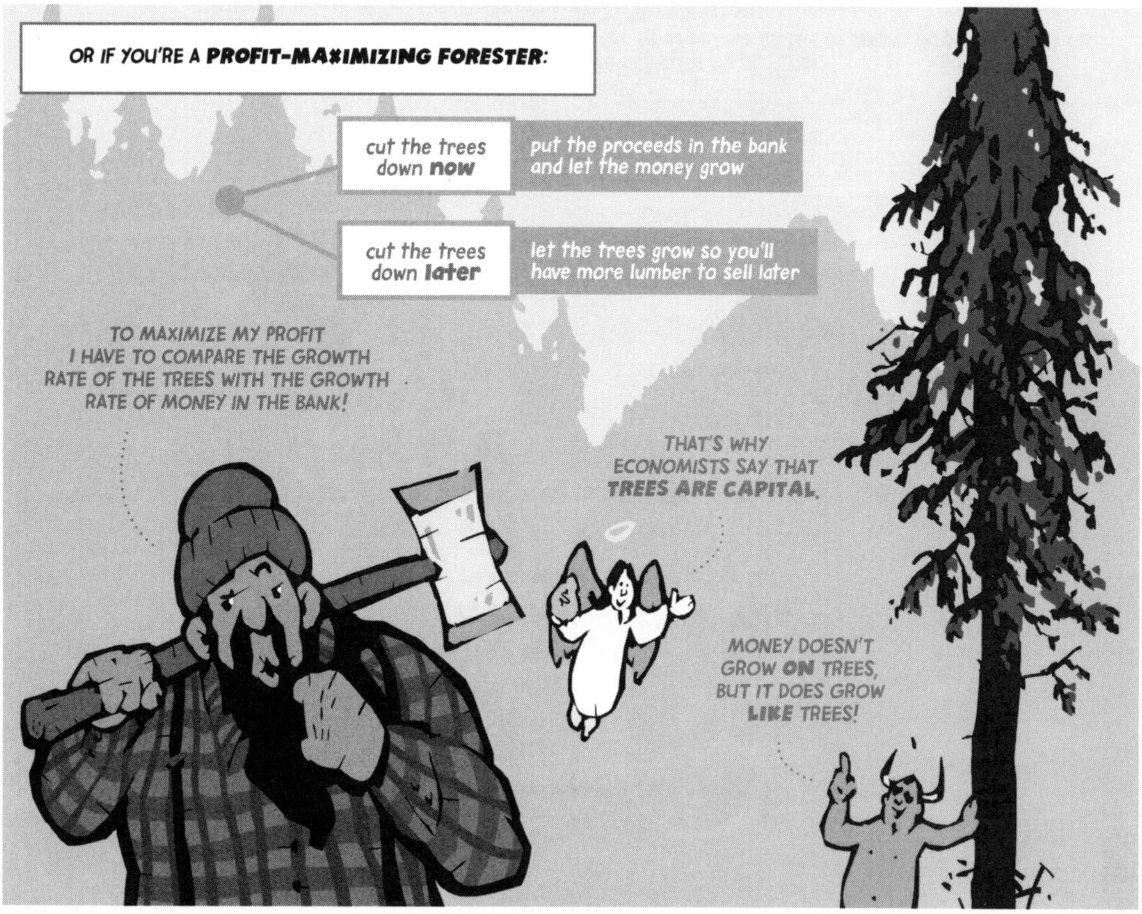
OR IF YOU'RE A **PROFIT-MAXIMIZING FORESTER**:
cut the trees down **now**
put the proceeds in the bank and let the money grow
cut the trees down **later**
let the trees grow so you'll have more lumber to sell later
TO MAXIMIZE MY PROFIT I HAVE TO COMPARE THE GROWTH RATE OF THE TREES WITH THE GROWTH RATE OF MONEY IN THE BANK!
THAT'S WHY ECONOMISTS SAY THAT **TREES ARE CAPITAL**.
MONEY DOESN'T GROW **ON** TREES, BUT IT DOES GROW **LIKE** TREES!

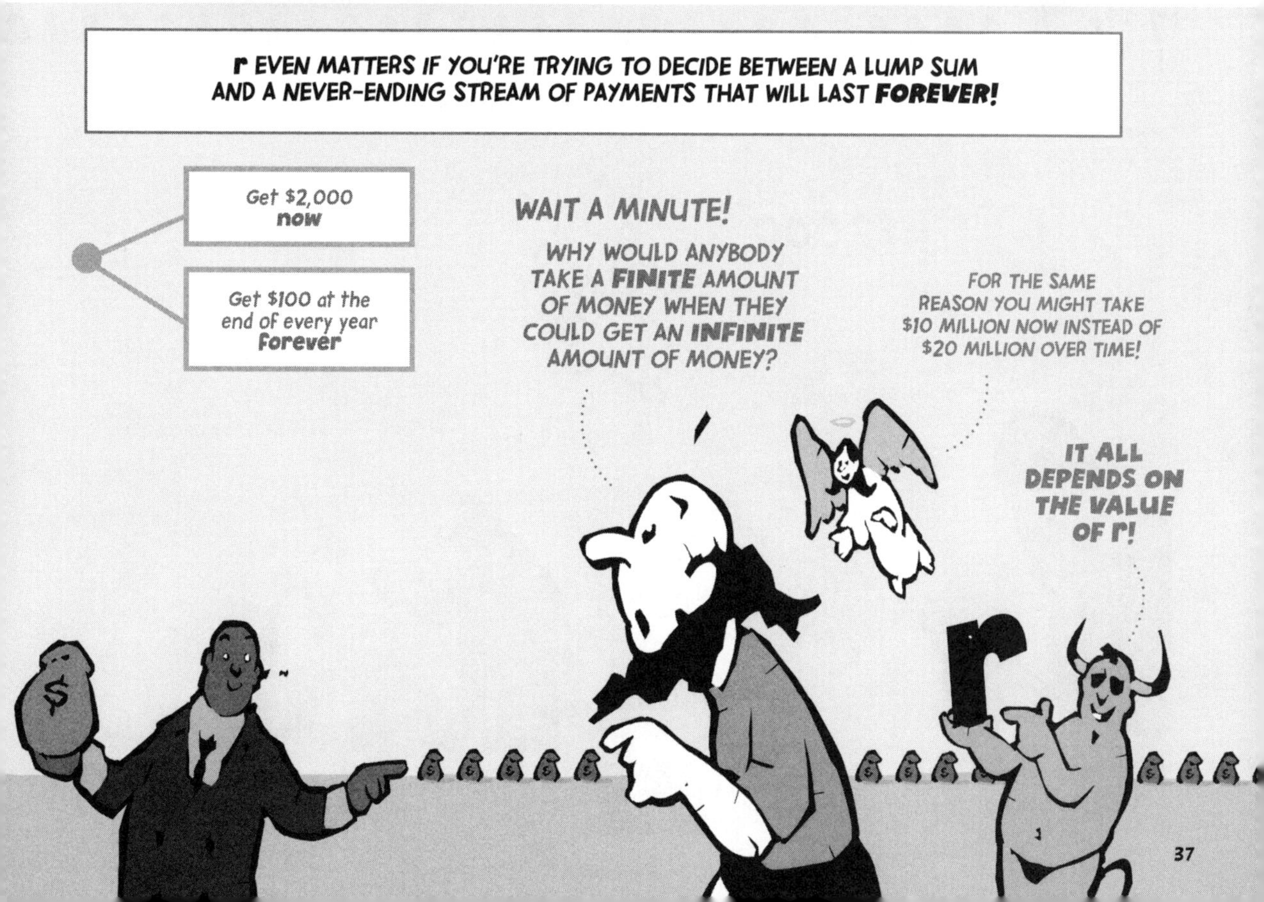
r EVEN MATTERS IF YOU'RE TRYING TO DECIDE BETWEEN A LUMP SUM AND A NEVER-ENDING STREAM OF PAYMENTS THAT WILL LAST **FOREVER!**
Get $2,000 **now**
Get $100 at the end of every year **forever**
WAIT A MINUTE!
WHY WOULD ANYBODY TAKE A **FINITE** AMOUNT OF MONEY WHEN THEY COULD GET AN **INFINITE** AMOUNT OF MONEY?
FOR THE SAME REASON YOU MIGHT TAKE $10 MILLION NOW INSTEAD OF $20 MILLION OVER TIME!
IT ALL DEPENDS ON THE VALUE OF r!
r

TO SEE WHY $2,000 **NOW** MIGHT BE BETTER THAN $100 AT THE END OF EVERY YEAR **FOREVER**, CONSIDER AN INTEREST RATE OF 10%:

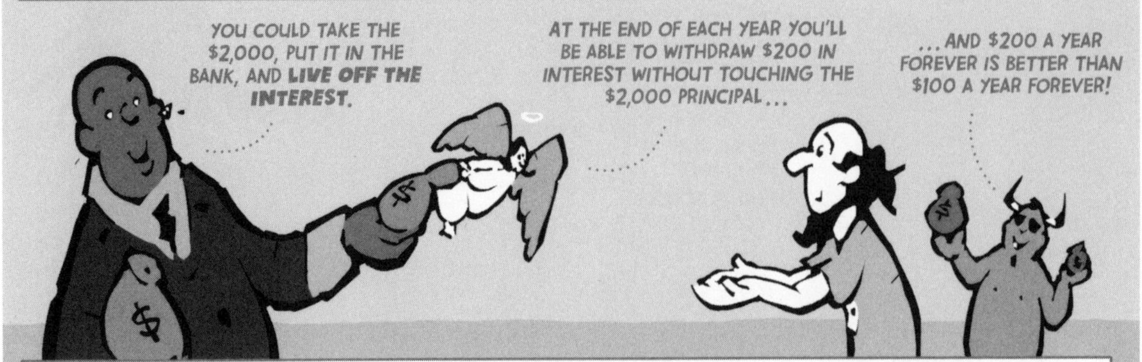

YOU COULD TAKE THE $2,000, PUT IT IN THE BANK, AND **LIVE OFF THE INTEREST**.
AT THE END OF EACH YEAR YOU'LL BE ABLE TO WITHDRAW $200 IN INTEREST WITHOUT TOUCHING THE $2,000 PRINCIPAL...
...AND $200 A YEAR FOREVER IS BETTER THAN $100 A YEAR FOREVER!

IN FACT, THE PRESENT VALUE OF GETTING A FIXED AMOUNT OF MONEY ON AN ANNUAL BASIS **FOREVER** IS GIVEN BY:

A **PERPETUITY** IS SIMPLY A PERPETUAL ANNUITY...

...IN OTHER WORDS, IT'S AN ANNUITY THAT LASTS **FOREVER!**

THE **FORMULA** FOR **THE PRESENT VALUE OF A PERPETUITY**

$$PV = \frac{x}{r}$$

x is the amount to be received at the end of each year forever.

r is the all-powerful interest rate.

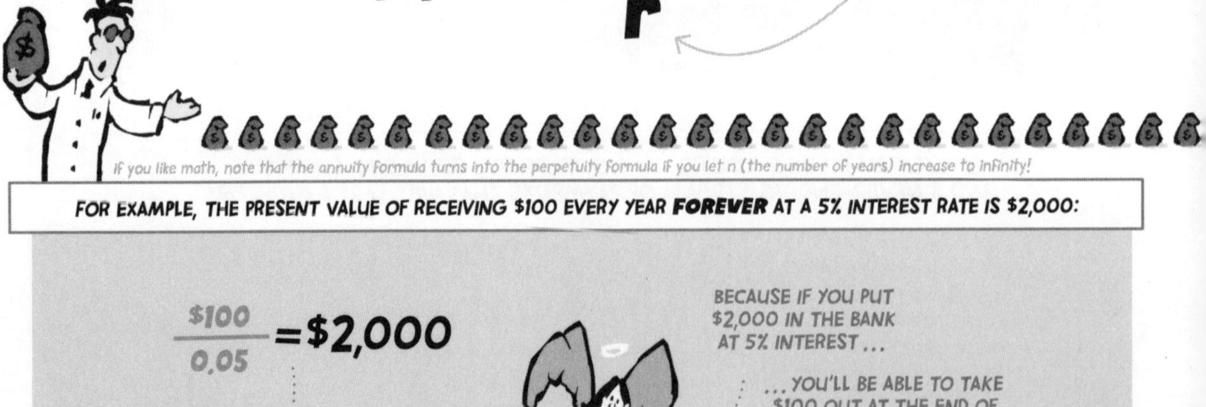

If you like math, note that the annuity formula turns into the perpetuity formula if you let n (the number of years) increase to infinity!

FOR EXAMPLE, THE PRESENT VALUE OF RECEIVING $100 EVERY YEAR **FOREVER** AT A 5% INTEREST RATE IS $2,000:

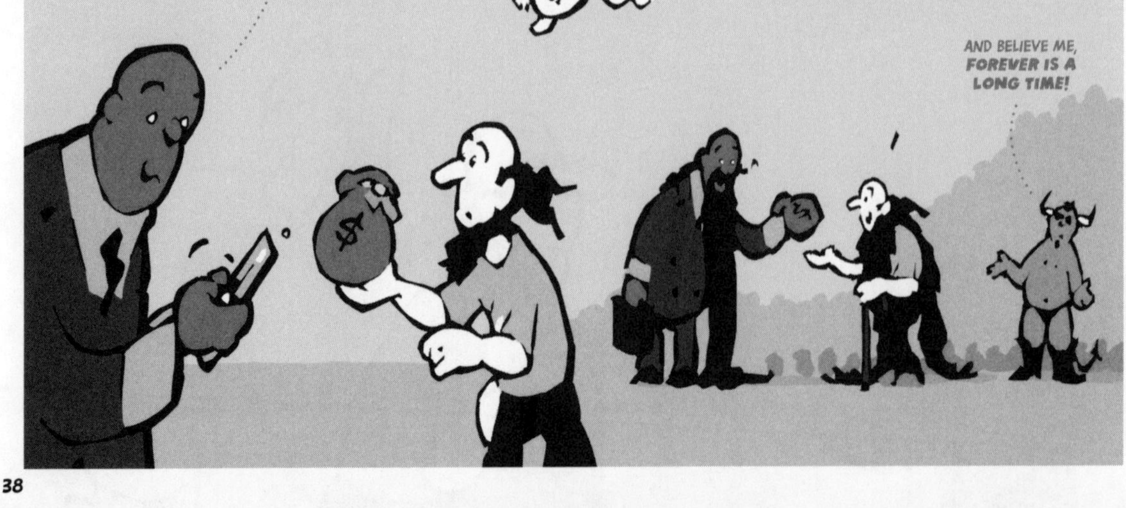

$\frac{\$100}{0.05} = \$2,000$
BECAUSE IF YOU PUT $2,000 IN THE BANK AT 5% INTEREST...
...YOU'LL BE ABLE TO TAKE $100 OUT AT THE END OF EACH YEAR **FOREVER**.
AND BELIEVE ME, **FOREVER IS A LONG TIME!**

CHAPTER 4
RISK

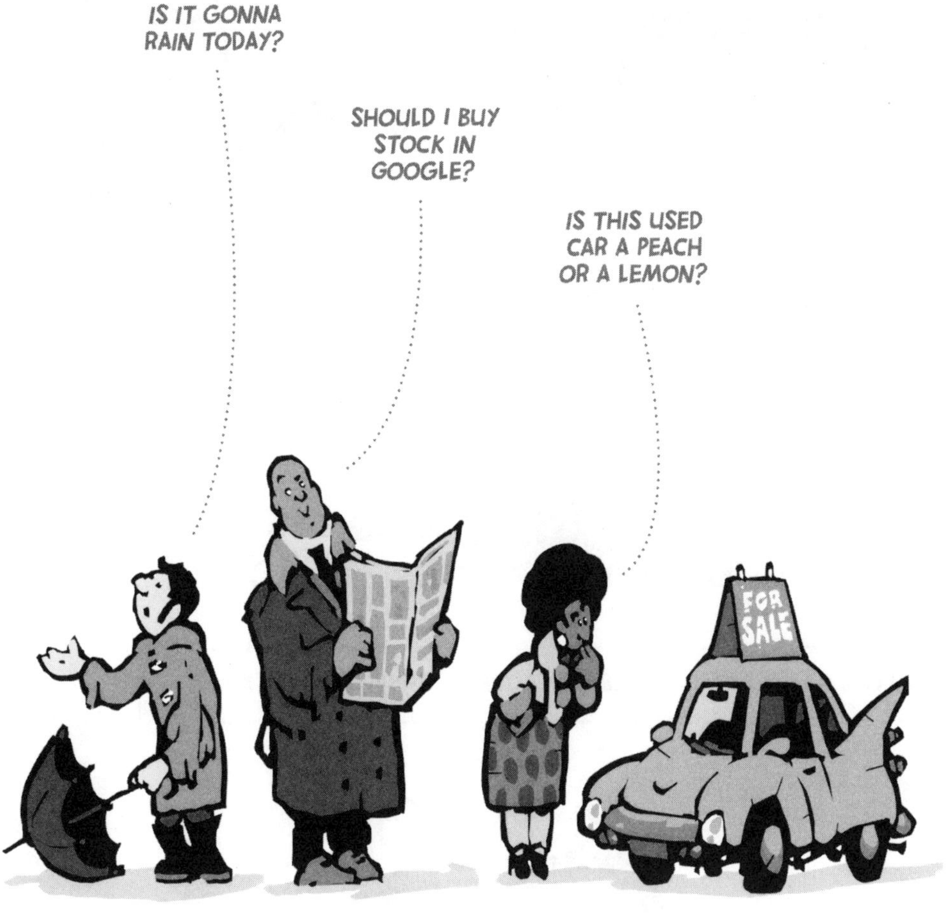
IS IT GONNA RAIN TODAY?
SHOULD I BUY STOCK IN GOOGLE?
IS THIS USED CAR A PEACH OR A LEMON?
FOR SALE

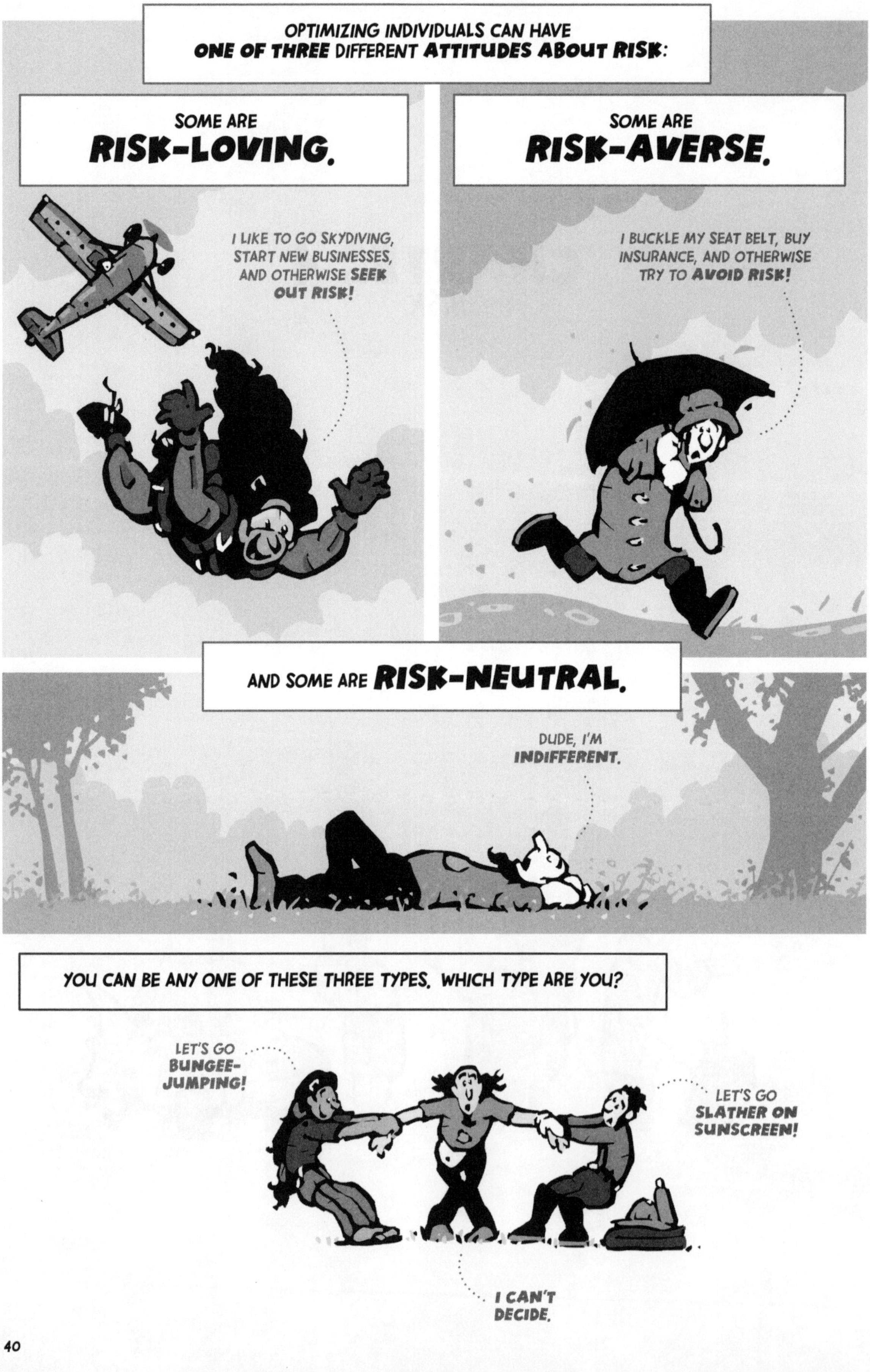
OPTIMIZING INDIVIDUALS CAN HAVE ONE OF THREE DIFFERENT ATTITUDES ABOUT RISK:
SOME ARE RISK-LOVING.
I LIKE TO GO SKYDIVING, START NEW BUSINESSES, AND OTHERWISE SEEK OUT RISK!
SOME ARE RISK-AVERSE.
I BUCKLE MY SEAT BELT, BUY INSURANCE, AND OTHERWISE TRY TO AVOID RISK!
AND SOME ARE RISK-NEUTRAL.
DUDE, I'M INDIFFERENT.
YOU CAN BE ANY ONE OF THESE THREE TYPES. WHICH TYPE ARE YOU?
LET'S GO BUNGEE-JUMPING!
LET'S GO SLATHER ON SUNSCREEN!
I CAN'T DECIDE.

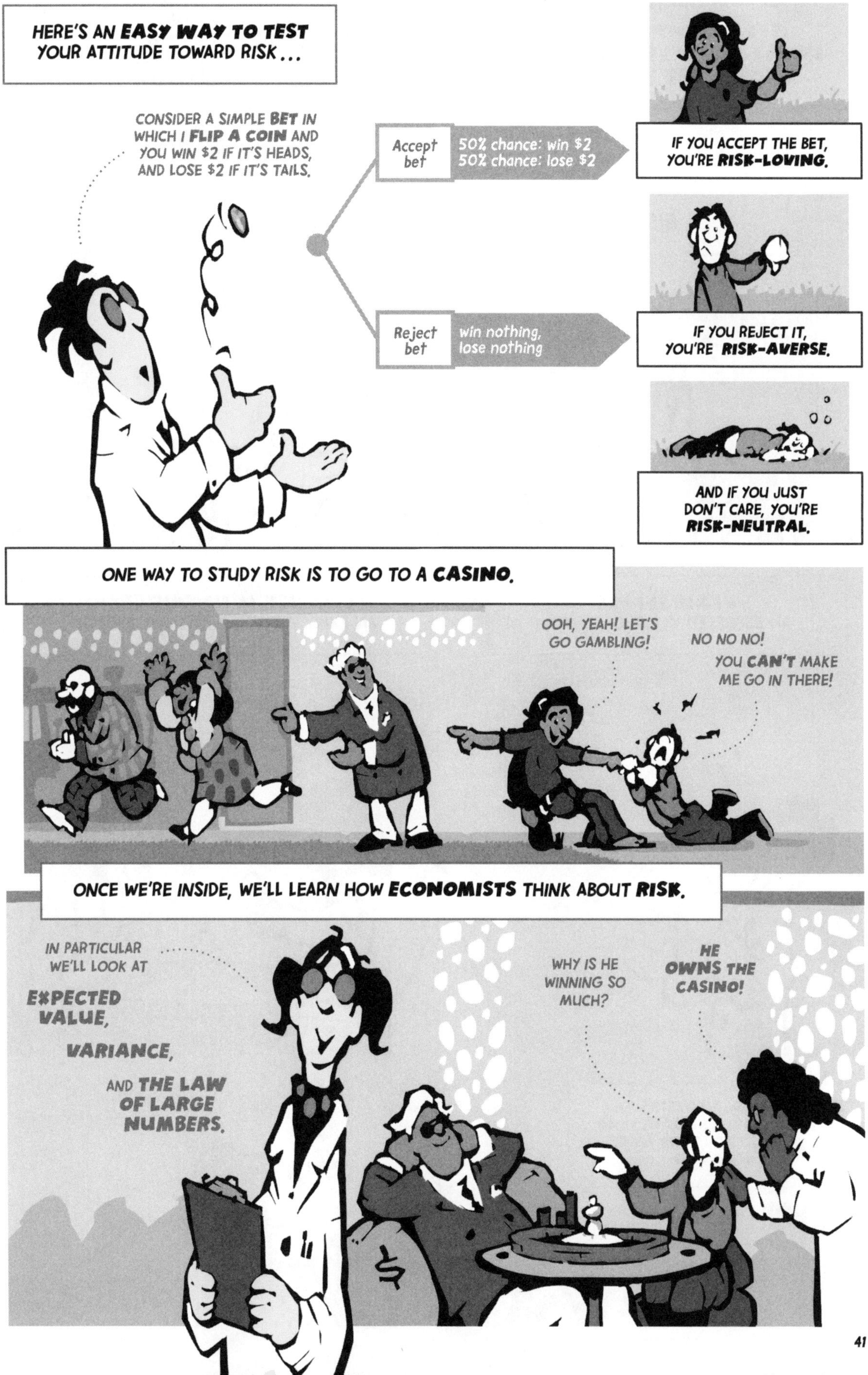
HERE'S AN EASY WAY TO TEST YOUR ATTITUDE TOWARD RISK...
CONSIDER A SIMPLE BET IN WHICH I FLIP A COIN AND YOU WIN $2 IF IT'S HEADS, AND LOSE $2 IF IT'S TAILS.
Accept bet
50% chance: win $2
50% chance: lose $2
IF YOU ACCEPT THE BET, YOU'RE RISK-LOVING.
Reject bet
win nothing, lose nothing
IF YOU REJECT IT, YOU'RE RISK-AVERSE.
AND IF YOU JUST DON'T CARE, YOU'RE RISK-NEUTRAL.
ONE WAY TO STUDY RISK IS TO GO TO A CASINO.
OOH, YEAH! LET'S GO GAMBLING!
NO NO NO! YOU CAN'T MAKE ME GO IN THERE!
ONCE WE'RE INSIDE, WE'LL LEARN HOW ECONOMISTS THINK ABOUT RISK.
IN PARTICULAR WE'LL LOOK AT EXPECTED VALUE, VARIANCE, AND THE LAW OF LARGE NUMBERS.
WHY IS HE WINNING SO MUCH?
HE OWNS THE CASINO!

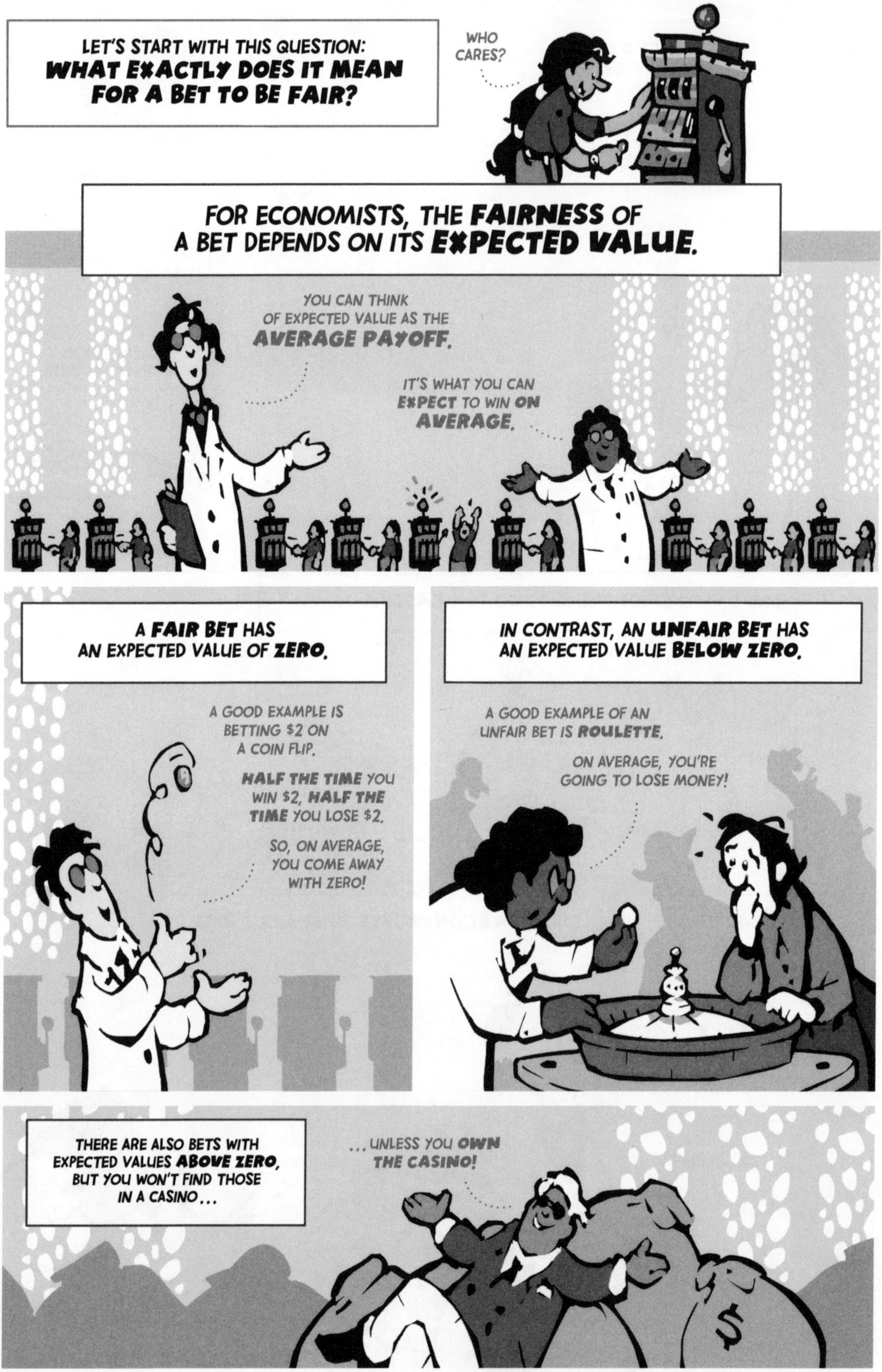
LET'S START WITH THIS QUESTION:
WHAT EXACTLY DOES IT MEAN FOR A BET TO BE FAIR?
WHO CARES?
FOR ECONOMISTS, THE **FAIRNESS** OF A BET DEPENDS ON ITS **EXPECTED VALUE.**
YOU CAN THINK OF EXPECTED VALUE AS THE **AVERAGE PAYOFF.**
IT'S WHAT YOU CAN **EXPECT** TO WIN **ON AVERAGE.**
A **FAIR BET** HAS AN EXPECTED VALUE OF **ZERO.**
A GOOD EXAMPLE IS BETTING $2 ON A COIN FLIP.
HALF THE TIME YOU WIN $2, **HALF THE TIME** YOU LOSE $2.
SO, ON AVERAGE, YOU COME AWAY WITH ZERO!
IN CONTRAST, AN **UNFAIR BET** HAS AN EXPECTED VALUE **BELOW ZERO.**
A GOOD EXAMPLE OF AN UNFAIR BET IS **ROULETTE.**
ON AVERAGE, YOU'RE GOING TO LOSE MONEY!
THERE ARE ALSO BETS WITH EXPECTED VALUES **ABOVE ZERO,** BUT YOU WON'T FIND THOSE IN A CASINO...
...UNLESS YOU **OWN THE CASINO!**
$

LET'S USE A $1 BET ON ROULETTE TO LOOK MORE CLOSELY AT **HOW EXPECTED VALUE WORKS.**

YOU PICK ONE NUMBER OUT OF THE 38 NUMBERS ON THE ROULETTE WHEEL...

...AND THEN I SPIN THE WHEEL.

IF THE MARBLE LANDS ON YOUR NUMBER, **YOU WIN $35!**

...AND IF IT DOESN'T, **YOU LOSE $1!**

TO CALCULATE THE EXPECTED VALUE, WE NEED TO DETERMINE **THE WEIGHTED AVERAGE OF ALL THE POSSIBLE OUTCOMES.**

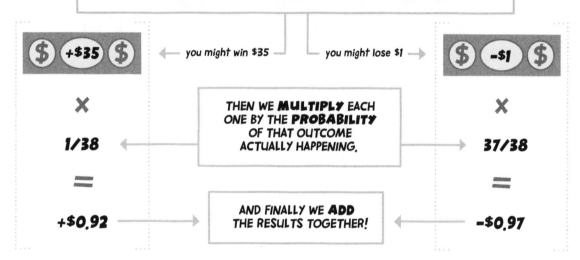

IN OUR ROULETTE GAME THERE ARE TWO POSSIBLE OUTCOMES, SO FIRST WE **LOOK AT EACH POSSIBLE OUTCOME.**

$ +$35 $ ← you might win $35 — you might lose $1 → $ –$1 $

×   ×

1/38   THEN WE **MULTIPLY** EACH ONE BY THE **PROBABILITY** OF THAT OUTCOME ACTUALLY HAPPENING.   37/38

=   =

+$0.92   AND FINALLY WE **ADD** THE RESULTS TOGETHER!   –$0.97

+0.92 – $0.97 = –$0.05

Math details are in the glossary and online at **www.cartooneconomics.com.**

ON AVERAGE, YOU'LL LOSE **5 CENTS** FOR EVERY DOLLAR YOU BET!

HEH HEH.

BY CALCULATING ITS EXPECTED VALUE, WE'VE PROVEN THAT ROULETTE IS AN **UNFAIR BET** FOR THE GAMBLER!

BUT THAT'S NOT WHAT MAKES IT **RISKY**...

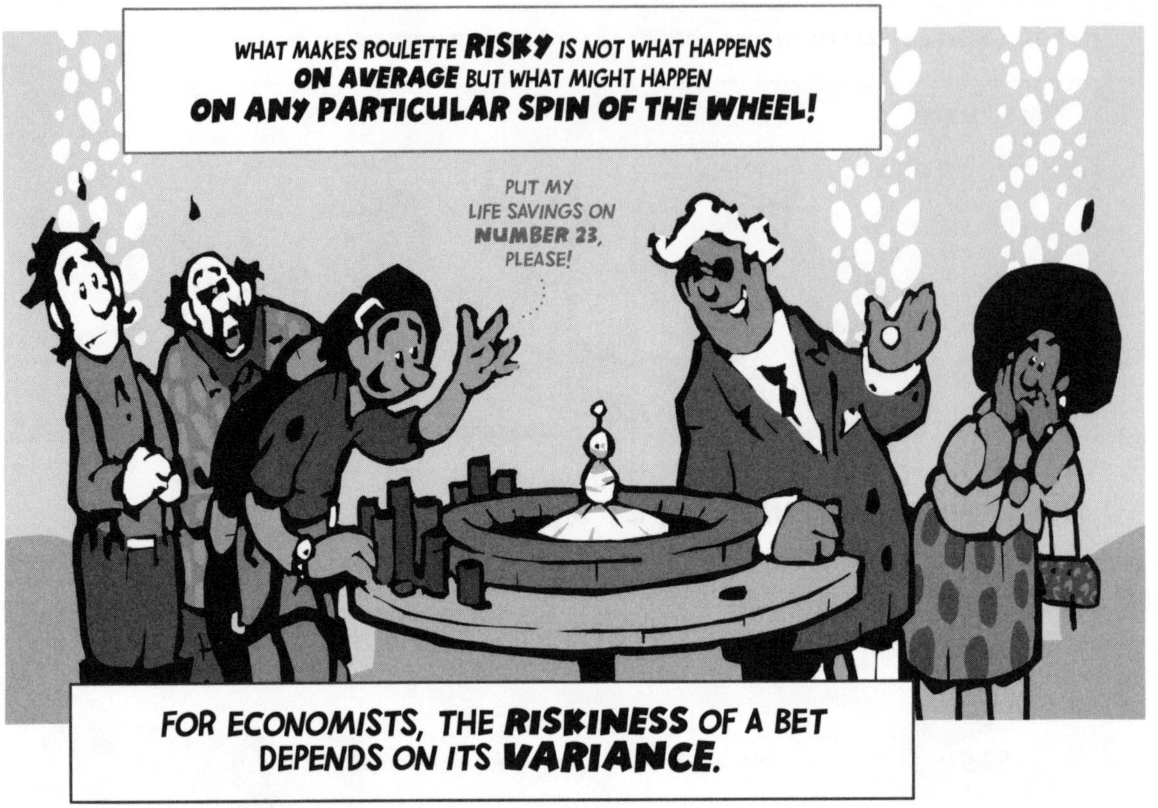
WHAT MAKES ROULETTE **RISKY** IS NOT WHAT HAPPENS **ON AVERAGE** BUT WHAT MIGHT HAPPEN **ON ANY PARTICULAR SPIN OF THE WHEEL!**
PUT MY LIFE SAVINGS ON **NUMBER 23**, PLEASE!
FOR ECONOMISTS, THE **RISKINESS** OF A BET DEPENDS ON ITS **VARIANCE.**

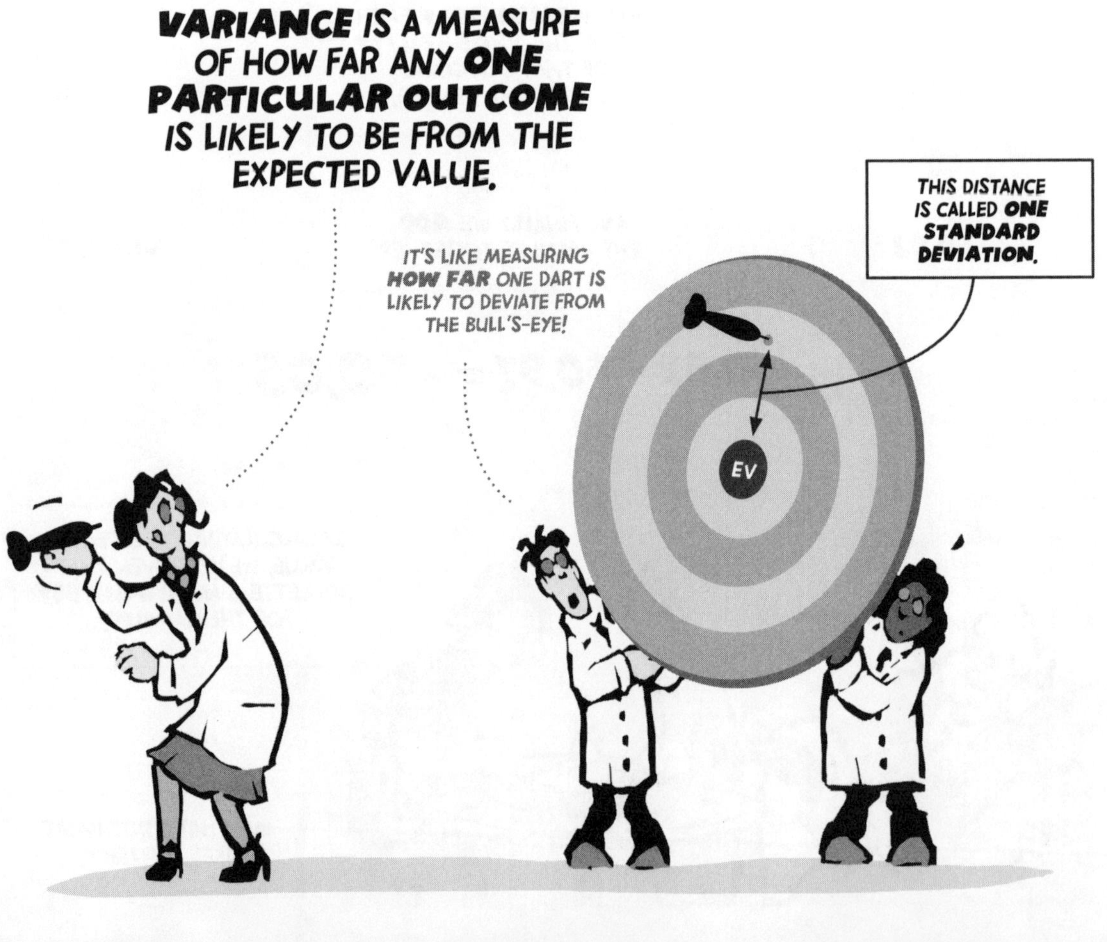
VARIANCE IS A MEASURE OF HOW FAR ANY **ONE PARTICULAR OUTCOME** IS LIKELY TO BE FROM THE EXPECTED VALUE.
IT'S LIKE MEASURING **HOW FAR** ONE DART IS LIKELY TO DEVIATE FROM THE BULL'S-EYE!
THIS DISTANCE IS CALLED **ONE STANDARD DEVIATION.**
EV

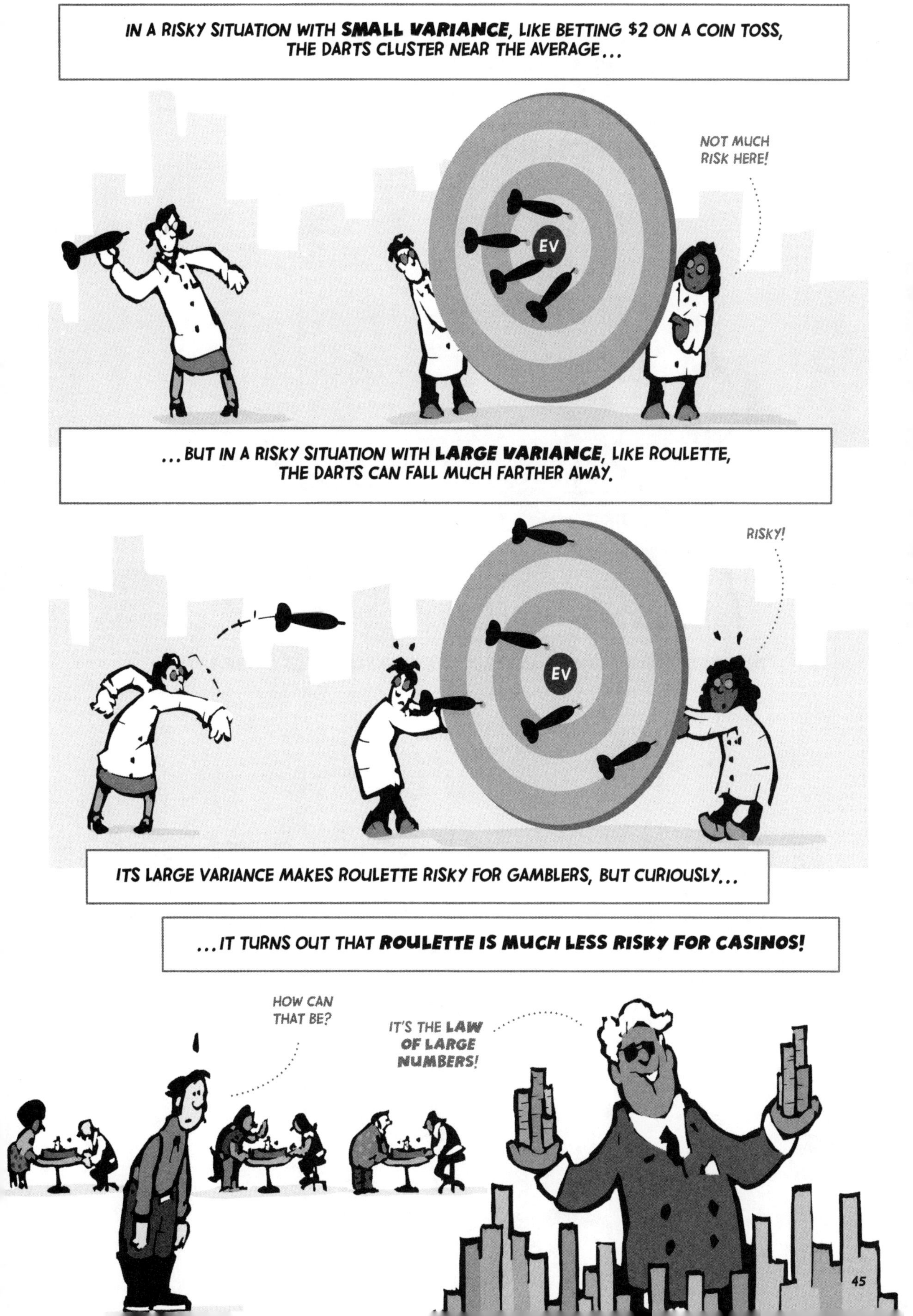
IN A RISKY SITUATION WITH SMALL VARIANCE, LIKE BETTING $2 ON A COIN TOSS, THE DARTS CLUSTER NEAR THE AVERAGE...
EV
NOT MUCH RISK HERE!
...BUT IN A RISKY SITUATION WITH LARGE VARIANCE, LIKE ROULETTE, THE DARTS CAN FALL MUCH FARTHER AWAY.
EV
RISKY!
ITS LARGE VARIANCE MAKES ROULETTE RISKY FOR GAMBLERS, BUT CURIOUSLY...
...IT TURNS OUT THAT ROULETTE IS MUCH LESS RISKY FOR CASINOS!
HOW CAN THAT BE?
IT'S THE LAW OF LARGE NUMBERS!

THE LAW OF LARGE NUMBERS

SAYS THAT PLAYING A GAME LIKE ROULETTE OVER AND OVER IS LIKELY TO PRODUCE **AN AVERAGE RESULT CLOSE TO THE EXPECTED VALUE!**

EACH GAMBLER ONLY PLAYS ROULETTE A FEW TIMES, BUT THE CASINO PLAYS ROULETTE THOUSANDS OF TIMES,

SO I'M CONFIDENT THAT *ON AVERAGE* I WILL MAKE ABOUT 5 CENTS FOR EACH DOLLAR WAGERED!

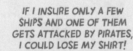

THE LAW OF LARGE NUMBERS ALSO WORKS FOR **INSURANCE COMPANIES**,

IF I INSURE ONLY A FEW SHIPS AND ONE OF THEM GETS ATTACKED BY PIRATES, I COULD LOSE MY SHIRT!

BUT IF I'M COVERING LOTS OF SHIPS, THE **LAW OF LARGE NUMBERS** HELPS ME MANAGE MY RISK,

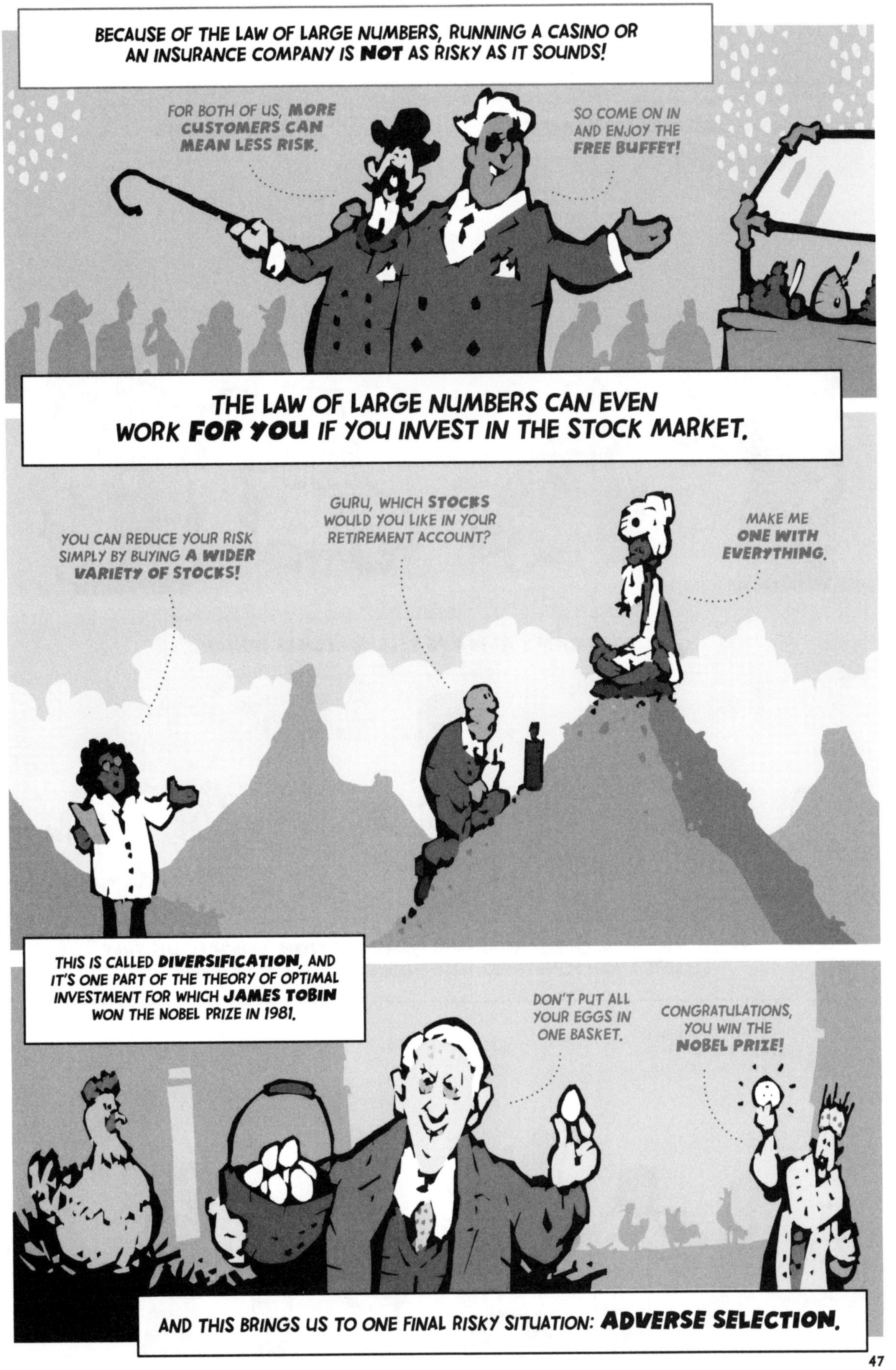
BECAUSE OF THE LAW OF LARGE NUMBERS, RUNNING A CASINO OR AN INSURANCE COMPANY IS NOT AS RISKY AS IT SOUNDS!
FOR BOTH OF US, MORE CUSTOMERS CAN MEAN LESS RISK.
SO COME ON IN AND ENJOY THE FREE BUFFET!
THE LAW OF LARGE NUMBERS CAN EVEN WORK FOR YOU IF YOU INVEST IN THE STOCK MARKET.
YOU CAN REDUCE YOUR RISK SIMPLY BY BUYING A WIDER VARIETY OF STOCKS!
GURU, WHICH STOCKS WOULD YOU LIKE IN YOUR RETIREMENT ACCOUNT?
MAKE ME ONE WITH EVERYTHING.
THIS IS CALLED DIVERSIFICATION, AND IT'S ONE PART OF THE THEORY OF OPTIMAL INVESTMENT FOR WHICH JAMES TOBIN WON THE NOBEL PRIZE IN 1981.
DON'T PUT ALL YOUR EGGS IN ONE BASKET.
CONGRATULATIONS, YOU WIN THE NOBEL PRIZE!
AND THIS BRINGS US TO ONE FINAL RISKY SITUATION: ADVERSE SELECTION.

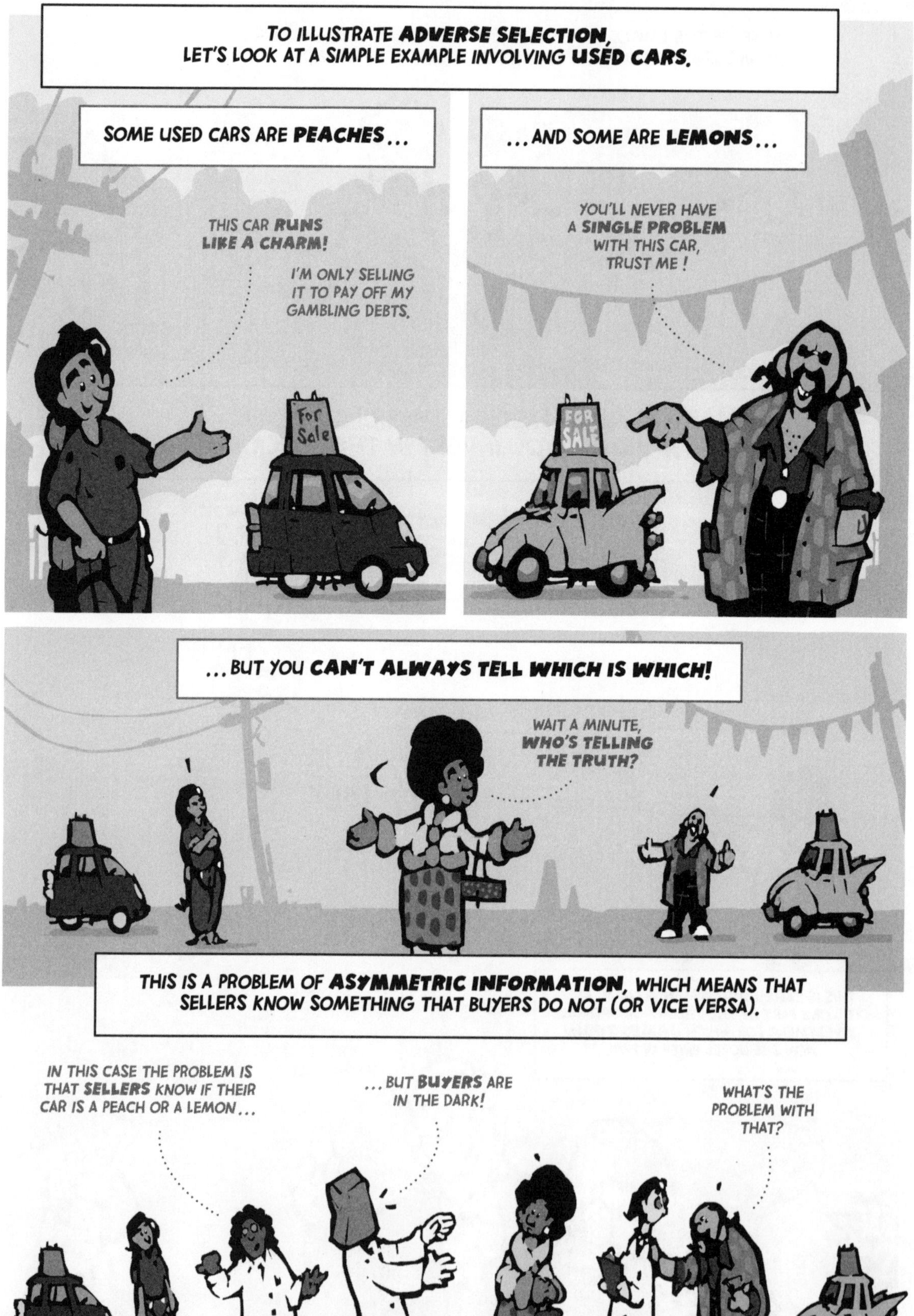
TO ILLUSTRATE ADVERSE SELECTION, LET'S LOOK AT A SIMPLE EXAMPLE INVOLVING USED CARS.
SOME USED CARS ARE PEACHES...
THIS CAR RUNS LIKE A CHARM!
I'M ONLY SELLING IT TO PAY OFF MY GAMBLING DEBTS.
For Sale
...AND SOME ARE LEMONS...
YOU'LL NEVER HAVE A SINGLE PROBLEM WITH THIS CAR, TRUST ME!
FOR SALE
...BUT YOU CAN'T ALWAYS TELL WHICH IS WHICH!
WAIT A MINUTE, WHO'S TELLING THE TRUTH?
THIS IS A PROBLEM OF ASYMMETRIC INFORMATION, WHICH MEANS THAT SELLERS KNOW SOMETHING THAT BUYERS DO NOT (OR VICE VERSA).
IN THIS CASE THE PROBLEM IS THAT SELLERS KNOW IF THEIR CAR IS A PEACH OR A LEMON...
...BUT BUYERS ARE IN THE DARK!
WHAT'S THE PROBLEM WITH THAT?

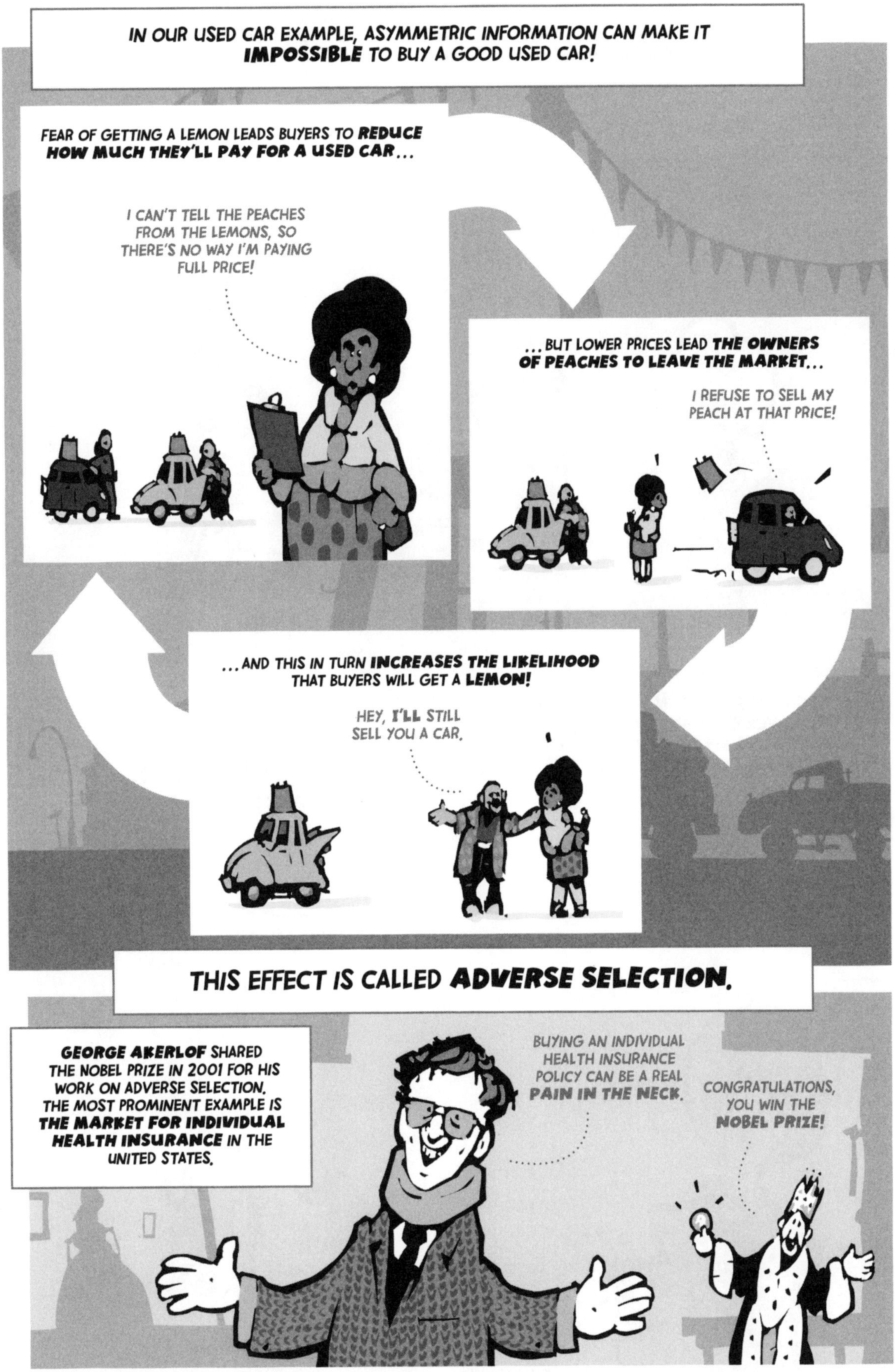
IN OUR USED CAR EXAMPLE, ASYMMETRIC INFORMATION CAN MAKE IT **IMPOSSIBLE** TO BUY A GOOD USED CAR!
FEAR OF GETTING A LEMON LEADS BUYERS TO **REDUCE HOW MUCH THEY'LL PAY FOR A USED CAR**...
I CAN'T TELL THE PEACHES FROM THE LEMONS, SO THERE'S NO WAY I'M PAYING FULL PRICE!
...BUT LOWER PRICES LEAD **THE OWNERS OF PEACHES TO LEAVE THE MARKET**...
I REFUSE TO SELL MY PEACH AT THAT PRICE!
...AND THIS IN TURN **INCREASES THE LIKELIHOOD** THAT BUYERS WILL GET A **LEMON!**
HEY, **I'LL** STILL SELL YOU A CAR.
THIS EFFECT IS CALLED **ADVERSE SELECTION.**
GEORGE AKERLOF SHARED THE NOBEL PRIZE IN 2001 FOR HIS WORK ON ADVERSE SELECTION. THE MOST PROMINENT EXAMPLE IS **THE MARKET FOR INDIVIDUAL HEALTH INSURANCE** IN THE UNITED STATES.
BUYING AN INDIVIDUAL HEALTH INSURANCE POLICY CAN BE A REAL **PAIN IN THE NECK.**
CONGRATULATIONS, YOU WIN THE **NOBEL PRIZE!**

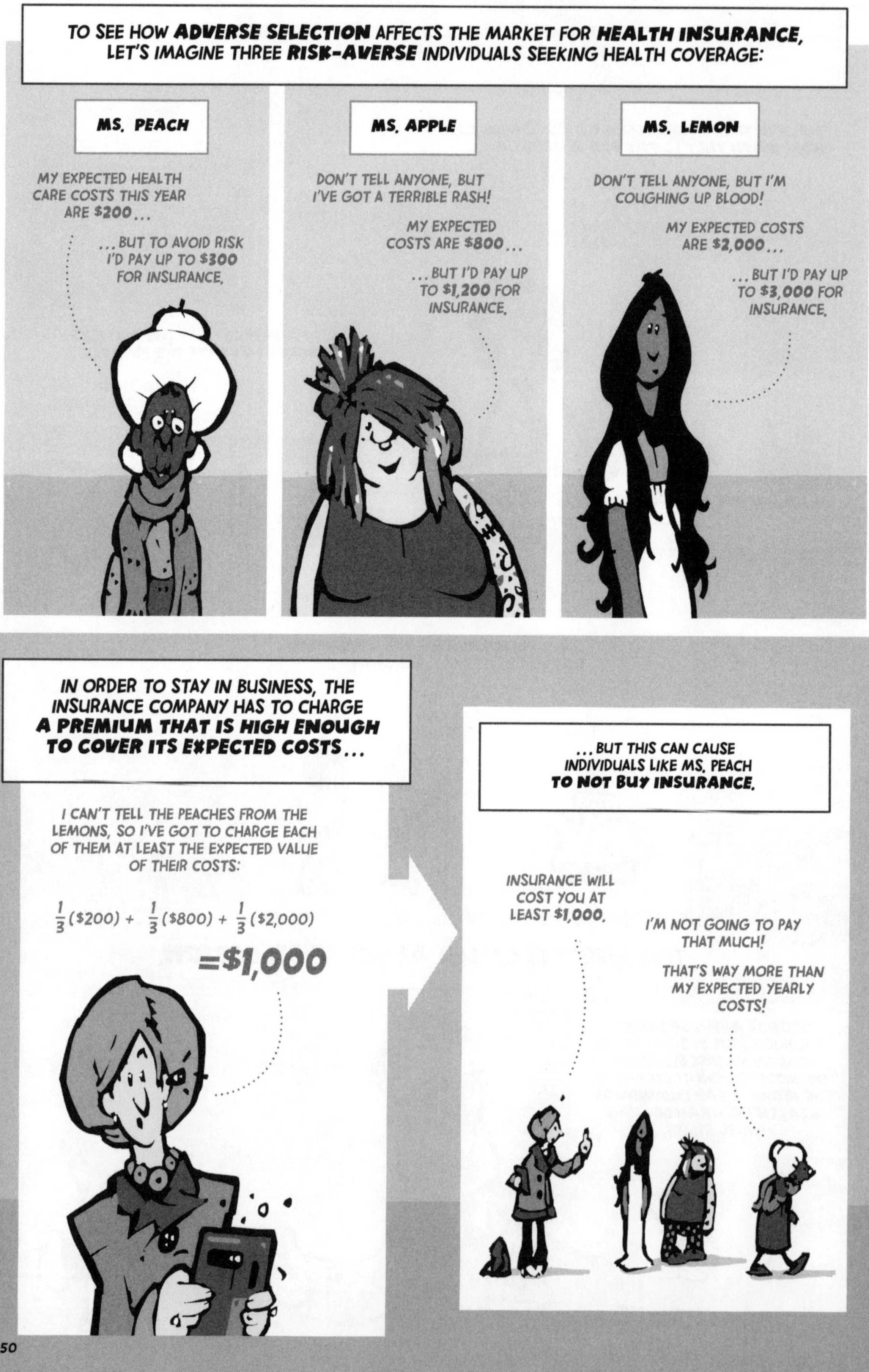
TO SEE HOW ADVERSE SELECTION AFFECTS THE MARKET FOR HEALTH INSURANCE, LET'S IMAGINE THREE RISK-AVERSE INDIVIDUALS SEEKING HEALTH COVERAGE:
MS. PEACH
MY EXPECTED HEALTH CARE COSTS THIS YEAR ARE $200...
...BUT TO AVOID RISK I'D PAY UP TO $300 FOR INSURANCE.
MS. APPLE
DON'T TELL ANYONE, BUT I'VE GOT A TERRIBLE RASH!
MY EXPECTED COSTS ARE $800...
...BUT I'D PAY UP TO $1,200 FOR INSURANCE.
MS. LEMON
DON'T TELL ANYONE, BUT I'M COUGHING UP BLOOD!
MY EXPECTED COSTS ARE $2,000...
...BUT I'D PAY UP TO $3,000 FOR INSURANCE.
IN ORDER TO STAY IN BUSINESS, THE INSURANCE COMPANY HAS TO CHARGE A PREMIUM THAT IS HIGH ENOUGH TO COVER ITS EXPECTED COSTS...
I CAN'T TELL THE PEACHES FROM THE LEMONS, SO I'VE GOT TO CHARGE EACH OF THEM AT LEAST THE EXPECTED VALUE OF THEIR COSTS:
$\frac{1}{3}(\$200) + \frac{1}{3}(\$800) + \frac{1}{3}(\$2,000)$
=$1,000
...BUT THIS CAN CAUSE INDIVIDUALS LIKE MS. PEACH TO NOT BUY INSURANCE.
INSURANCE WILL COST YOU AT LEAST $1,000.
I'M NOT GOING TO PAY THAT MUCH!
THAT'S WAY MORE THAN MY EXPECTED YEARLY COSTS!

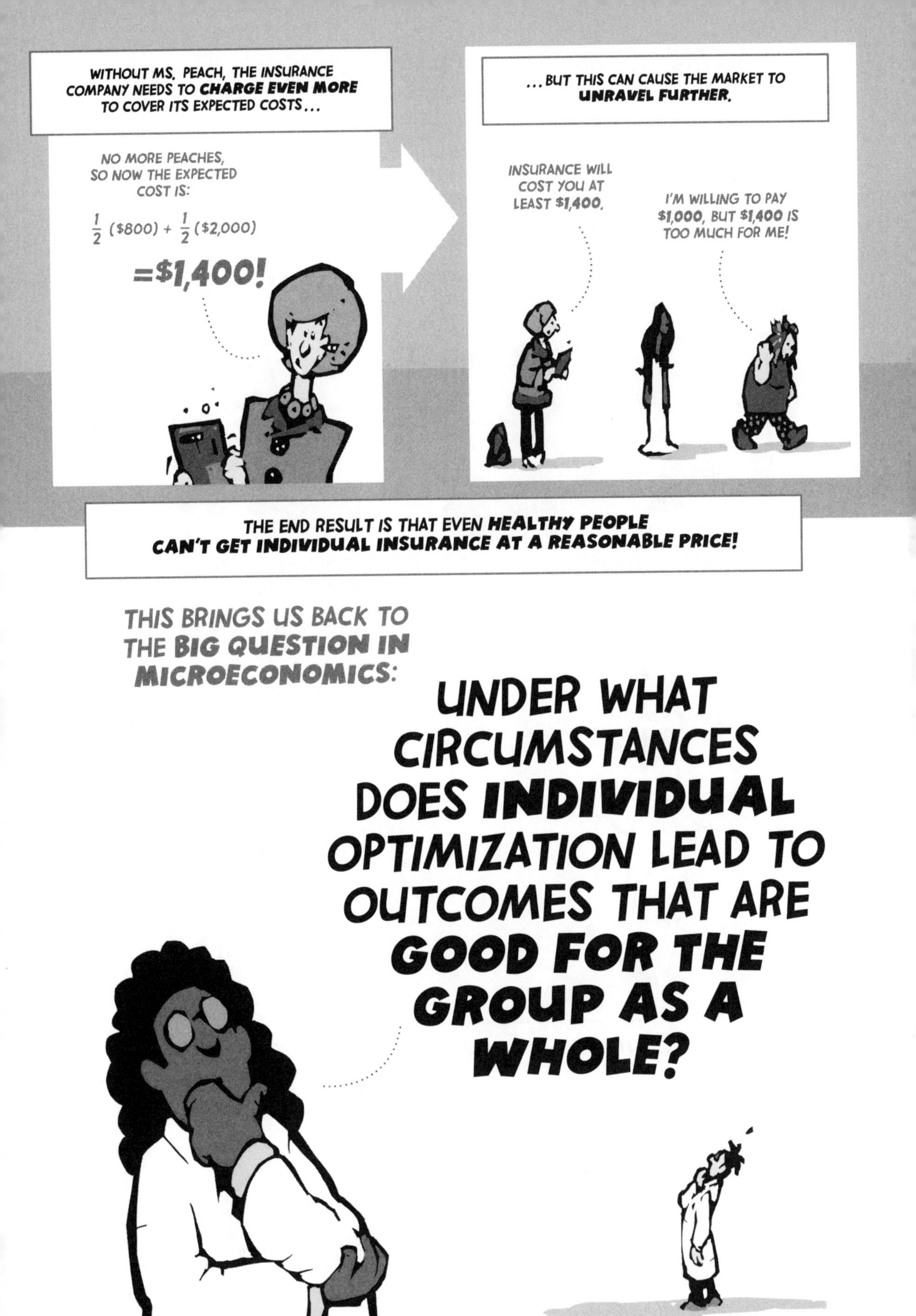
WITHOUT MS. PEACH, THE INSURANCE COMPANY NEEDS TO CHARGE EVEN MORE TO COVER ITS EXPECTED COSTS...
NO MORE PEACHES, SO NOW THE EXPECTED COST IS:
$\frac{1}{2}$ (\$800) + $\frac{1}{2}$ (\$2,000)
=\$1,400!
...BUT THIS CAN CAUSE THE MARKET TO UNRAVEL FURTHER.
INSURANCE WILL COST YOU AT LEAST \$1,400.
I'M WILLING TO PAY \$1,000, BUT \$1,400 IS TOO MUCH FOR ME!
THE END RESULT IS THAT EVEN HEALTHY PEOPLE CAN'T GET INDIVIDUAL INSURANCE AT A REASONABLE PRICE!
THIS BRINGS US BACK TO THE BIG QUESTION IN MICROECONOMICS:
UNDER WHAT CIRCUMSTANCES DOES INDIVIDUAL OPTIMIZATION LEAD TO OUTCOMES THAT ARE GOOD FOR THE GROUP AS A WHOLE?

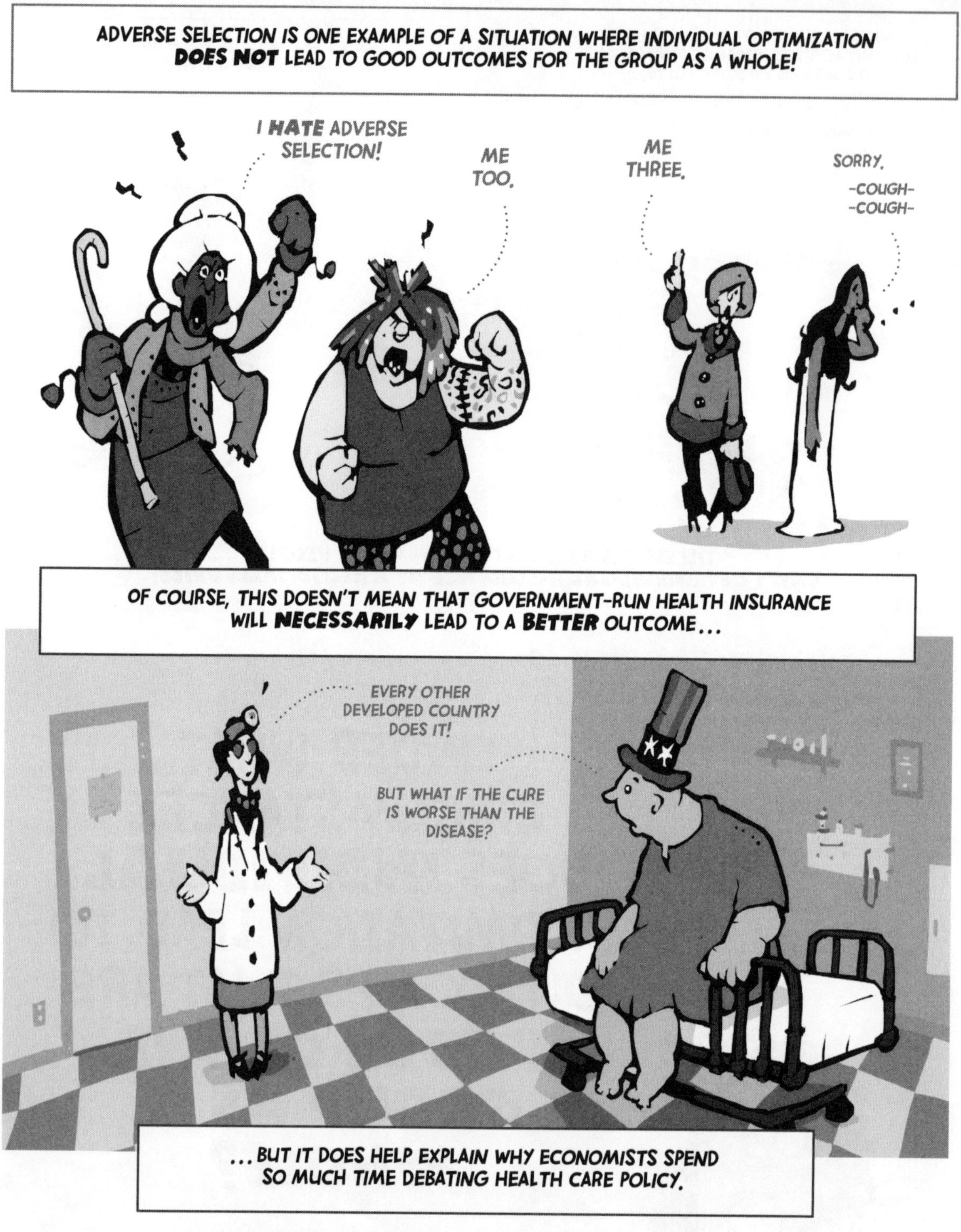
ADVERSE SELECTION IS ONE EXAMPLE OF A SITUATION WHERE INDIVIDUAL OPTIMIZATION **DOES NOT** LEAD TO GOOD OUTCOMES FOR THE GROUP AS A WHOLE!
I **HATE** ADVERSE SELECTION!
ME TOO.
ME THREE.
SORRY.
-COUGH- -COUGH-
OF COURSE, THIS DOESN'T MEAN THAT GOVERNMENT-RUN HEALTH INSURANCE WILL **NECESSARILY** LEAD TO A **BETTER** OUTCOME...
EVERY OTHER DEVELOPED COUNTRY DOES IT!
BUT WHAT IF THE CURE IS WORSE THAN THE DISEASE?
...BUT IT DOES HELP EXPLAIN WHY ECONOMISTS SPEND SO MUCH TIME DEBATING HEALTH CARE POLICY.
ON THE ONE HAND...
BUT ON THE OTHER HAND...

CHAPTER 5
FROM ONE TO SOME

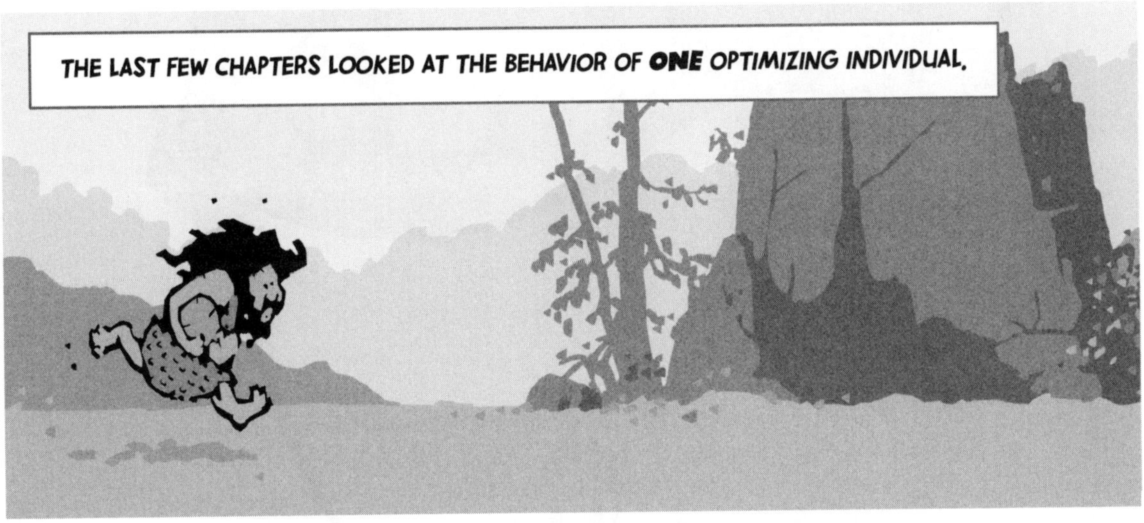
THE LAST FEW CHAPTERS LOOKED AT THE BEHAVIOR OF **ONE** OPTIMIZING INDIVIDUAL.

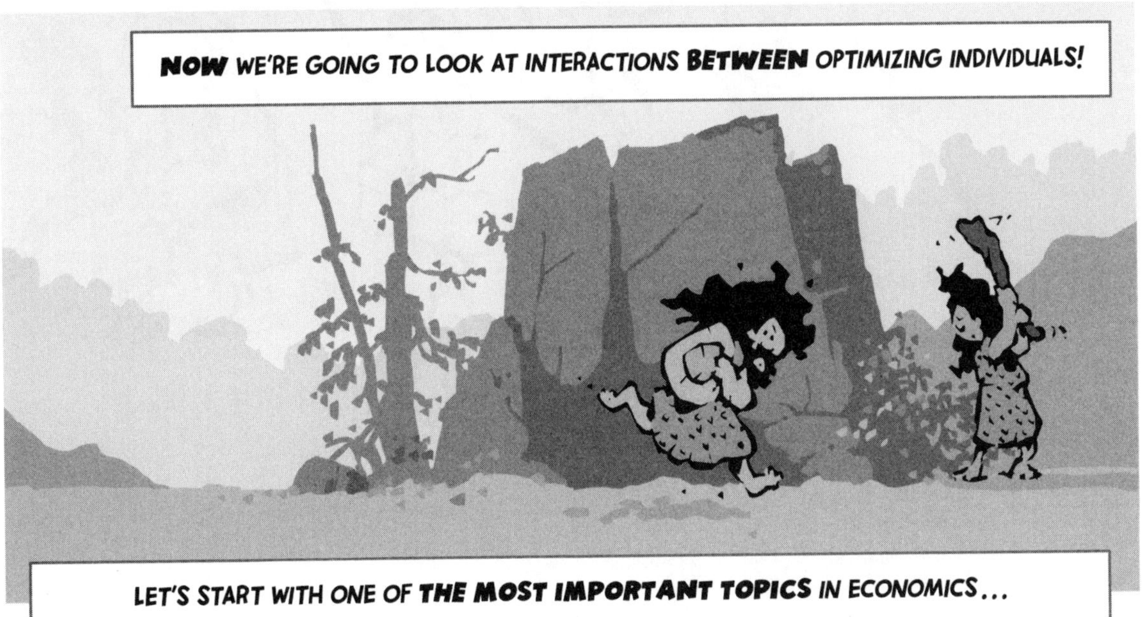
NOW WE'RE GOING TO LOOK AT INTERACTIONS **BETWEEN** OPTIMIZING INDIVIDUALS!
LET'S START WITH ONE OF **THE MOST IMPORTANT TOPICS** IN ECONOMICS...

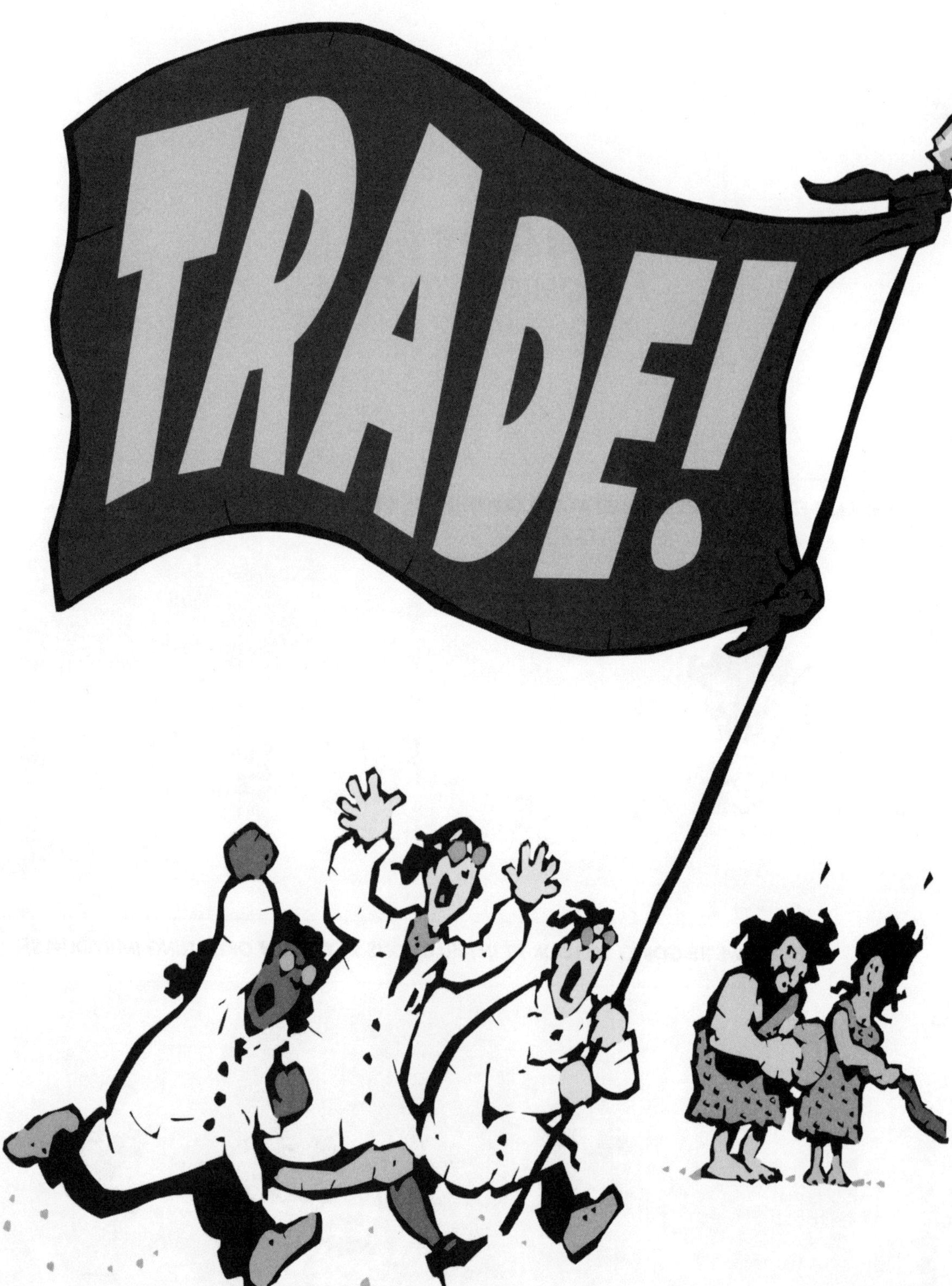
TRADE!

TRADING IS SOMETHING WE'VE **ALL** DONE SINCE WE WERE CHILDREN...

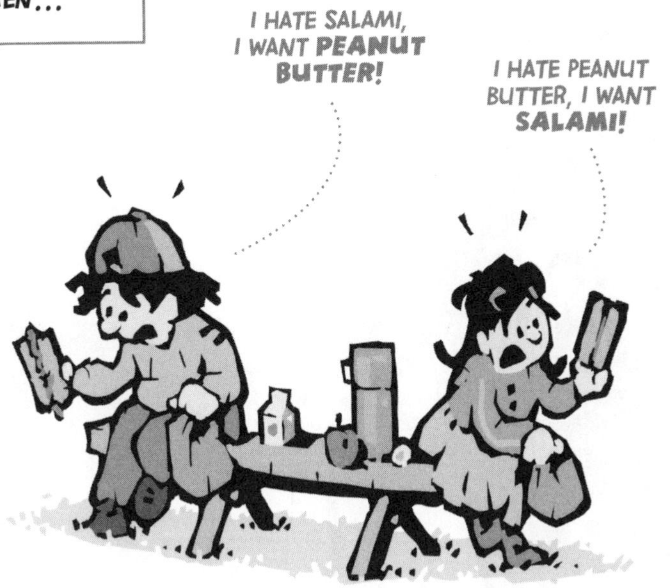
I HATE SALAMI, I WANT **PEANUT BUTTER!**
I HATE PEANUT BUTTER, I WANT **SALAMI!**

...AND IT'S PROBABLY SOMETHING HUMANS HAVE **ALWAYS** DONE!

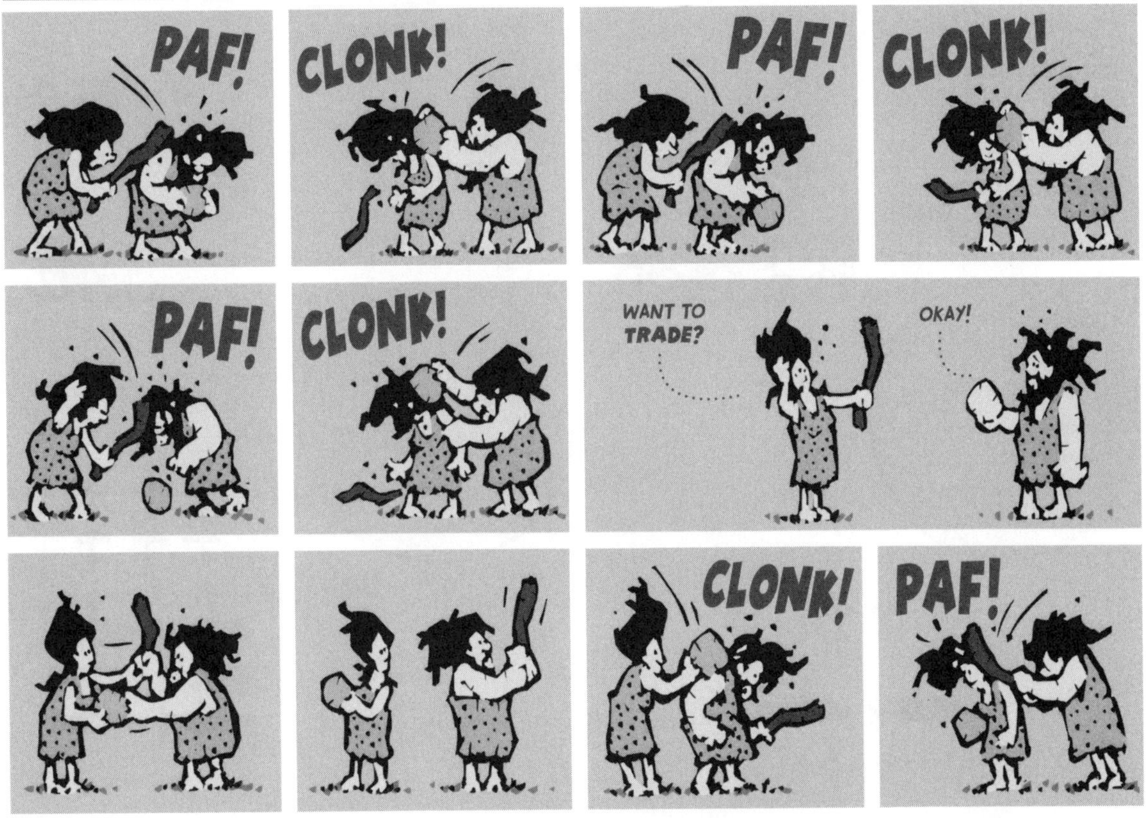
PAF!
CLONK!
PAF!
CLONK!
PAF!
CLONK!
WANT TO **TRADE?**
OKAY!
CLONK!
PAF!

JOKING ASIDE, WE TRADE BECAUSE IT MAKES US **BETTER OFF.**

IN FACT, INDIVIDUALS CAN GET **MUTUAL BENEFITS FROM TRADE** EVEN IN **UNLIKELY SITUATIONS** LIKE THIS ONE:

MOG
(Homo neanderthalensis)

OOGA
(Homo sapiens)

thick skull

cranium stuffed with brains

tongue-tied

recites poetry

arm wrestling champion

destined for global domination

IMAGINE THAT **MOG** AND **OOGA** EACH DEVOTE 3 HOURS A DAY TO GETTING A BALANCED DIET THAT HAS **EQUAL NUMBERS** OF FISH AND MUSHROOMS:

MOG **BY HIMSELF** CAN CATCH **1 FISH** OR GATHER **2 MUSHROOMS** PER HOUR...

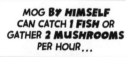

...SO TO GET A **BALANCED DIET,** THIS IS HOW HE MUST SPEND HIS **3 HOURS:**

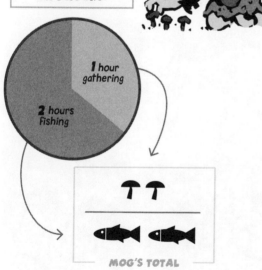

1 hour gathering

2 hours fishing

MOG'S TOTAL

OOGA **BY HERSELF** CAN CATCH **6 FISH** OR GATHER **3 MUSHROOMS** PER HOUR...

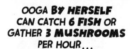

...SO TO GET A **BALANCED DIET,** THIS IS HOW SHE MUST SPEND HER **3 HOURS:**

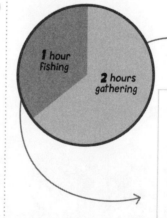

1 hour Fishing

2 hours gathering

OOGA'S TOTAL

NEXT LET'S SEE WHAT CAN HAPPEN IF THEY **TRADE** WITH EACH OTHER...

WAIT A MINUTE!

I'M BETTER THAN THAT NEANDERTHAL AT **EVERYTHING!**

HOW CAN TRADING WITH **HIM** POSSIBLY HELP **ME?**

MOG GETTING MAD ANGRY!

BELIEVE IT OR NOT, BOTH MOG AND OOGA **CAN** GAIN FROM TRADE! HERE'S ONE WAY:

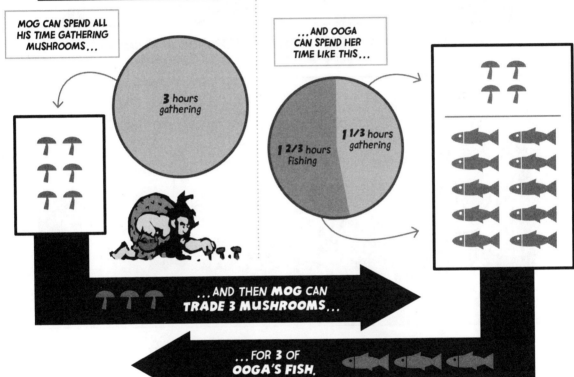

MOG CAN SPEND ALL HIS TIME GATHERING MUSHROOMS...

3 hours gathering

...AND OOGA CAN SPEND HER TIME LIKE THIS...

1 2/3 hours fishing

1 1/3 hours gathering

...AND THEN **MOG** CAN **TRADE 3 MUSHROOMS...**

...FOR **3** OF **OOGA'S FISH.**

WHOA!

BY MYSELF I COULD ONLY GET 6 OF EACH, BUT NOW I CAN GET 7!

MOG'S TOTAL (AFTER TRADE)

INSTEAD OF 2 OF EACH, MOG NOW HAVE...

UM...

UM...

...**MORE!**

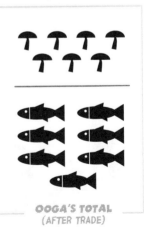

OOGA'S TOTAL (AFTER TRADE)

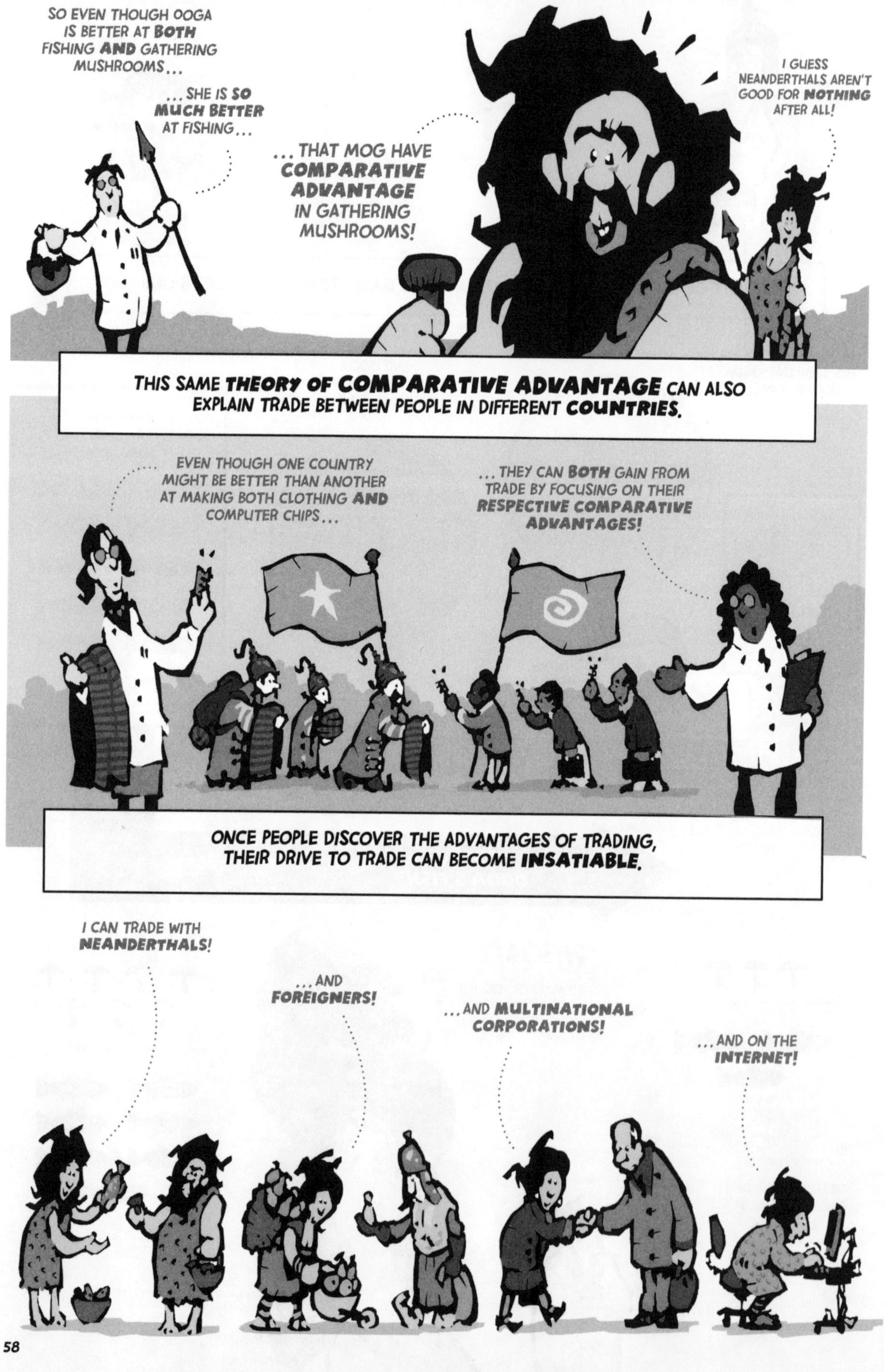

SO EVEN THOUGH OOGA IS BETTER AT BOTH FISHING AND GATHERING MUSHROOMS...
...SHE IS SO MUCH BETTER AT FISHING...
...THAT MOG HAVE COMPARATIVE ADVANTAGE IN GATHERING MUSHROOMS!
I GUESS NEANDERTHALS AREN'T GOOD FOR NOTHING AFTER ALL!
THIS SAME THEORY OF COMPARATIVE ADVANTAGE CAN ALSO EXPLAIN TRADE BETWEEN PEOPLE IN DIFFERENT COUNTRIES.
EVEN THOUGH ONE COUNTRY MIGHT BE BETTER THAN ANOTHER AT MAKING BOTH CLOTHING AND COMPUTER CHIPS...
...THEY CAN BOTH GAIN FROM TRADE BY FOCUSING ON THEIR RESPECTIVE COMPARATIVE ADVANTAGES!
ONCE PEOPLE DISCOVER THE ADVANTAGES OF TRADING, THEIR DRIVE TO TRADE CAN BECOME INSATIABLE.
I CAN TRADE WITH NEANDERTHALS!
...AND FOREIGNERS!
...AND MULTINATIONAL CORPORATIONS!
...AND ON THE INTERNET!

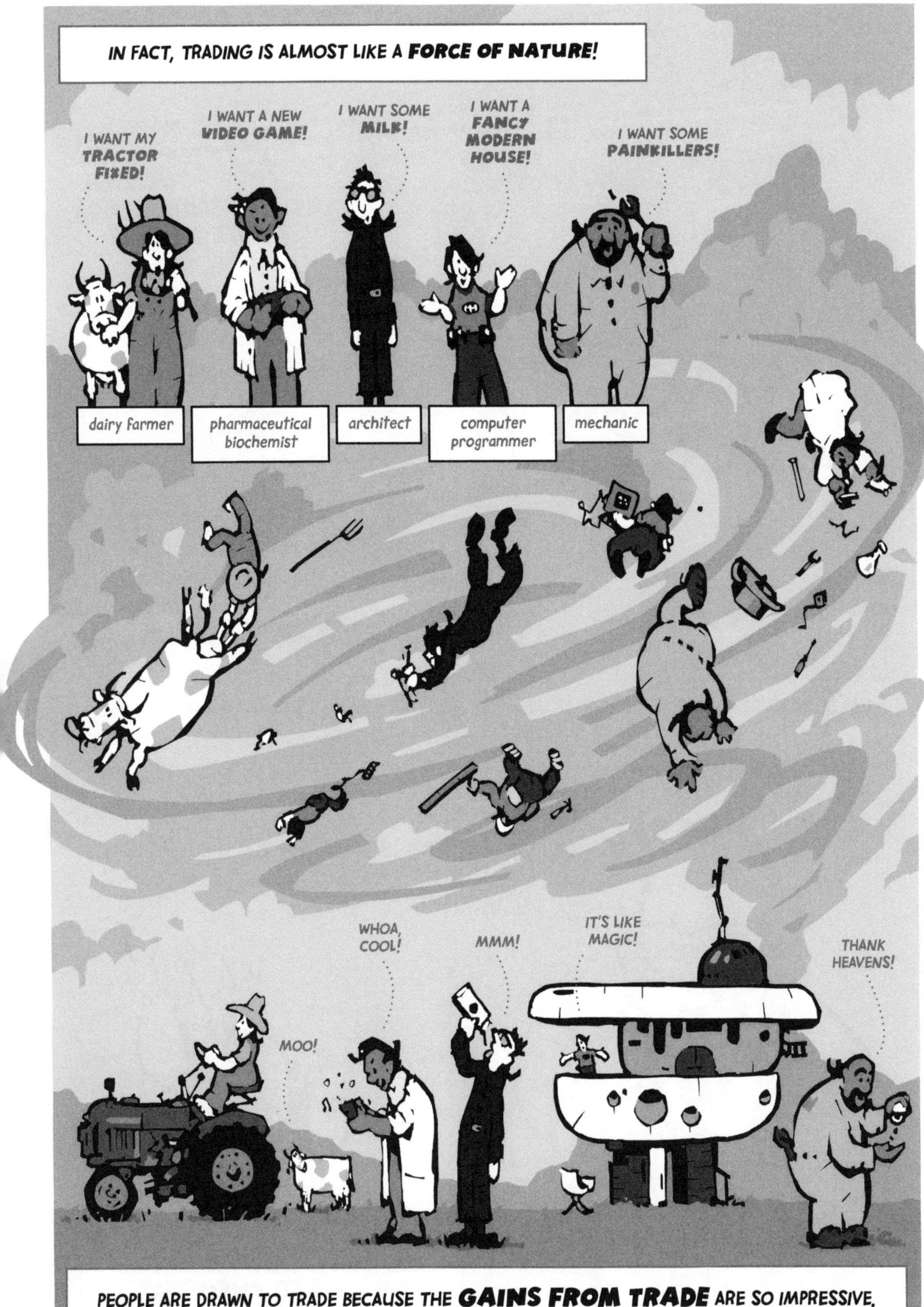
IN FACT, TRADING IS ALMOST LIKE A **FORCE OF NATURE!**
I WANT MY **TRACTOR FIXED!**
I WANT A NEW **VIDEO GAME!**
I WANT SOME **MILK!**
I WANT A **FANCY MODERN HOUSE!**
I WANT SOME **PAINKILLERS!**
dairy farmer
pharmaceutical biochemist
architect
computer programmer
mechanic
MOO!
WHOA, COOL!
MMM!
IT'S LIKE MAGIC!
THANK HEAVENS!
PEOPLE ARE DRAWN TO TRADE BECAUSE THE **GAINS FROM TRADE** ARE SO IMPRESSIVE.

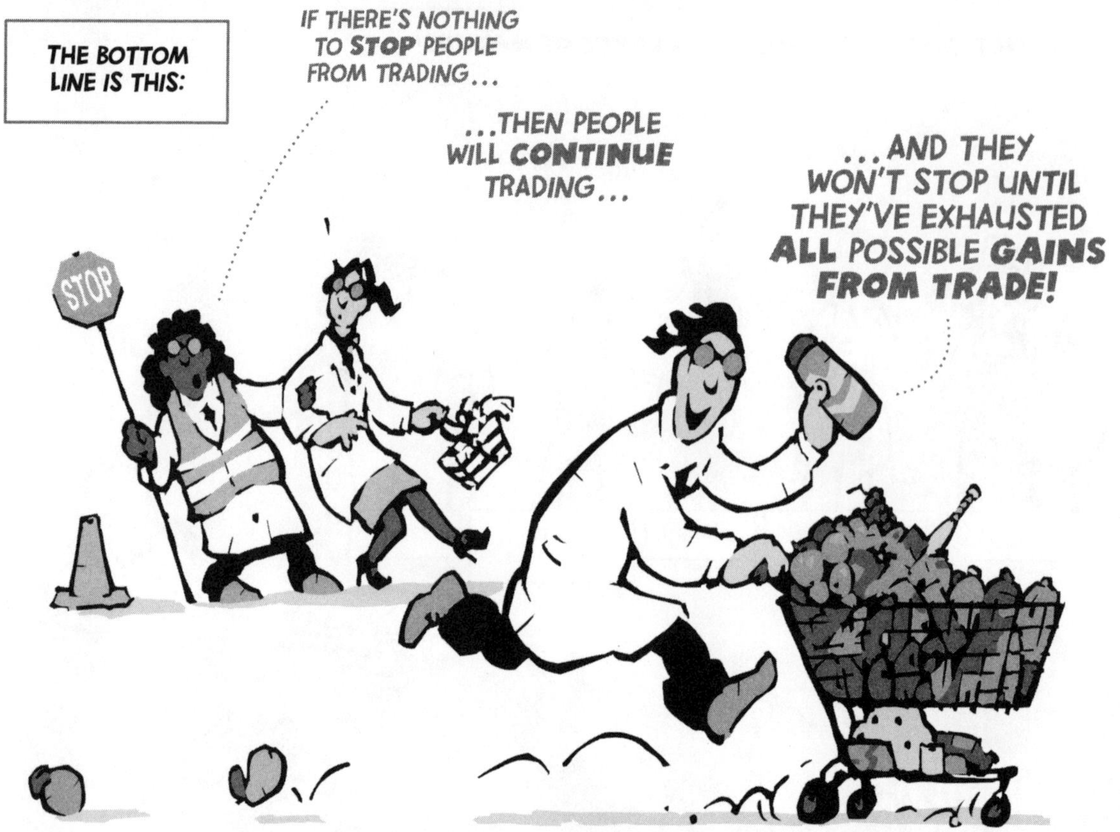
THE BOTTOM LINE IS THIS:
IF THERE'S NOTHING TO **STOP** PEOPLE FROM TRADING...
...THEN PEOPLE WILL **CONTINUE** TRADING...
...AND THEY WON'T STOP UNTIL THEY'VE EXHAUSTED **ALL** POSSIBLE **GAINS FROM TRADE!**
STOP

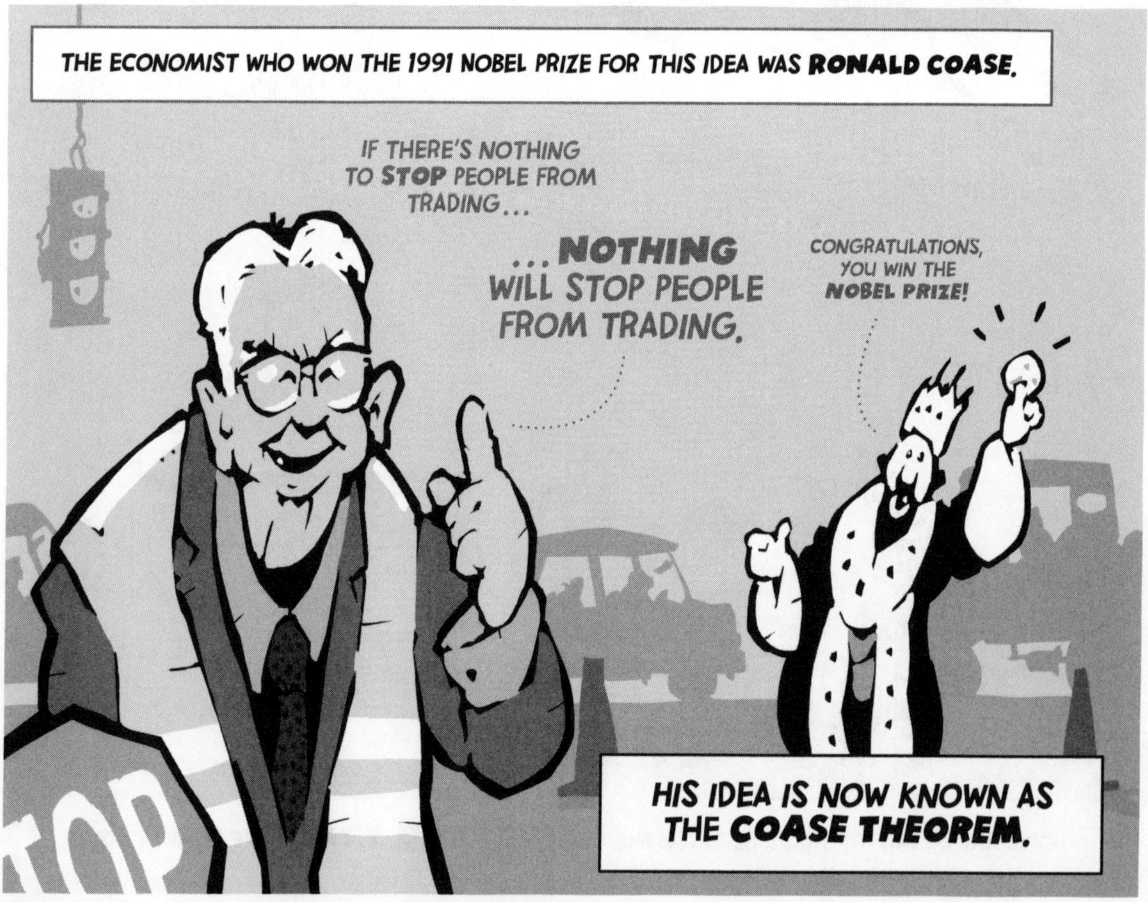
THE ECONOMIST WHO WON THE 1991 NOBEL PRIZE FOR THIS IDEA WAS **RONALD COASE.**
IF THERE'S NOTHING TO **STOP** PEOPLE FROM TRADING...
...**NOTHING** WILL STOP PEOPLE FROM TRADING.
CONGRATULATIONS, YOU WIN THE **NOBEL PRIZE!**
HIS IDEA IS NOW KNOWN AS THE **COASE THEOREM.**

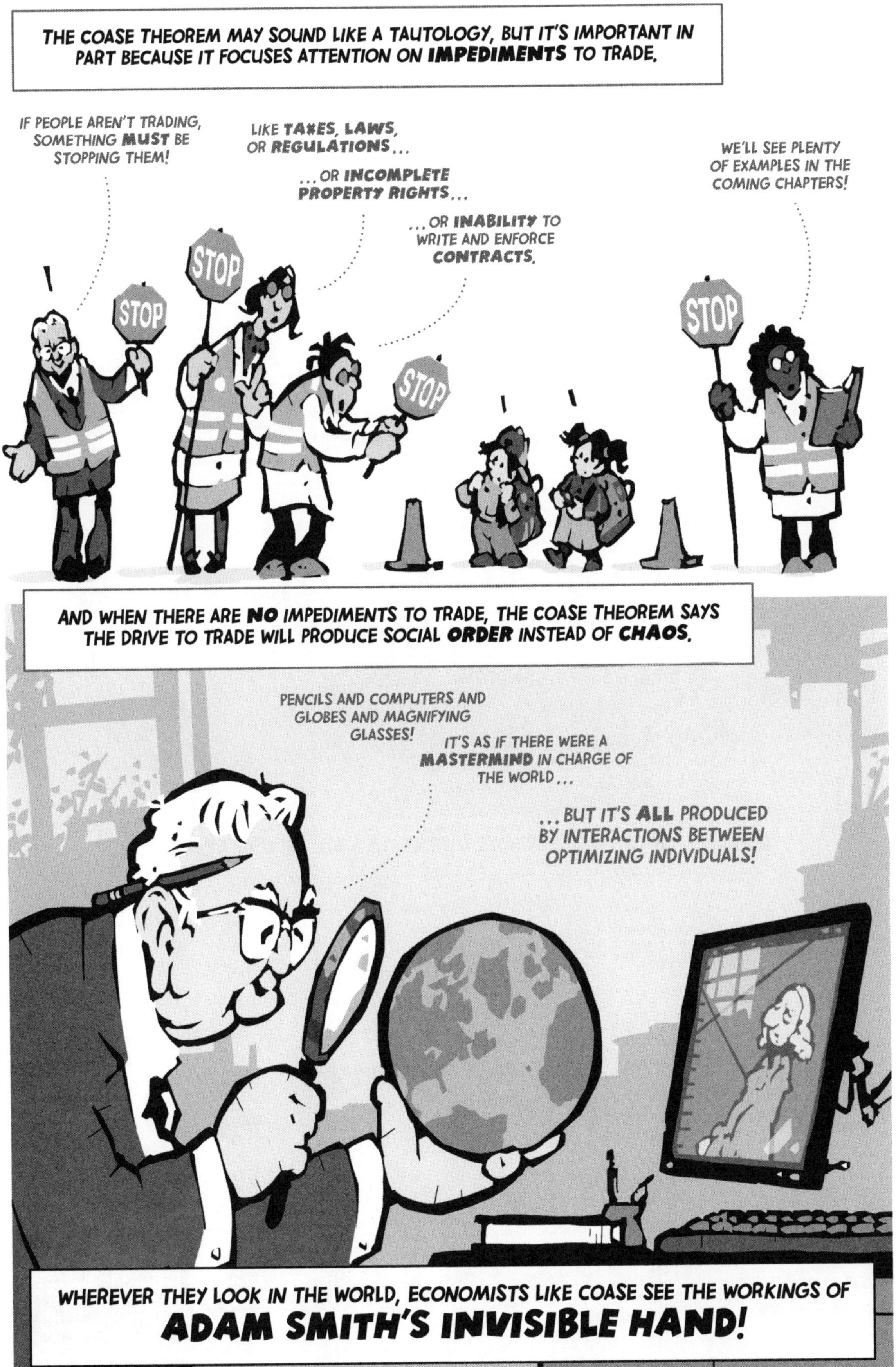
THE COASE THEOREM MAY SOUND LIKE A TAUTOLOGY, BUT IT'S IMPORTANT IN PART BECAUSE IT FOCUSES ATTENTION ON **IMPEDIMENTS** TO TRADE.
IF PEOPLE AREN'T TRADING, SOMETHING **MUST** BE STOPPING THEM!
LIKE **TAXES, LAWS,** OR **REGULATIONS**...
...OR **INCOMPLETE PROPERTY RIGHTS**...
...OR **INABILITY** TO WRITE AND ENFORCE **CONTRACTS.**
WE'LL SEE PLENTY OF EXAMPLES IN THE COMING CHAPTERS!
STOP
STOP
STOP
STOP
STOP
AND WHEN THERE ARE **NO** IMPEDIMENTS TO TRADE, THE COASE THEOREM SAYS THE DRIVE TO TRADE WILL PRODUCE SOCIAL **ORDER** INSTEAD OF **CHAOS.**
PENCILS AND COMPUTERS AND GLOBES AND MAGNIFYING GLASSES!
IT'S AS IF THERE WERE A **MASTERMIND** IN CHARGE OF THE WORLD...
...BUT IT'S **ALL** PRODUCED BY INTERACTIONS BETWEEN OPTIMIZING INDIVIDUALS!
WHEREVER THEY LOOK IN THE WORLD, ECONOMISTS LIKE COASE SEE THE WORKINGS OF
ADAM SMITH'S INVISIBLE HAND!

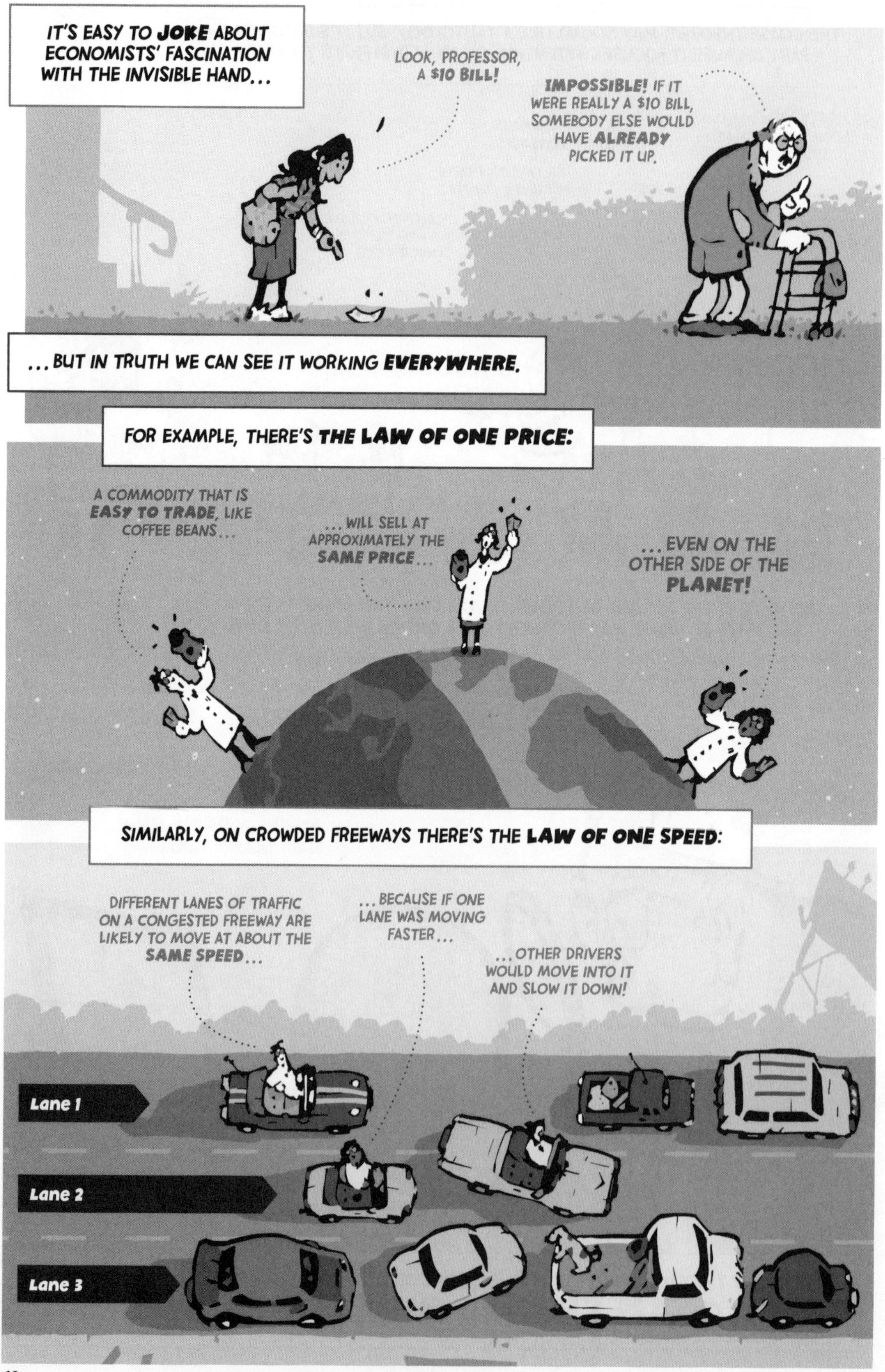
IT'S EASY TO JOKE ABOUT ECONOMISTS' FASCINATION WITH THE INVISIBLE HAND...
LOOK, PROFESSOR, A $10 BILL!
IMPOSSIBLE! IF IT WERE REALLY A $10 BILL, SOMEBODY ELSE WOULD HAVE ALREADY PICKED IT UP.
...BUT IN TRUTH WE CAN SEE IT WORKING EVERYWHERE.
FOR EXAMPLE, THERE'S THE LAW OF ONE PRICE:
A COMMODITY THAT IS EASY TO TRADE, LIKE COFFEE BEANS...
...WILL SELL AT APPROXIMATELY THE SAME PRICE...
...EVEN ON THE OTHER SIDE OF THE PLANET!
SIMILARLY, ON CROWDED FREEWAYS THERE'S THE LAW OF ONE SPEED:
DIFFERENT LANES OF TRAFFIC ON A CONGESTED FREEWAY ARE LIKELY TO MOVE AT ABOUT THE SAME SPEED...
...BECAUSE IF ONE LANE WAS MOVING FASTER...
...OTHER DRIVERS WOULD MOVE INTO IT AND SLOW IT DOWN!
Lane 1
Lane 2
Lane 3

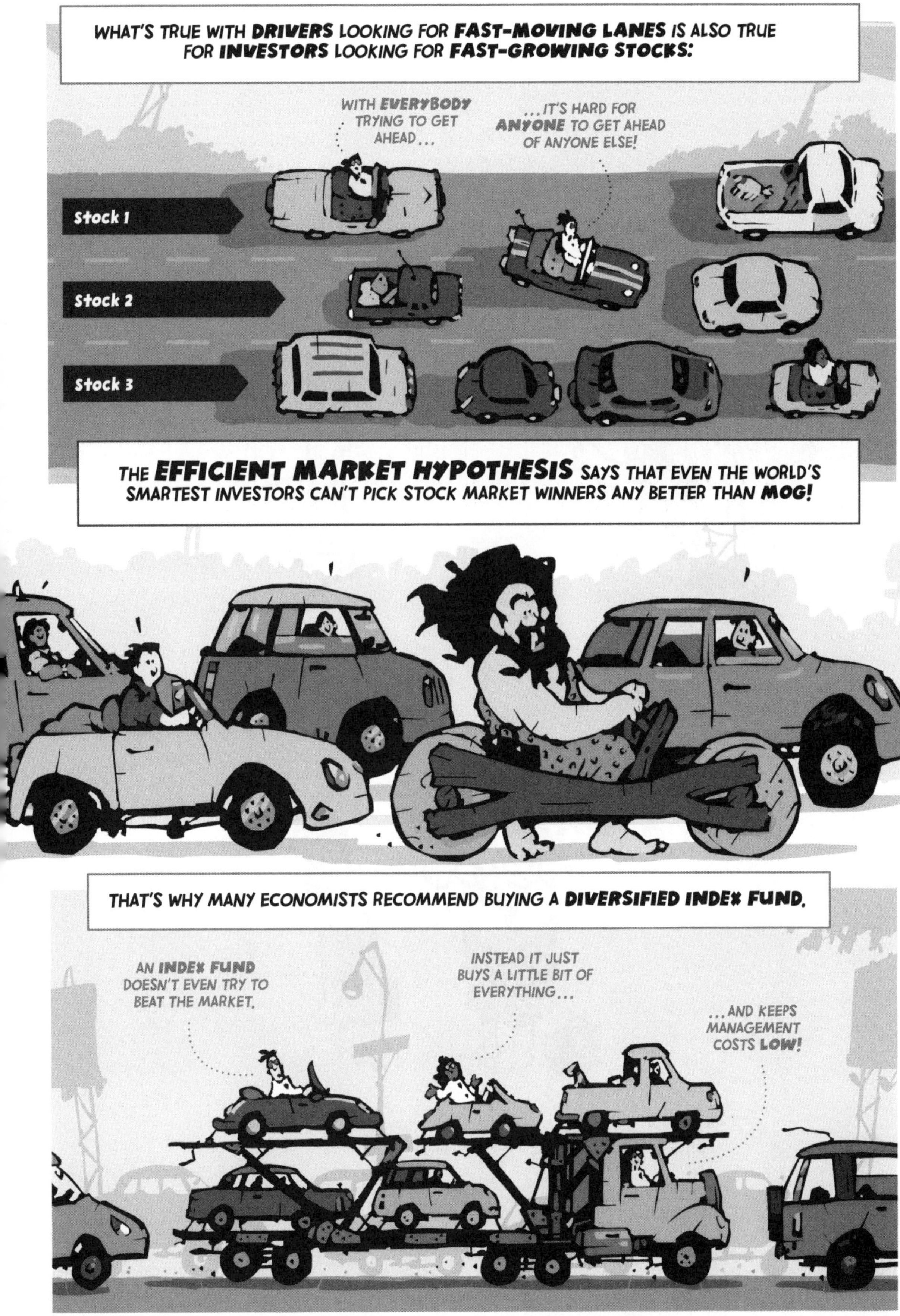
WHAT'S TRUE WITH DRIVERS LOOKING FOR FAST-MOVING LANES IS ALSO TRUE FOR INVESTORS LOOKING FOR FAST-GROWING STOCKS:
WITH EVERYBODY TRYING TO GET AHEAD...
...IT'S HARD FOR ANYONE TO GET AHEAD OF ANYONE ELSE!
Stock 1
Stock 2
Stock 3
THE EFFICIENT MARKET HYPOTHESIS SAYS THAT EVEN THE WORLD'S SMARTEST INVESTORS CAN'T PICK STOCK MARKET WINNERS ANY BETTER THAN MOG!
THAT'S WHY MANY ECONOMISTS RECOMMEND BUYING A DIVERSIFIED INDEX FUND.
AN INDEX FUND DOESN'T EVEN TRY TO BEAT THE MARKET.
INSTEAD IT JUST BUYS A LITTLE BIT OF EVERYTHING...
...AND KEEPS MANAGEMENT COSTS LOW!

HEY, OOGA! MOG DEVELOP **FANCY STOCK-PICKING TECHNIQUE!**
LEMME GUESS...
...YOU USE **ROCK PAPER SCISSORS?**
NO!
COURSE NOT!
MOG USE **ROCK ROCK ROCK!**

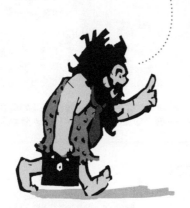

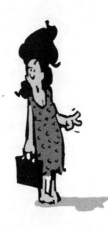

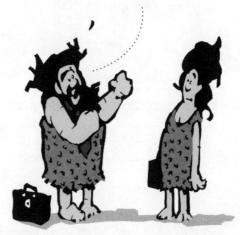

PART TWO
STRATEGIC INTERACTIONS

CHAPTER 6
CAKE CUTTING

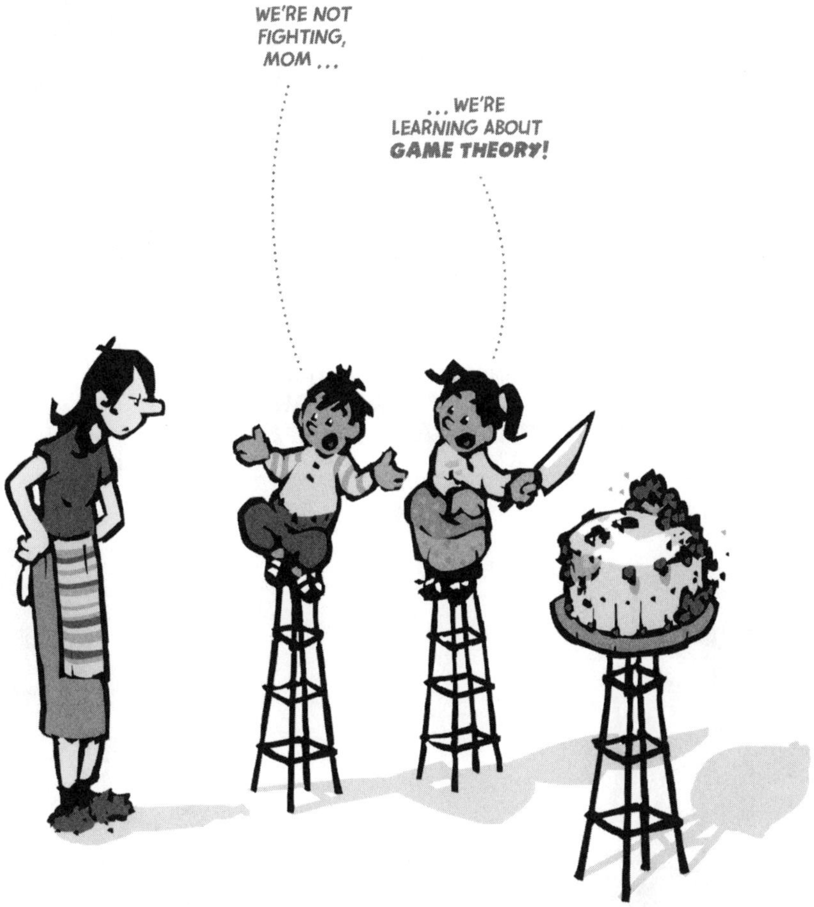
WE'RE NOT FIGHTING, MOM . . .
. . . WE'RE LEARNING ABOUT GAME THEORY!

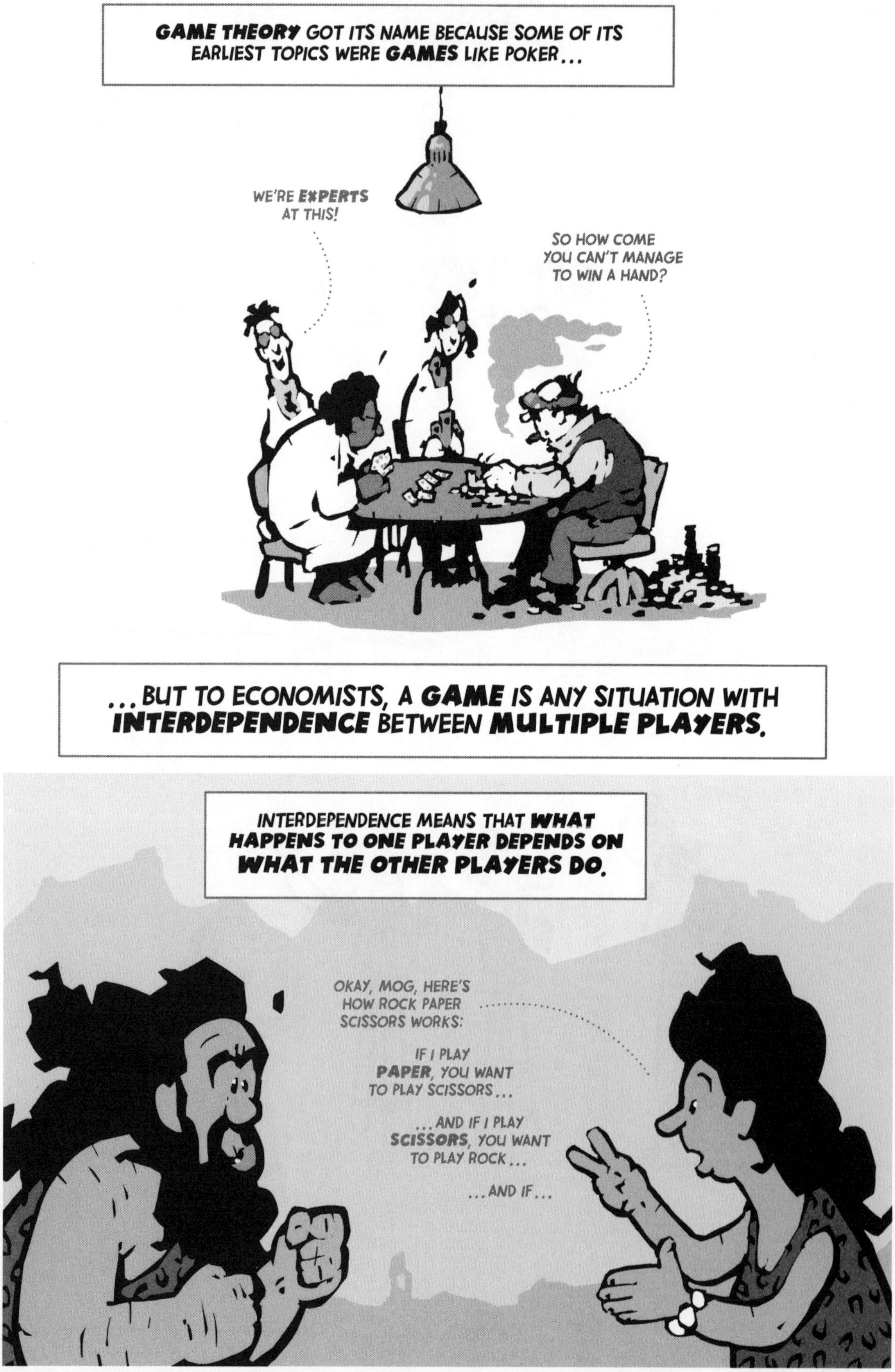
GAME THEORY GOT ITS NAME BECAUSE SOME OF ITS EARLIEST TOPICS WERE GAMES LIKE POKER...
WE'RE EXPERTS AT THIS!
SO HOW COME YOU CAN'T MANAGE TO WIN A HAND?
...BUT TO ECONOMISTS, A GAME IS ANY SITUATION WITH INTERDEPENDENCE BETWEEN MULTIPLE PLAYERS.
INTERDEPENDENCE MEANS THAT WHAT HAPPENS TO ONE PLAYER DEPENDS ON WHAT THE OTHER PLAYERS DO.
OKAY, MOG, HERE'S HOW ROCK PAPER SCISSORS WORKS:
IF I PLAY PAPER, YOU WANT TO PLAY SCISSORS...
...AND IF I PLAY SCISSORS, YOU WANT TO PLAY ROCK...
...AND IF...

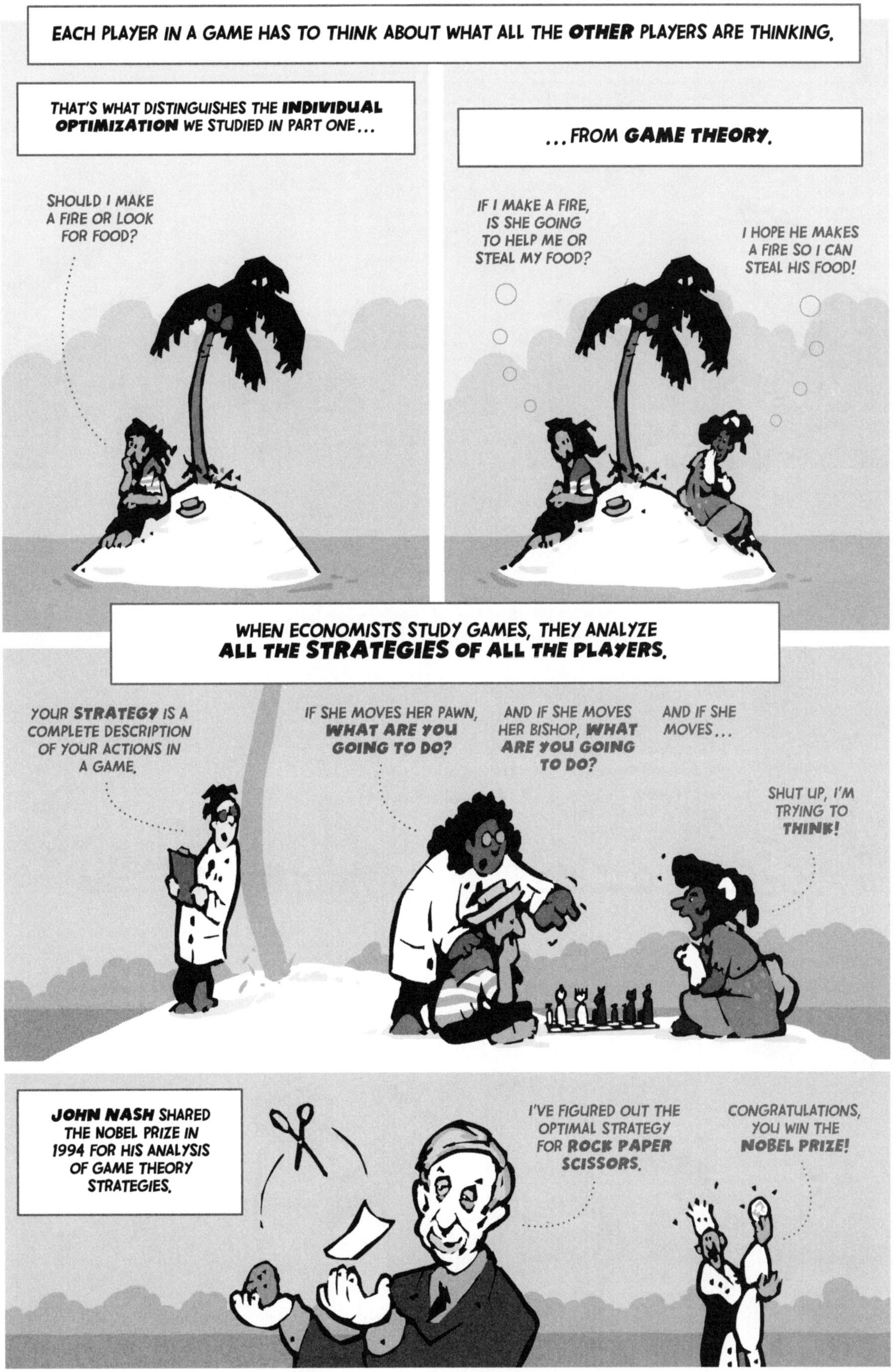
EACH PLAYER IN A GAME HAS TO THINK ABOUT WHAT ALL THE OTHER PLAYERS ARE THINKING.
THAT'S WHAT DISTINGUISHES THE INDIVIDUAL OPTIMIZATION WE STUDIED IN PART ONE...
SHOULD I MAKE A FIRE OR LOOK FOR FOOD?
...FROM GAME THEORY.
IF I MAKE A FIRE, IS SHE GOING TO HELP ME OR STEAL MY FOOD?
I HOPE HE MAKES A FIRE SO I CAN STEAL HIS FOOD!
WHEN ECONOMISTS STUDY GAMES, THEY ANALYZE ALL THE STRATEGIES OF ALL THE PLAYERS.
YOUR STRATEGY IS A COMPLETE DESCRIPTION OF YOUR ACTIONS IN A GAME.
IF SHE MOVES HER PAWN, WHAT ARE YOU GOING TO DO?
AND IF SHE MOVES HER BISHOP, WHAT ARE YOU GOING TO DO?
AND IF SHE MOVES...
SHUT UP, I'M TRYING TO THINK!
JOHN NASH SHARED THE NOBEL PRIZE IN 1994 FOR HIS ANALYSIS OF GAME THEORY STRATEGIES.
I'VE FIGURED OUT THE OPTIMAL STRATEGY FOR ROCK PAPER SCISSORS.
CONGRATULATIONS, YOU WIN THE NOBEL PRIZE!

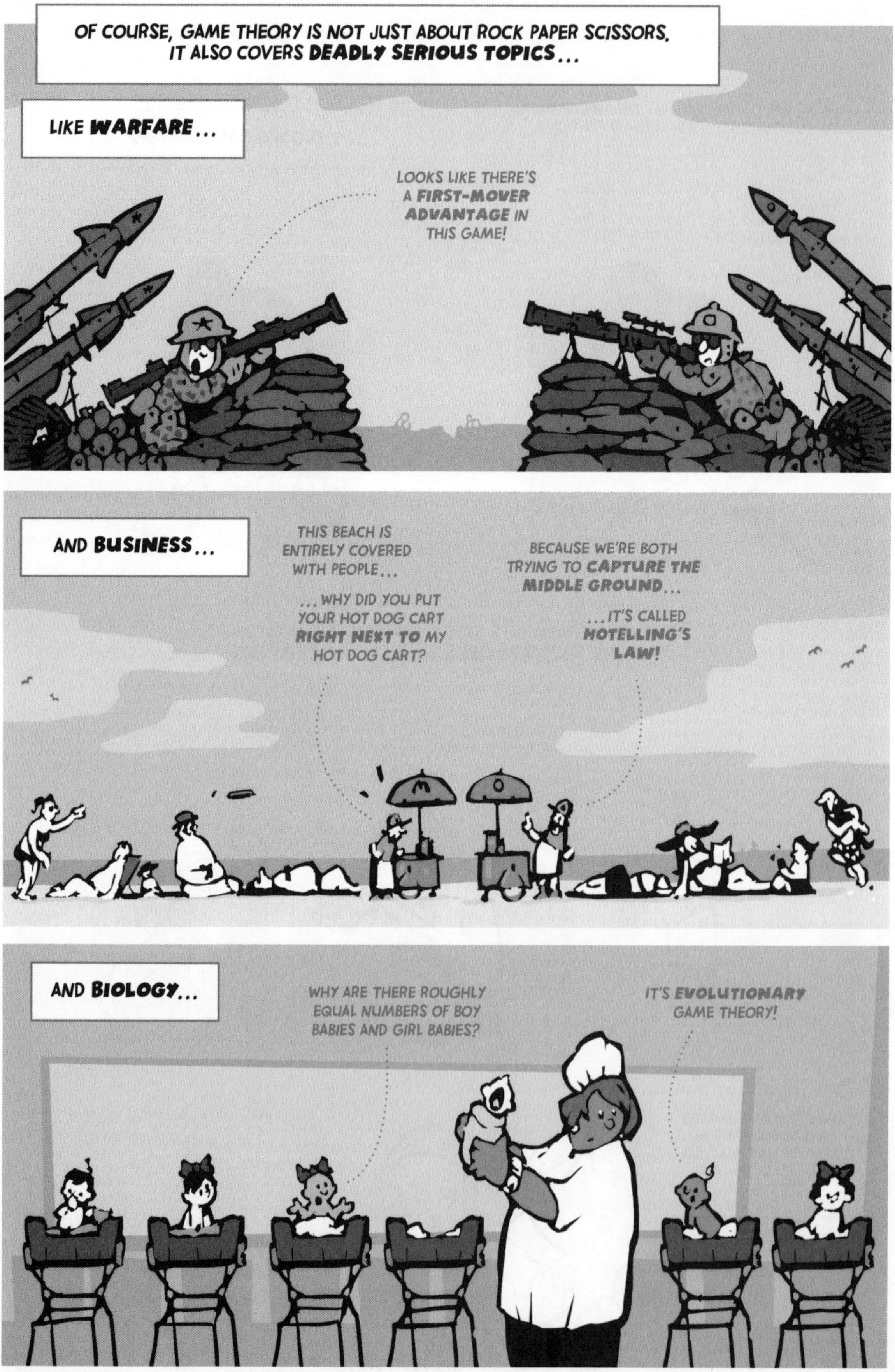
OF COURSE, GAME THEORY IS NOT JUST ABOUT ROCK PAPER SCISSORS. IT ALSO COVERS DEADLY SERIOUS TOPICS...
LIKE WARFARE...
LOOKS LIKE THERE'S A FIRST-MOVER ADVANTAGE IN THIS GAME!
AND BUSINESS...
THIS BEACH IS ENTIRELY COVERED WITH PEOPLE...
...WHY DID YOU PUT YOUR HOT DOG CART RIGHT NEXT TO MY HOT DOG CART?
BECAUSE WE'RE BOTH TRYING TO CAPTURE THE MIDDLE GROUND...
...IT'S CALLED HOTELLING'S LAW!
AND BIOLOGY...
WHY ARE THERE ROUGHLY EQUAL NUMBERS OF BOY BABIES AND GIRL BABIES?
IT'S EVOLUTIONARY GAME THEORY!

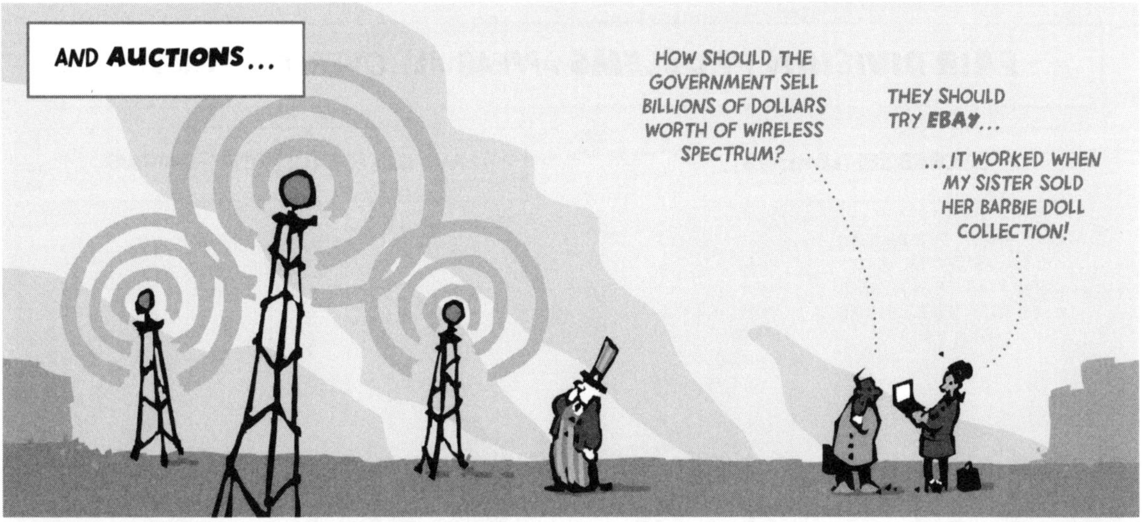
AND **AUCTIONS**...
HOW SHOULD THE GOVERNMENT SELL BILLIONS OF DOLLARS WORTH OF WIRELESS SPECTRUM?
THEY SHOULD TRY **EBAY**...
...IT WORKED WHEN MY SISTER SOLD HER BARBIE DOLL COLLECTION!

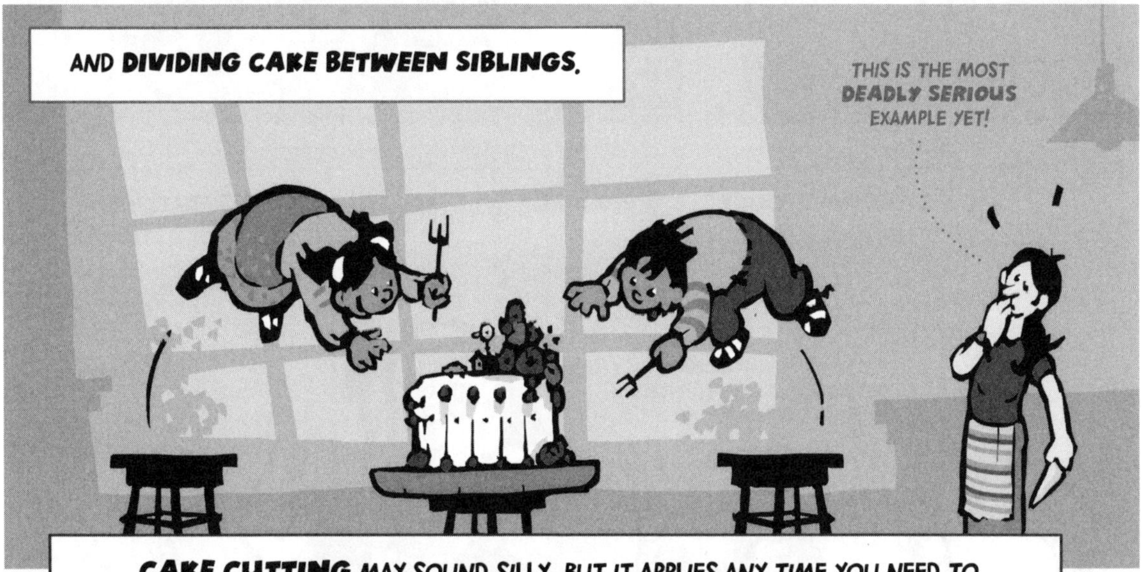
AND **DIVIDING CAKE BETWEEN SIBLINGS.**
THIS IS THE MOST **DEADLY SERIOUS** EXAMPLE YET!

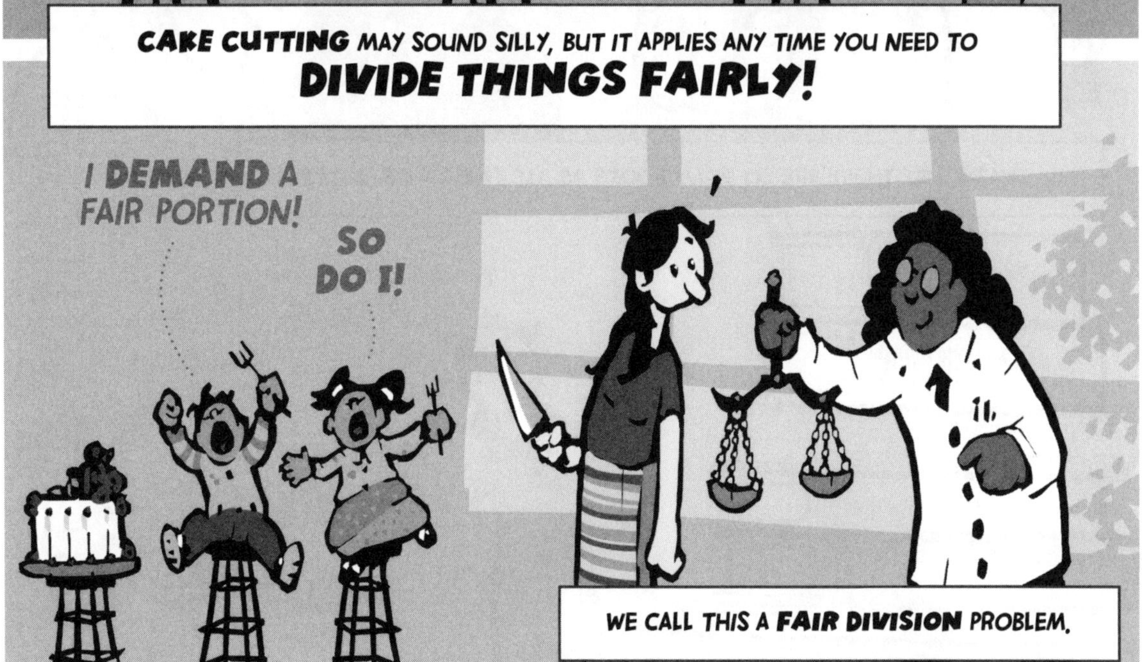
CAKE CUTTING MAY SOUND SILLY, BUT IT APPLIES ANY TIME YOU NEED TO **DIVIDE THINGS FAIRLY!**
I **DEMAND** A FAIR PORTION!
SO DO I!
WE CALL THIS A **FAIR DIVISION** PROBLEM.

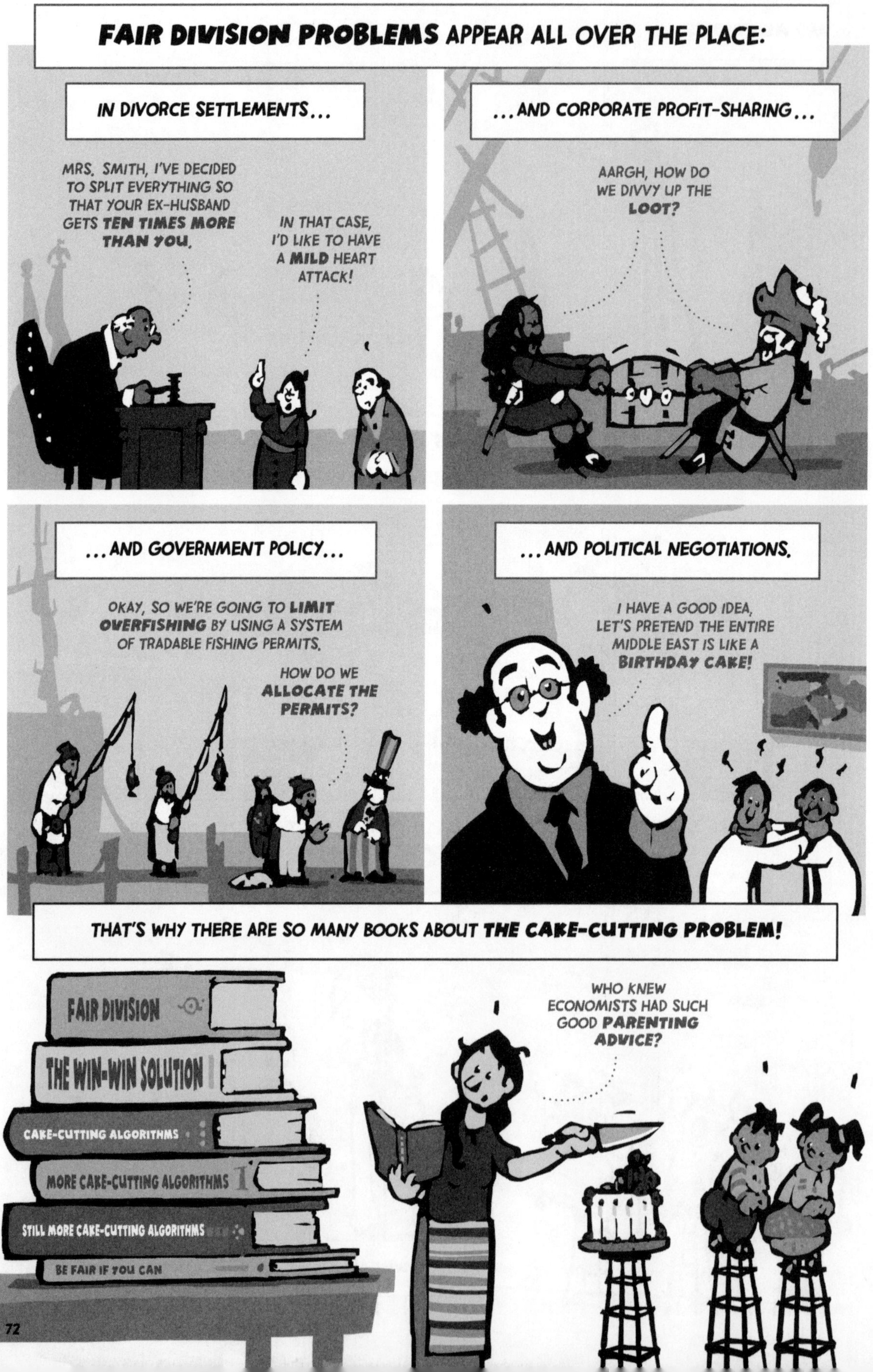
FAIR DIVISION PROBLEMS APPEAR ALL OVER THE PLACE:
IN DIVORCE SETTLEMENTS...
MRS. SMITH, I'VE DECIDED TO SPLIT EVERYTHING SO THAT YOUR EX-HUSBAND GETS TEN TIMES MORE THAN YOU.
IN THAT CASE, I'D LIKE TO HAVE A MILD HEART ATTACK!
...AND CORPORATE PROFIT-SHARING...
AARGH, HOW DO WE DIVVY UP THE LOOT?
...AND GOVERNMENT POLICY...
OKAY, SO WE'RE GOING TO LIMIT OVERFISHING BY USING A SYSTEM OF TRADABLE FISHING PERMITS.
HOW DO WE ALLOCATE THE PERMITS?
...AND POLITICAL NEGOTIATIONS.
I HAVE A GOOD IDEA, LET'S PRETEND THE ENTIRE MIDDLE EAST IS LIKE A BIRTHDAY CAKE!
THAT'S WHY THERE ARE SO MANY BOOKS ABOUT THE CAKE-CUTTING PROBLEM!
FAIR DIVISION
THE WIN-WIN SOLUTION
CAKE-CUTTING ALGORITHMS
MORE CAKE-CUTTING ALGORITHMS
STILL MORE CAKE-CUTTING ALGORITHMS
BE FAIR IF YOU CAN
WHO KNEW ECONOMISTS HAD SUCH GOOD PARENTING ADVICE?

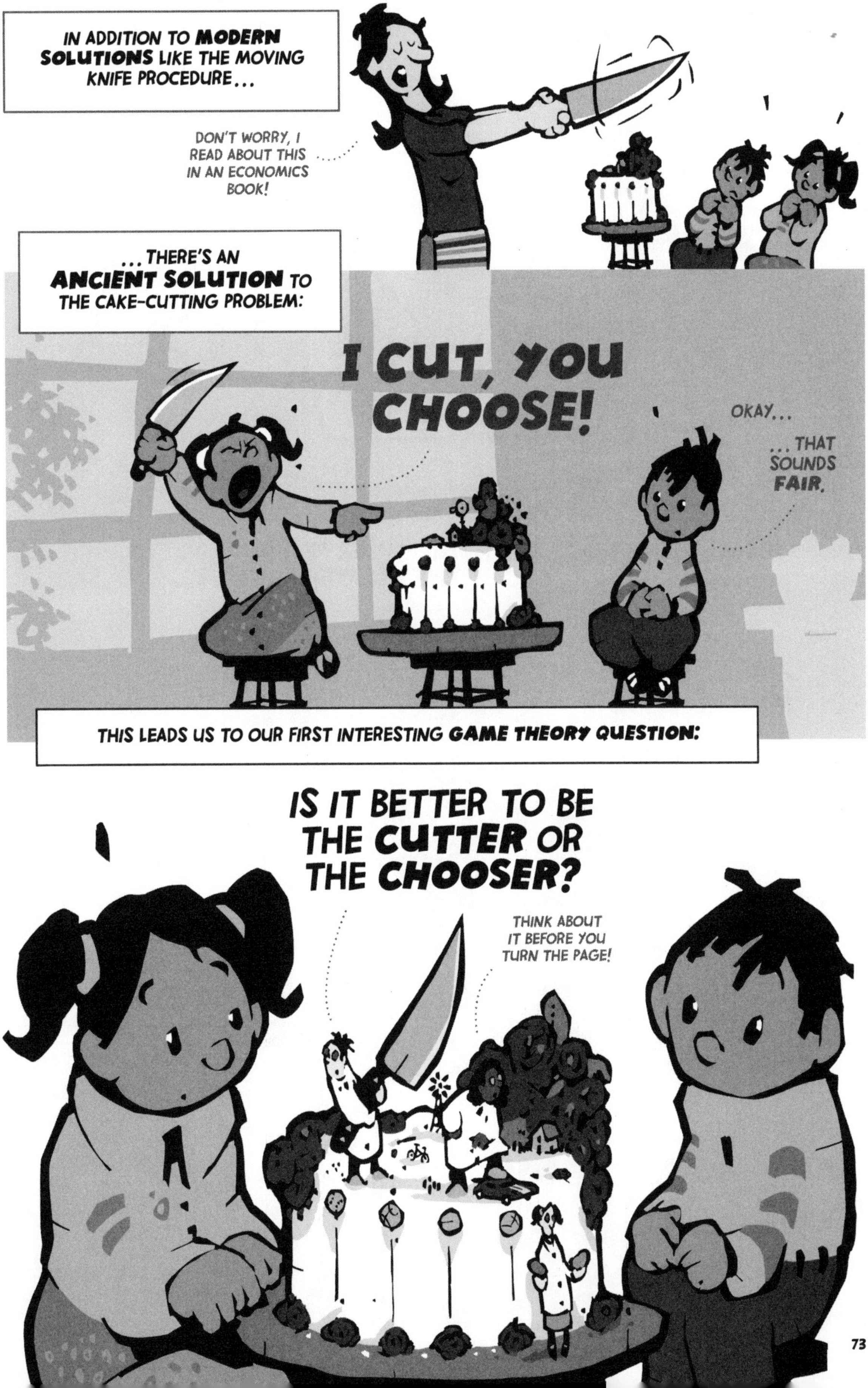
IN ADDITION TO **MODERN SOLUTIONS** LIKE THE MOVING KNIFE PROCEDURE...
DON'T WORRY, I READ ABOUT THIS IN AN ECONOMICS BOOK!
...THERE'S AN **ANCIENT SOLUTION** TO THE CAKE-CUTTING PROBLEM:
I CUT, YOU CHOOSE!
OKAY...
...THAT SOUNDS **FAIR.**
THIS LEADS US TO OUR FIRST INTERESTING **GAME THEORY QUESTION:**
IS IT BETTER TO BE THE **CUTTER** OR THE **CHOOSER?**
THINK ABOUT IT BEFORE YOU TURN THE PAGE!

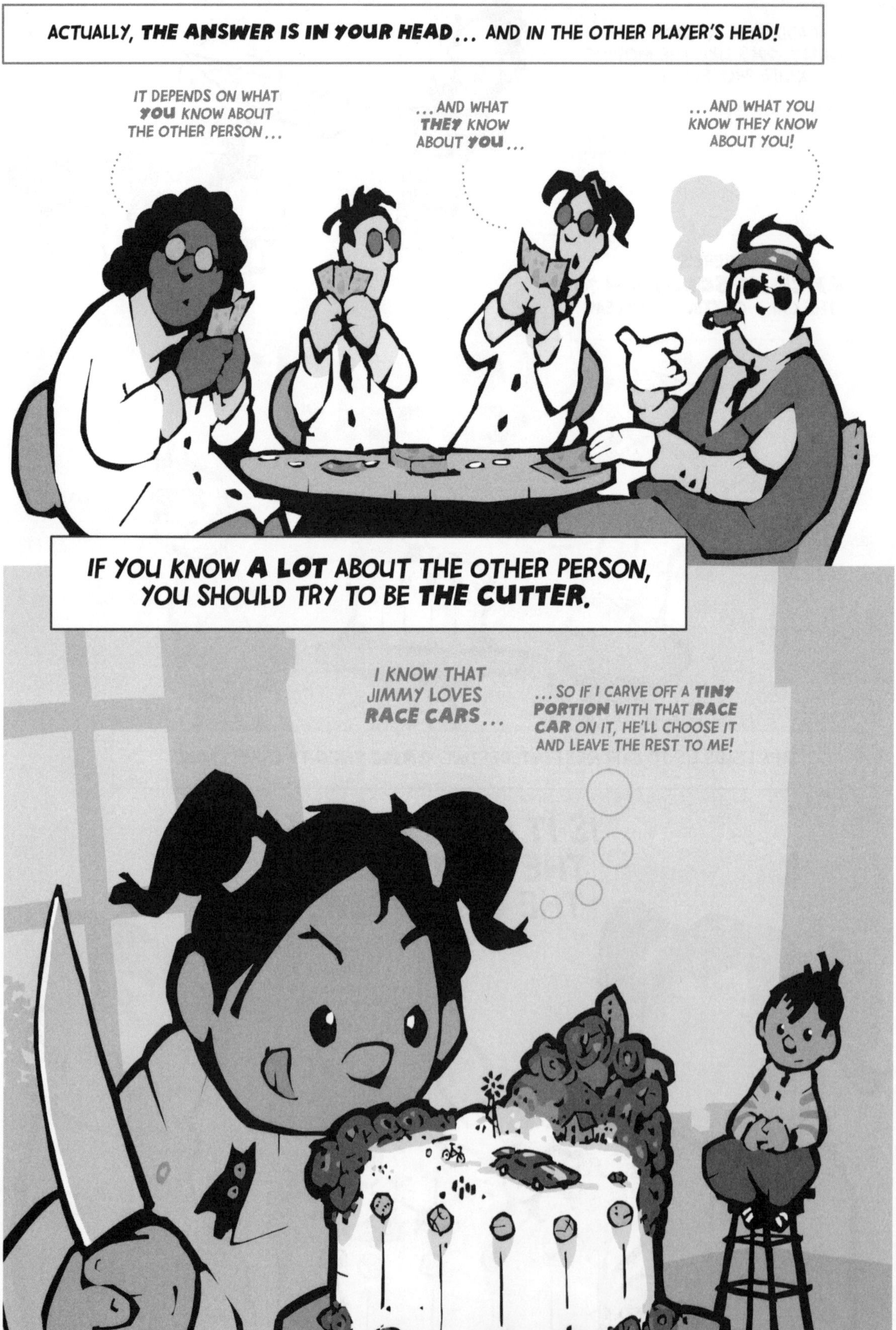
ACTUALLY, THE ANSWER IS IN YOUR HEAD... AND IN THE OTHER PLAYER'S HEAD!
IT DEPENDS ON WHAT YOU KNOW ABOUT THE OTHER PERSON...
...AND WHAT THEY KNOW ABOUT YOU...
...AND WHAT YOU KNOW THEY KNOW ABOUT YOU!
IF YOU KNOW A LOT ABOUT THE OTHER PERSON, YOU SHOULD TRY TO BE THE CUTTER.
I KNOW THAT JIMMY LOVES RACE CARS...
...SO IF I CARVE OFF A TINY PORTION WITH THAT RACE CAR ON IT, HE'LL CHOOSE IT AND LEAVE THE REST TO ME!

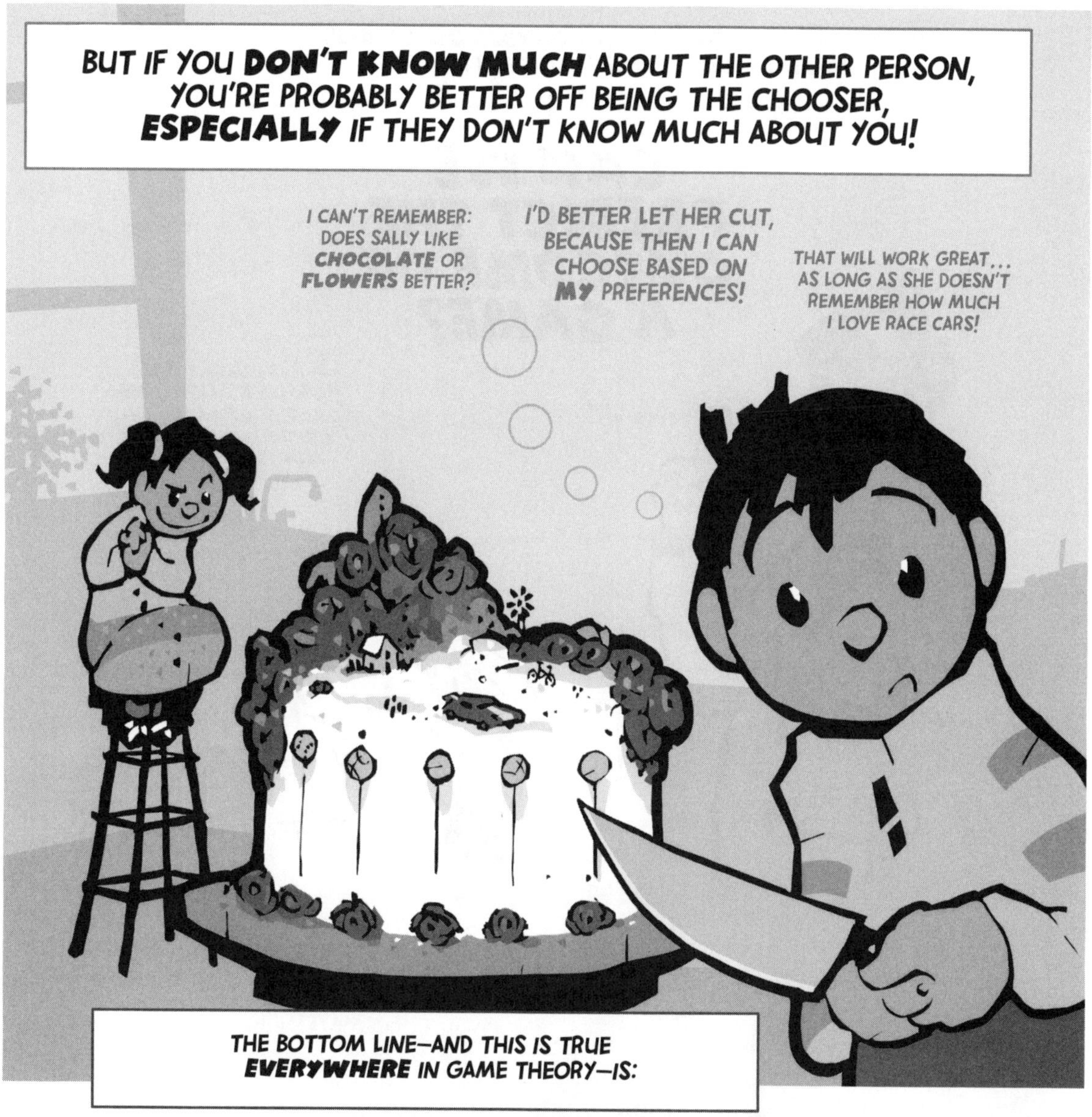
BUT IF YOU DON'T KNOW MUCH ABOUT THE OTHER PERSON, YOU'RE PROBABLY BETTER OFF BEING THE CHOOSER, ESPECIALLY IF THEY DON'T KNOW MUCH ABOUT YOU!
I CAN'T REMEMBER: DOES SALLY LIKE CHOCOLATE OR FLOWERS BETTER?
I'D BETTER LET HER CUT, BECAUSE THEN I CAN CHOOSE BASED ON MY PREFERENCES!
THAT WILL WORK GREAT... AS LONG AS SHE DOESN'T REMEMBER HOW MUCH I LOVE RACE CARS!
THE BOTTOM LINE—AND THIS IS TRUE EVERYWHERE IN GAME THEORY—IS:

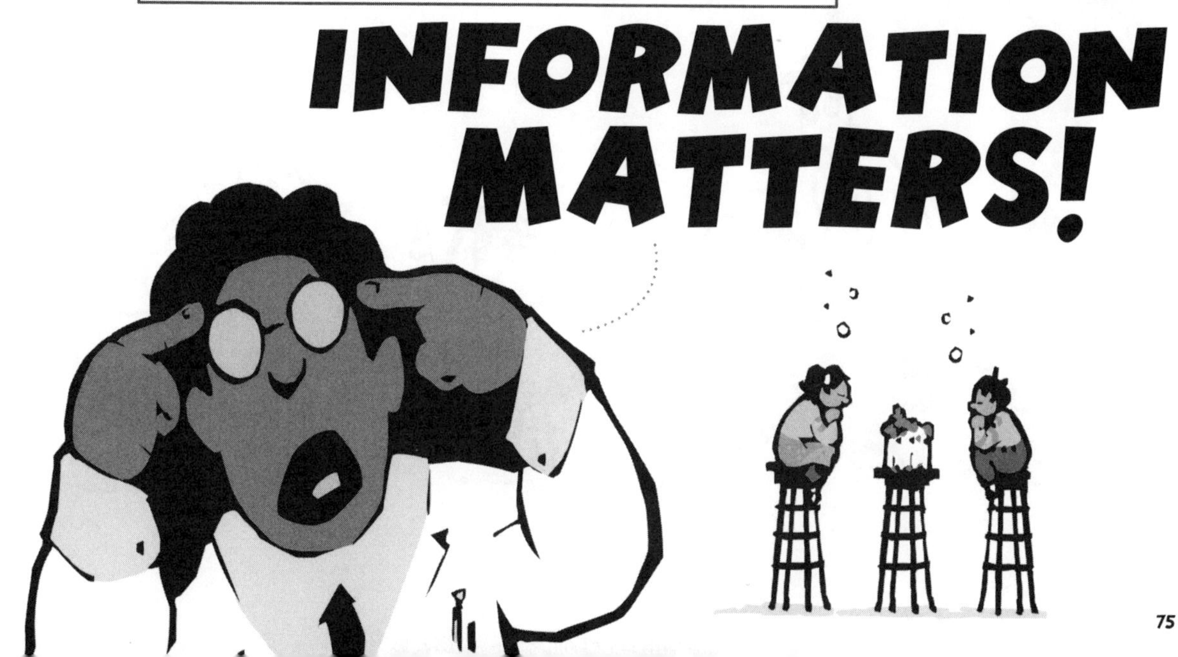
INFORMATION MATTERS!

ECONOMISTS WHO STUDY GAMES FOCUS ON **TWO QUESTIONS**.
THE **FIRST** GAME THEORY QUESTION IS:

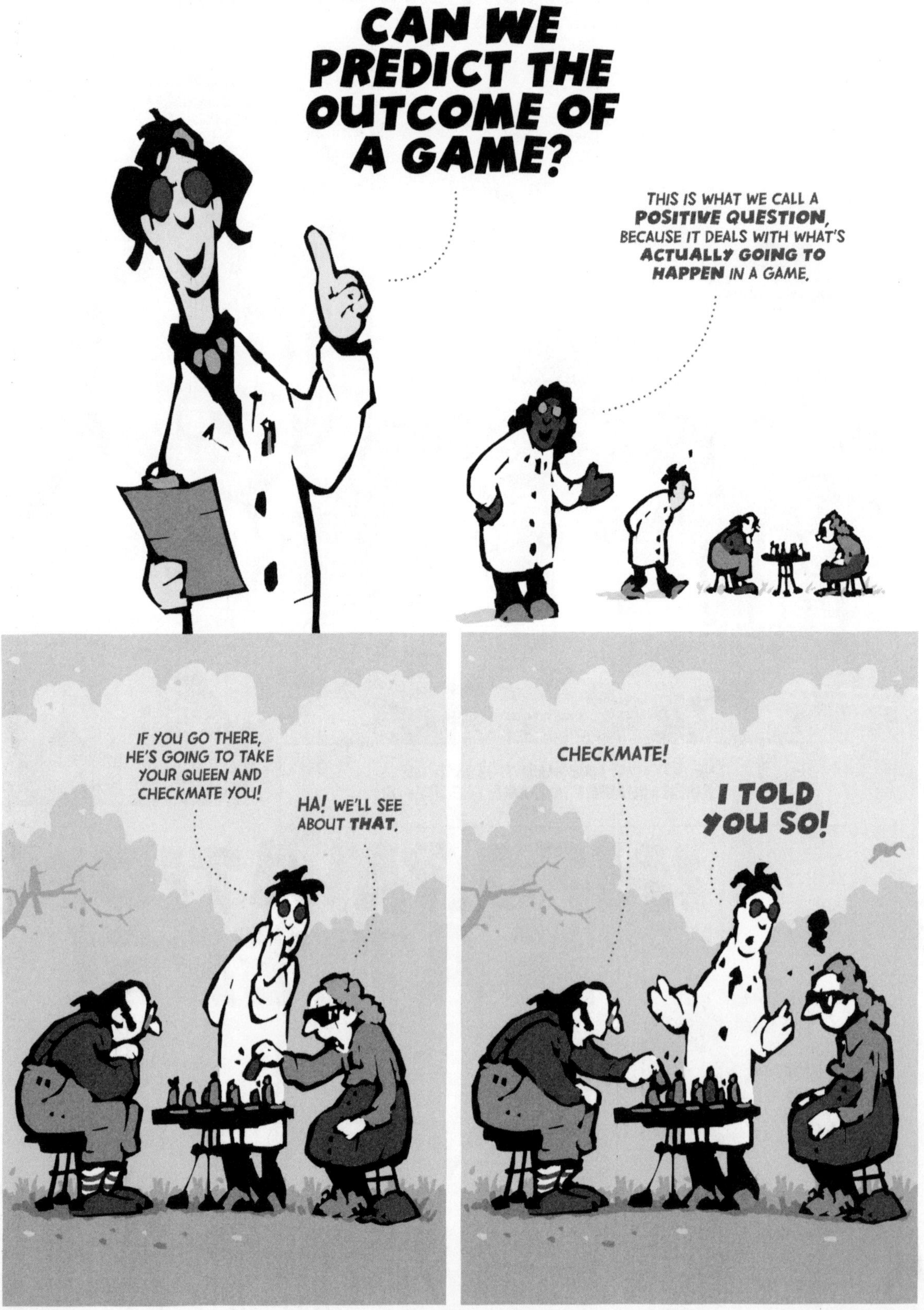
CAN WE PREDICT THE OUTCOME OF A GAME?
THIS IS WHAT WE CALL A POSITIVE QUESTION, BECAUSE IT DEALS WITH WHAT'S ACTUALLY GOING TO HAPPEN IN A GAME.
IF YOU GO THERE, HE'S GOING TO TAKE YOUR QUEEN AND CHECKMATE YOU!
HA! WE'LL SEE ABOUT THAT.
CHECKMATE!
I TOLD YOU SO!

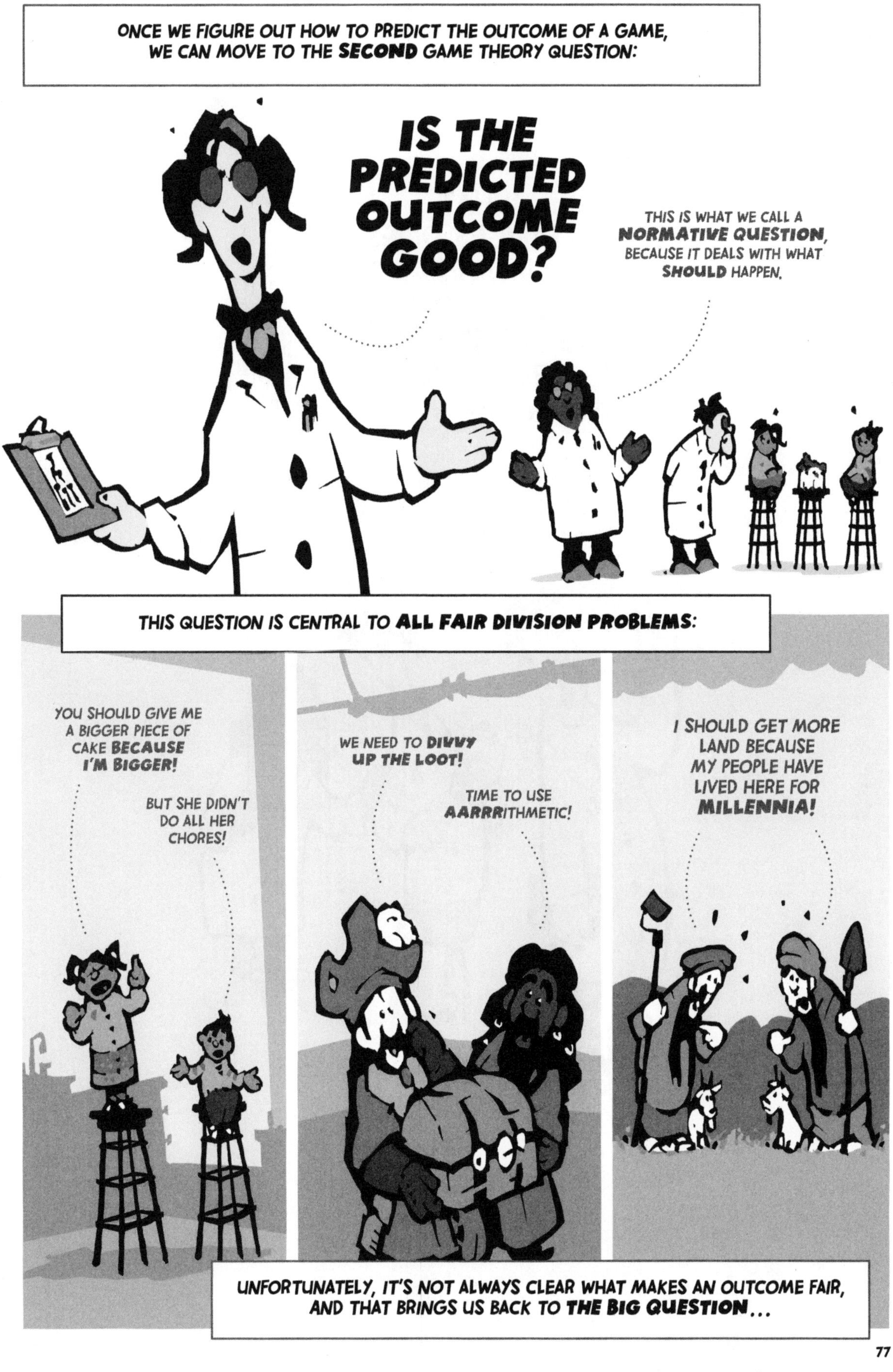
ONCE WE FIGURE OUT HOW TO PREDICT THE OUTCOME OF A GAME, WE CAN MOVE TO THE SECOND GAME THEORY QUESTION:
IS THE PREDICTED OUTCOME GOOD?
THIS IS WHAT WE CALL A NORMATIVE QUESTION, BECAUSE IT DEALS WITH WHAT SHOULD HAPPEN.
THIS QUESTION IS CENTRAL TO ALL FAIR DIVISION PROBLEMS:
YOU SHOULD GIVE ME A BIGGER PIECE OF CAKE BECAUSE I'M BIGGER!
BUT SHE DIDN'T DO ALL HER CHORES!
WE NEED TO DIVVY UP THE LOOT!
TIME TO USE AARRRITHMETIC!
I SHOULD GET MORE LAND BECAUSE MY PEOPLE HAVE LIVED HERE FOR MILLENNIA!
UNFORTUNATELY, IT'S NOT ALWAYS CLEAR WHAT MAKES AN OUTCOME FAIR, AND THAT BRINGS US BACK TO THE BIG QUESTION...

UNDER WHAT CIRCUMSTANCES DOES INDIVIDUAL OPTIMIZATION LEAD TO OUTCOMES THAT ARE **GOOD** FOR THE GROUP AS A WHOLE?

UM, WHAT EXACTLY DOES "**GOOD**" MEAN, ANYWAY?

CHAPTER 7
PARETO EFFICIENCY

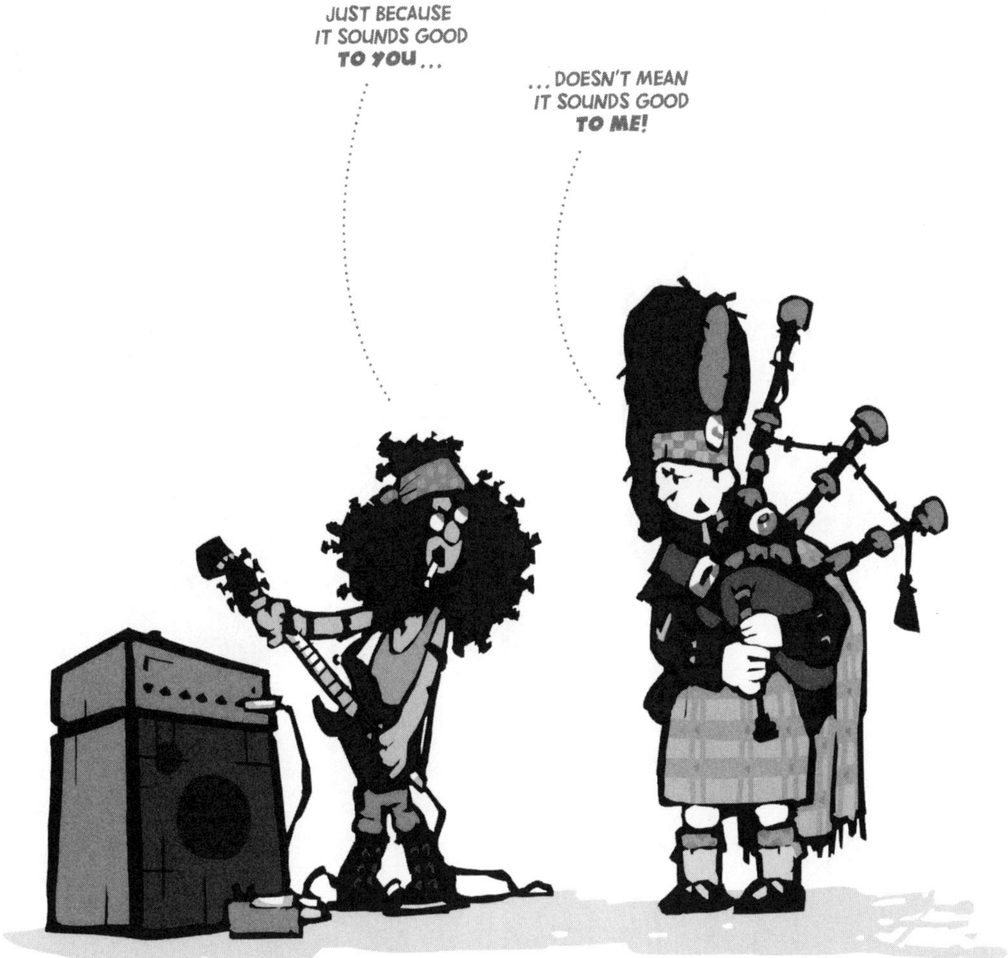
JUST BECAUSE IT SOUNDS GOOD **TO YOU**...
...DOESN'T MEAN IT SOUNDS GOOD **TO ME!**

THE QUESTION OF **WHAT MAKES AN OUTCOME GOOD** HAS OCCUPIED PHILOSOPHERS AND THINKERS FOR CENTURIES.

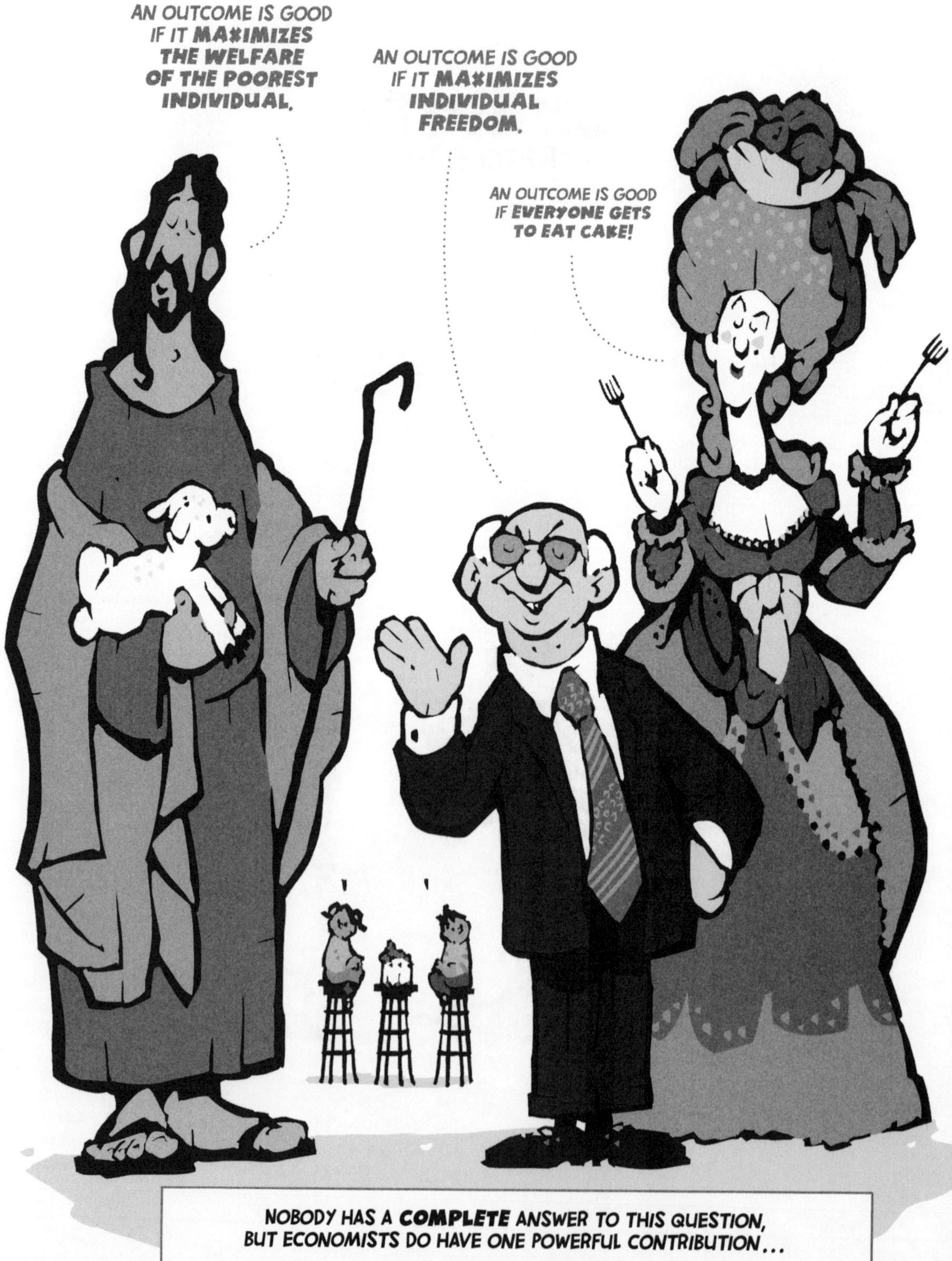
AN OUTCOME IS GOOD IF IT MAXIMIZES THE WELFARE OF THE POOREST INDIVIDUAL.
AN OUTCOME IS GOOD IF IT MAXIMIZES INDIVIDUAL FREEDOM.
AN OUTCOME IS GOOD IF EVERYONE GETS TO EAT CAKE!

NOBODY HAS A **COMPLETE** ANSWER TO THIS QUESTION, BUT ECONOMISTS DO HAVE ONE POWERFUL CONTRIBUTION...

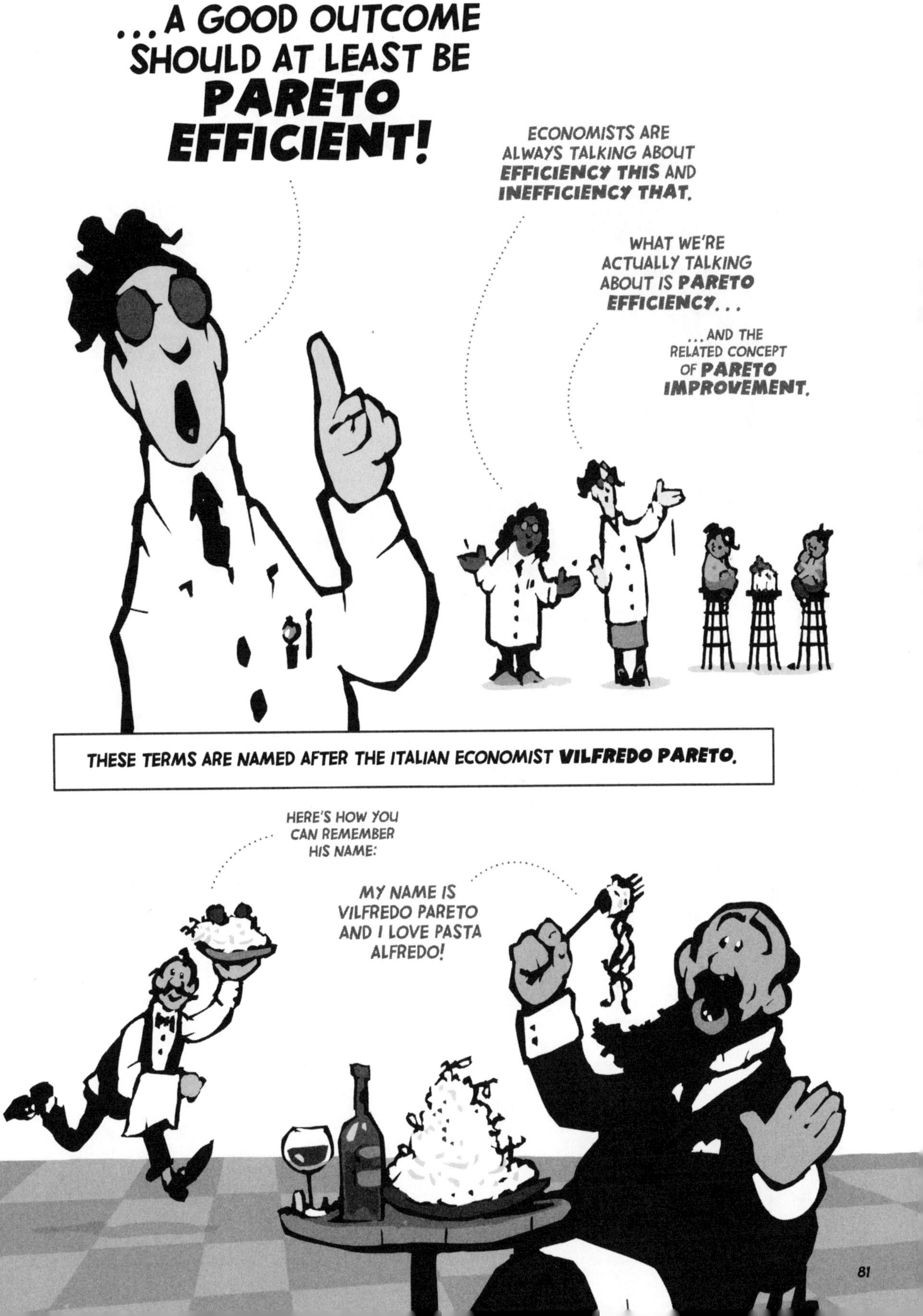
...A GOOD OUTCOME SHOULD AT LEAST BE **PARETO EFFICIENT!**
ECONOMISTS ARE ALWAYS TALKING ABOUT **EFFICIENCY THIS** AND **INEFFICIENCY THAT.**
WHAT WE'RE ACTUALLY TALKING ABOUT IS **PARETO EFFICIENCY...**
...AND THE RELATED CONCEPT OF **PARETO IMPROVEMENT.**
THESE TERMS ARE NAMED AFTER THE ITALIAN ECONOMIST **VILFREDO PARETO.**
HERE'S HOW YOU CAN REMEMBER HIS NAME:
MY NAME IS VILFREDO PARETO AND I LOVE PASTA ALFREDO!

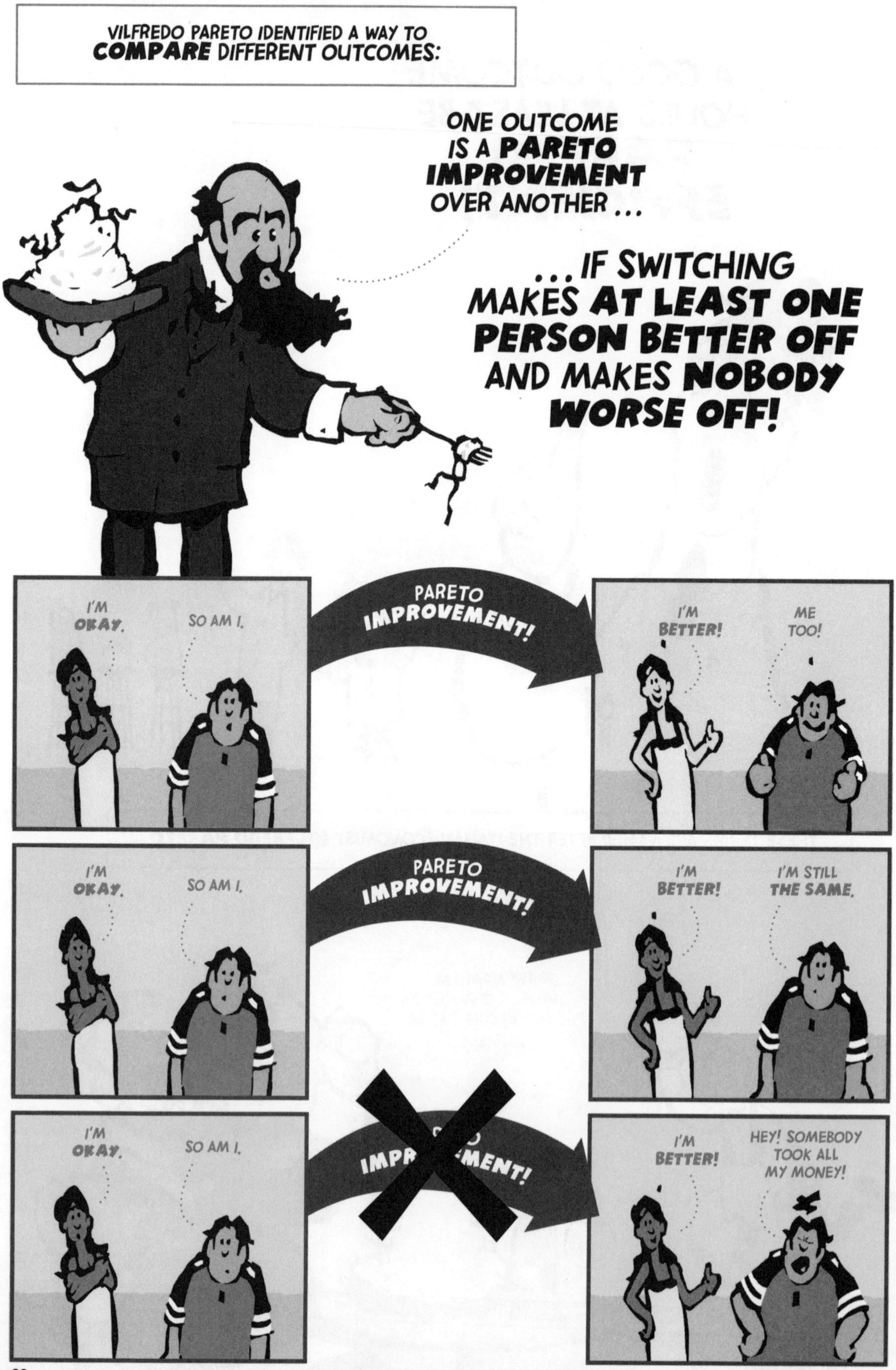
VILFREDO PARETO IDENTIFIED A WAY TO **COMPARE** DIFFERENT OUTCOMES:
ONE OUTCOME IS A **PARETO IMPROVEMENT** OVER ANOTHER ...
... IF SWITCHING MAKES **AT LEAST ONE PERSON BETTER OFF** AND MAKES **NOBODY WORSE OFF!**
I'M **OKAY.**
SO AM I.
PARETO **IMPROVEMENT!**
I'M **BETTER!**
ME TOO!
I'M **OKAY.**
SO AM I.
PARETO **IMPROVEMENT!**
I'M **BETTER!**
I'M STILL **THE SAME.**
I'M **OKAY.**
SO AM I.
I'M **BETTER!**
HEY! SOMEBODY TOOK ALL MY MONEY!

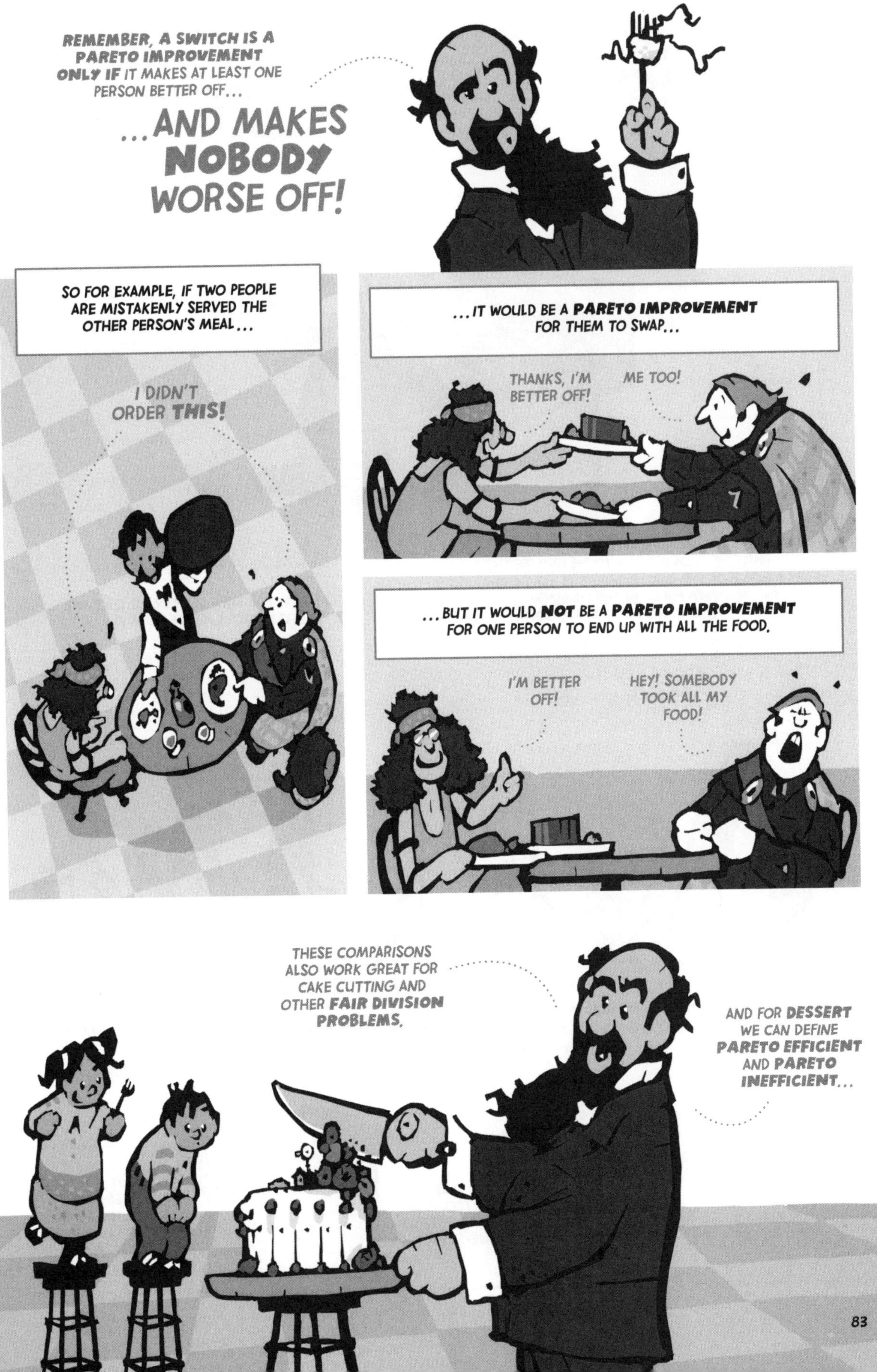

REMEMBER, A SWITCH IS A PARETO IMPROVEMENT ONLY IF IT MAKES AT LEAST ONE PERSON BETTER OFF...
...AND MAKES NOBODY WORSE OFF!
SO FOR EXAMPLE, IF TWO PEOPLE ARE MISTAKENLY SERVED THE OTHER PERSON'S MEAL...
I DIDN'T ORDER THIS!
...IT WOULD BE A PARETO IMPROVEMENT FOR THEM TO SWAP...
THANKS, I'M BETTER OFF!
ME TOO!
...BUT IT WOULD NOT BE A PARETO IMPROVEMENT FOR ONE PERSON TO END UP WITH ALL THE FOOD.
I'M BETTER OFF!
HEY! SOMEBODY TOOK ALL MY FOOD!
THESE COMPARISONS ALSO WORK GREAT FOR CAKE CUTTING AND OTHER FAIR DIVISION PROBLEMS.
AND FOR DESSERT WE CAN DEFINE PARETO EFFICIENT AND PARETO INEFFICIENT...

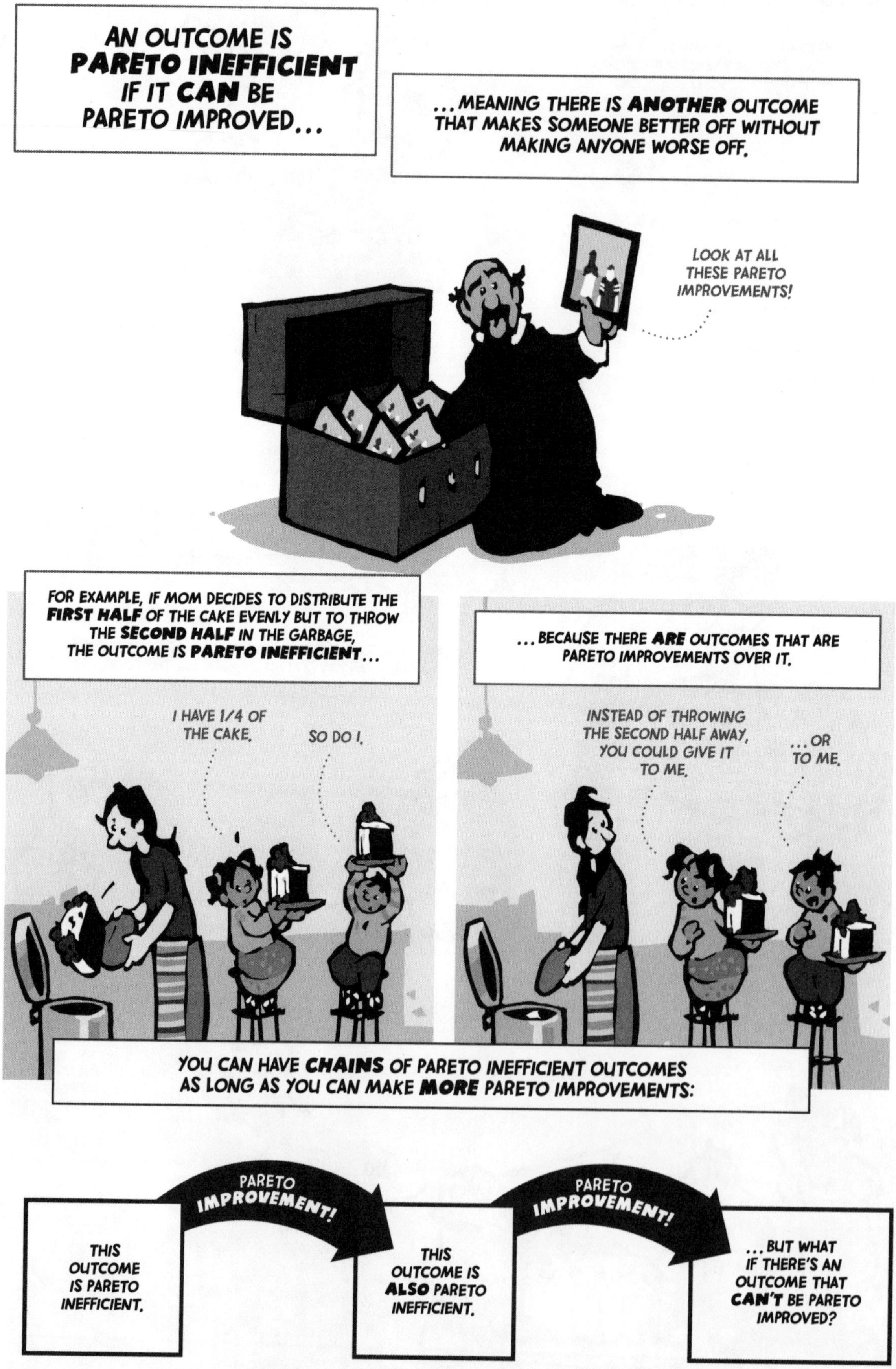
AN OUTCOME IS **PARETO INEFFICIENT** IF IT **CAN** BE PARETO IMPROVED...
...MEANING THERE IS **ANOTHER** OUTCOME THAT MAKES SOMEONE BETTER OFF WITHOUT MAKING ANYONE WORSE OFF.
LOOK AT ALL THESE PARETO IMPROVEMENTS!
FOR EXAMPLE, IF MOM DECIDES TO DISTRIBUTE THE **FIRST HALF** OF THE CAKE EVENLY BUT TO THROW THE **SECOND HALF** IN THE GARBAGE, THE OUTCOME IS **PARETO INEFFICIENT**...
I HAVE 1/4 OF THE CAKE.
SO DO I.
...BECAUSE THERE **ARE** OUTCOMES THAT ARE PARETO IMPROVEMENTS OVER IT.
INSTEAD OF THROWING THE SECOND HALF AWAY, YOU COULD GIVE IT TO ME.
...OR TO ME.
YOU CAN HAVE **CHAINS** OF PARETO INEFFICIENT OUTCOMES AS LONG AS YOU CAN MAKE **MORE** PARETO IMPROVEMENTS:
THIS OUTCOME IS PARETO INEFFICIENT.
PARETO **IMPROVEMENT!**
THIS OUTCOME IS **ALSO** PARETO INEFFICIENT.
PARETO **IMPROVEMENT!**
...BUT WHAT IF THERE'S AN OUTCOME THAT **CAN'T** BE PARETO IMPROVED?

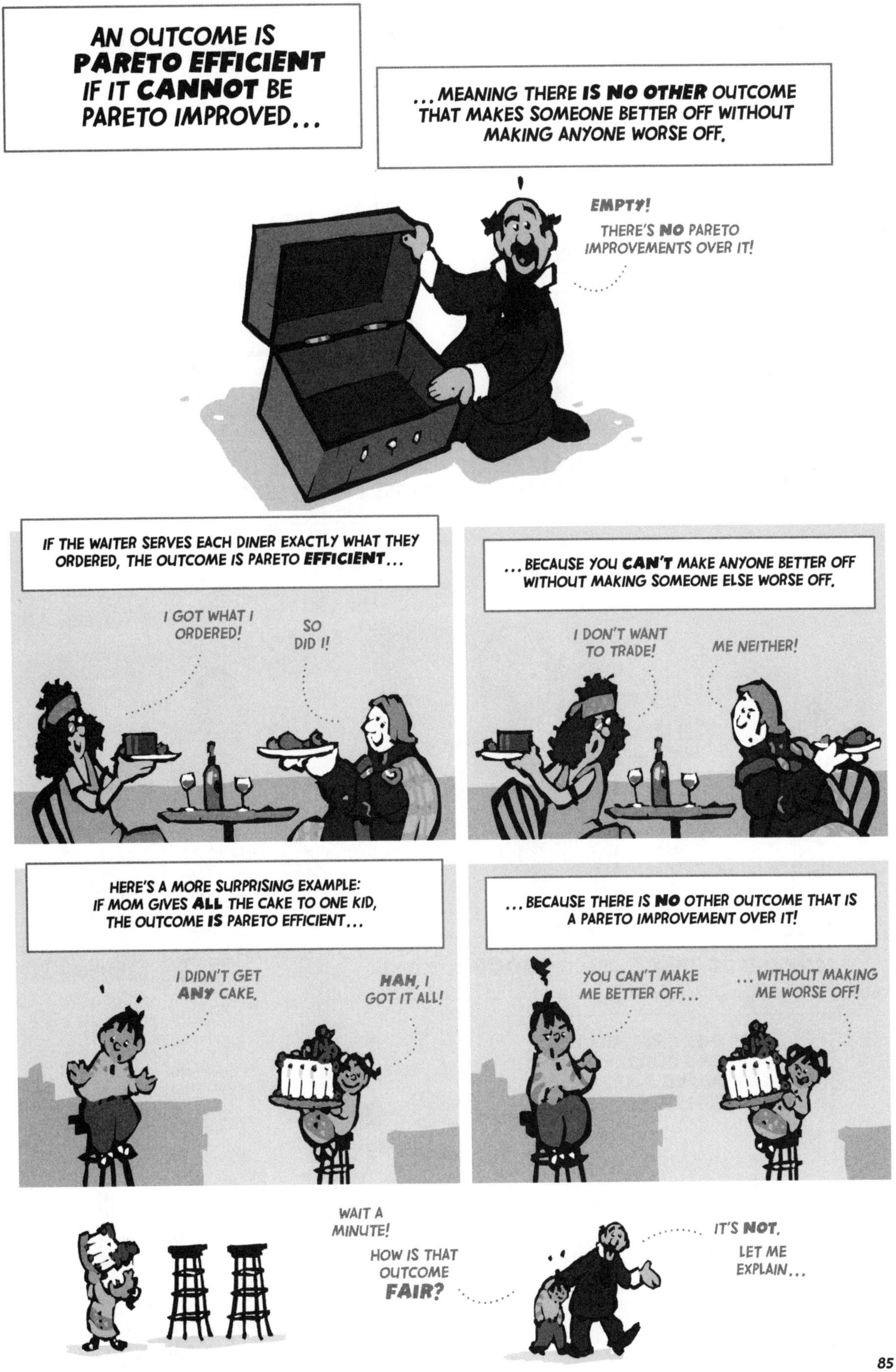
AN OUTCOME IS **PARETO EFFICIENT** IF IT **CANNOT** BE PARETO IMPROVED...
...MEANING THERE **IS NO OTHER** OUTCOME THAT MAKES SOMEONE BETTER OFF WITHOUT MAKING ANYONE WORSE OFF.
EMPTY!
THERE'S **NO** PARETO IMPROVEMENTS OVER IT!
IF THE WAITER SERVES EACH DINER EXACTLY WHAT THEY ORDERED, THE OUTCOME IS PARETO **EFFICIENT**...
I GOT WHAT I ORDERED!
SO DID I!
...BECAUSE YOU **CAN'T** MAKE ANYONE BETTER OFF WITHOUT MAKING SOMEONE ELSE WORSE OFF.
I DON'T WANT TO TRADE!
ME NEITHER!
HERE'S A MORE SURPRISING EXAMPLE: IF MOM GIVES **ALL** THE CAKE TO ONE KID, THE OUTCOME **IS** PARETO EFFICIENT...
I DIDN'T GET **ANY** CAKE.
HAH, I GOT IT ALL!
...BECAUSE THERE IS **NO** OTHER OUTCOME THAT IS A PARETO IMPROVEMENT OVER IT!
YOU CAN'T MAKE ME BETTER OFF...
...WITHOUT MAKING ME WORSE OFF!
WAIT A MINUTE!
HOW IS THAT OUTCOME **FAIR?**
IT'S **NOT**.
LET ME EXPLAIN...

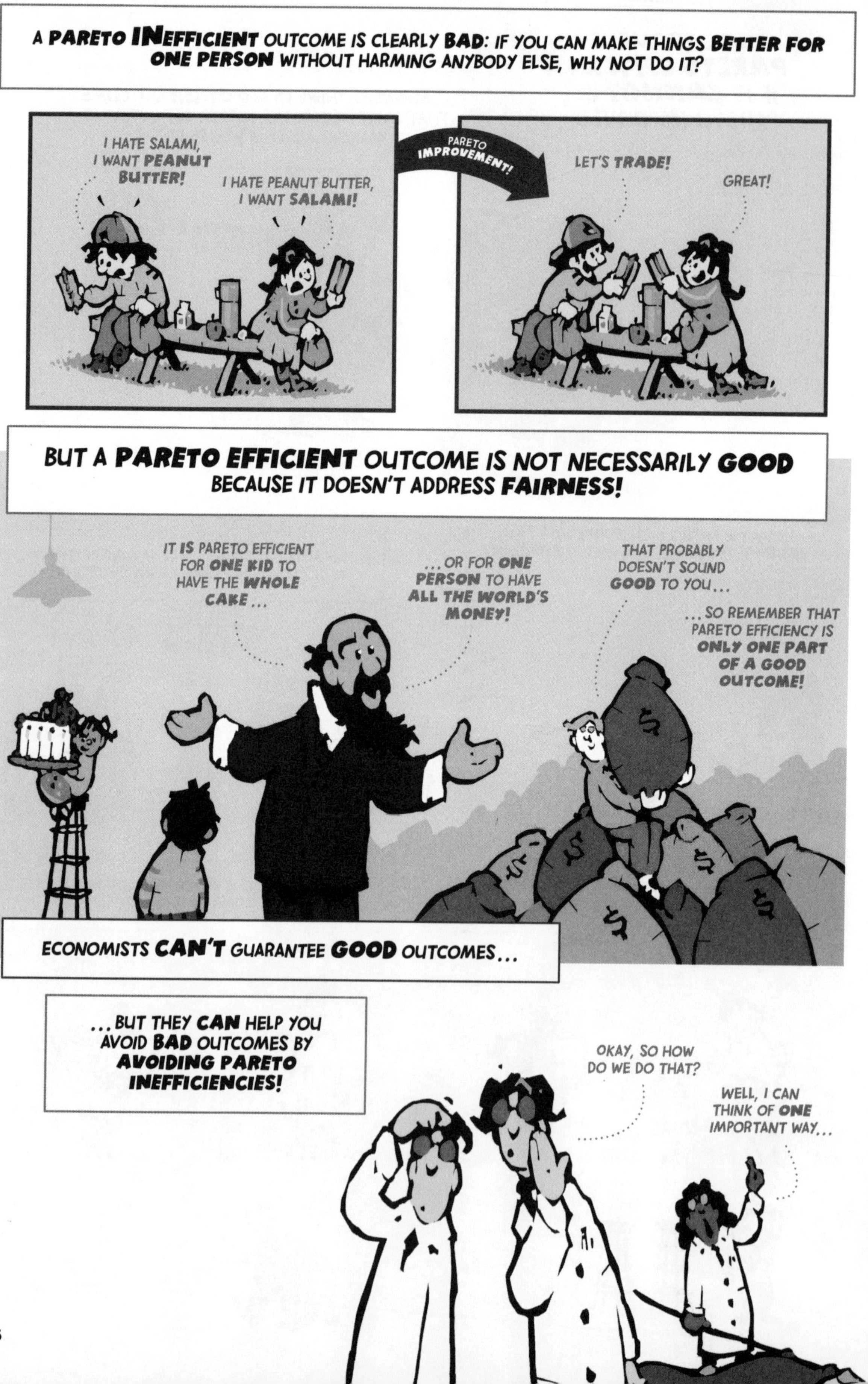
A PARETO INEFFICIENT OUTCOME IS CLEARLY BAD: IF YOU CAN MAKE THINGS BETTER FOR ONE PERSON WITHOUT HARMING ANYBODY ELSE, WHY NOT DO IT?
I HATE SALAMI, I WANT PEANUT BUTTER!
I HATE PEANUT BUTTER, I WANT SALAMI!
PARETO IMPROVEMENT!
LET'S TRADE!
GREAT!
BUT A PARETO EFFICIENT OUTCOME IS NOT NECESSARILY GOOD BECAUSE IT DOESN'T ADDRESS FAIRNESS!
IT IS PARETO EFFICIENT FOR ONE KID TO HAVE THE WHOLE CAKE...
...OR FOR ONE PERSON TO HAVE ALL THE WORLD'S MONEY!
THAT PROBABLY DOESN'T SOUND GOOD TO YOU...
...SO REMEMBER THAT PARETO EFFICIENCY IS ONLY ONE PART OF A GOOD OUTCOME!
ECONOMISTS CAN'T GUARANTEE GOOD OUTCOMES...
...BUT THEY CAN HELP YOU AVOID BAD OUTCOMES BY AVOIDING PARETO INEFFICIENCIES!
OKAY, SO HOW DO WE DO THAT?
WELL, I CAN THINK OF ONE IMPORTANT WAY...

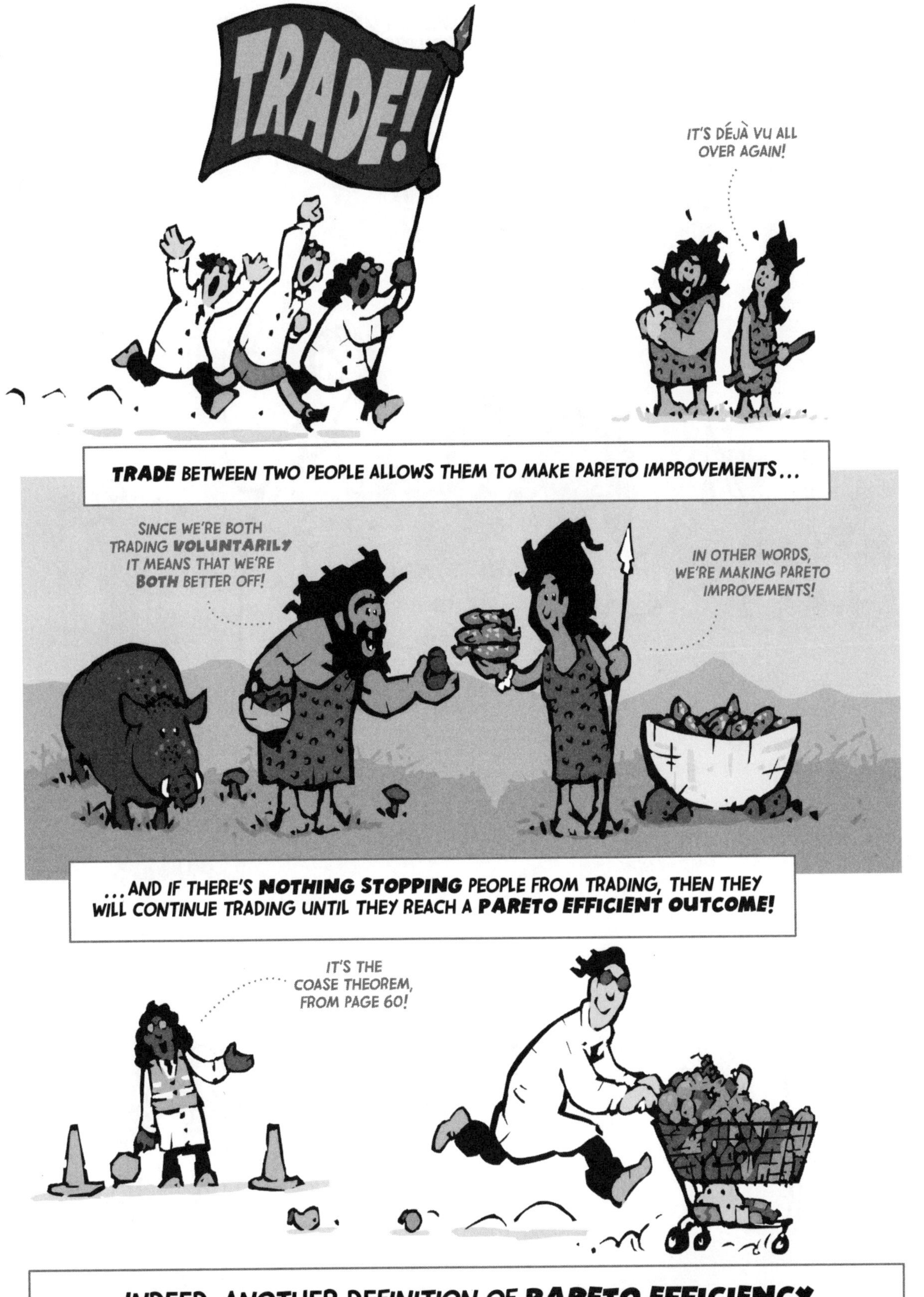
TRADE!
IT'S DÉJÀ VU ALL OVER AGAIN!
TRADE BETWEEN TWO PEOPLE ALLOWS THEM TO MAKE PARETO IMPROVEMENTS...
SINCE WE'RE BOTH TRADING VOLUNTARILY IT MEANS THAT WE'RE BOTH BETTER OFF!
IN OTHER WORDS, WE'RE MAKING PARETO IMPROVEMENTS!
...AND IF THERE'S NOTHING STOPPING PEOPLE FROM TRADING, THEN THEY WILL CONTINUE TRADING UNTIL THEY REACH A PARETO EFFICIENT OUTCOME!
IT'S THE COASE THEOREM, FROM PAGE 60!
INDEED, ANOTHER DEFINITION OF PARETO EFFICIENCY IS THAT ALL POTENTIAL GAINS FROM TRADE HAVE BEEN EXHAUSTED!

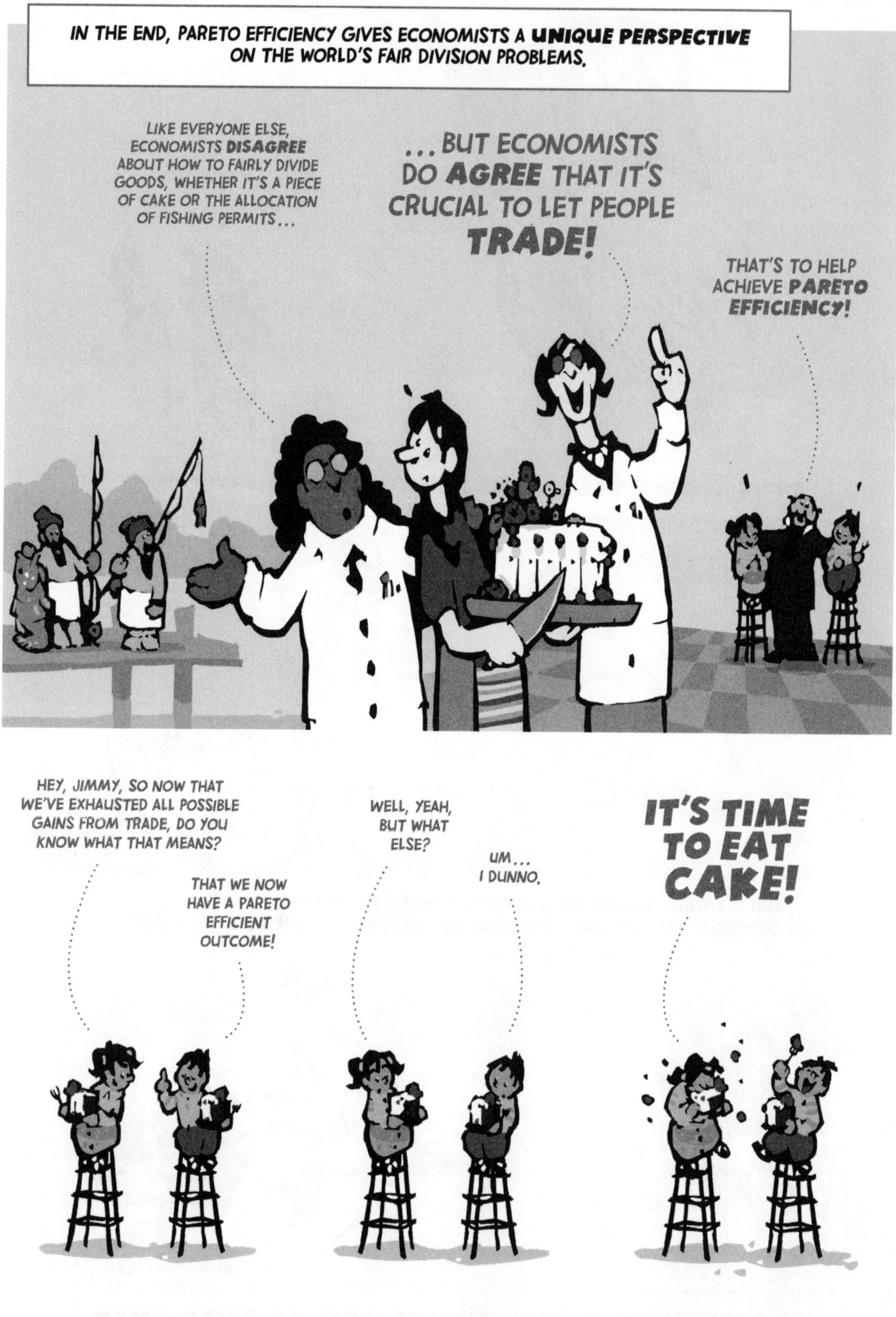
IN THE END, PARETO EFFICIENCY GIVES ECONOMISTS A UNIQUE PERSPECTIVE ON THE WORLD'S FAIR DIVISION PROBLEMS.
LIKE EVERYONE ELSE, ECONOMISTS DISAGREE ABOUT HOW TO FAIRLY DIVIDE GOODS, WHETHER IT'S A PIECE OF CAKE OR THE ALLOCATION OF FISHING PERMITS...
...BUT ECONOMISTS DO AGREE THAT IT'S CRUCIAL TO LET PEOPLE TRADE!
THAT'S TO HELP ACHIEVE PARETO EFFICIENCY!
HEY, JIMMY, SO NOW THAT WE'VE EXHAUSTED ALL POSSIBLE GAINS FROM TRADE, DO YOU KNOW WHAT THAT MEANS?
THAT WE NOW HAVE A PARETO EFFICIENT OUTCOME!
WELL, YEAH, BUT WHAT ELSE?
UM... I DUNNO.
IT'S TIME TO EAT CAKE!
...AND THEN LET'S PLAY MORE GAMES!

CHAPTER 8
SIMULTANEOUS-MOVE GAMES

OKAY, OOGA, MOG UNDERSTAND RULES!
READY?
1...
2...
3...
ROCK!
PAPER!

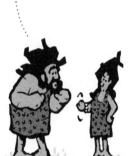

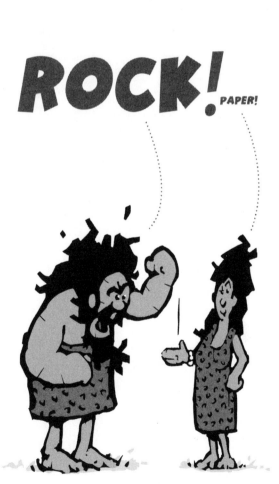

ALL GAMES CAN BE ANALYZED AS SIMULTANEOUS-MOVE GAMES IN WHICH PLAYERS MOVE **AT THE SAME TIME.**

MOG WANT TO PLAY AGAIN!

WE CAN ANALYZE SIMULTANEOUS-MOVE GAMES BETWEEN TWO PLAYERS USING A **PAYOFF MATRIX.**

EACH CHOICE FOR **THE FIRST PLAYER GETS A ROW**...

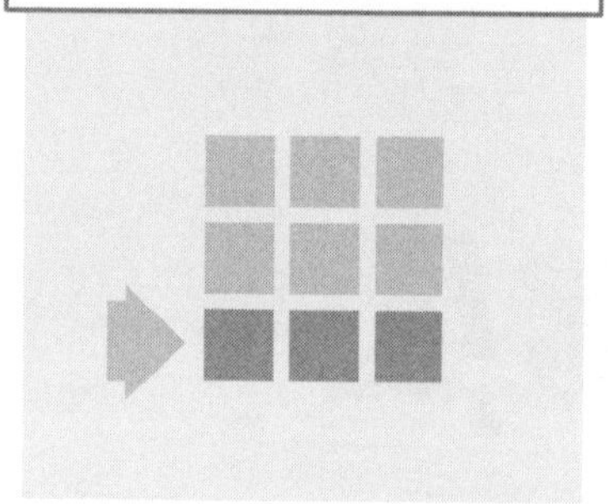

...AND EACH CHOICE FOR **THE SECOND PLAYER GETS A COLUMN**...

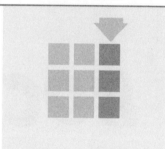

...AND THE **OUTCOME** FROM THOSE CHOICES APPEARS AT THE **INTERSECTION.**

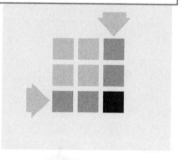

HERE'S A SIMPLE EXAMPLE: THE PAYOFF MATRIX FOR ROCK PAPER SCISSORS IF MOG AND OOGA PLAY FOR $5.

READY?
1...
2...
3...

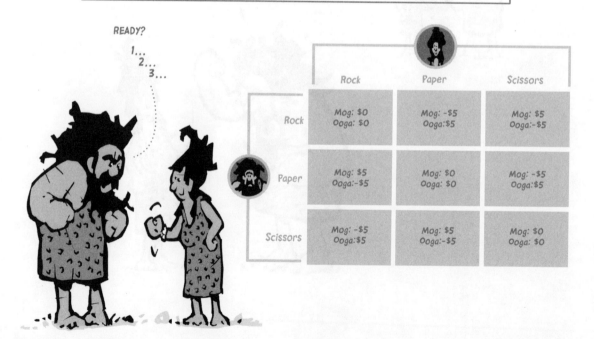

	Rock	Paper	Scissors
Rock	Mog: $0 Ooga: $0	Mog: -$5 Ooga: $5	Mog: $5 Ooga: -$5
Paper	Mog: $5 Ooga: -$5	Mog: $0 Ooga: $0	Mog: -$5 Ooga: $5
Scissors	Mog: -$5 Ooga: $5	Mog: $5 Ooga: -$5	Mog: $0 Ooga: $0

ANOTHER EXAMPLE OF A SIMULTANEOUS-MOVE GAME IS THE GAME OF **CHICKEN**.

I'LL BET YOU $5 I CAN BEAT YOU AT CHICKEN, BONNIE!

SURE, CLYDE, ANYTIME!

IN CHICKEN, EACH PLAYER CHOOSES TO **EITHER** DRIVE STRAIGHT AT THE OTHER CAR AT TOP SPEED **OR** CHICKEN OUT BY TURNING AWAY.

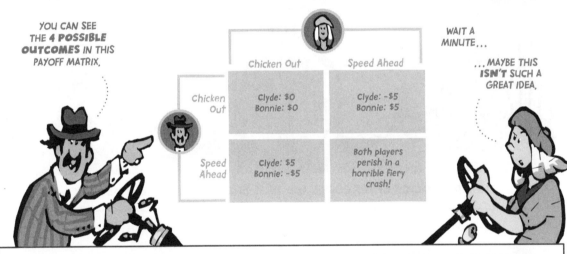

YOU CAN SEE THE 4 **POSSIBLE OUTCOMES** IN THIS PAYOFF MATRIX.

WAIT A MINUTE...

...MAYBE THIS **ISN'T** SUCH A GREAT IDEA.

	Chicken Out	Speed Ahead
Chicken Out	Clyde: $0 Bonnie: $0	Clyde: -$5 Bonnie: $5
Speed Ahead	Clyde: $5 Bonnie: -$5	Both players perish in a horrible fiery crash!

IN THIS CHAPTER WE'RE GOING TO FOCUS ON THE MOST FAMOUS SIMULTANEOUS-MOVE GAME:

THE PRISONERS' DILEMMA!

HOW DID WE BOTH END UP IN THIS ROTTEN JAIL FOR 10 YEARS?

TURN THE PAGE AND FIND OUT!

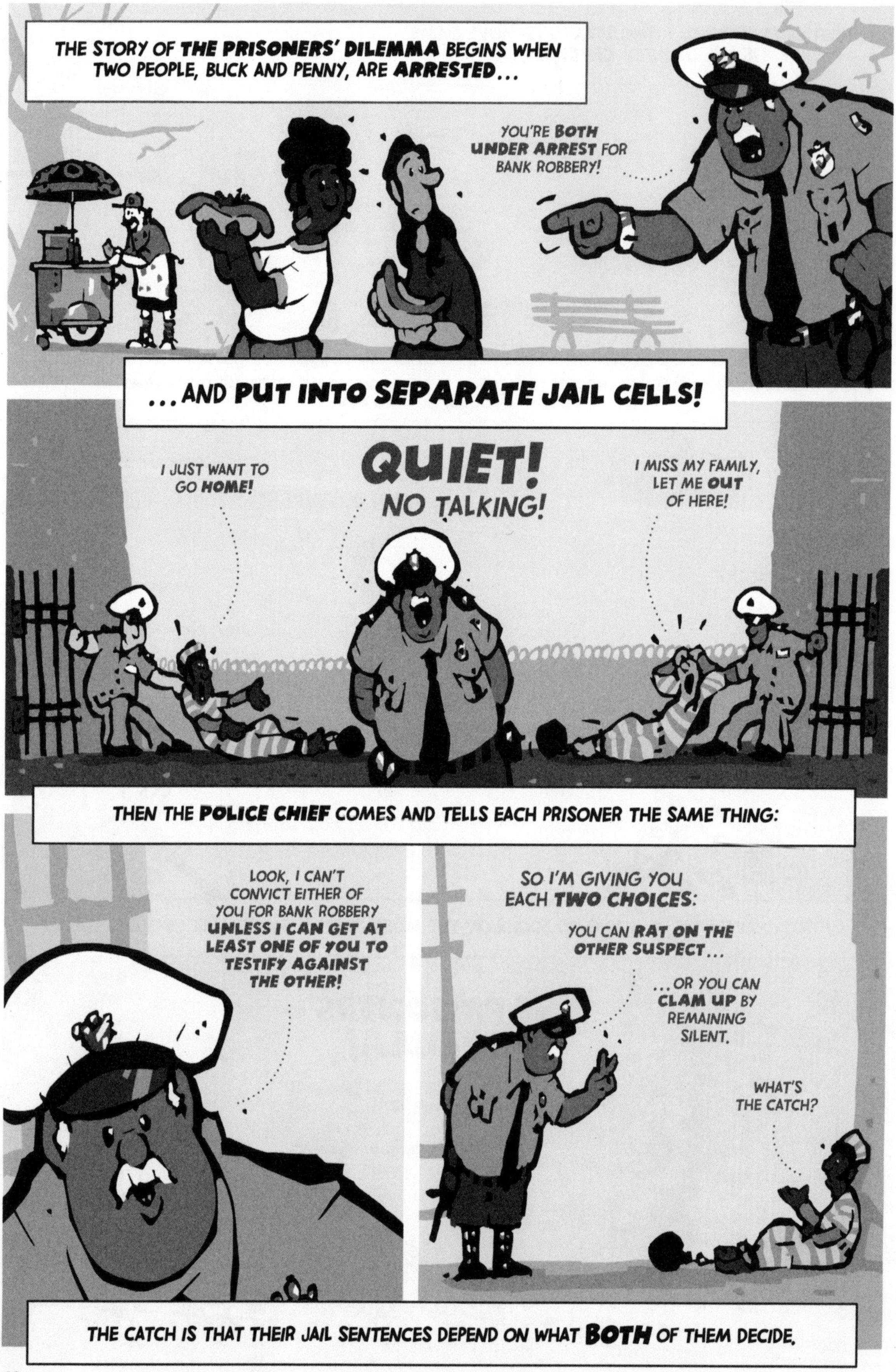
THE STORY OF THE PRISONERS' DILEMMA BEGINS WHEN TWO PEOPLE, BUCK AND PENNY, ARE ARRESTED...
YOU'RE BOTH UNDER ARREST FOR BANK ROBBERY!
...AND PUT INTO SEPARATE JAIL CELLS!
I JUST WANT TO GO HOME!
QUIET! NO TALKING!
I MISS MY FAMILY, LET ME OUT OF HERE!
THEN THE POLICE CHIEF COMES AND TELLS EACH PRISONER THE SAME THING:
LOOK, I CAN'T CONVICT EITHER OF YOU FOR BANK ROBBERY UNLESS I CAN GET AT LEAST ONE OF YOU TO TESTIFY AGAINST THE OTHER!
SO I'M GIVING YOU EACH TWO CHOICES:
YOU CAN RAT ON THE OTHER SUSPECT...
...OR YOU CAN CLAM UP BY REMAINING SILENT.
WHAT'S THE CATCH?
THE CATCH IS THAT THEIR JAIL SENTENCES DEPEND ON WHAT BOTH OF THEM DECIDE.

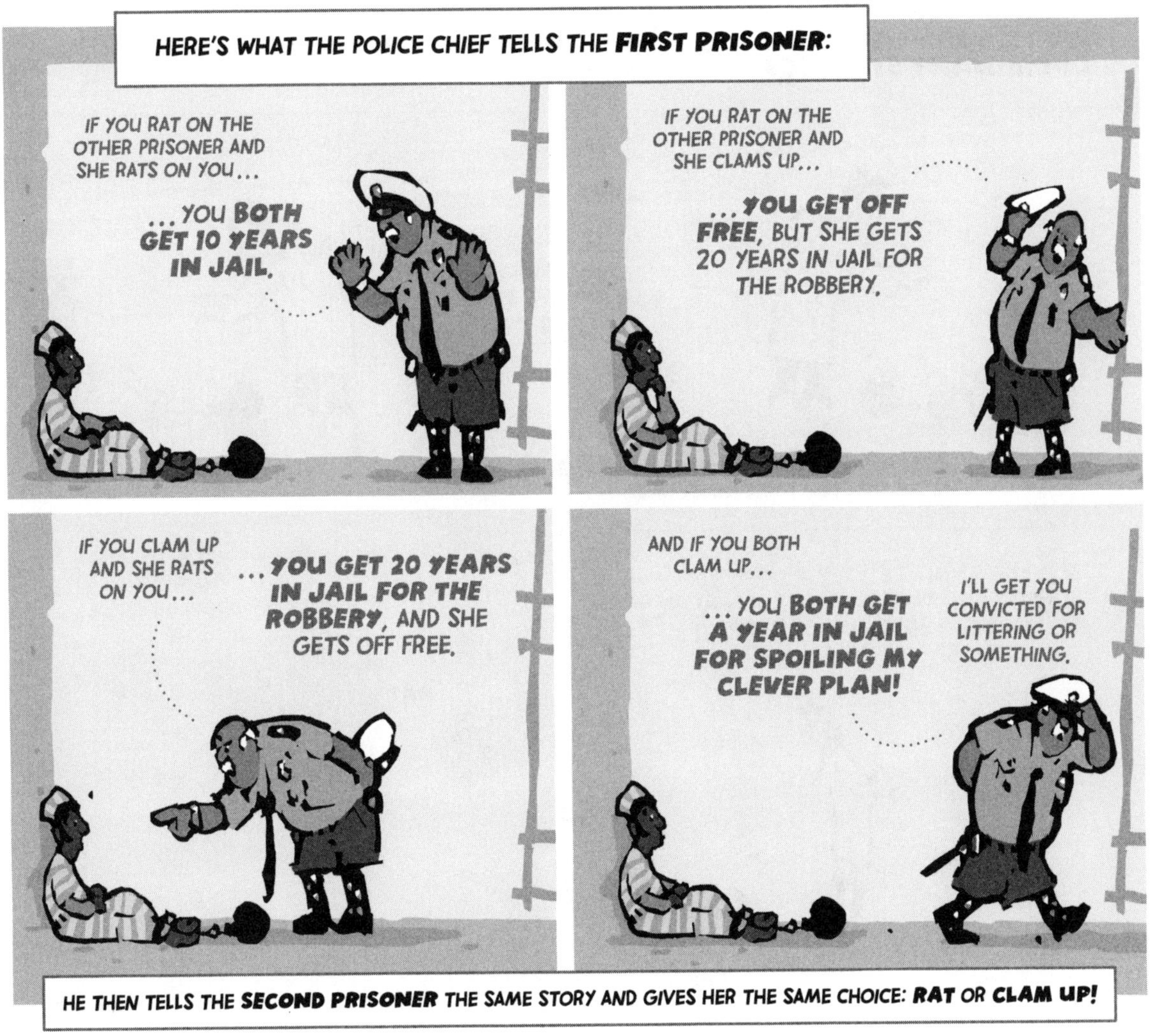
HERE'S WHAT THE POLICE CHIEF TELLS THE **FIRST PRISONER**:
IF YOU RAT ON THE OTHER PRISONER AND SHE RATS ON YOU...
...YOU **BOTH GET 10 YEARS IN JAIL.**
IF YOU RAT ON THE OTHER PRISONER AND SHE CLAMS UP...
...YOU GET OFF FREE, BUT SHE GETS 20 YEARS IN JAIL FOR THE ROBBERY.
IF YOU CLAM UP AND SHE RATS ON YOU...
...YOU GET 20 YEARS IN JAIL FOR THE ROBBERY, AND SHE GETS OFF FREE.
AND IF YOU BOTH CLAM UP...
...YOU **BOTH GET A YEAR IN JAIL FOR SPOILING MY CLEVER PLAN!**
I'LL GET YOU CONVICTED FOR LITTERING OR SOMETHING.
HE THEN TELLS THE **SECOND PRISONER** THE SAME STORY AND GIVES HER THE SAME CHOICE: **RAT** OR **CLAM UP!**

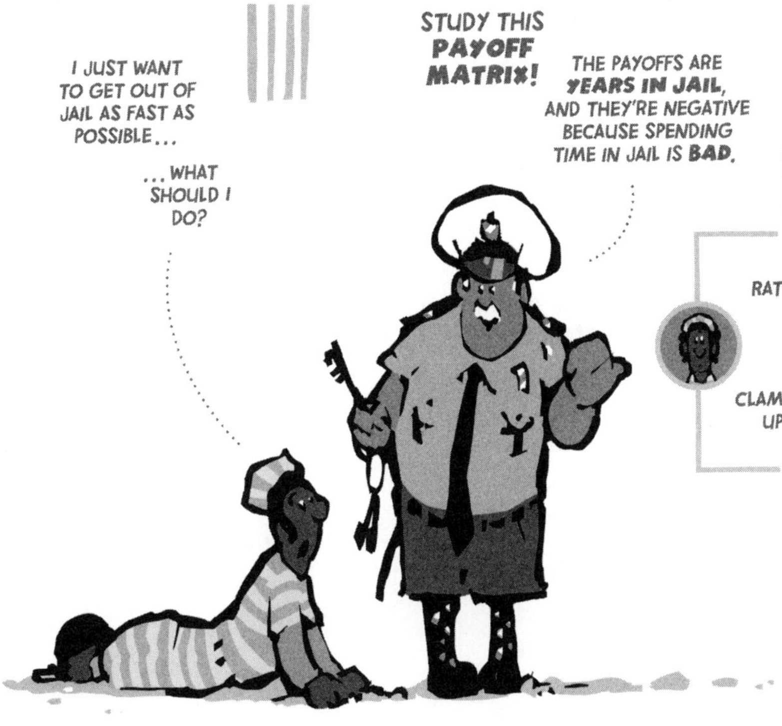
I JUST WANT TO GET OUT OF JAIL AS FAST AS POSSIBLE...
...WHAT SHOULD I DO?
STUDY THIS **PAYOFF MATRIX!**
THE PAYOFFS ARE **YEARS IN JAIL**, AND THEY'RE NEGATIVE BECAUSE SPENDING TIME IN JAIL IS **BAD**.

	RAT	CLAM UP
RAT	Buck: -10 Penny: -10	Buck: 0 Penny: -20
CLAM UP	Buck: -20 Penny: 0	Buck: -1 Penny: -1

TWO THINGS MAKE THE PRISONERS' DILEMMA **SPECIAL**. THE **FIRST** IS THAT EACH PLAYER HAS A **DOMINANT STRATEGY** IF THEY JUST WANT TO GET OUT OF JAIL AS SOON AS POSSIBLE.

HAVING A **DOMINANT STRATEGY** MEANS THAT YOUR BEST CHOICE IS ALWAYS THE SAME...

... **NO MATTER WHAT THE OTHER PLAYER DOES!**

TO SEE THE **FIRST PRISONER'S DOMINANT STRATEGY**, WE JUST ASK HIM THESE QUESTIONS:

IF PENNY CHOOSES TO **RAT ON YOU**, WHAT'S YOUR BEST CHOICE?

TO **RAT ON HER**, BECAUSE THEN I GET **TEN** YEARS IN JAIL INSTEAD OF THE **TWENTY** I GET IF I CLAM UP.

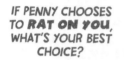

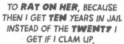

		RAT	CLAM UP
RAT		Buck: **-10** Penny: -10	Buck: 0 Penny: -20
CLAM UP		Buck: **-20** Penny: 0	Buck: -1 Penny: -1

AND IF PENNY CHOOSES TO **KEEP QUIET**, WHAT'S YOUR BEST CHOICE?

TO **RAT ON HER**, BECAUSE THEN I GET **ZERO** YEARS IN JAIL INSTEAD OF THE **ONE** I GET IF I CLAM UP.

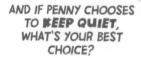

		RAT	**CLAM UP**
RAT		Buck: -10 Penny: -10	Buck: **0** Penny: -20
CLAM UP		Buck: -20 Penny: 0	Buck: **-1** Penny: -1

REGARDLESS OF WHAT PENNY DOES, BUCK CAN MINIMIZE HIS JAIL SENTENCE BY RATTING. SO RATTING IS HIS **DOMINANT STRATEGY**.

AND THE SAME IS TRUE FOR **PENNY**:

NO MATTER WHAT BUCK DOES, PENNY CAN MINIMIZE **HER** JAIL SENTENCE BY RATTING ON **HIM**.

SO RATTING IS MY **DOMINANT STRATEGY** TOO!

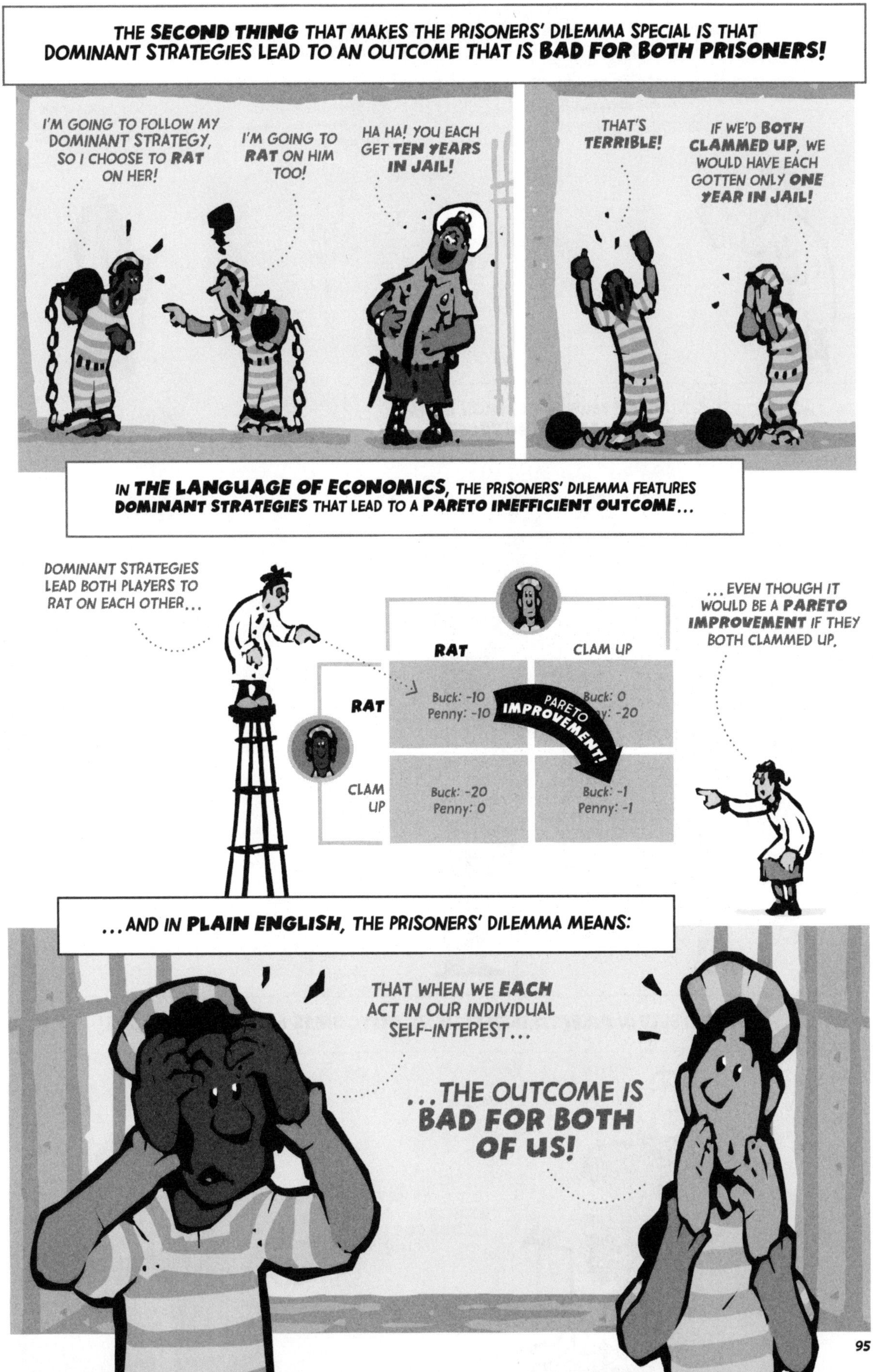
THE SECOND THING THAT MAKES THE PRISONERS' DILEMMA SPECIAL IS THAT DOMINANT STRATEGIES LEAD TO AN OUTCOME THAT IS BAD FOR BOTH PRISONERS!
I'M GOING TO FOLLOW MY DOMINANT STRATEGY, SO I CHOOSE TO RAT ON HER!
I'M GOING TO RAT ON HIM TOO!
HA HA! YOU EACH GET TEN YEARS IN JAIL!
THAT'S TERRIBLE!
IF WE'D BOTH CLAMMED UP, WE WOULD HAVE EACH GOTTEN ONLY ONE YEAR IN JAIL!
IN THE LANGUAGE OF ECONOMICS, THE PRISONERS' DILEMMA FEATURES DOMINANT STRATEGIES THAT LEAD TO A PARETO INEFFICIENT OUTCOME...
DOMINANT STRATEGIES LEAD BOTH PLAYERS TO RAT ON EACH OTHER...
RAT
CLAM UP
RAT
Buck: -10
Penny: -10
Buck: 0
Penny: -20
CLAM UP
Buck: -20
Penny: 0
Buck: -1
Penny: -1
PARETO IMPROVEMENT!
...EVEN THOUGH IT WOULD BE A PARETO IMPROVEMENT IF THEY BOTH CLAMMED UP.
...AND IN PLAIN ENGLISH, THE PRISONERS' DILEMMA MEANS:
THAT WHEN WE EACH ACT IN OUR INDIVIDUAL SELF-INTEREST...
...THE OUTCOME IS BAD FOR BOTH OF US!

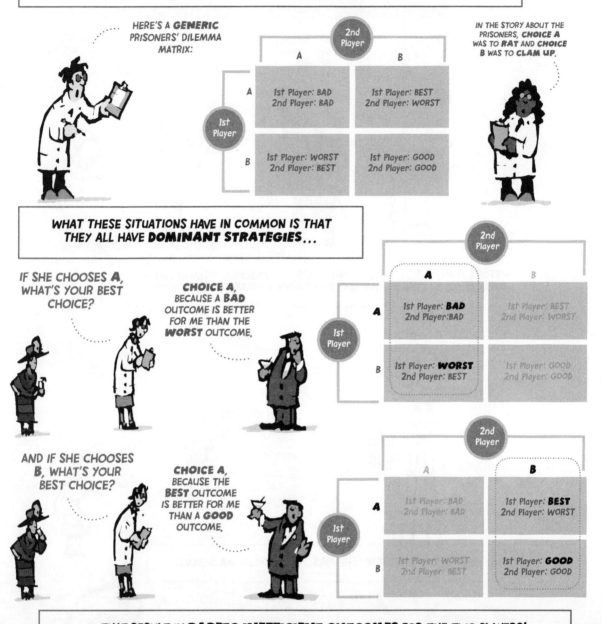

ECONOMISTS USE THE PHRASE PRISONERS' DILEMMA TO REFER TO ANY SITUATION WITH A SIMILAR INCENTIVE STRUCTURE.

HERE'S A GENERIC PRISONERS' DILEMMA MATRIX:

IN THE STORY ABOUT THE PRISONERS, CHOICE A WAS TO RAT AND CHOICE B WAS TO CLAM UP.

2nd Player

		A	B
1st Player	A	1st Player: BAD / 2nd Player: BAD	1st Player: BEST / 2nd Player: WORST
	B	1st Player: WORST / 2nd Player: BEST	1st Player: GOOD / 2nd Player: GOOD

WHAT THESE SITUATIONS HAVE IN COMMON IS THAT THEY ALL HAVE DOMINANT STRATEGIES...

IF SHE CHOOSES A, WHAT'S YOUR BEST CHOICE?

CHOICE A, BECAUSE A BAD OUTCOME IS BETTER FOR ME THAN THE WORST OUTCOME.

2nd Player

		A	B
1st Player	A	1st Player: **BAD** / 2nd Player: BAD	1st Player: BEST / 2nd Player: WORST
	B	1st Player: **WORST** / 2nd Player: BEST	1st Player: GOOD / 2nd Player: GOOD

AND IF SHE CHOOSES B, WHAT'S YOUR BEST CHOICE?

CHOICE A, BECAUSE THE BEST OUTCOME IS BETTER FOR ME THAN A GOOD OUTCOME.

2nd Player

		A	B
1st Player	A	1st Player: BAD / 2nd Player: BAD	1st Player: **BEST** / 2nd Player: WORST
	B	1st Player: WORST / 2nd Player: BEST	1st Player: **GOOD** / 2nd Player: GOOD

... THAT RESULT IN PARETO INEFFICIENT OUTCOMES FOR THE TWO PLAYERS!

CHOICE A IS MY DOMINANT STRATEGY TOO.

BUT WHEN WE BOTH CHOOSE A THE OUTCOME IS BAD FOR BOTH OF US!

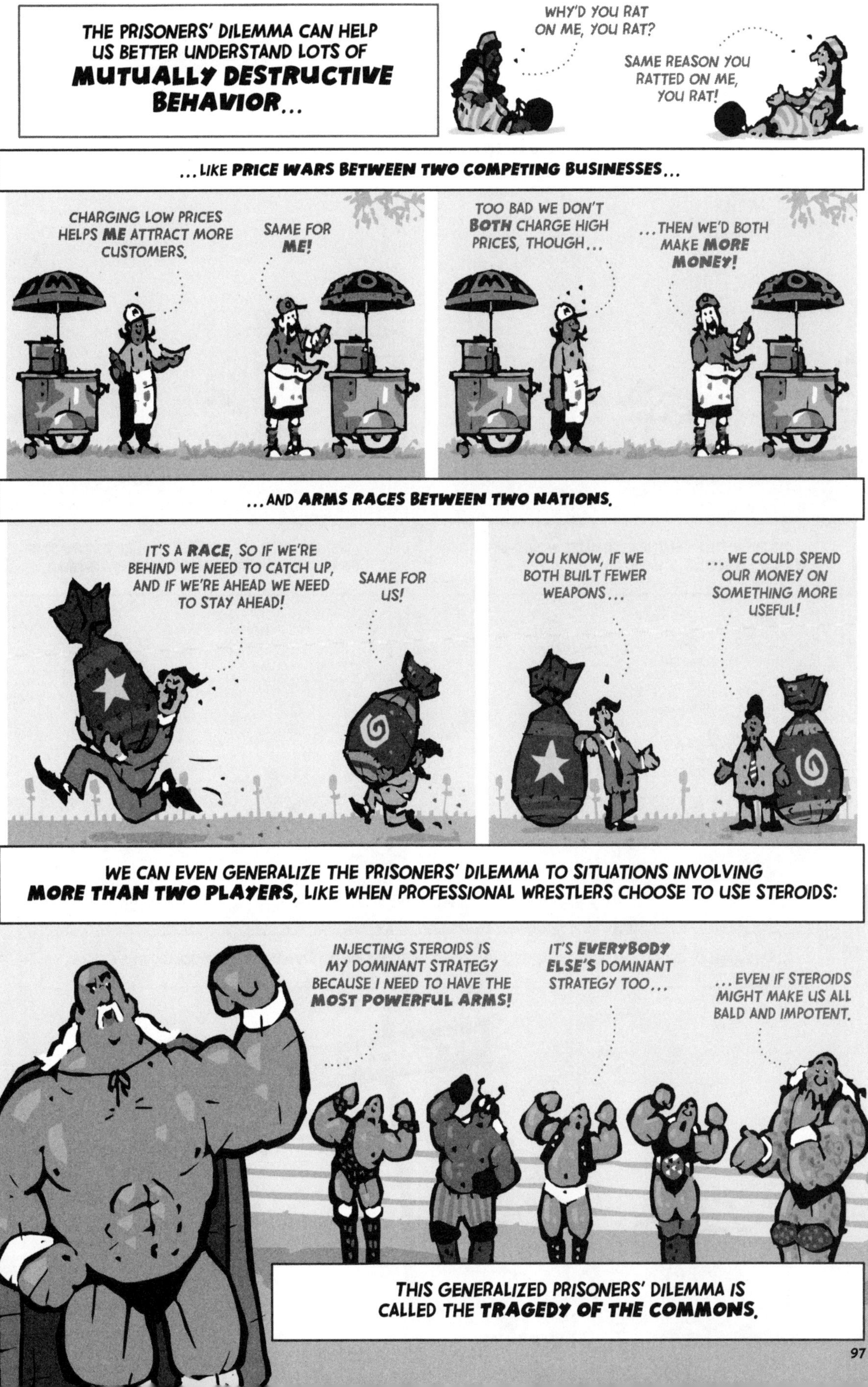
THE PRISONERS' DILEMMA CAN HELP US BETTER UNDERSTAND LOTS OF MUTUALLY DESTRUCTIVE BEHAVIOR...
WHY'D YOU RAT ON ME, YOU RAT?
SAME REASON YOU RATTED ON ME, YOU RAT!
...LIKE PRICE WARS BETWEEN TWO COMPETING BUSINESSES...
CHARGING LOW PRICES HELPS ME ATTRACT MORE CUSTOMERS.
SAME FOR ME!
TOO BAD WE DON'T BOTH CHARGE HIGH PRICES, THOUGH...
...THEN WE'D BOTH MAKE MORE MONEY!
...AND ARMS RACES BETWEEN TWO NATIONS.
IT'S A RACE, SO IF WE'RE BEHIND WE NEED TO CATCH UP, AND IF WE'RE AHEAD WE NEED TO STAY AHEAD!
SAME FOR US!
YOU KNOW, IF WE BOTH BUILT FEWER WEAPONS...
...WE COULD SPEND OUR MONEY ON SOMETHING MORE USEFUL!
WE CAN EVEN GENERALIZE THE PRISONERS' DILEMMA TO SITUATIONS INVOLVING MORE THAN TWO PLAYERS, LIKE WHEN PROFESSIONAL WRESTLERS CHOOSE TO USE STEROIDS:
INJECTING STEROIDS IS MY DOMINANT STRATEGY BECAUSE I NEED TO HAVE THE MOST POWERFUL ARMS!
IT'S EVERYBODY ELSE'S DOMINANT STRATEGY TOO...
...EVEN IF STEROIDS MIGHT MAKE US ALL BALD AND IMPOTENT.
THIS GENERALIZED PRISONERS' DILEMMA IS CALLED THE TRAGEDY OF THE COMMONS.

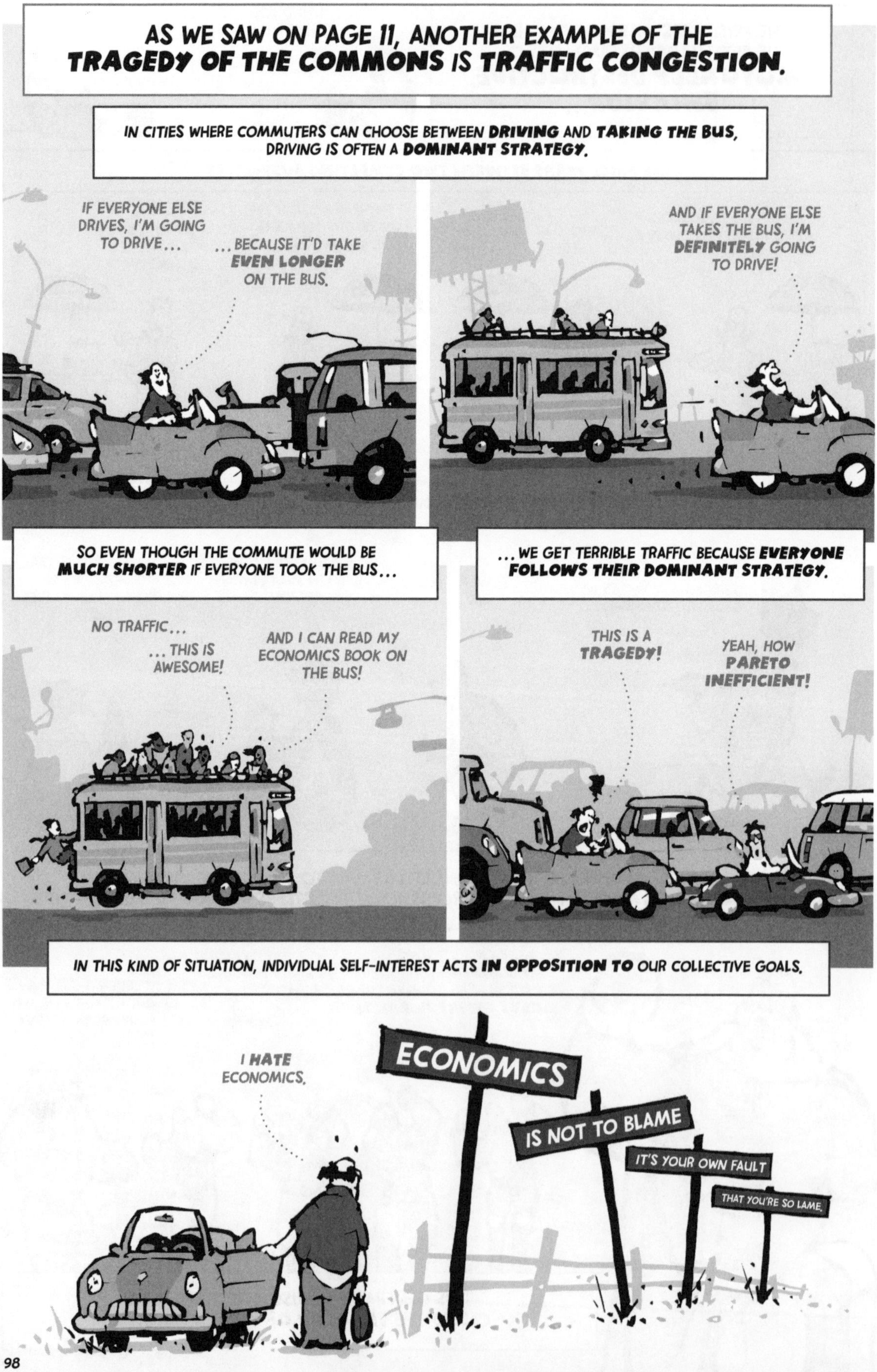
AS WE SAW ON PAGE 11, ANOTHER EXAMPLE OF THE TRAGEDY OF THE COMMONS IS TRAFFIC CONGESTION.
IN CITIES WHERE COMMUTERS CAN CHOOSE BETWEEN DRIVING AND TAKING THE BUS, DRIVING IS OFTEN A DOMINANT STRATEGY.
IF EVERYONE ELSE DRIVES, I'M GOING TO DRIVE...
...BECAUSE IT'D TAKE EVEN LONGER ON THE BUS.
AND IF EVERYONE ELSE TAKES THE BUS, I'M DEFINITELY GOING TO DRIVE!
SO EVEN THOUGH THE COMMUTE WOULD BE MUCH SHORTER IF EVERYONE TOOK THE BUS...
NO TRAFFIC...
...THIS IS AWESOME!
AND I CAN READ MY ECONOMICS BOOK ON THE BUS!
...WE GET TERRIBLE TRAFFIC BECAUSE EVERYONE FOLLOWS THEIR DOMINANT STRATEGY.
THIS IS A TRAGEDY!
YEAH, HOW PARETO INEFFICIENT!
IN THIS KIND OF SITUATION, INDIVIDUAL SELF-INTEREST ACTS IN OPPOSITION TO OUR COLLECTIVE GOALS.
I HATE ECONOMICS.
ECONOMICS
IS NOT TO BLAME
IT'S YOUR OWN FAULT
THAT YOU'RE SO LAME.

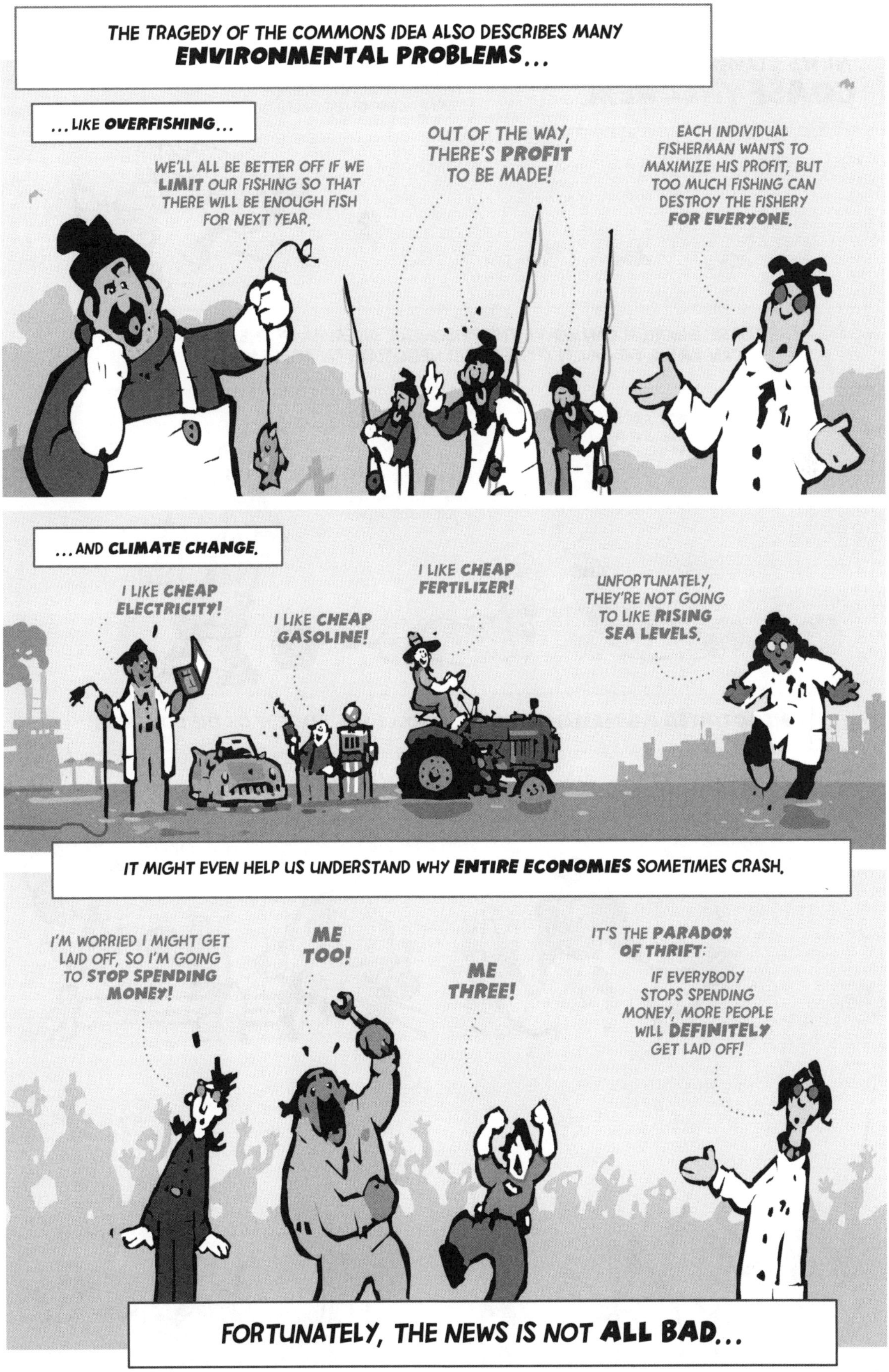
THE TRAGEDY OF THE COMMONS IDEA ALSO DESCRIBES MANY **ENVIRONMENTAL PROBLEMS**...
...LIKE **OVERFISHING**...
WE'LL ALL BE BETTER OFF IF WE **LIMIT** OUR FISHING SO THAT THERE WILL BE ENOUGH FISH FOR NEXT YEAR.
OUT OF THE WAY, THERE'S **PROFIT** TO BE MADE!
EACH INDIVIDUAL FISHERMAN WANTS TO MAXIMIZE HIS PROFIT, BUT TOO MUCH FISHING CAN DESTROY THE FISHERY **FOR EVERYONE**.
...AND **CLIMATE CHANGE**.
I LIKE **CHEAP ELECTRICITY**!
I LIKE **CHEAP GASOLINE**!
I LIKE **CHEAP FERTILIZER**!
UNFORTUNATELY, THEY'RE NOT GOING TO LIKE **RISING SEA LEVELS**.
IT MIGHT EVEN HELP US UNDERSTAND WHY **ENTIRE ECONOMIES** SOMETIMES CRASH.
I'M WORRIED I MIGHT GET LAID OFF, SO I'M GOING TO **STOP SPENDING MONEY**!
ME TOO!
ME THREE!
IT'S THE **PARADOX OF THRIFT**:
IF EVERYBODY STOPS SPENDING MONEY, MORE PEOPLE WILL **DEFINITELY** GET LAID OFF!
FORTUNATELY, THE NEWS IS NOT **ALL BAD**...

ONE PIECE OF GOOD NEWS COMES FROM THE **COASE THEOREM.**

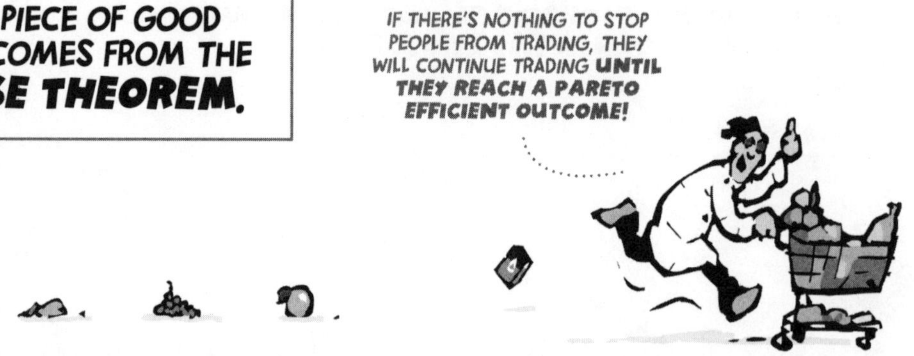
IF THERE'S NOTHING TO STOP PEOPLE FROM TRADING, THEY WILL CONTINUE TRADING UNTIL THEY REACH A PARETO EFFICIENT OUTCOME!

THE COASE THEOREM CAN SOLVE THE PRISONERS' DILEMMA **IF** THE PRISONERS CAN **TALK TO EACH OTHER** AND NEGOTIATE AN AGREEMENT.

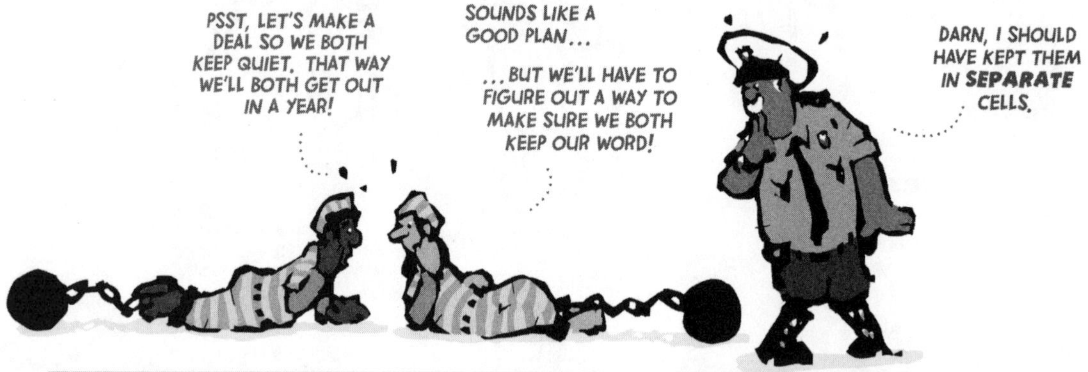
PSST, LET'S MAKE A DEAL SO WE BOTH KEEP QUIET. THAT WAY WE'LL BOTH GET OUT IN A YEAR!
SOUNDS LIKE A GOOD PLAN...
...BUT WE'LL HAVE TO FIGURE OUT A WAY TO MAKE SURE WE BOTH KEEP OUR WORD!
DARN, I SHOULD HAVE KEPT THEM IN SEPARATE CELLS.

NEGOTIATED AGREEMENTS CAN ALSO SOLVE THE TRAGEDY OF THE COMMONS!

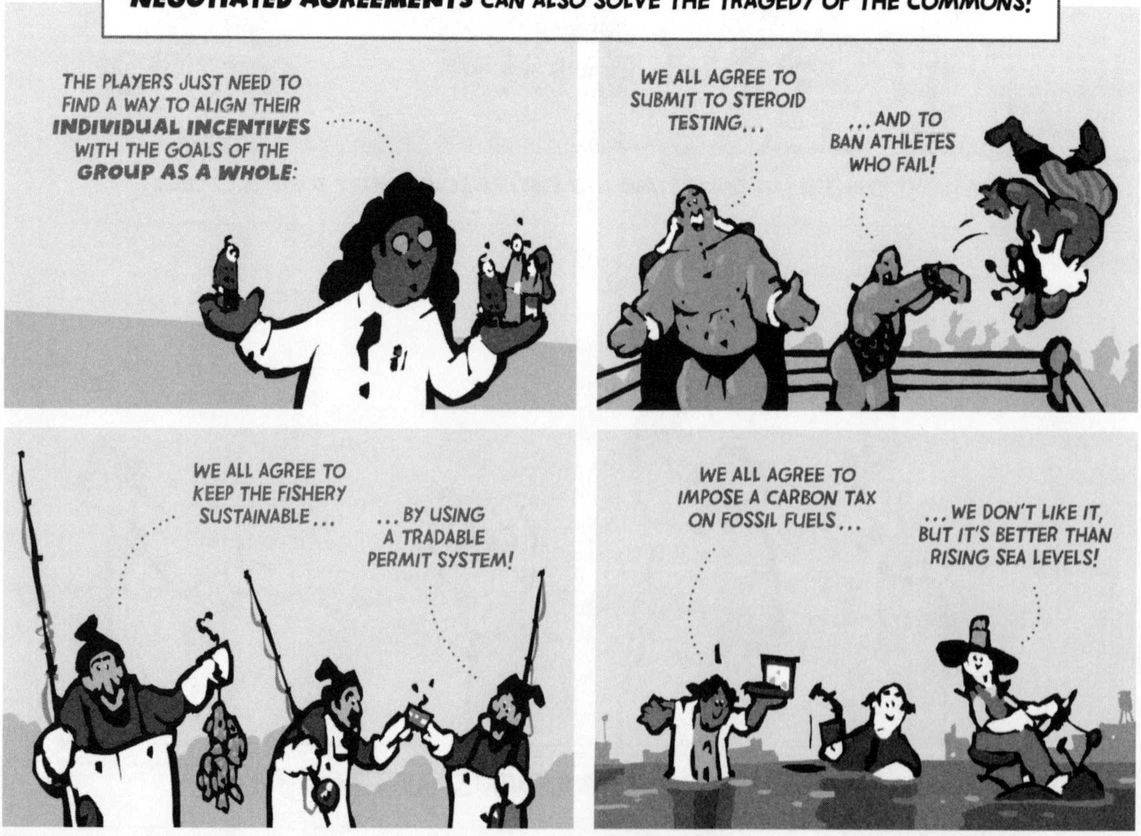
THE PLAYERS JUST NEED TO FIND A WAY TO ALIGN THEIR INDIVIDUAL INCENTIVES WITH THE GOALS OF THE GROUP AS A WHOLE:
WE ALL AGREE TO SUBMIT TO STEROID TESTING...
...AND TO BAN ATHLETES WHO FAIL!
WE ALL AGREE TO KEEP THE FISHERY SUSTAINABLE...
...BY USING A TRADABLE PERMIT SYSTEM!
WE ALL AGREE TO IMPOSE A CARBON TAX ON FOSSIL FUELS...
...WE DON'T LIKE IT, BUT IT'S BETTER THAN RISING SEA LEVELS!

ANOTHER PIECE OF GOOD NEWS IS THAT **LOTS** OF SIMULTANEOUS-MOVE GAMES **AREN'T LIKE THE PRISONERS' DILEMMA.**

MANY GAMES **DON'T HAVE DOMINANT STRATEGIES**...

LIKE ROCK PAPER SCISSORS, WHERE YOUR BEST STRATEGY DEPENDS ON WHAT THE OTHER PLAYER DOES.

YOU MEAN MOG NOT **ALWAYS** SUPPOSED TO PLAY ROCK?

...AND SOME GAMES WITH DOMINANT STRATEGIES **DON'T HAVE PARETO INEFFICIENT OUTCOMES.**

LIKE THIS GAME, WHICH MIGHT BE CALLED THE **PRISONERS' DELIGHT.**

IN THIS PAYOFF MATRIX OUR **INCENTIVE** IS TO **COOPERATE** BY CHOOSING **A!**

		A	B
A		1st Player: GOOD 2nd Player: GOOD	1st Player: BEST 2nd Player: WORST
B		1st Player: WORST 2nd Player: BEST	1st Player: BAD 2nd Player: BAD

BUT THE BEST NEWS OF ALL IS THAT **SOME** PRISONERS' DILEMMA SITUATIONS HAVE **UNEXPECTED BENEFITS!**

ESPECIALLY IF WE TAKE A **BROADER PERSPECTIVE** ON SITUATIONS LIKE THIS ONE...

CHARGING LOW PRICES HELPS **ME** ATTRACT MORE CUSTOMERS.

SAME FOR **ME!**

WE CAN SEE THESE **UNEXPECTED BENEFITS** MOST CLEARLY IN THE CASE OF **TWO COMPETING BUSINESSES** WHO EACH HAVE A **DOMINANT STRATEGY** OF SETTING **LOW PRICES.**

I'M GOING TO SET **LOW** PRICES FOR MY HOT DOGS.

OTHERWISE **OSCAR** WILL STEAL MY CUSTOMERS!

I'M GOING TO SET **LOW** PRICES FOR MY HOT DOGS.

OTHERWISE **MAYA** WILL STEAL MY CUSTOMERS!

FROM THE **NARROW PERSPECTIVE** OF THE BUSINESSES, THIS IS A CLASSIC PRISONERS' DILEMMA SITUATION...

BOTH PLAYERS HAVE A **DOMINANT STRATEGY** THAT LEADS TO A **PARETO INEFFICIENT** OUTCOME FOR THEM.

IF THEY **BOTH** SET HIGHER PRICES, THEY'D **BOTH** MAKE MORE MONEY!

	SET LOW PRICE	SET HIGHER PRICE
SET LOW PRICE	Oscar: $2m / Maya: $2m	Oscar: $5m / Maya: $0m
SET HIGHER PRICE	Oscar: $0m / Maya: $5m	Oscar: $4m / Maya: $4m

PARETO IMPROVEMENT!

... BUT FOR CONSUMERS THE RESULT IS **FANTASTIC!**

IT'S AS IF AN **INVISIBLE HAND** WERE GUIDING THEM TO PROVIDE ME WITH HOT DOGS AT LOW PRICES!

GEE, THANKS FOR THE LOW PRICES!

DON'T THANK ME— I'M JUST TRYING TO **MAXIMIZE MY PROFIT!**

SELFISH JERK!

CHAPTER 9
AUCTIONS

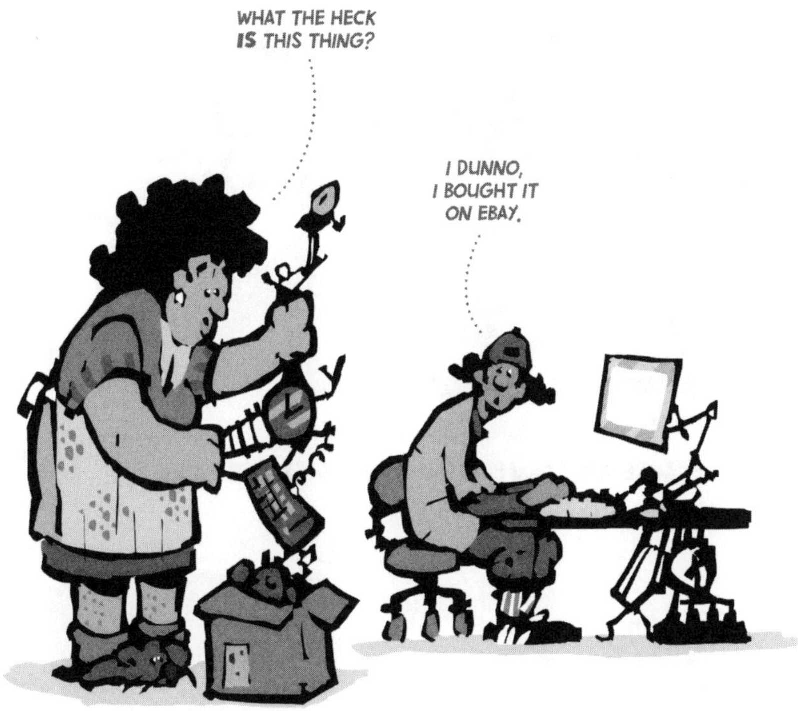
WHAT THE HECK **IS** THIS THING?
I DUNNO, I BOUGHT IT ON EBAY.

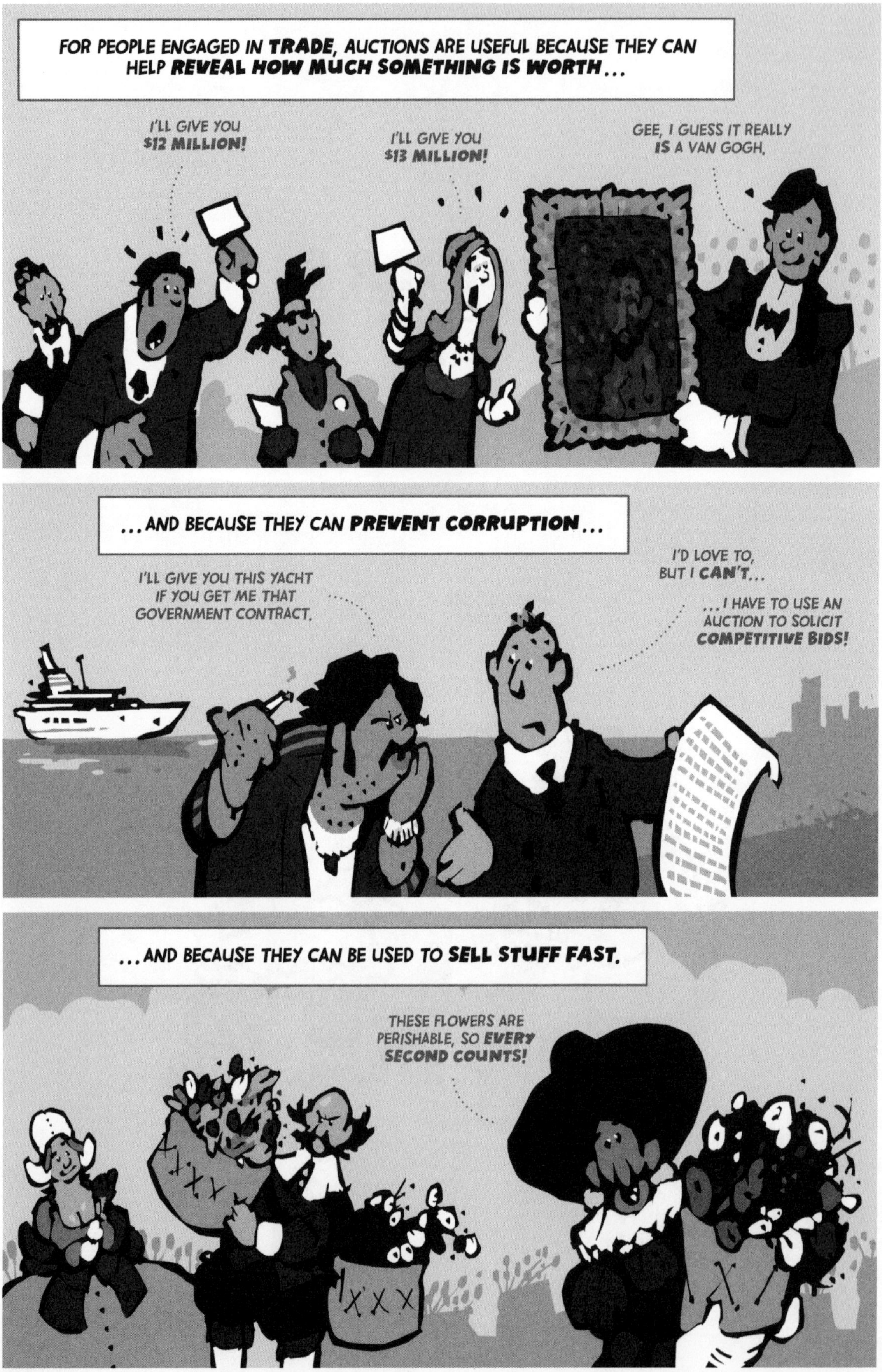
FOR PEOPLE ENGAGED IN TRADE, AUCTIONS ARE USEFUL BECAUSE THEY CAN HELP REVEAL HOW MUCH SOMETHING IS WORTH...
I'LL GIVE YOU $12 MILLION!
I'LL GIVE YOU $13 MILLION!
GEE, I GUESS IT REALLY IS A VAN GOGH.
...AND BECAUSE THEY CAN PREVENT CORRUPTION...
I'LL GIVE YOU THIS YACHT IF YOU GET ME THAT GOVERNMENT CONTRACT.
I'D LOVE TO, BUT I CAN'T...
...I HAVE TO USE AN AUCTION TO SOLICIT COMPETITIVE BIDS!
...AND BECAUSE THEY CAN BE USED TO SELL STUFF FAST.
THESE FLOWERS ARE PERISHABLE, SO EVERY SECOND COUNTS!

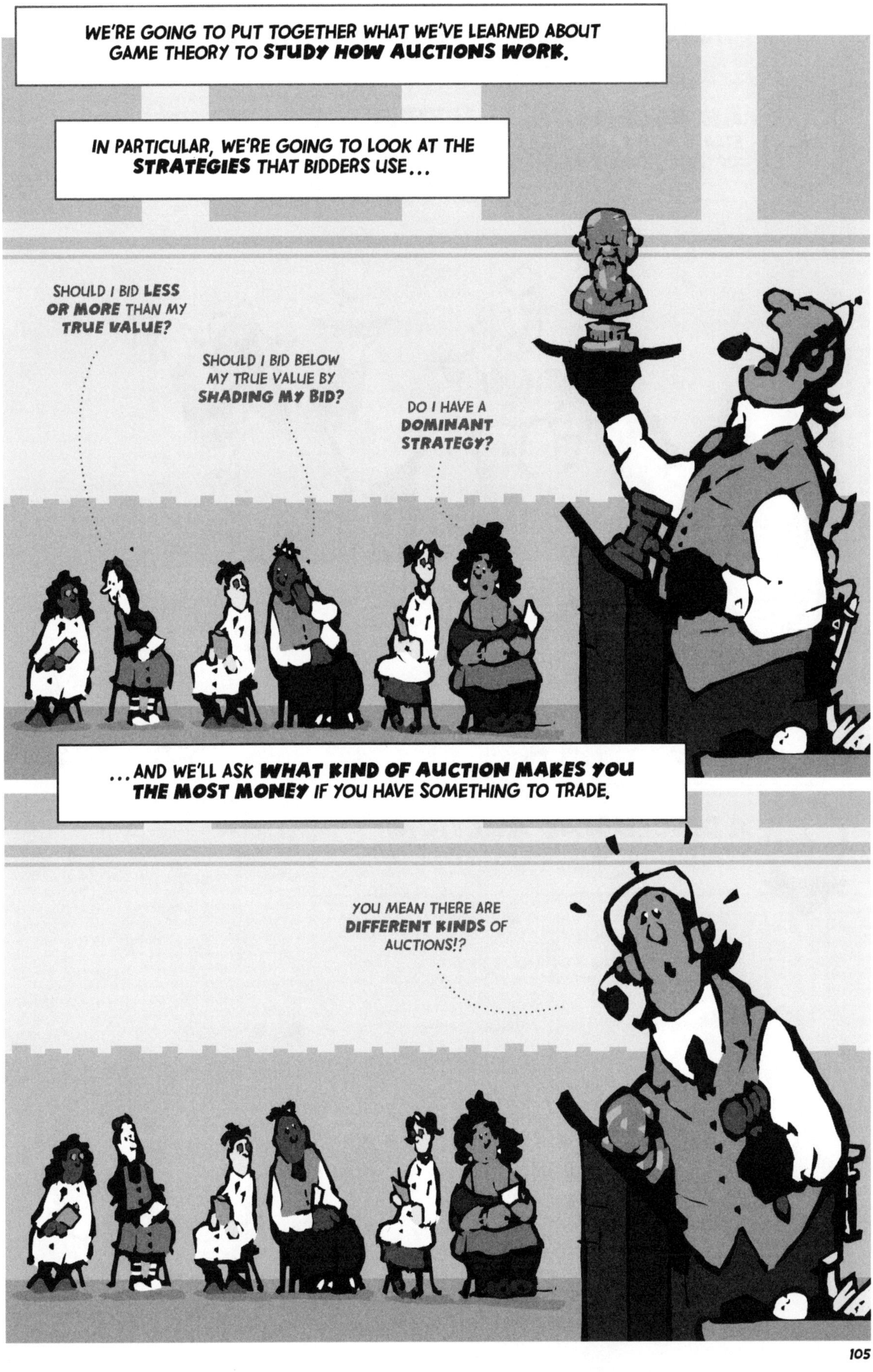
WE'RE GOING TO PUT TOGETHER WHAT WE'VE LEARNED ABOUT GAME THEORY TO **STUDY HOW AUCTIONS WORK.**
IN PARTICULAR, WE'RE GOING TO LOOK AT THE **STRATEGIES** THAT BIDDERS USE...
SHOULD I BID **LESS OR MORE** THAN MY **TRUE VALUE?**
SHOULD I BID BELOW MY TRUE VALUE BY **SHADING MY BID?**
DO I HAVE A **DOMINANT STRATEGY?**
...AND WE'LL ASK **WHAT KIND OF AUCTION MAKES YOU THE MOST MONEY** IF YOU HAVE SOMETHING TO TRADE.
YOU MEAN THERE ARE **DIFFERENT KINDS** OF AUCTIONS!?

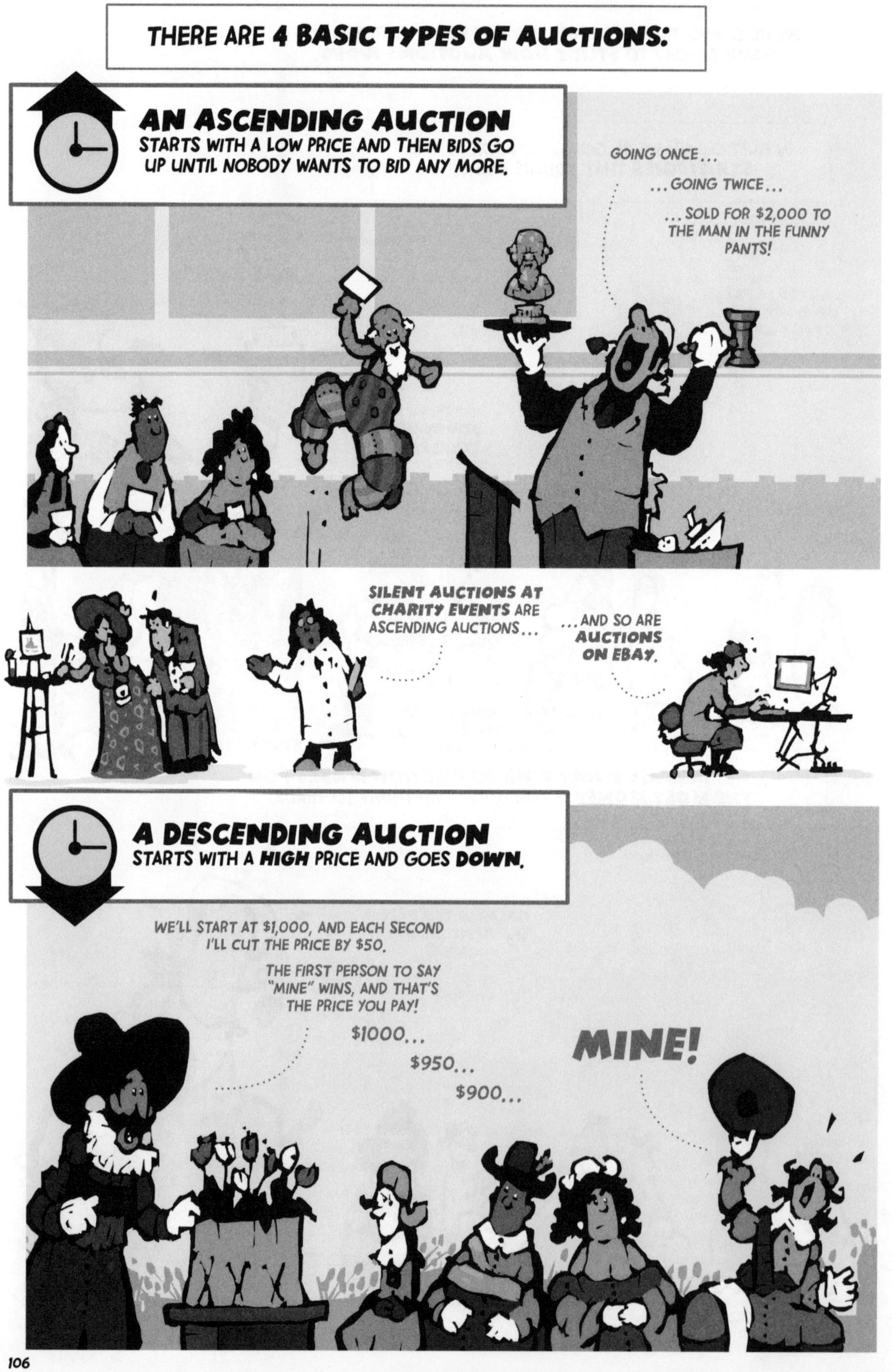
THERE ARE 4 BASIC TYPES OF AUCTIONS:
AN ASCENDING AUCTION
STARTS WITH A LOW PRICE AND THEN BIDS GO UP UNTIL NOBODY WANTS TO BID ANY MORE.
GOING ONCE...
...GOING TWICE...
...SOLD FOR $2,000 TO THE MAN IN THE FUNNY PANTS!
SILENT AUCTIONS AT CHARITY EVENTS ARE ASCENDING AUCTIONS...
...AND SO ARE AUCTIONS ON EBAY.
A DESCENDING AUCTION
STARTS WITH A HIGH PRICE AND GOES DOWN.
WE'LL START AT $1,000, AND EACH SECOND I'LL CUT THE PRICE BY $50.
THE FIRST PERSON TO SAY "MINE" WINS, AND THAT'S THE PRICE YOU PAY!
$1000...
$950...
$900...
MINE!

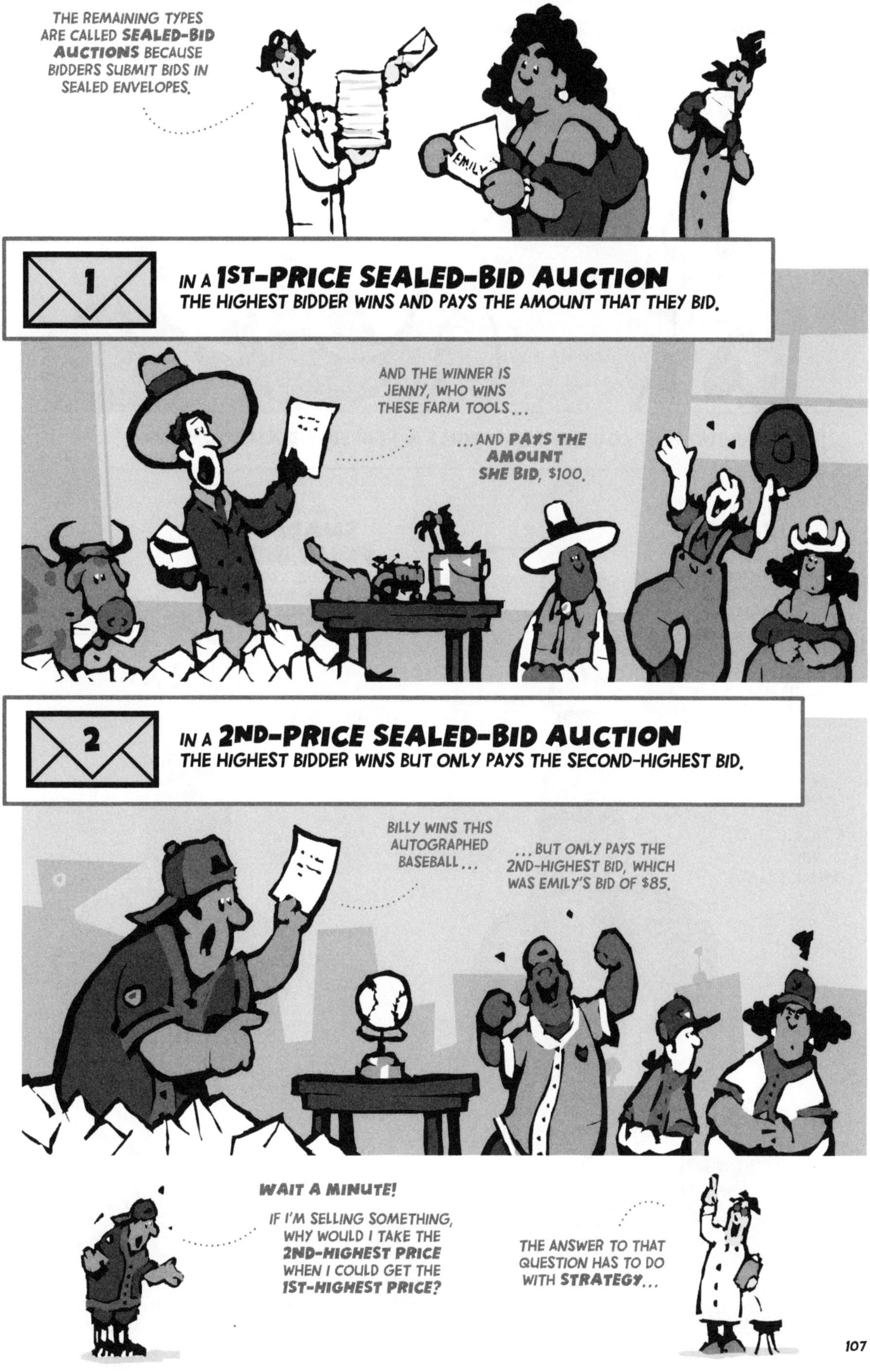
THE REMAINING TYPES ARE CALLED SEALED-BID AUCTIONS BECAUSE BIDDERS SUBMIT BIDS IN SEALED ENVELOPES.
EMILY
1
IN A 1ST-PRICE SEALED-BID AUCTION
THE HIGHEST BIDDER WINS AND PAYS THE AMOUNT THAT THEY BID.
AND THE WINNER IS JENNY, WHO WINS THESE FARM TOOLS...
...AND PAYS THE AMOUNT SHE BID, $100.
2
IN A 2ND-PRICE SEALED-BID AUCTION
THE HIGHEST BIDDER WINS BUT ONLY PAYS THE SECOND-HIGHEST BID.
BILLY WINS THIS AUTOGRAPHED BASEBALL...
...BUT ONLY PAYS THE 2ND-HIGHEST BID, WHICH WAS EMILY'S BID OF $85.
WAIT A MINUTE!
IF I'M SELLING SOMETHING, WHY WOULD I TAKE THE 2ND-HIGHEST PRICE WHEN I COULD GET THE 1ST-HIGHEST PRICE?
THE ANSWER TO THAT QUESTION HAS TO DO WITH STRATEGY...

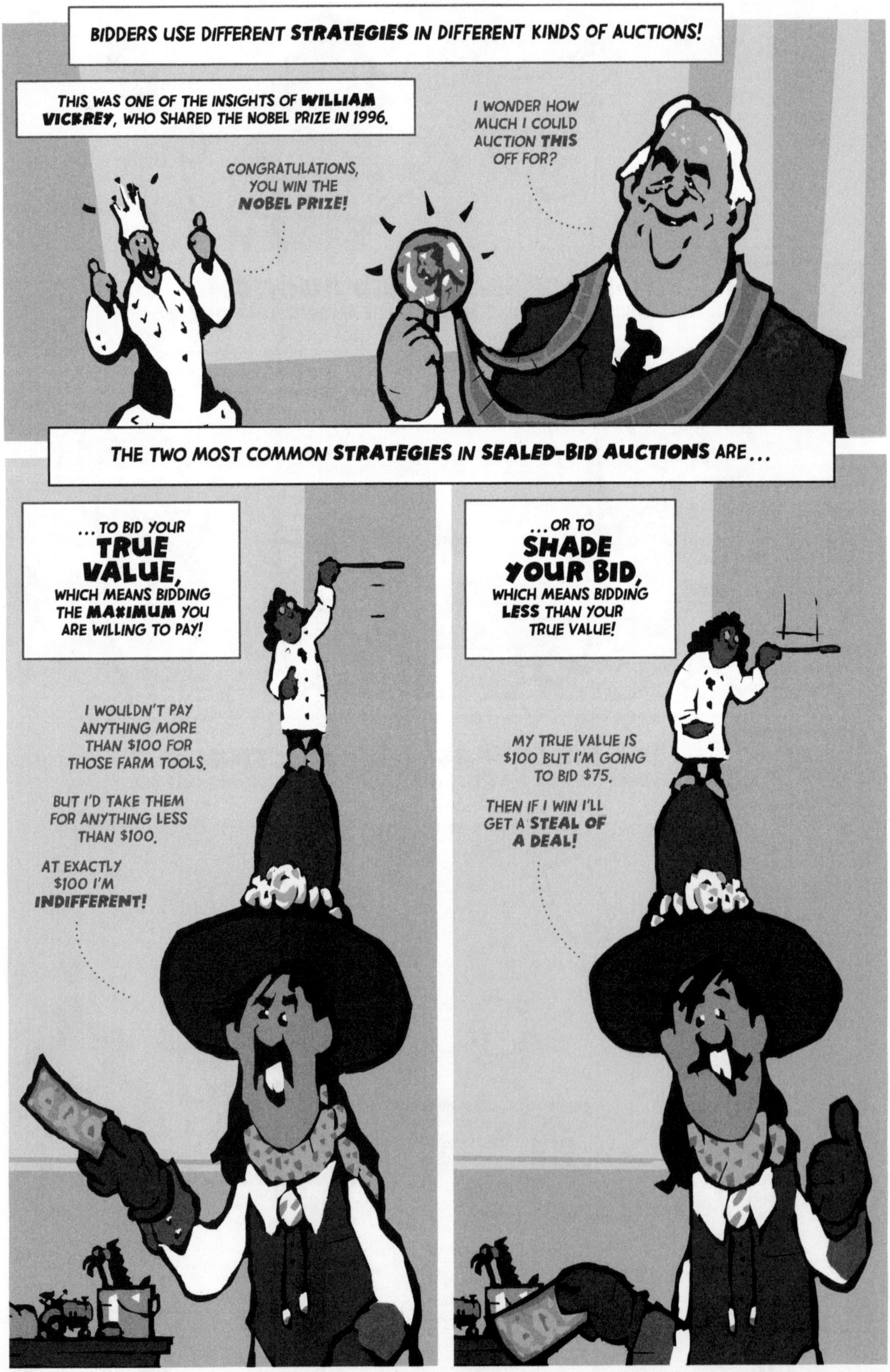
BIDDERS USE DIFFERENT STRATEGIES IN DIFFERENT KINDS OF AUCTIONS!
THIS WAS ONE OF THE INSIGHTS OF WILLIAM VICKREY, WHO SHARED THE NOBEL PRIZE IN 1996.
CONGRATULATIONS, YOU WIN THE NOBEL PRIZE!
I WONDER HOW MUCH I COULD AUCTION THIS OFF FOR?
THE TWO MOST COMMON STRATEGIES IN SEALED-BID AUCTIONS ARE...
...TO BID YOUR TRUE VALUE, WHICH MEANS BIDDING THE MAXIMUM YOU ARE WILLING TO PAY!
I WOULDN'T PAY ANYTHING MORE THAN $100 FOR THOSE FARM TOOLS.
BUT I'D TAKE THEM FOR ANYTHING LESS THAN $100.
AT EXACTLY $100 I'M INDIFFERENT!
...OR TO SHADE YOUR BID, WHICH MEANS BIDDING LESS THAN YOUR TRUE VALUE!
MY TRUE VALUE IS $100 BUT I'M GOING TO BID $75.
THEN IF I WIN I'LL GET A STEAL OF A DEAL!

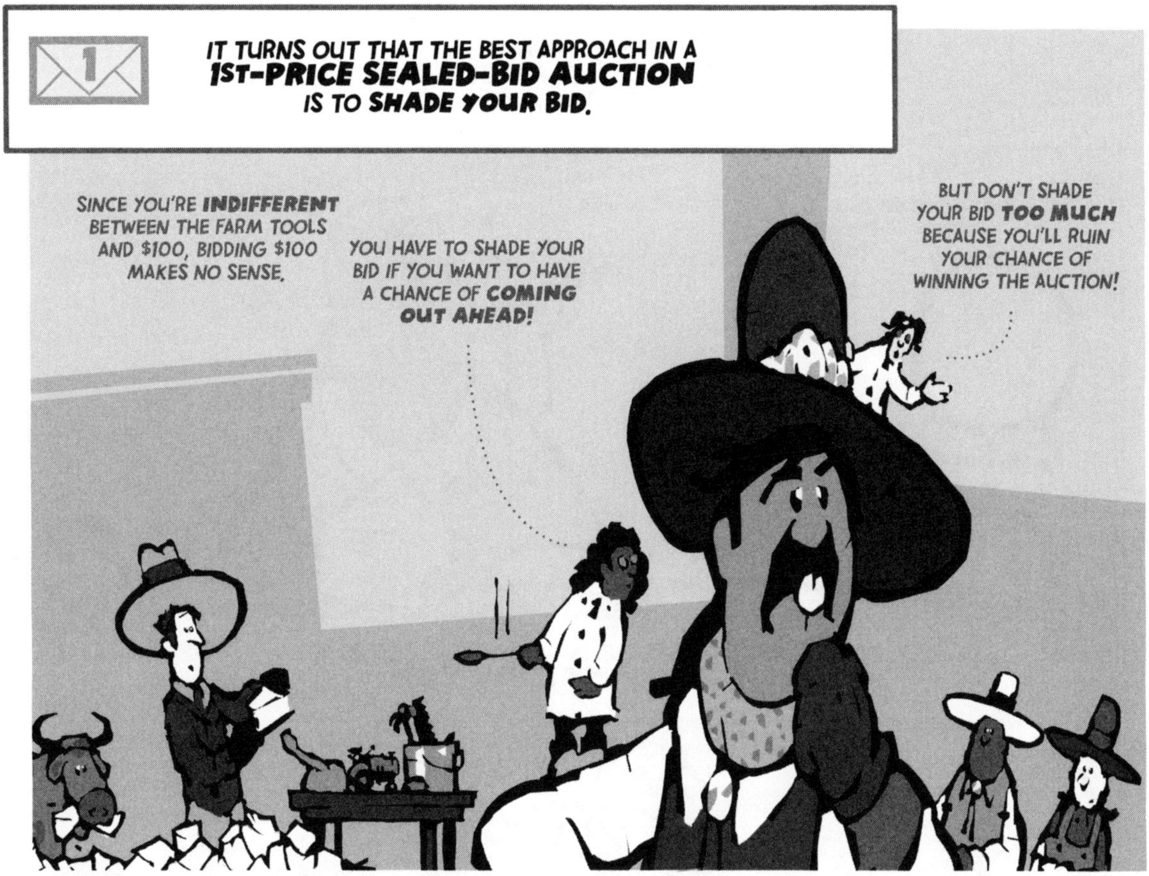
IT TURNS OUT THAT THE BEST APPROACH IN A
1ST-PRICE SEALED-BID AUCTION
IS TO SHADE YOUR BID.
SINCE YOU'RE INDIFFERENT BETWEEN THE FARM TOOLS AND $100, BIDDING $100 MAKES NO SENSE.
YOU HAVE TO SHADE YOUR BID IF YOU WANT TO HAVE A CHANCE OF COMING OUT AHEAD!
BUT DON'T SHADE YOUR BID TOO MUCH BECAUSE YOU'LL RUIN YOUR CHANCE OF WINNING THE AUCTION!

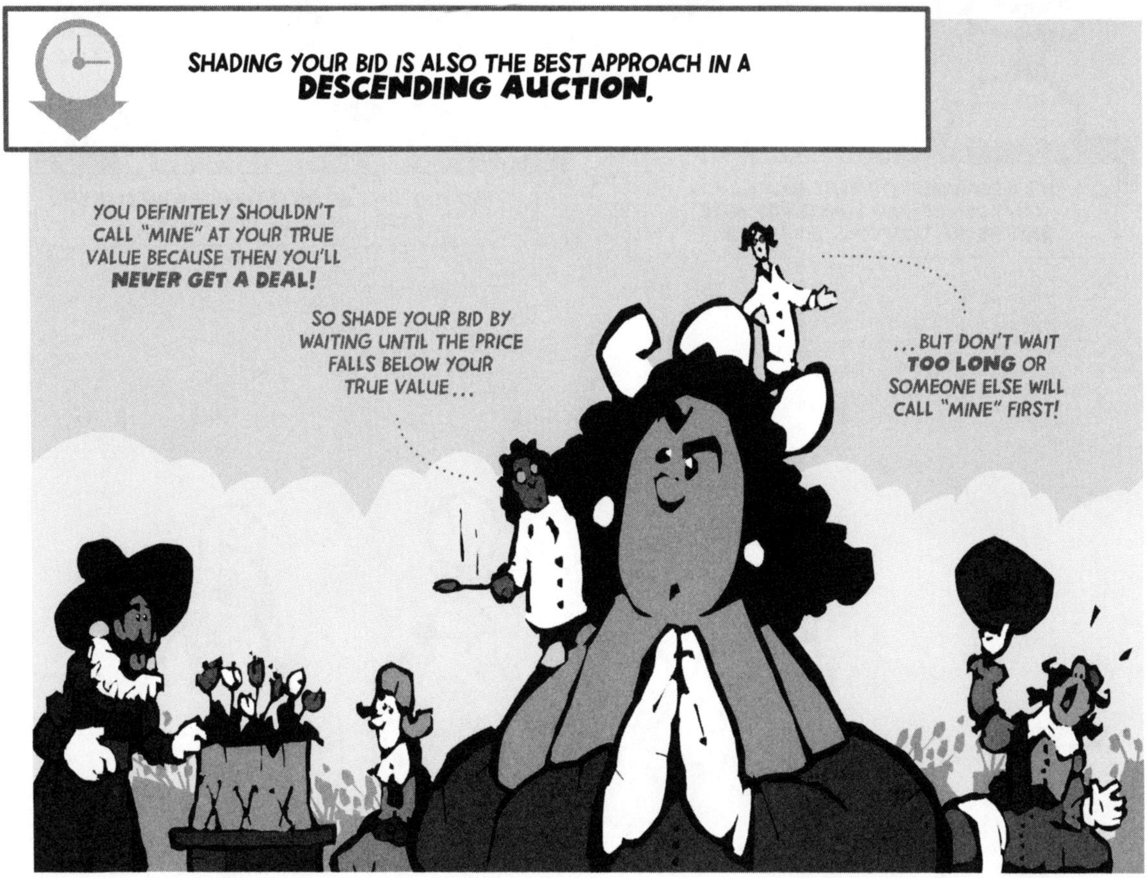
SHADING YOUR BID IS ALSO THE BEST APPROACH IN A
DESCENDING AUCTION.
YOU DEFINITELY SHOULDN'T CALL "MINE" AT YOUR TRUE VALUE BECAUSE THEN YOU'LL NEVER GET A DEAL!
SO SHADE YOUR BID BY WAITING UNTIL THE PRICE FALLS BELOW YOUR TRUE VALUE...
...BUT DON'T WAIT TOO LONG OR SOMEONE ELSE WILL CALL "MINE" FIRST!

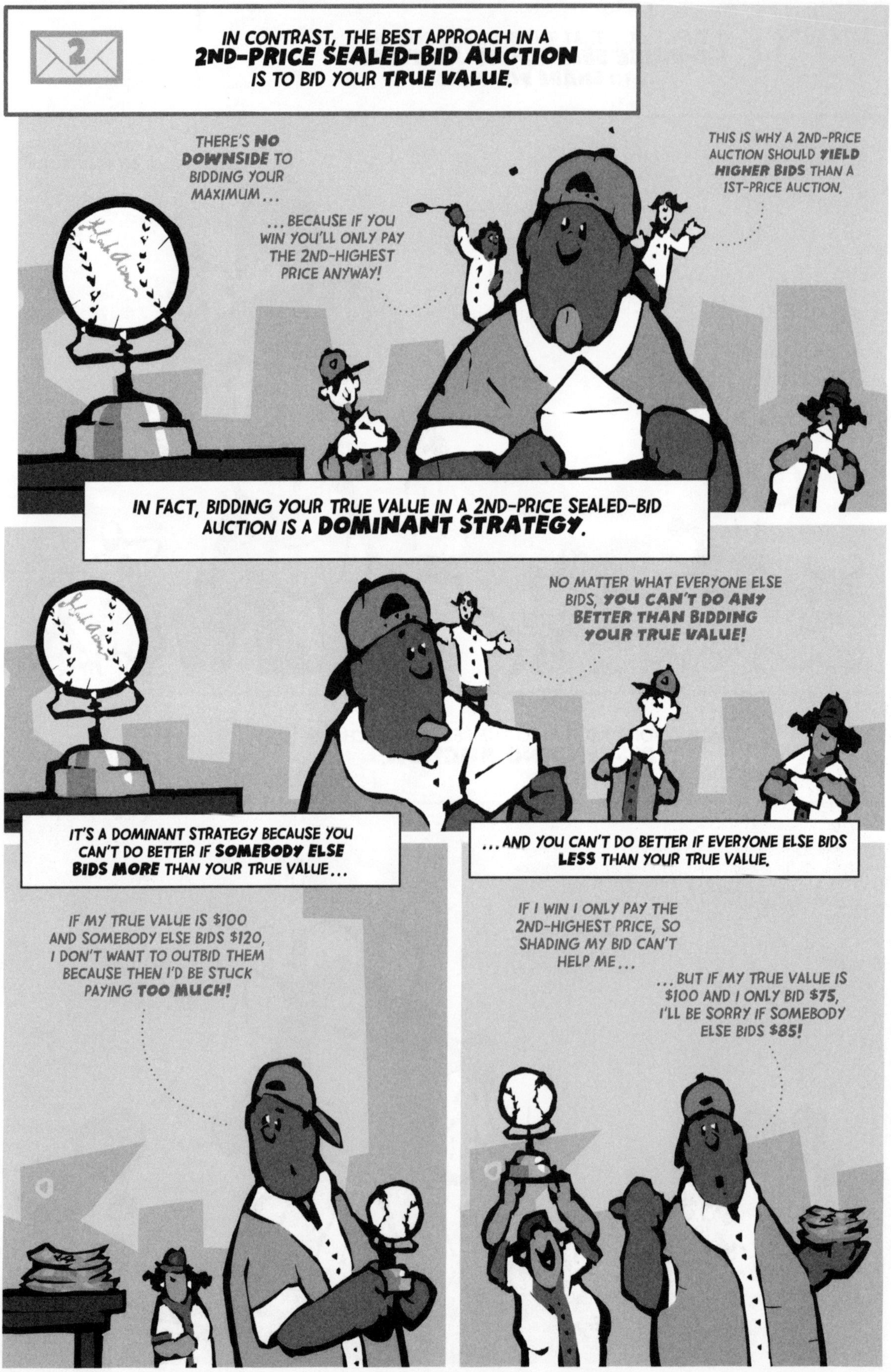
IN CONTRAST, THE BEST APPROACH IN A
2ND-PRICE SEALED-BID AUCTION
IS TO BID YOUR TRUE VALUE.
THERE'S NO DOWNSIDE TO BIDDING YOUR MAXIMUM...
...BECAUSE IF YOU WIN YOU'LL ONLY PAY THE 2ND-HIGHEST PRICE ANYWAY!
THIS IS WHY A 2ND-PRICE AUCTION SHOULD YIELD HIGHER BIDS THAN A 1ST-PRICE AUCTION.
IN FACT, BIDDING YOUR TRUE VALUE IN A 2ND-PRICE SEALED-BID AUCTION IS A DOMINANT STRATEGY.
NO MATTER WHAT EVERYONE ELSE BIDS, YOU CAN'T DO ANY BETTER THAN BIDDING YOUR TRUE VALUE!
IT'S A DOMINANT STRATEGY BECAUSE YOU CAN'T DO BETTER IF SOMEBODY ELSE BIDS MORE THAN YOUR TRUE VALUE...
IF MY TRUE VALUE IS $100 AND SOMEBODY ELSE BIDS $120, I DON'T WANT TO OUTBID THEM BECAUSE THEN I'D BE STUCK PAYING TOO MUCH!
...AND YOU CAN'T DO BETTER IF EVERYONE ELSE BIDS LESS THAN YOUR TRUE VALUE.
IF I WIN I ONLY PAY THE 2ND-HIGHEST PRICE, SO SHADING MY BID CAN'T HELP ME...
...BUT IF MY TRUE VALUE IS $100 AND I ONLY BID $75, I'LL BE SORRY IF SOMEBODY ELSE BIDS $85!

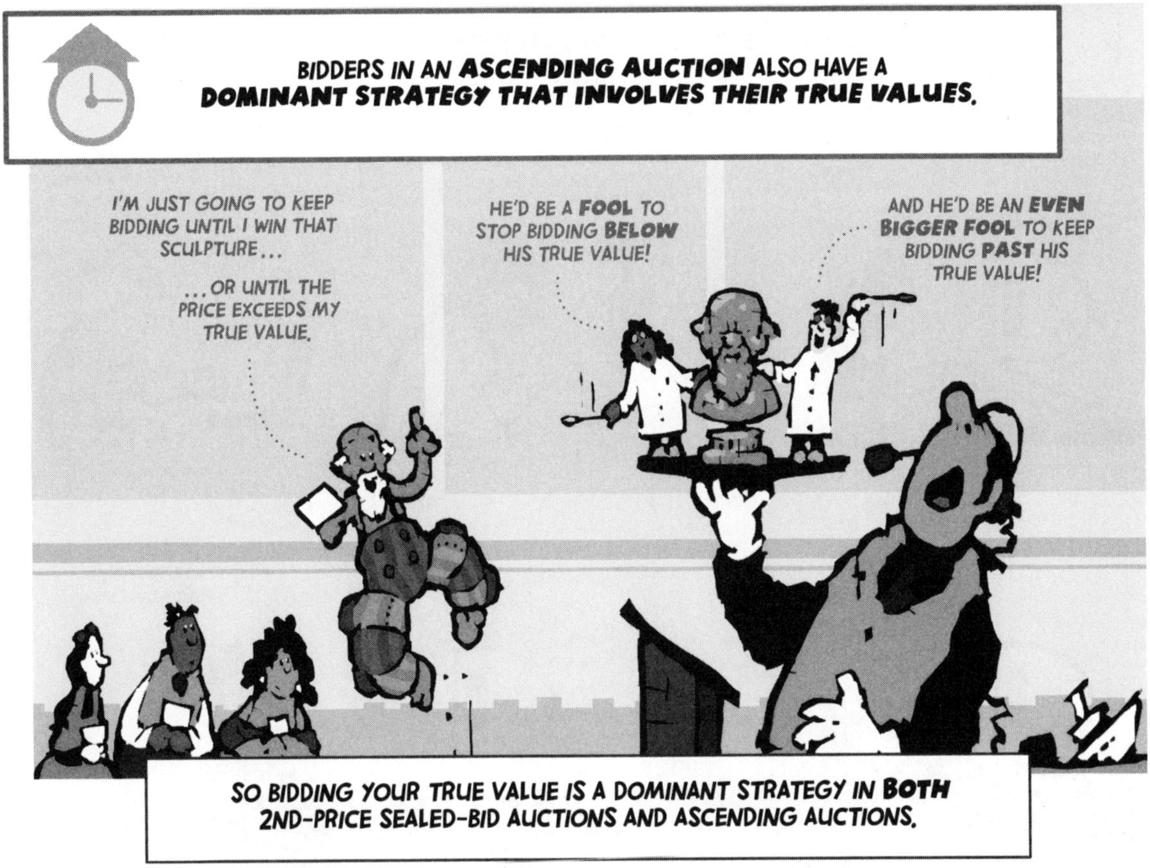
BIDDERS IN AN **ASCENDING AUCTION** ALSO HAVE A **DOMINANT STRATEGY THAT INVOLVES THEIR TRUE VALUES.**
I'M JUST GOING TO KEEP BIDDING UNTIL I WIN THAT SCULPTURE...
...OR UNTIL THE PRICE EXCEEDS MY TRUE VALUE.
HE'D BE A **FOOL** TO STOP BIDDING **BELOW** HIS TRUE VALUE!
AND HE'D BE AN **EVEN BIGGER FOOL** TO KEEP BIDDING **PAST** HIS TRUE VALUE!
SO BIDDING YOUR TRUE VALUE IS A DOMINANT STRATEGY IN **BOTH** 2ND-PRICE SEALED-BID AUCTIONS AND ASCENDING AUCTIONS.

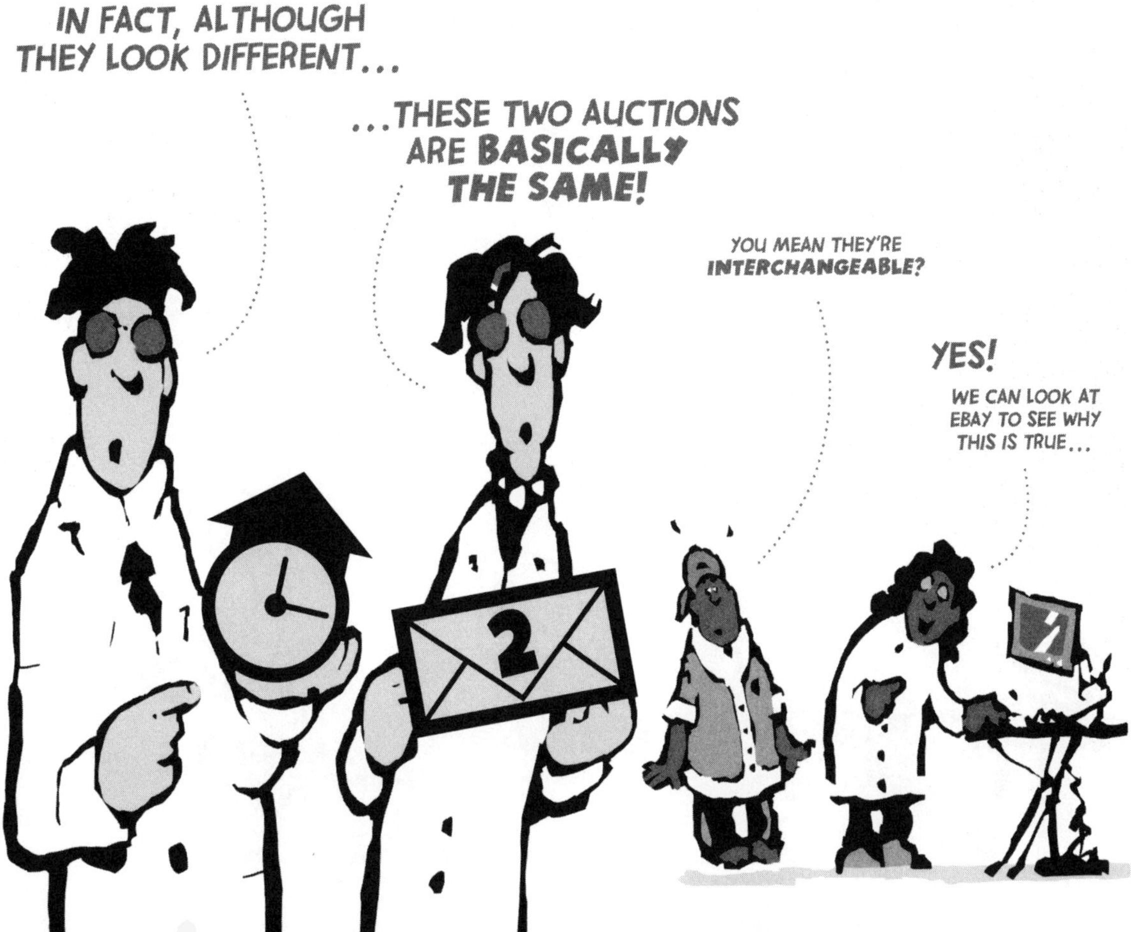
IN FACT, ALTHOUGH THEY LOOK DIFFERENT...
...THESE TWO AUCTIONS ARE **BASICALLY THE SAME!**
YOU MEAN THEY'RE **INTERCHANGEABLE?**
YES!
WE CAN LOOK AT EBAY TO SEE WHY THIS IS TRUE...

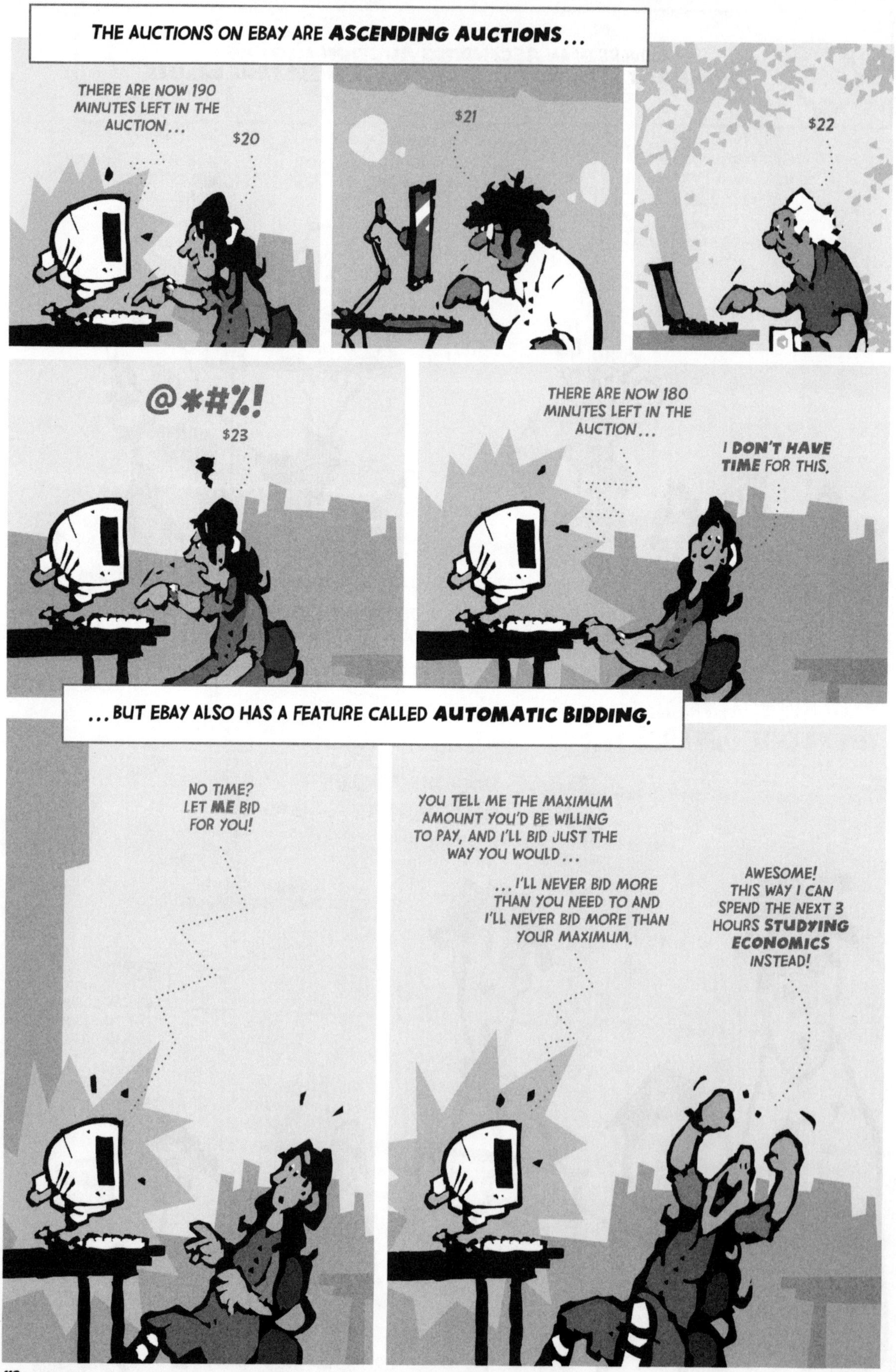
THE AUCTIONS ON EBAY ARE ASCENDING AUCTIONS...
THERE ARE NOW 190 MINUTES LEFT IN THE AUCTION...
$20
$21
$22
@*#%!
$23
THERE ARE NOW 180 MINUTES LEFT IN THE AUCTION...
I DON'T HAVE TIME FOR THIS.
...BUT EBAY ALSO HAS A FEATURE CALLED AUTOMATIC BIDDING.
NO TIME? LET ME BID FOR YOU!
YOU TELL ME THE MAXIMUM AMOUNT YOU'D BE WILLING TO PAY, AND I'LL BID JUST THE WAY YOU WOULD...
...I'LL NEVER BID MORE THAN YOU NEED TO AND I'LL NEVER BID MORE THAN YOUR MAXIMUM.
AWESOME! THIS WAY I CAN SPEND THE NEXT 3 HOURS STUDYING ECONOMICS INSTEAD!

NOW IMAGINE WHAT HAPPENS IF **EVERYBODY** USES AUTOMATIC BIDDING.

MAX: $100

MAX: $175

MAX: $125

EBAY'S COMPUTER DOES THE CALCULATIONS AND CAN EASILY PREDICT THE OUTCOME:

I'M GOING TO WIN AND PAY ABOUT $125, BECAUSE AT THAT POINT THE 2ND-HIGHEST BIDDER WILL DROP OUT!

WITH AUTOMATIC BIDDING, EBAY HAS BASICALLY **TURNED AN ASCENDING AUCTION INTO A 2ND-PRICE SEALED-BID AUCTION!**

THIS IS WHY WE SAY THAT ASCENDING-PRICE AUCTIONS AND 2ND-PRICE SEALED-BID AUCTIONS ARE **STRATEGICALLY EQUIVALENT!**

BIDDING YOUR TRUE VALUE IS A **DOMINANT STRATEGY** IN BOTH AUCTIONS...

...AND THE WINNING BIDDER IN EACH AUCTION WILL **PAY ONLY THE 2ND-HIGHEST BID.**

WHAT A BARGAIN!

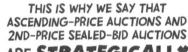

STRATEGICALLY EQUIVALENT

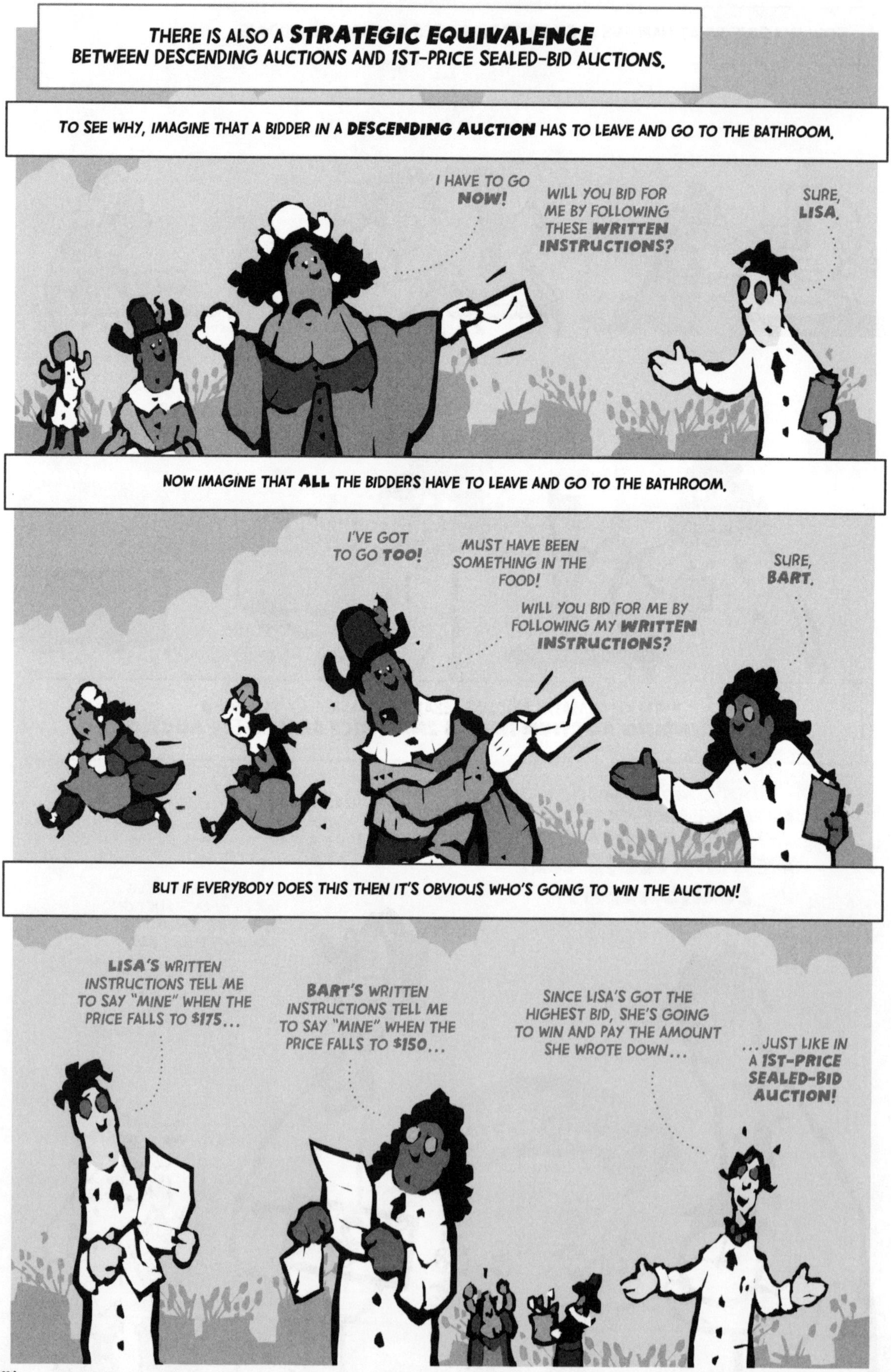
THERE IS ALSO A STRATEGIC EQUIVALENCE BETWEEN DESCENDING AUCTIONS AND 1ST-PRICE SEALED-BID AUCTIONS.
TO SEE WHY, IMAGINE THAT A BIDDER IN A DESCENDING AUCTION HAS TO LEAVE AND GO TO THE BATHROOM.
I HAVE TO GO NOW!
WILL YOU BID FOR ME BY FOLLOWING THESE WRITTEN INSTRUCTIONS?
SURE, LISA.
NOW IMAGINE THAT ALL THE BIDDERS HAVE TO LEAVE AND GO TO THE BATHROOM.
I'VE GOT TO GO TOO!
MUST HAVE BEEN SOMETHING IN THE FOOD!
WILL YOU BID FOR ME BY FOLLOWING MY WRITTEN INSTRUCTIONS?
SURE, BART.
BUT IF EVERYBODY DOES THIS THEN IT'S OBVIOUS WHO'S GOING TO WIN THE AUCTION!
LISA'S WRITTEN INSTRUCTIONS TELL ME TO SAY "MINE" WHEN THE PRICE FALLS TO $175...
BART'S WRITTEN INSTRUCTIONS TELL ME TO SAY "MINE" WHEN THE PRICE FALLS TO $150...
SINCE LISA'S GOT THE HIGHEST BID, SHE'S GOING TO WIN AND PAY THE AMOUNT SHE WROTE DOWN...
...JUST LIKE IN A 1ST-PRICE SEALED-BID AUCTION!

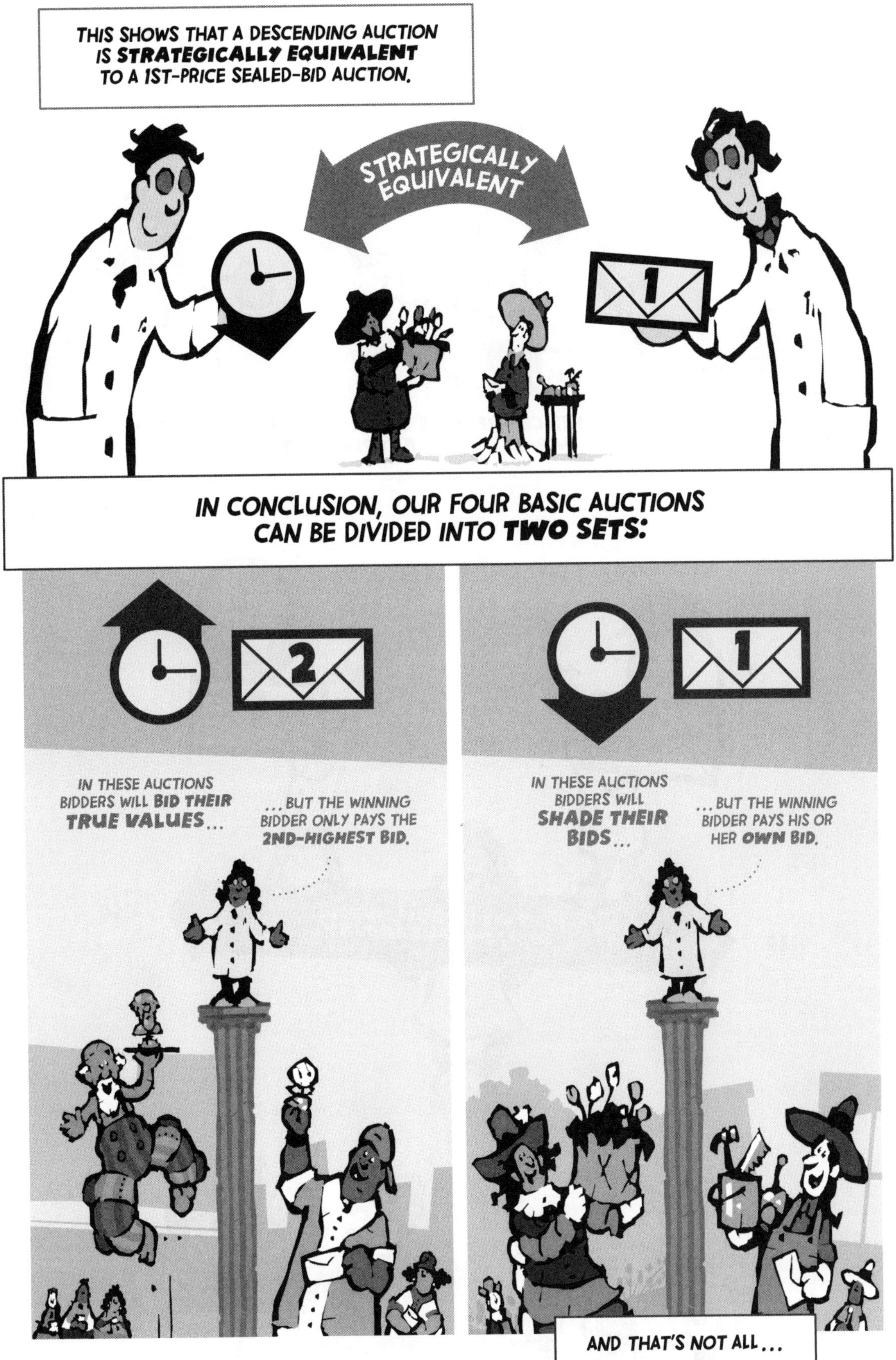
THIS SHOWS THAT A DESCENDING AUCTION IS STRATEGICALLY EQUIVALENT TO A 1ST-PRICE SEALED-BID AUCTION.
STRATEGICALLY EQUIVALENT
1
IN CONCLUSION, OUR FOUR BASIC AUCTIONS CAN BE DIVIDED INTO TWO SETS:
2
IN THESE AUCTIONS BIDDERS WILL BID THEIR TRUE VALUES...
...BUT THE WINNING BIDDER ONLY PAYS THE 2ND-HIGHEST BID.
1
IN THESE AUCTIONS BIDDERS WILL SHADE THEIR BIDS...
...BUT THE WINNING BIDDER PAYS HIS OR HER OWN BID.
AND THAT'S NOT ALL...

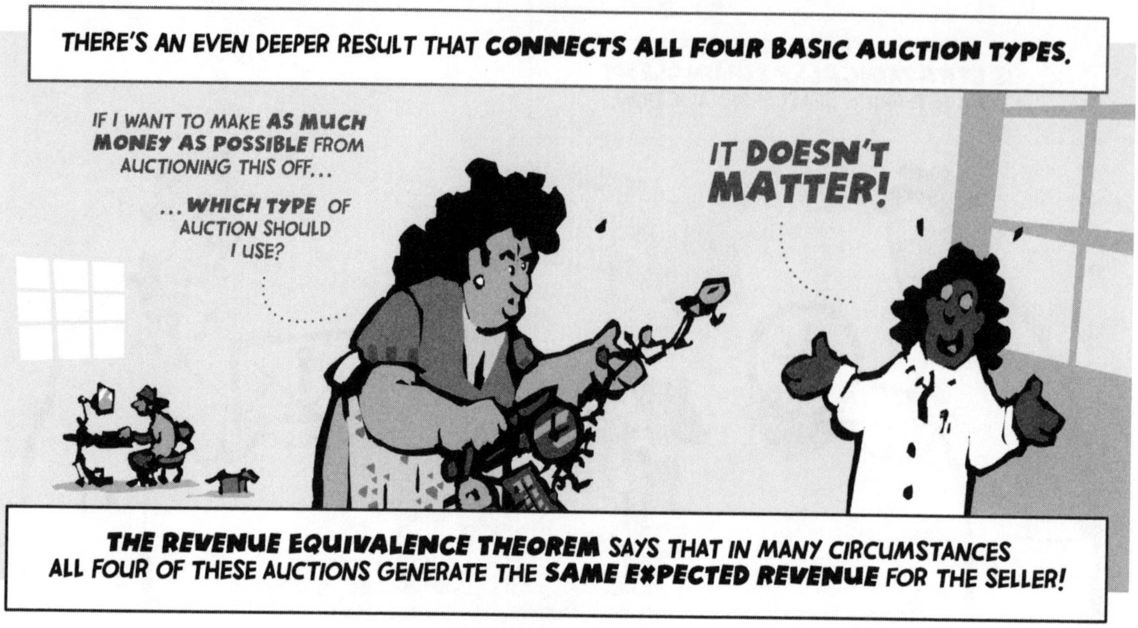
THERE'S AN EVEN DEEPER RESULT THAT CONNECTS ALL FOUR BASIC AUCTION TYPES.
IF I WANT TO MAKE AS MUCH MONEY AS POSSIBLE FROM AUCTIONING THIS OFF...
...WHICH TYPE OF AUCTION SHOULD I USE?
IT DOESN'T MATTER!
THE REVENUE EQUIVALENCE THEOREM SAYS THAT IN MANY CIRCUMSTANCES ALL FOUR OF THESE AUCTIONS GENERATE THE SAME EXPECTED REVENUE FOR THE SELLER!

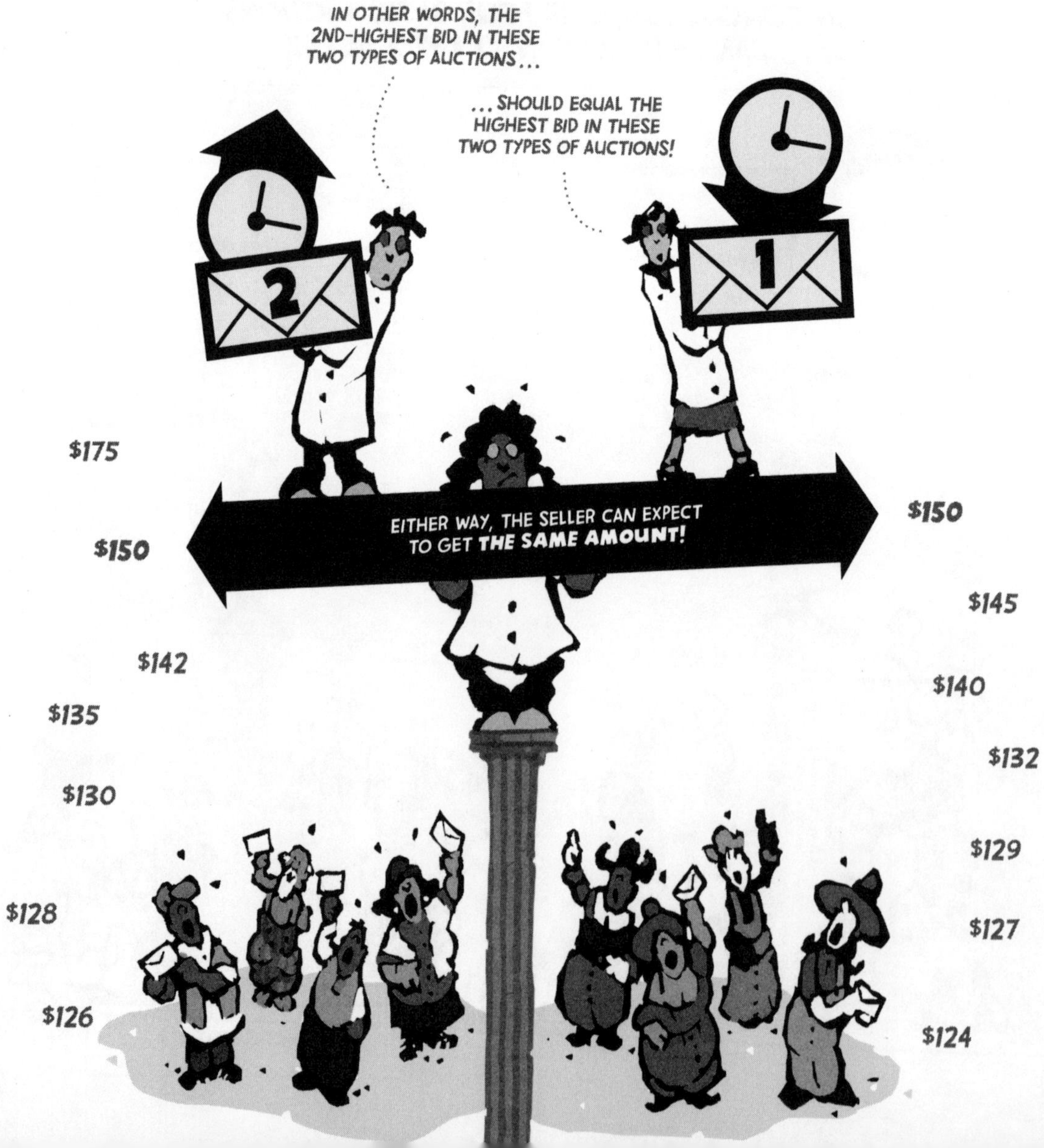
IN OTHER WORDS, THE 2ND-HIGHEST BID IN THESE TWO TYPES OF AUCTIONS...
...SHOULD EQUAL THE HIGHEST BID IN THESE TWO TYPES OF AUCTIONS!
2
1
EITHER WAY, THE SELLER CAN EXPECT TO GET THE SAME AMOUNT!
$175
$150
$142
$135
$130
$128
$126
$150
$145
$140
$132
$129
$127
$124

CHAPTER 10
FROM SOME TO MANY

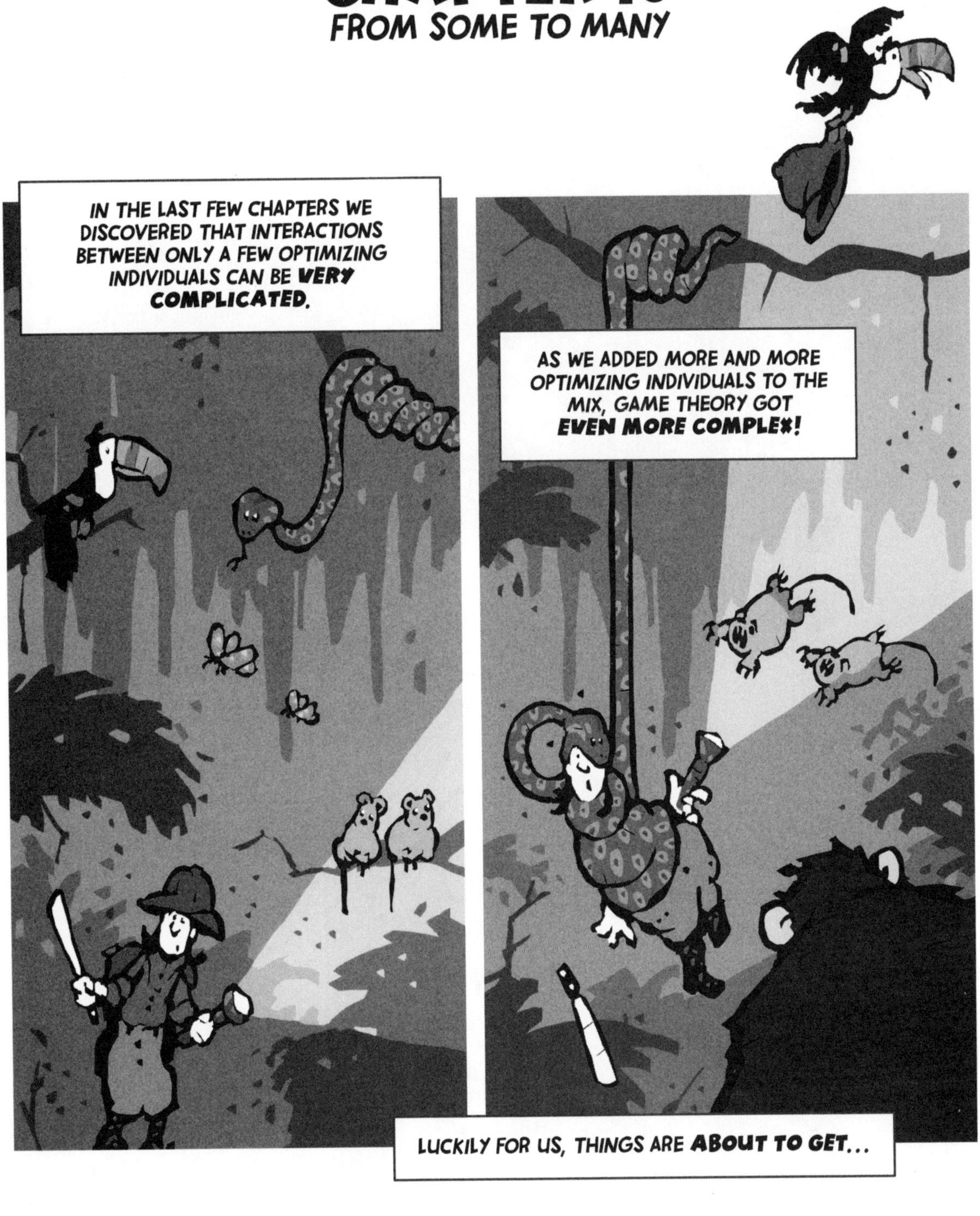

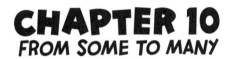

IN THE LAST FEW CHAPTERS WE DISCOVERED THAT INTERACTIONS BETWEEN ONLY A FEW OPTIMIZING INDIVIDUALS CAN BE **VERY COMPLICATED**.
AS WE ADDED MORE AND MORE OPTIMIZING INDIVIDUALS TO THE MIX, GAME THEORY GOT **EVEN MORE COMPLEX!**
LUCKILY FOR US, THINGS ARE **ABOUT TO GET**...

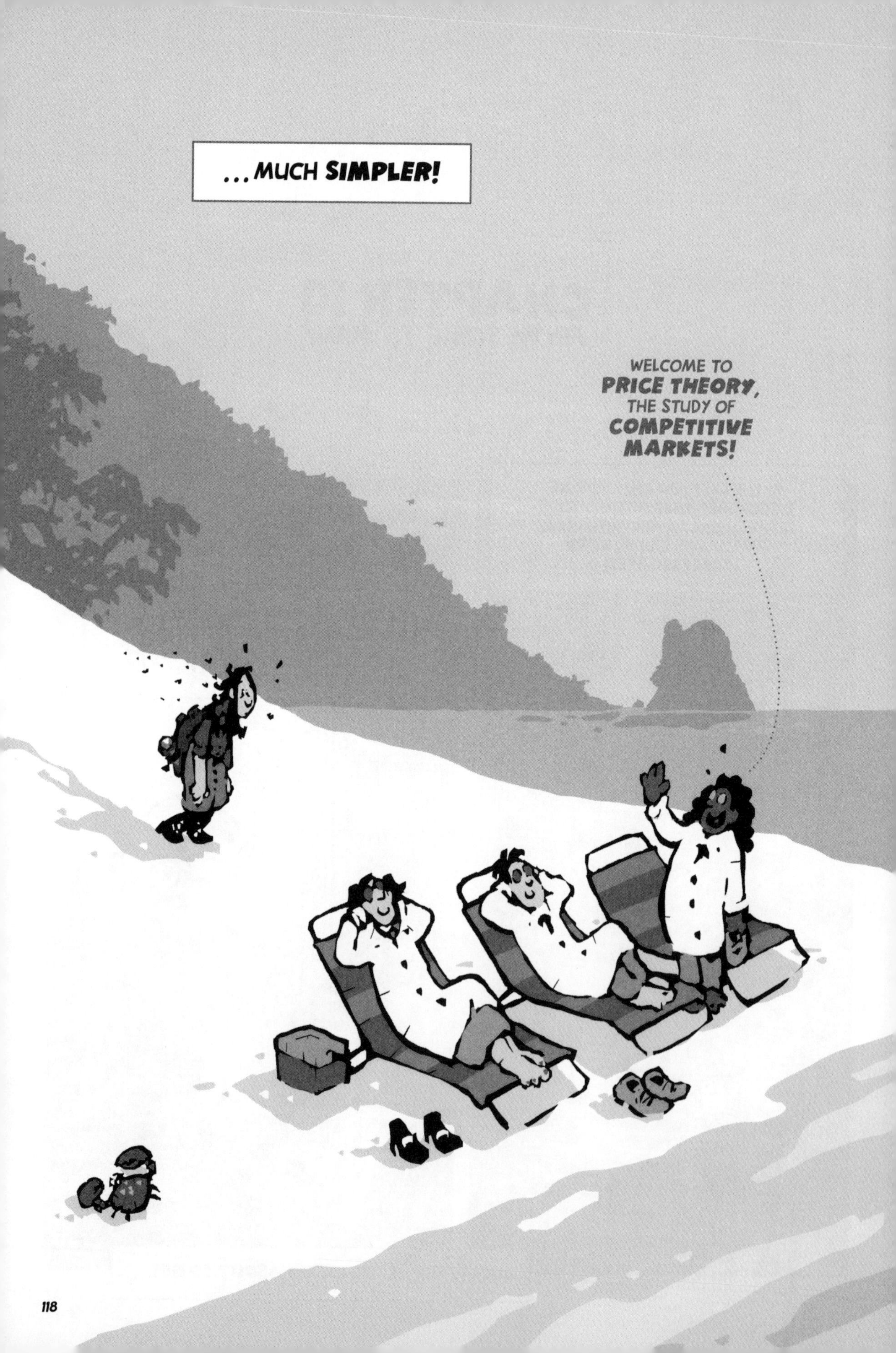
...MUCH SIMPLER!
WELCOME TO PRICE THEORY, THE STUDY OF COMPETITIVE MARKETS!

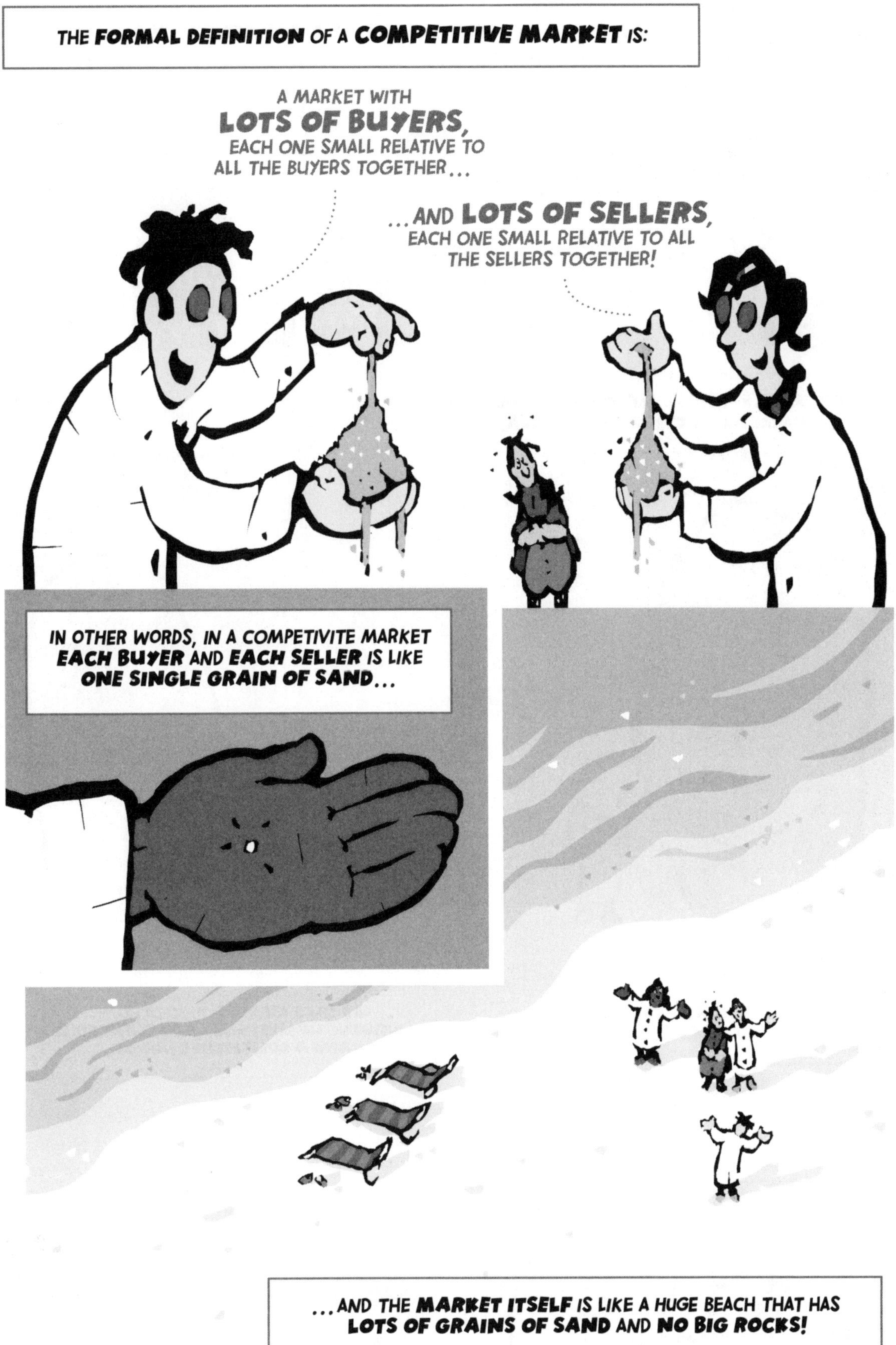
THE FORMAL DEFINITION OF A COMPETITIVE MARKET IS:
A MARKET WITH LOTS OF BUYERS, EACH ONE SMALL RELATIVE TO ALL THE BUYERS TOGETHER...
...AND LOTS OF SELLERS, EACH ONE SMALL RELATIVE TO ALL THE SELLERS TOGETHER!
IN OTHER WORDS, IN A COMPETIVITE MARKET EACH BUYER AND EACH SELLER IS LIKE ONE SINGLE GRAIN OF SAND...
...AND THE MARKET ITSELF IS LIKE A HUGE BEACH THAT HAS LOTS OF GRAINS OF SAND AND NO BIG ROCKS!

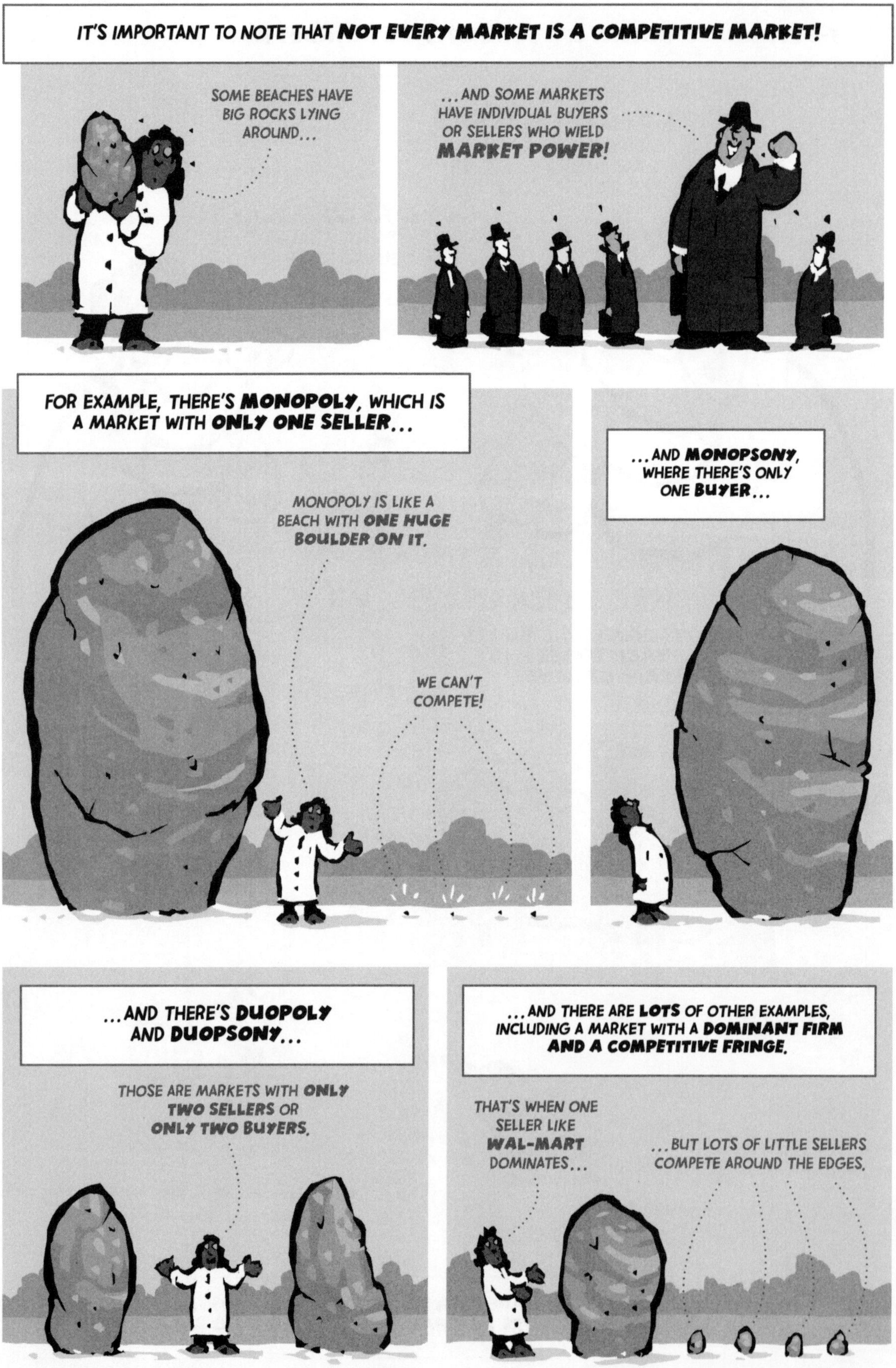
IT'S IMPORTANT TO NOTE THAT NOT EVERY MARKET IS A COMPETITIVE MARKET!
SOME BEACHES HAVE BIG ROCKS LYING AROUND...
...AND SOME MARKETS HAVE INDIVIDUAL BUYERS OR SELLERS WHO WIELD MARKET POWER!
FOR EXAMPLE, THERE'S MONOPOLY, WHICH IS A MARKET WITH ONLY ONE SELLER...
MONOPOLY IS LIKE A BEACH WITH ONE HUGE BOULDER ON IT.
WE CAN'T COMPETE!
...AND MONOPSONY, WHERE THERE'S ONLY ONE BUYER...
...AND THERE'S DUOPOLY AND DUOPSONY...
THOSE ARE MARKETS WITH ONLY TWO SELLERS OR ONLY TWO BUYERS.
...AND THERE ARE LOTS OF OTHER EXAMPLES, INCLUDING A MARKET WITH A DOMINANT FIRM AND A COMPETITIVE FRINGE.
THAT'S WHEN ONE SELLER LIKE WAL-MART DOMINATES...
...BUT LOTS OF LITTLE SELLERS COMPETE AROUND THE EDGES.

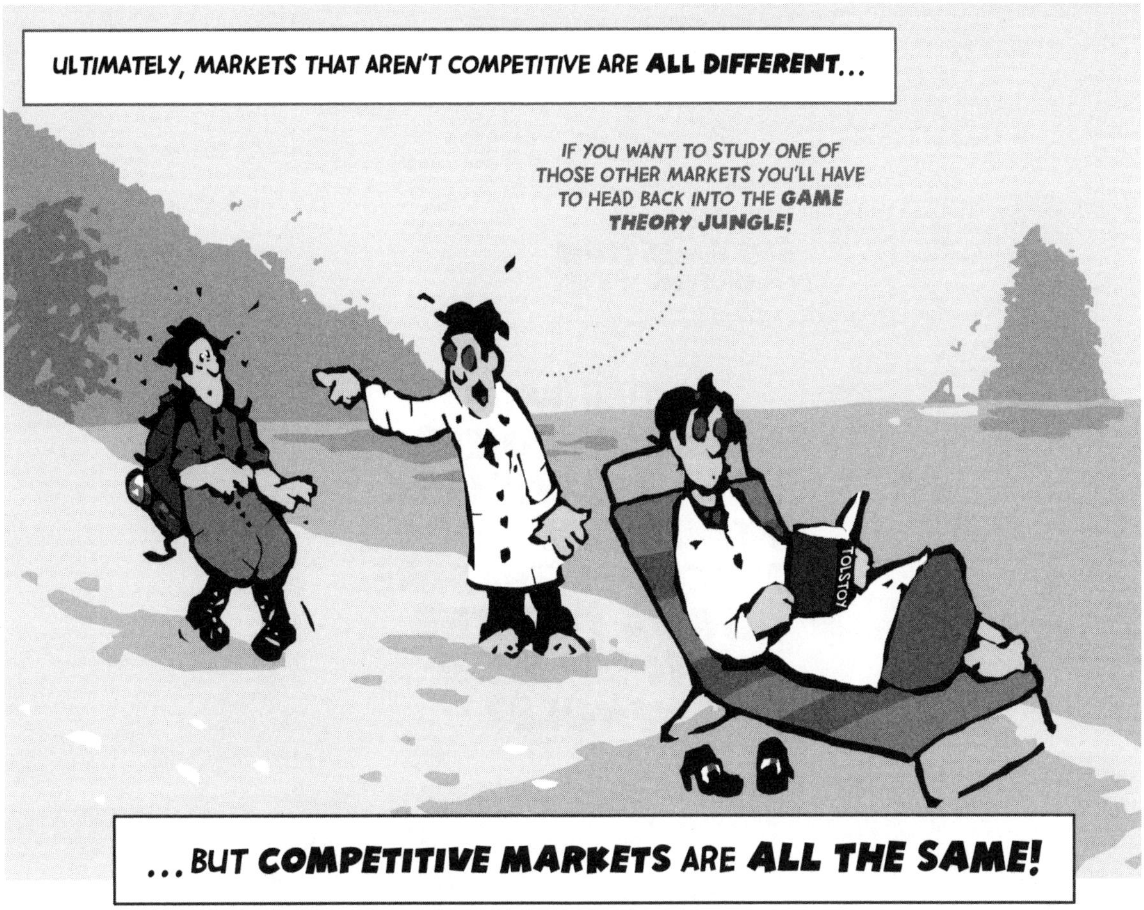
ULTIMATELY, MARKETS THAT AREN'T COMPETITIVE ARE ALL DIFFERENT...
IF YOU WANT TO STUDY ONE OF THOSE OTHER MARKETS YOU'LL HAVE TO HEAD BACK INTO THE GAME THEORY JUNGLE!
TOLSTOY
...BUT COMPETITIVE MARKETS ARE ALL THE SAME!

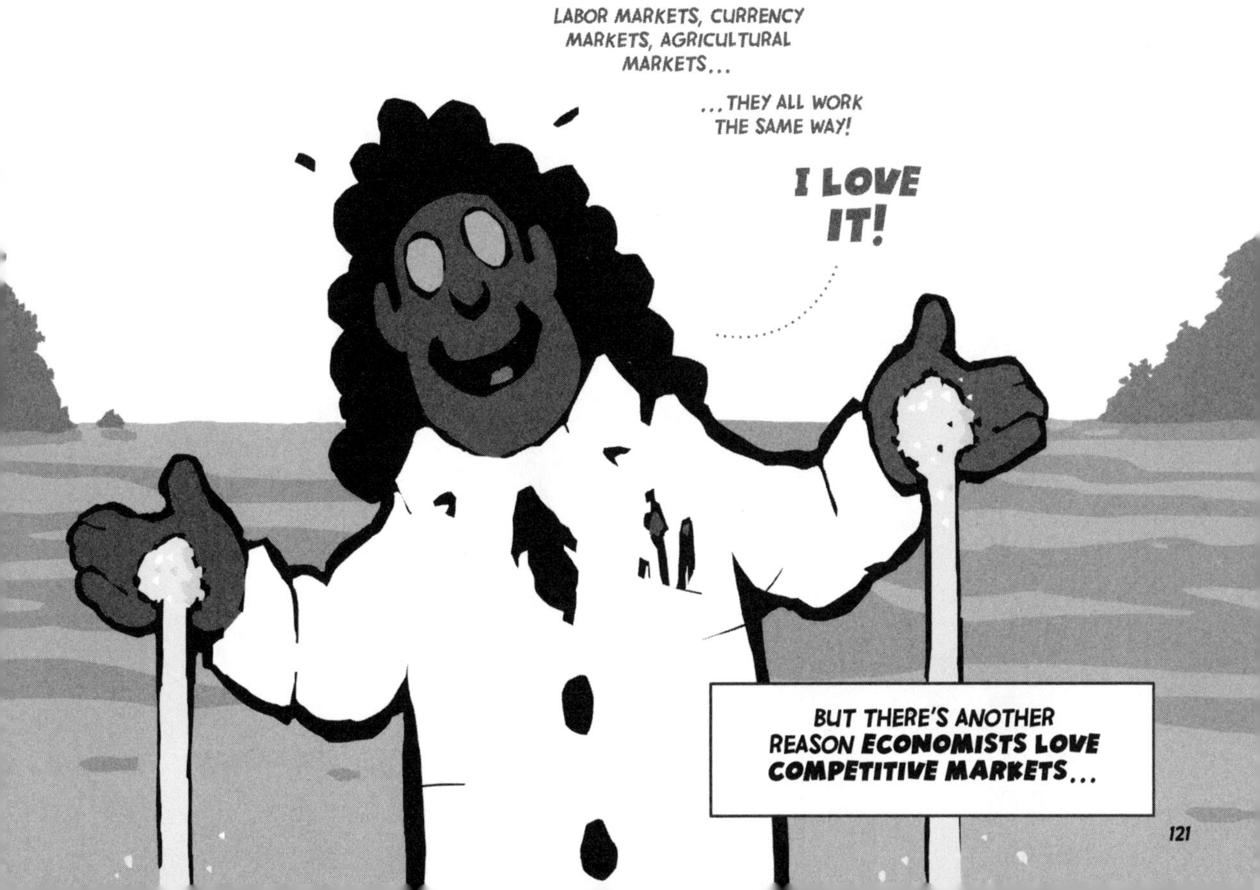
LABOR MARKETS, CURRENCY MARKETS, AGRICULTURAL MARKETS...
...THEY ALL WORK THE SAME WAY!
I LOVE IT!
BUT THERE'S ANOTHER REASON ECONOMISTS LOVE COMPETITIVE MARKETS...

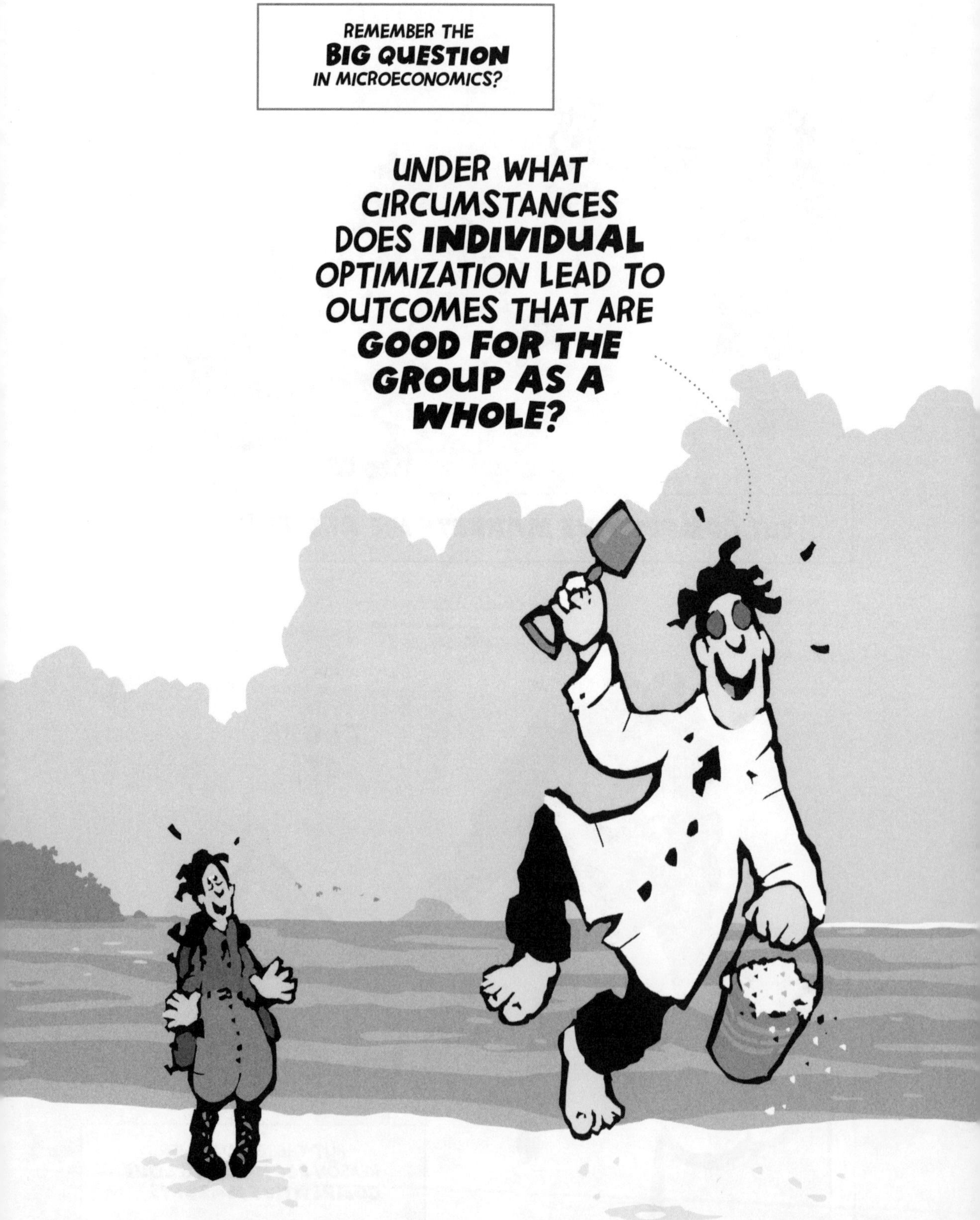
REMEMBER THE BIG QUESTION IN MICROECONOMICS?
UNDER WHAT CIRCUMSTANCES DOES INDIVIDUAL OPTIMIZATION LEAD TO OUTCOMES THAT ARE GOOD FOR THE GROUP AS A WHOLE?

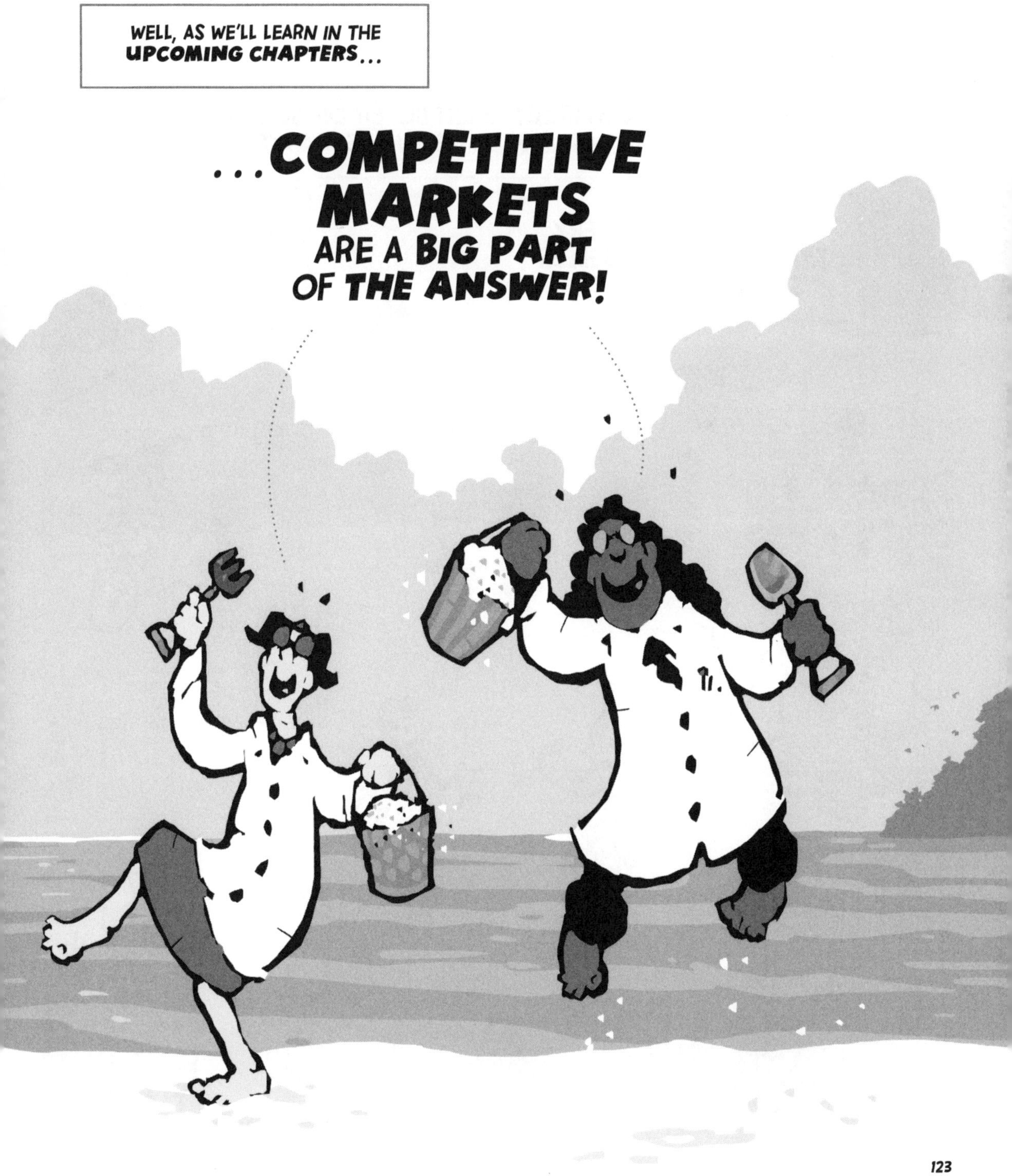
WELL, AS WE'LL LEARN IN THE UPCOMING CHAPTERS...
...COMPETITIVE MARKETS ARE A BIG PART OF THE ANSWER!

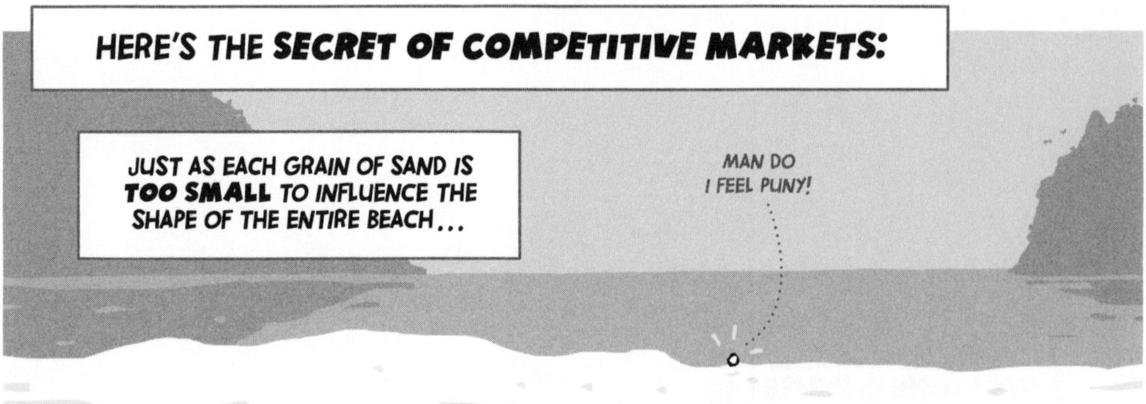
HERE'S THE **SECRET OF COMPETITIVE MARKETS:**
JUST AS EACH GRAIN OF SAND IS **TOO SMALL** TO INFLUENCE THE SHAPE OF THE ENTIRE BEACH...
MAN DO I FEEL PUNY!

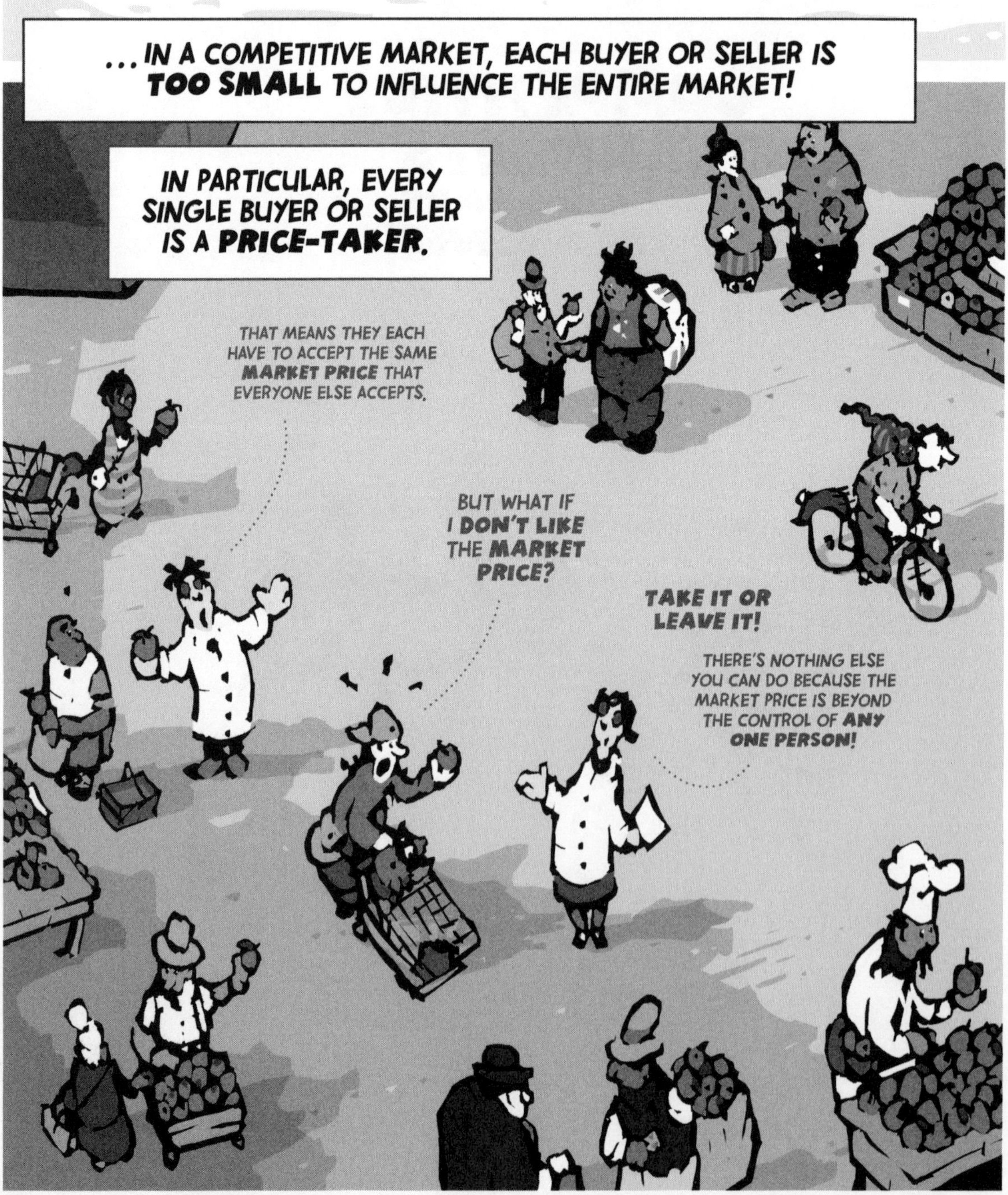
...IN A COMPETITIVE MARKET, EACH BUYER OR SELLER IS **TOO SMALL** TO INFLUENCE THE ENTIRE MARKET!
IN PARTICULAR, EVERY SINGLE BUYER OR SELLER IS A **PRICE-TAKER.**
THAT MEANS THEY EACH HAVE TO ACCEPT THE SAME **MARKET PRICE** THAT EVERYONE ELSE ACCEPTS.
BUT WHAT IF I **DON'T LIKE** THE **MARKET PRICE?**
TAKE IT OR LEAVE IT!
THERE'S NOTHING ELSE YOU CAN DO BECAUSE THE MARKET PRICE IS BEYOND THE CONTROL OF **ANY ONE PERSON!**

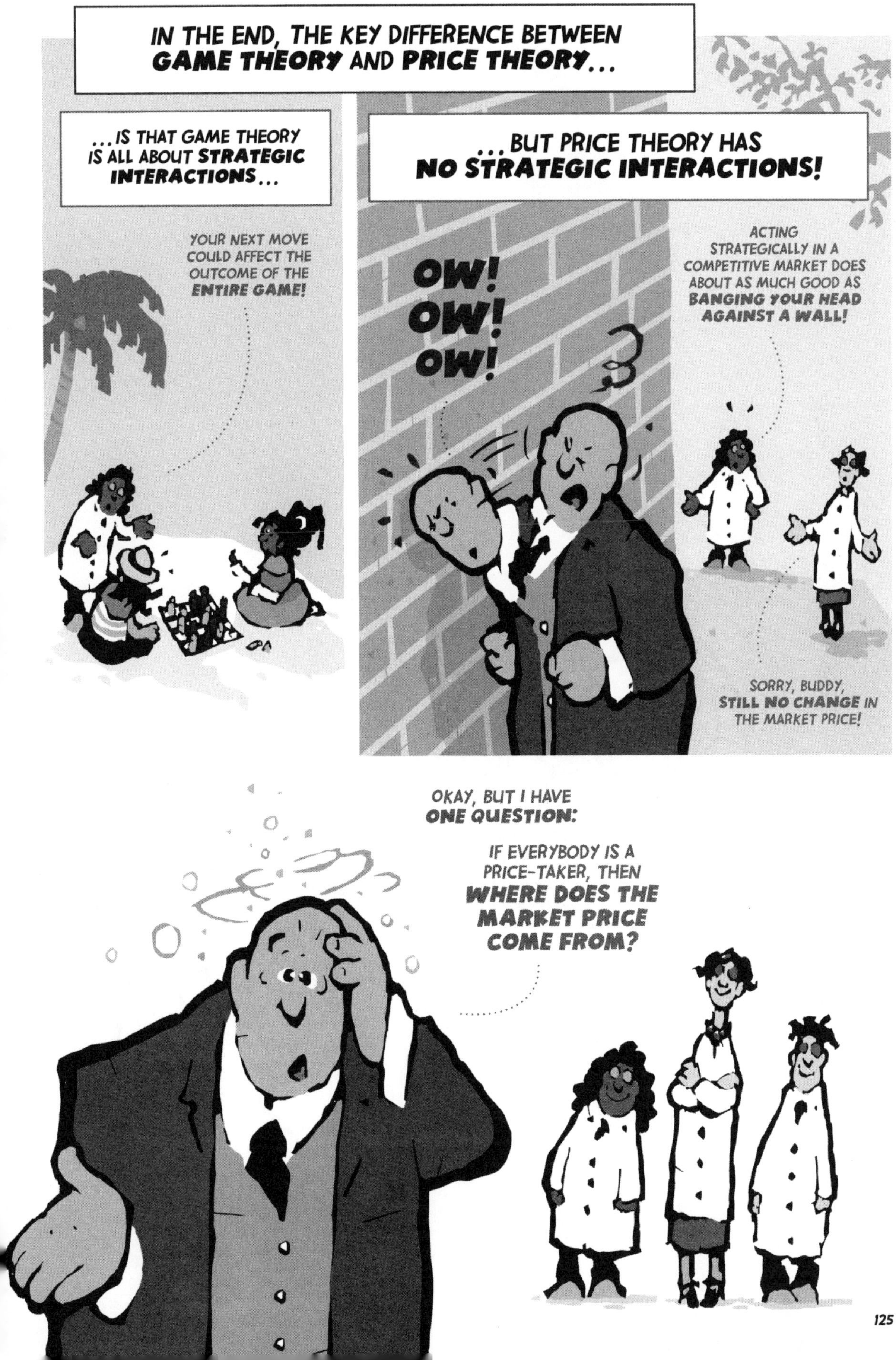
IN THE END, THE KEY DIFFERENCE BETWEEN GAME THEORY AND PRICE THEORY...
...IS THAT GAME THEORY IS ALL ABOUT STRATEGIC INTERACTIONS...
YOUR NEXT MOVE COULD AFFECT THE OUTCOME OF THE ENTIRE GAME!
...BUT PRICE THEORY HAS NO STRATEGIC INTERACTIONS!
OW! OW! OW!
ACTING STRATEGICALLY IN A COMPETITIVE MARKET DOES ABOUT AS MUCH GOOD AS BANGING YOUR HEAD AGAINST A WALL!
SORRY, BUDDY, STILL NO CHANGE IN THE MARKET PRICE!
OKAY, BUT I HAVE ONE QUESTION:
IF EVERYBODY IS A PRICE-TAKER, THEN WHERE DOES THE MARKET PRICE COME FROM?

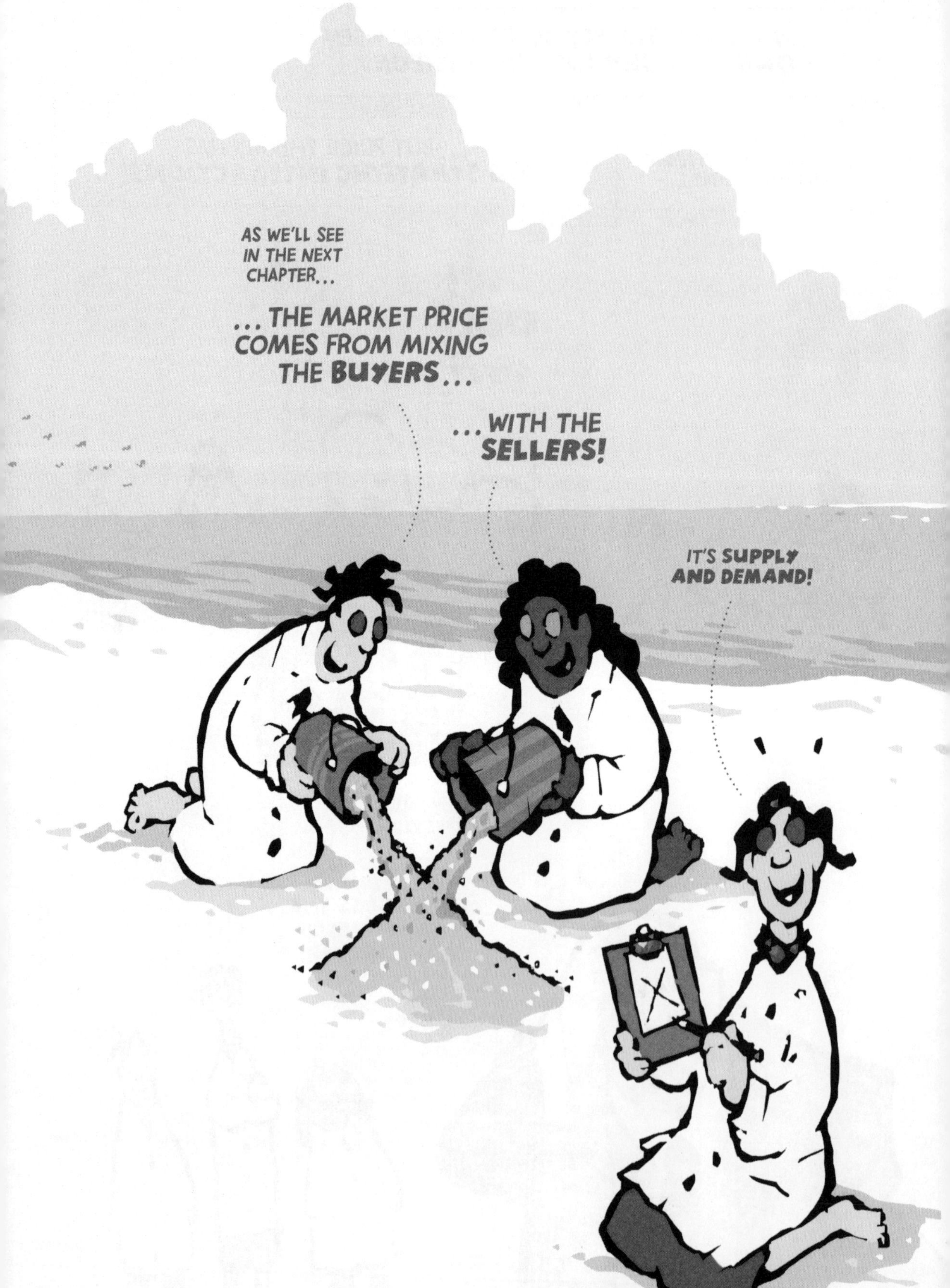
AS WE'LL SEE IN THE NEXT CHAPTER...
...THE MARKET PRICE COMES FROM MIXING THE BUYERS...
...WITH THE SELLERS!
IT'S SUPPLY AND DEMAND!

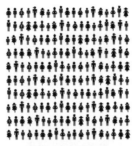

PART THREE
MARKET
INTERACTIONS

CHAPTER 11
SUPPLY AND DEMAND

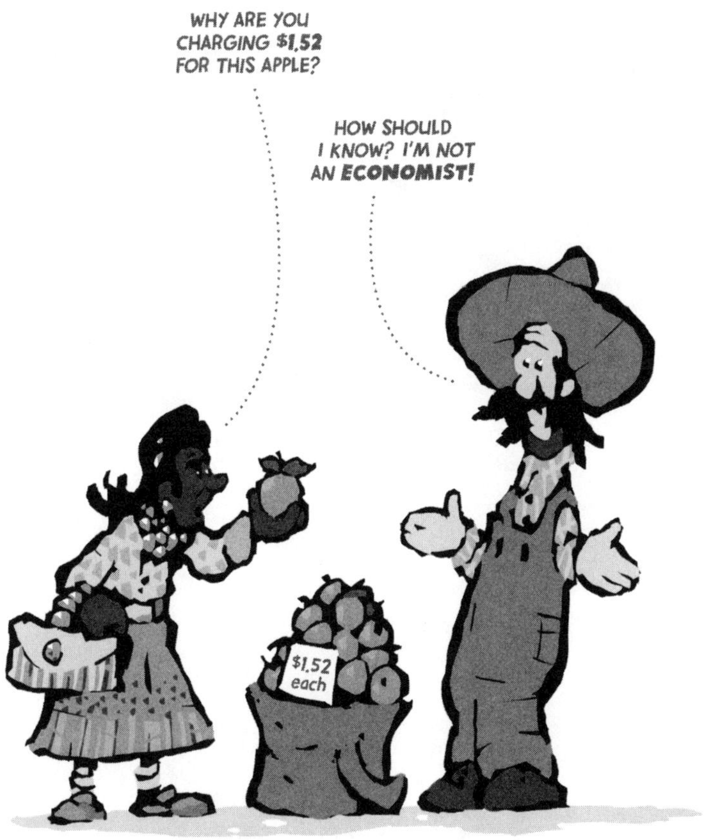
WHY ARE YOU CHARGING $1.52 FOR THIS APPLE?
HOW SHOULD I KNOW? I'M NOT AN ECONOMIST!
$1.52 each

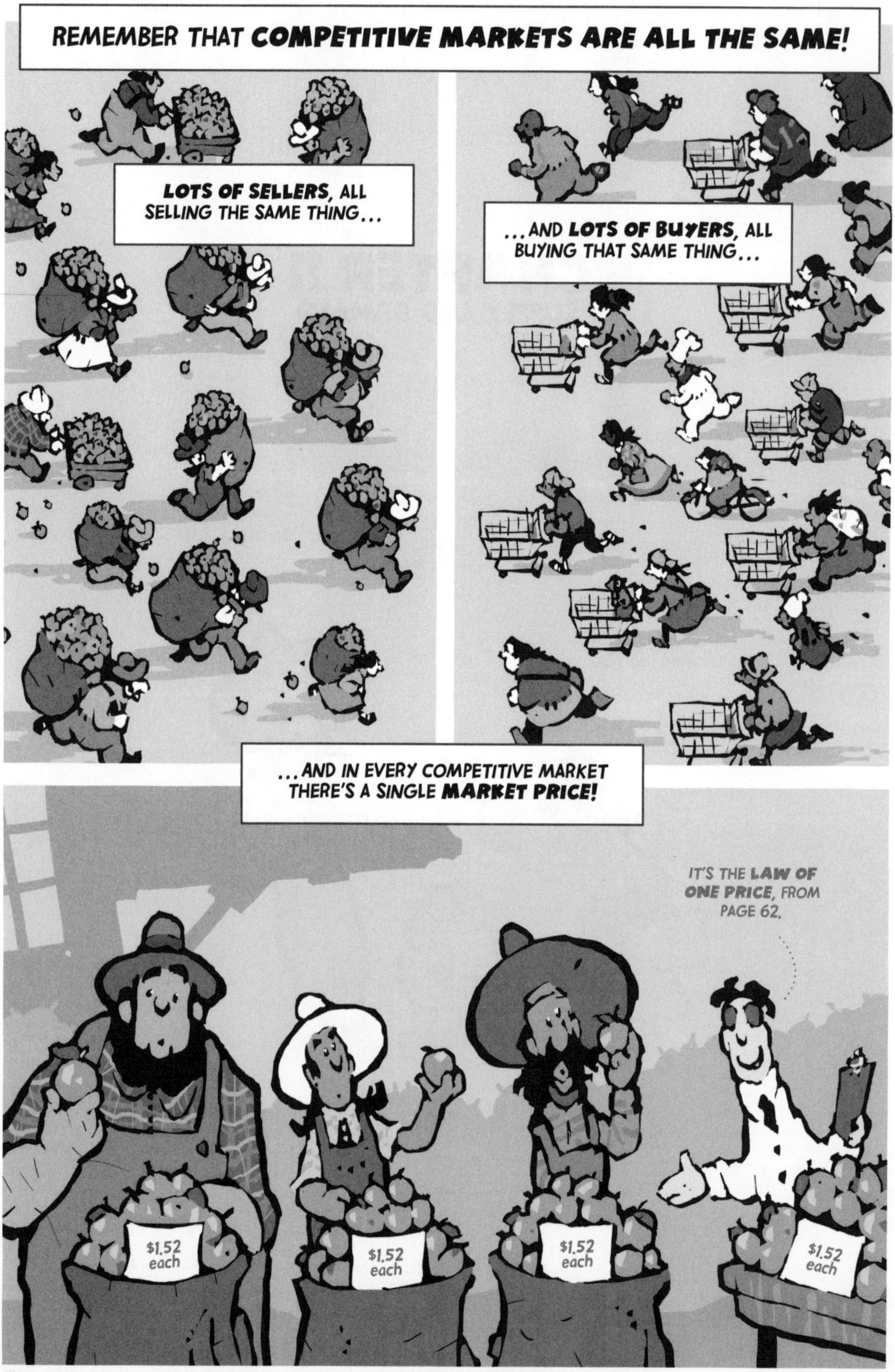
REMEMBER THAT **COMPETITIVE MARKETS ARE ALL THE SAME!**
LOTS OF SELLERS, ALL SELLING THE SAME THING...
...AND **LOTS OF BUYERS**, ALL BUYING THAT SAME THING...
...AND IN EVERY COMPETITIVE MARKET THERE'S A SINGLE **MARKET PRICE!**
IT'S THE **LAW OF ONE PRICE**, FROM PAGE 62.
$1.52 each
$1.52 each
$1.52 each
$1.52 each

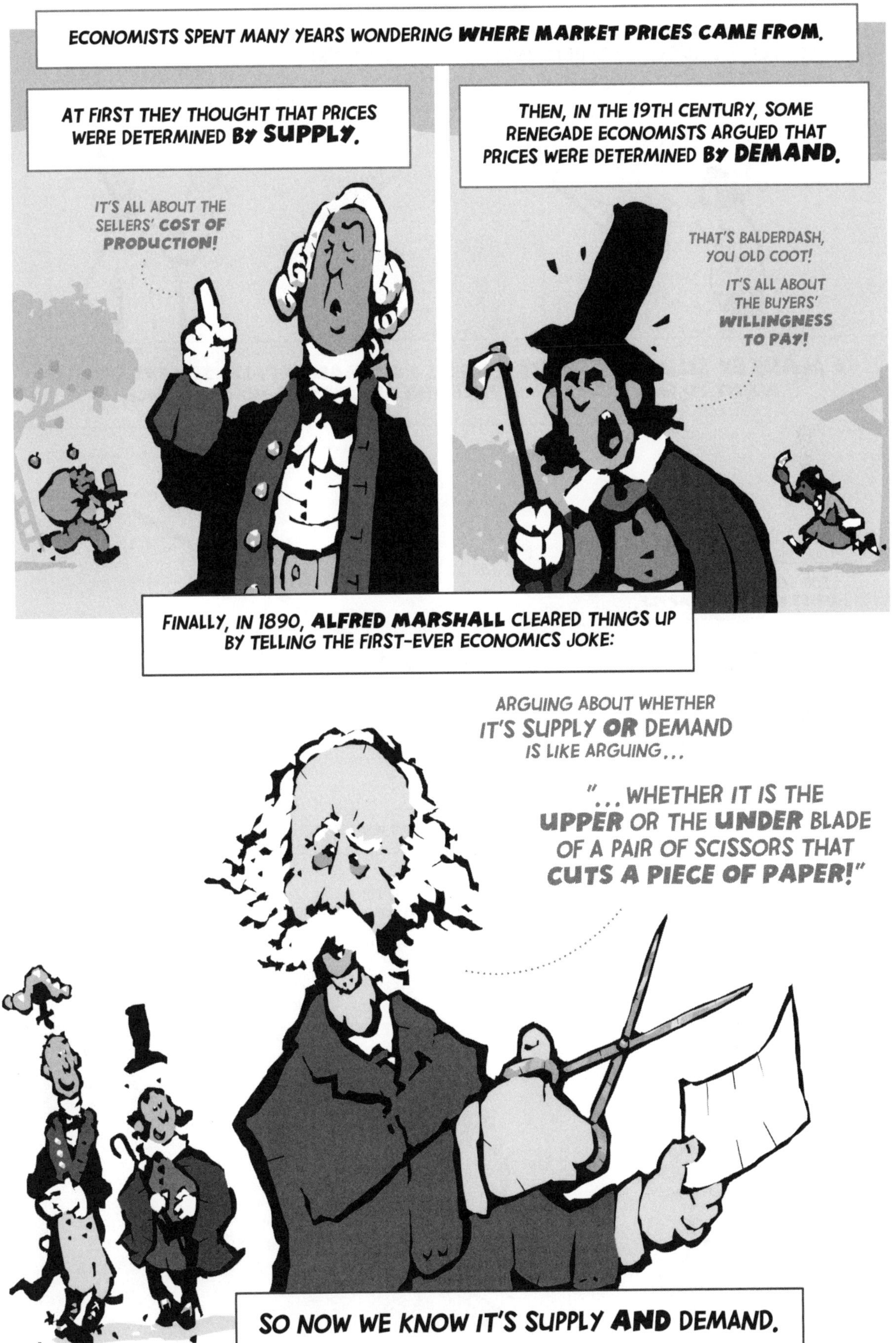
ECONOMISTS SPENT MANY YEARS WONDERING **WHERE MARKET PRICES CAME FROM.**
AT FIRST THEY THOUGHT THAT PRICES WERE DETERMINED **BY SUPPLY.**
IT'S ALL ABOUT THE SELLERS' **COST OF PRODUCTION!**
THEN, IN THE 19TH CENTURY, SOME RENEGADE ECONOMISTS ARGUED THAT PRICES WERE DETERMINED **BY DEMAND.**
THAT'S BALDERDASH, YOU OLD COOT!
IT'S ALL ABOUT THE BUYERS' **WILLINGNESS TO PAY!**
FINALLY, IN 1890, **ALFRED MARSHALL** CLEARED THINGS UP BY TELLING THE FIRST-EVER ECONOMICS JOKE:
ARGUING ABOUT WHETHER IT'S SUPPLY **OR** DEMAND IS LIKE ARGUING...
"...WHETHER IT IS THE **UPPER** OR THE **UNDER** BLADE OF A PAIR OF SCISSORS THAT **CUTS A PIECE OF PAPER!**"
SO NOW WE KNOW IT'S SUPPLY **AND** DEMAND.

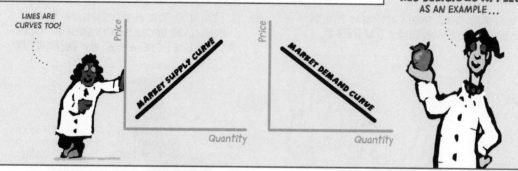

THE THEORY OF SUPPLY AND DEMAND SAYS THAT PRICES IN COMPETITIVE MARKETS ARE DETERMINED BY TWO CURVES:

LINES ARE CURVES TOO!

Price

MARKET SUPPLY CURVE

Quantity

Price

MARKET DEMAND CURVE

Quantity

LET'S USE THE MARKET FOR RED DELICIOUS APPLES AS AN EXAMPLE...

A MARKET SUPPLY CURVE DESCRIBES HOW MANY APPLES SELLERS WOULD WANT TO SELL IF THE MARKET PRICE WERE $2, OR $3, OR ANY OTHER PRICE.

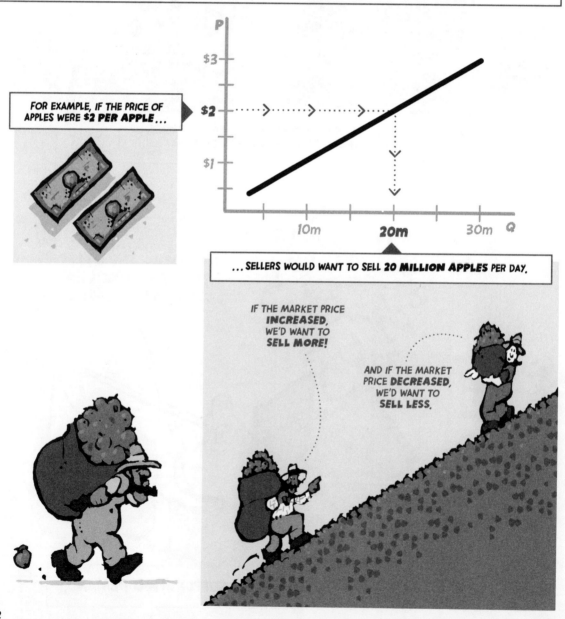

FOR EXAMPLE, IF THE PRICE OF APPLES WERE $2 PER APPLE...

P

$3

$2

$1

10m   20m   30m   Q

... SELLERS WOULD WANT TO SELL 20 MILLION APPLES PER DAY.

IF THE MARKET PRICE INCREASED, WE'D WANT TO SELL MORE!

AND IF THE MARKET PRICE DECREASED, WE'D WANT TO SELL LESS.

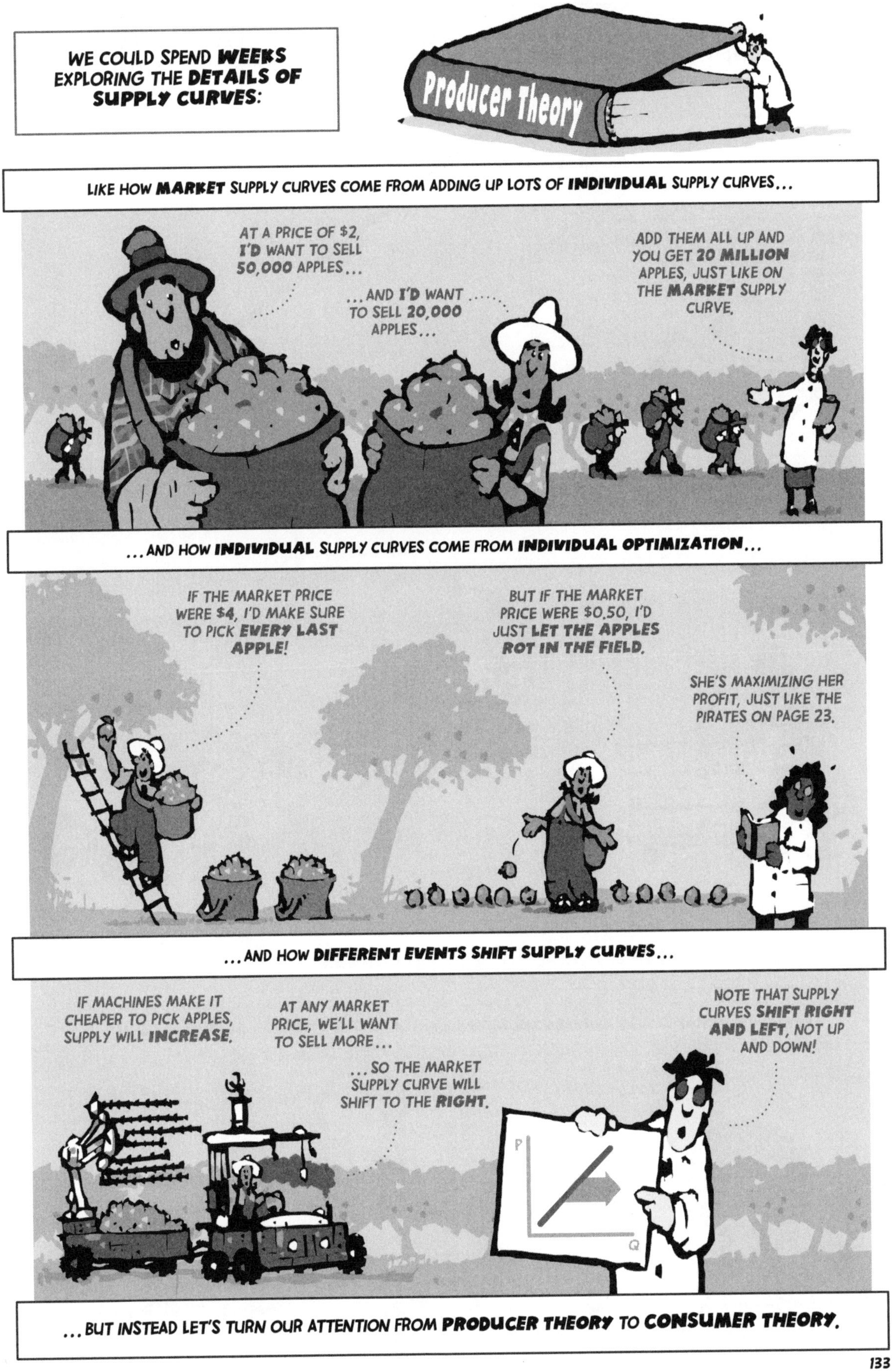
WE COULD SPEND WEEKS EXPLORING THE DETAILS OF SUPPLY CURVES:
Producer Theory
LIKE HOW MARKET SUPPLY CURVES COME FROM ADDING UP LOTS OF INDIVIDUAL SUPPLY CURVES...
AT A PRICE OF $2, I'D WANT TO SELL 50,000 APPLES...
...AND I'D WANT TO SELL 20,000 APPLES...
ADD THEM ALL UP AND YOU GET 20 MILLION APPLES, JUST LIKE ON THE MARKET SUPPLY CURVE.
...AND HOW INDIVIDUAL SUPPLY CURVES COME FROM INDIVIDUAL OPTIMIZATION...
IF THE MARKET PRICE WERE $4, I'D MAKE SURE TO PICK EVERY LAST APPLE!
BUT IF THE MARKET PRICE WERE $0.50, I'D JUST LET THE APPLES ROT IN THE FIELD.
SHE'S MAXIMIZING HER PROFIT, JUST LIKE THE PIRATES ON PAGE 23.
...AND HOW DIFFERENT EVENTS SHIFT SUPPLY CURVES...
IF MACHINES MAKE IT CHEAPER TO PICK APPLES, SUPPLY WILL INCREASE.
AT ANY MARKET PRICE, WE'LL WANT TO SELL MORE...
...SO THE MARKET SUPPLY CURVE WILL SHIFT TO THE RIGHT.
NOTE THAT SUPPLY CURVES SHIFT RIGHT AND LEFT, NOT UP AND DOWN!
P
Q
...BUT INSTEAD LET'S TURN OUR ATTENTION FROM PRODUCER THEORY TO CONSUMER THEORY.

A **MARKET DEMAND CURVE** DESCRIBES **HOW MANY APPLES BUYERS WOULD WANT TO BUY** IF THE MARKET PRICE WERE $2, OR $3, OR ANY OTHER PRICE.

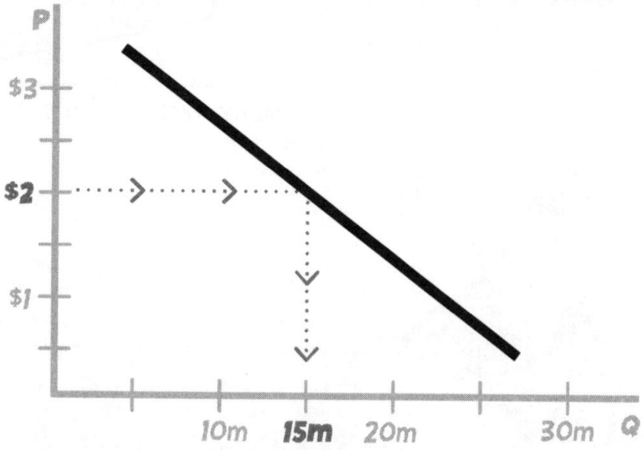
P
$3
$2
$1
10m
15m
20m
30m
Q

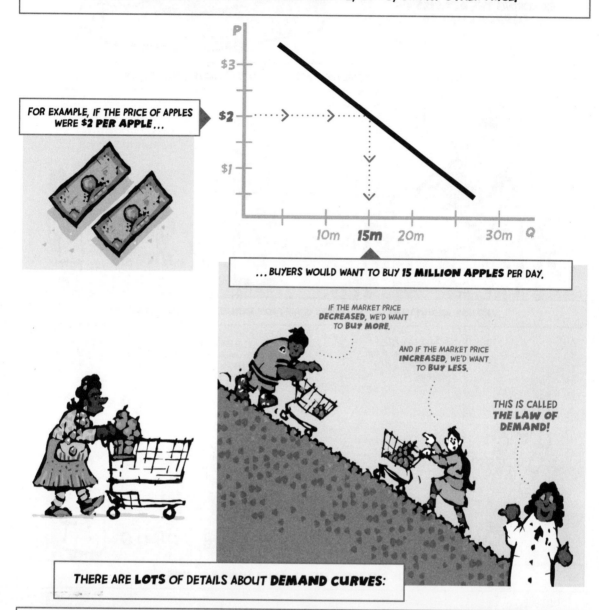

FOR EXAMPLE, IF THE PRICE OF APPLES WERE **$2 PER APPLE**...

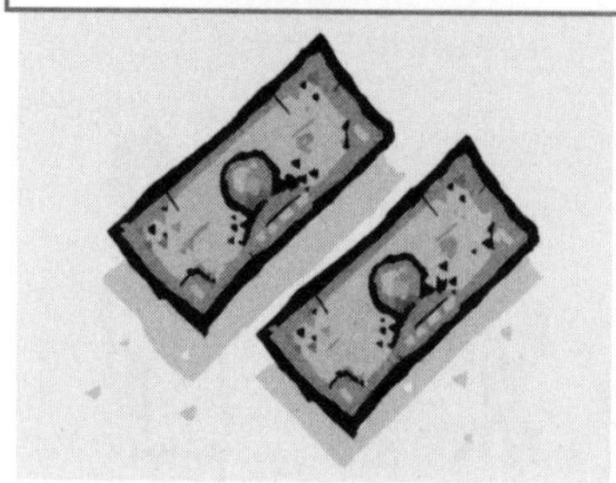

... BUYERS WOULD WANT TO BUY **15 MILLION APPLES** PER DAY.

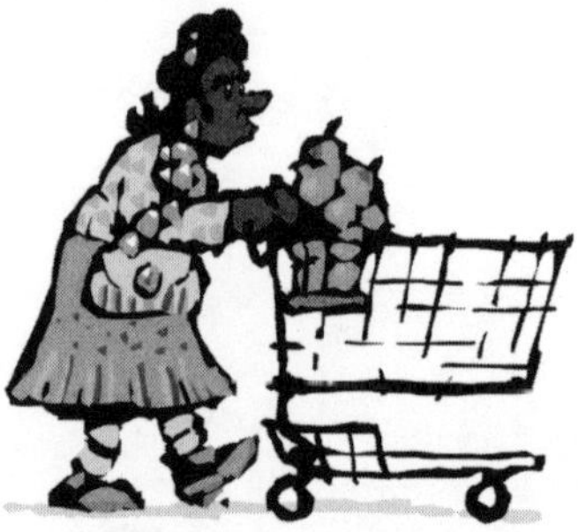

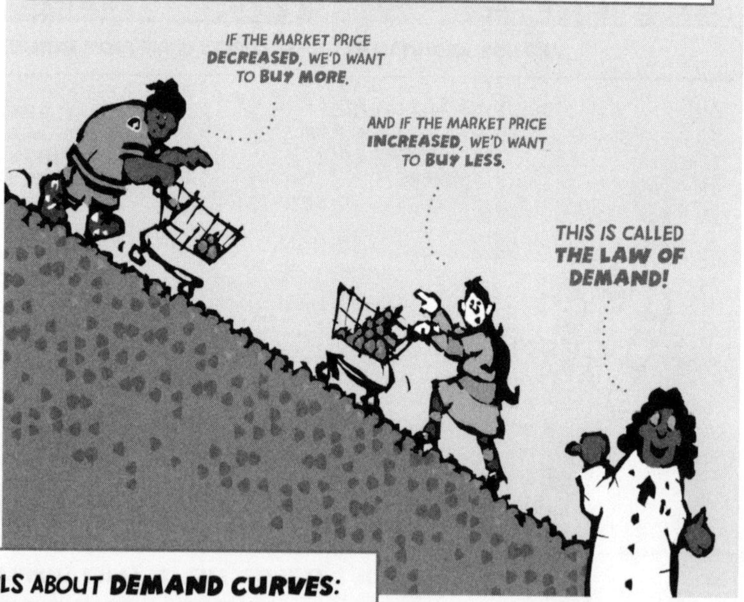
IF THE MARKET PRICE **DECREASED**, WE'D WANT TO **BUY MORE**.
AND IF THE MARKET PRICE **INCREASED**, WE'D WANT TO **BUY LESS**.
THIS IS CALLED **THE LAW OF DEMAND!**

THERE ARE **LOTS** OF DETAILS ABOUT **DEMAND CURVES**:

LIKE HOW **MARKET** DEMAND CURVES COME FROM ADDING UP LOTS OF **INDIVIDUAL** DEMAND CURVES...

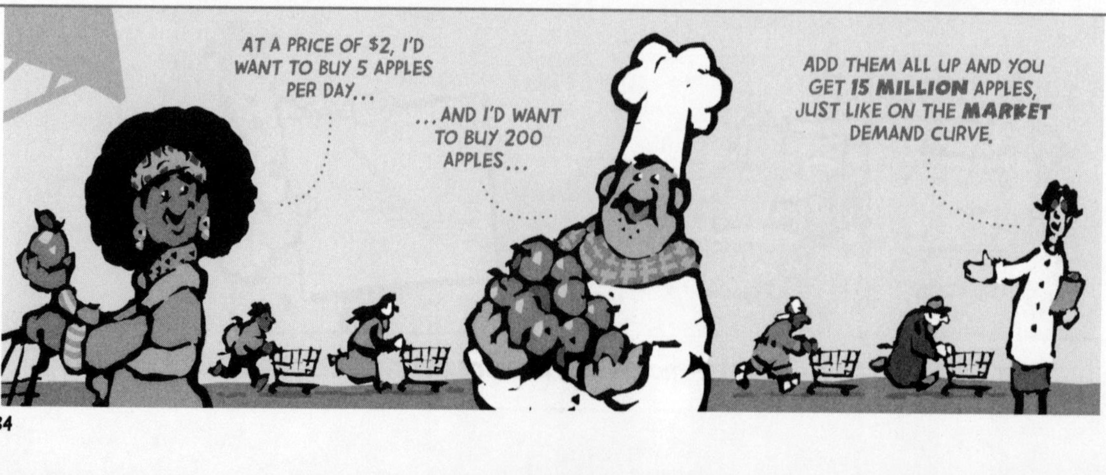
AT A PRICE OF $2, I'D WANT TO BUY 5 APPLES PER DAY...
...AND I'D WANT TO BUY 200 APPLES...
ADD THEM ALL UP AND YOU GET **15 MILLION** APPLES, JUST LIKE ON THE **MARKET** DEMAND CURVE.

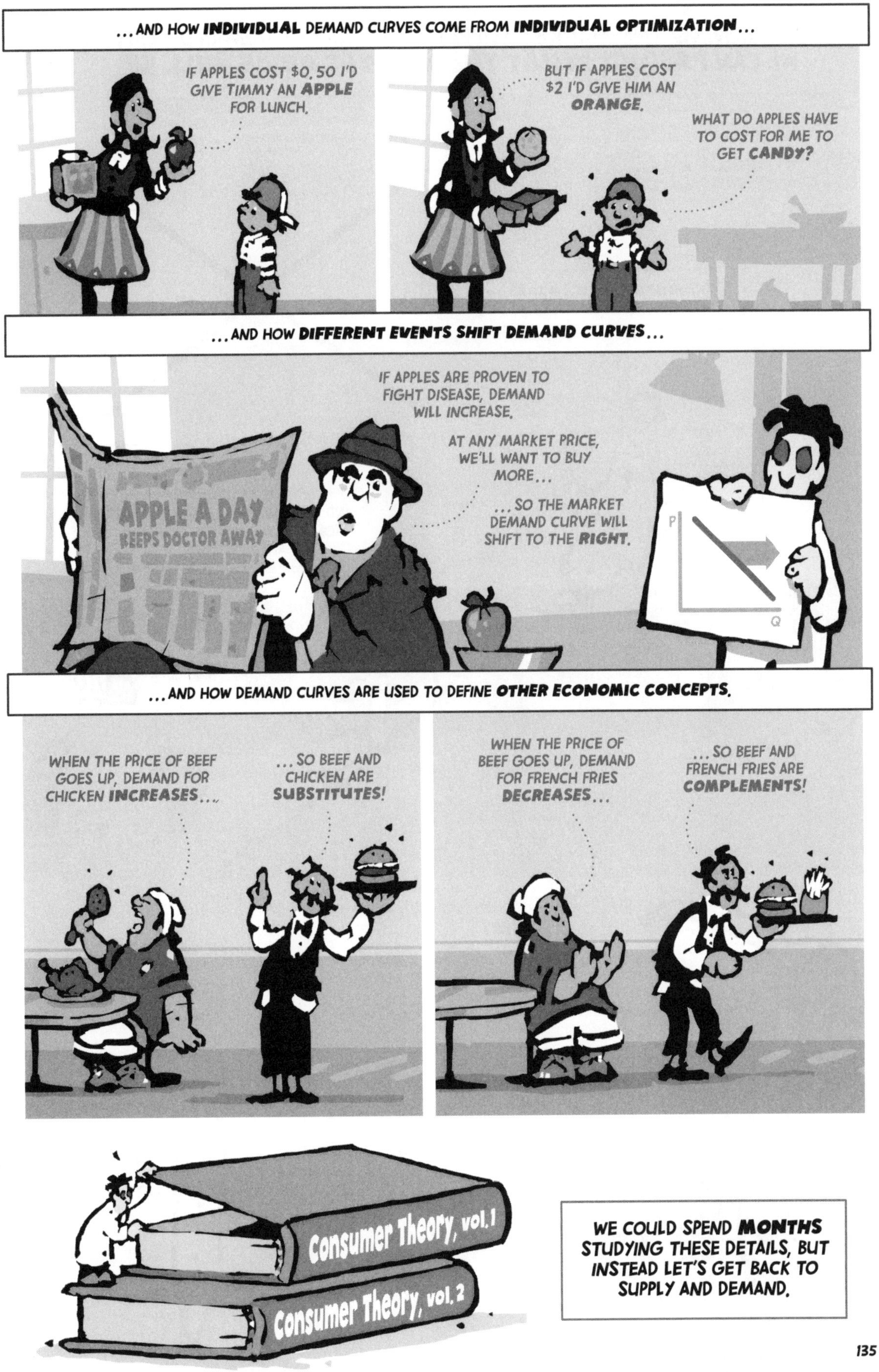

...AND HOW **INDIVIDUAL** DEMAND CURVES COME FROM **INDIVIDUAL OPTIMIZATION**...
IF APPLES COST $0.50 I'D GIVE TIMMY AN **APPLE** FOR LUNCH.
BUT IF APPLES COST $2 I'D GIVE HIM AN **ORANGE**.
WHAT DO APPLES HAVE TO COST FOR ME TO GET **CANDY?**
...AND HOW **DIFFERENT EVENTS SHIFT DEMAND CURVES**...
APPLE A DAY
KEEPS DOCTOR AWAY
IF APPLES ARE PROVEN TO FIGHT DISEASE, DEMAND WILL INCREASE.
AT ANY MARKET PRICE, WE'LL WANT TO BUY MORE...
...SO THE MARKET DEMAND CURVE WILL SHIFT TO THE **RIGHT**.
P
Q
...AND HOW DEMAND CURVES ARE USED TO DEFINE **OTHER ECONOMIC CONCEPTS**.
WHEN THE PRICE OF BEEF GOES UP, DEMAND FOR CHICKEN **INCREASES**...
...SO BEEF AND CHICKEN ARE **SUBSTITUTES!**
WHEN THE PRICE OF BEEF GOES UP, DEMAND FOR FRENCH FRIES **DECREASES**...
...SO BEEF AND FRENCH FRIES ARE **COMPLEMENTS!**
Consumer Theory, vol. 1
Consumer Theory, vol. 2
WE COULD SPEND **MONTHS** STUDYING THESE DETAILS, BUT INSTEAD LET'S GET BACK TO SUPPLY AND DEMAND.

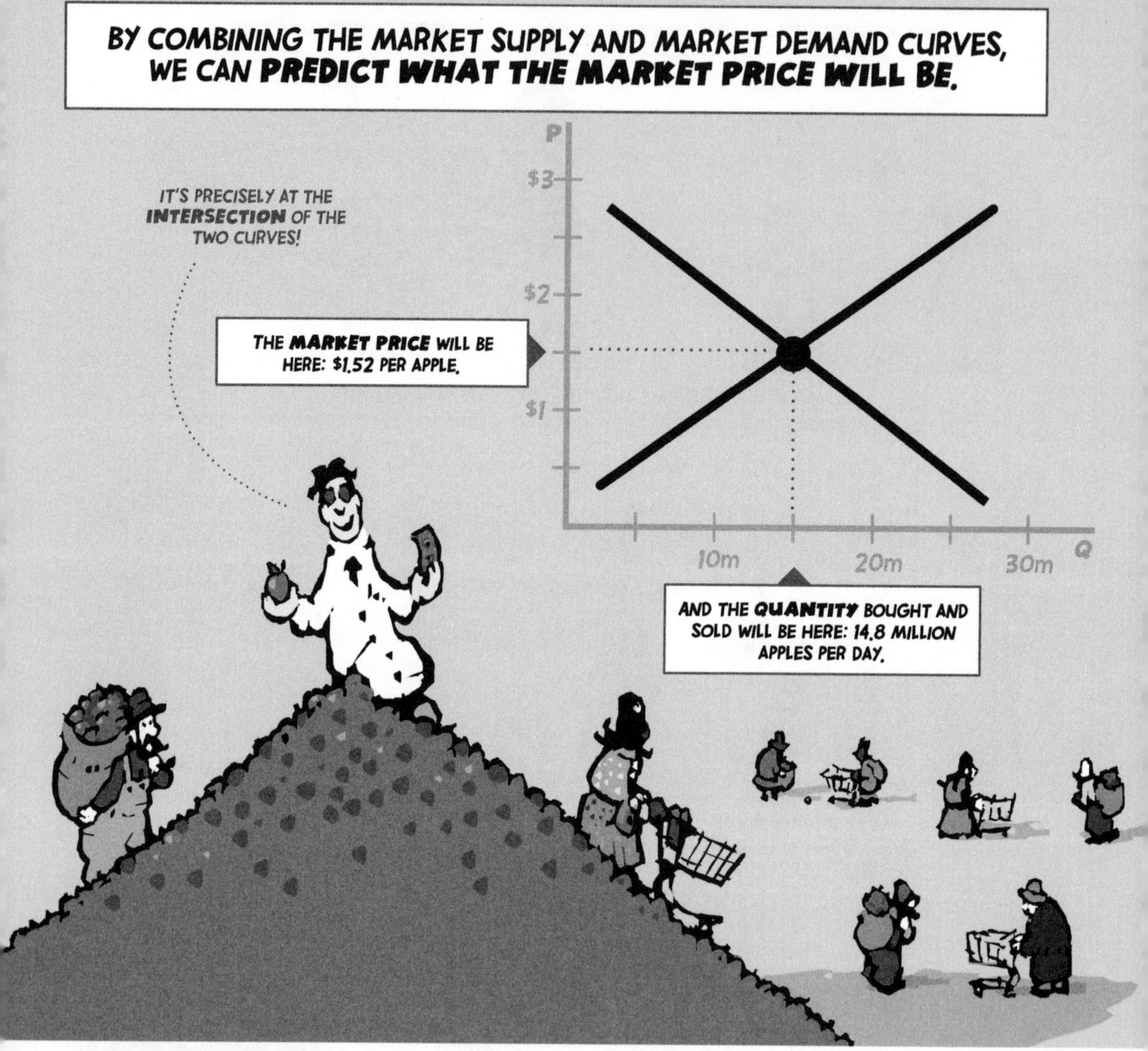
BY COMBINING THE MARKET SUPPLY AND MARKET DEMAND CURVES, WE CAN **PREDICT WHAT THE MARKET PRICE WILL BE.**
IT'S PRECISELY AT THE **INTERSECTION** OF THE TWO CURVES!
P
$3
$2
$1
Q
10m
20m
30m
THE **MARKET PRICE** WILL BE HERE: $1.52 PER APPLE.
AND THE **QUANTITY** BOUGHT AND SOLD WILL BE HERE: 14.8 MILLION APPLES PER DAY.

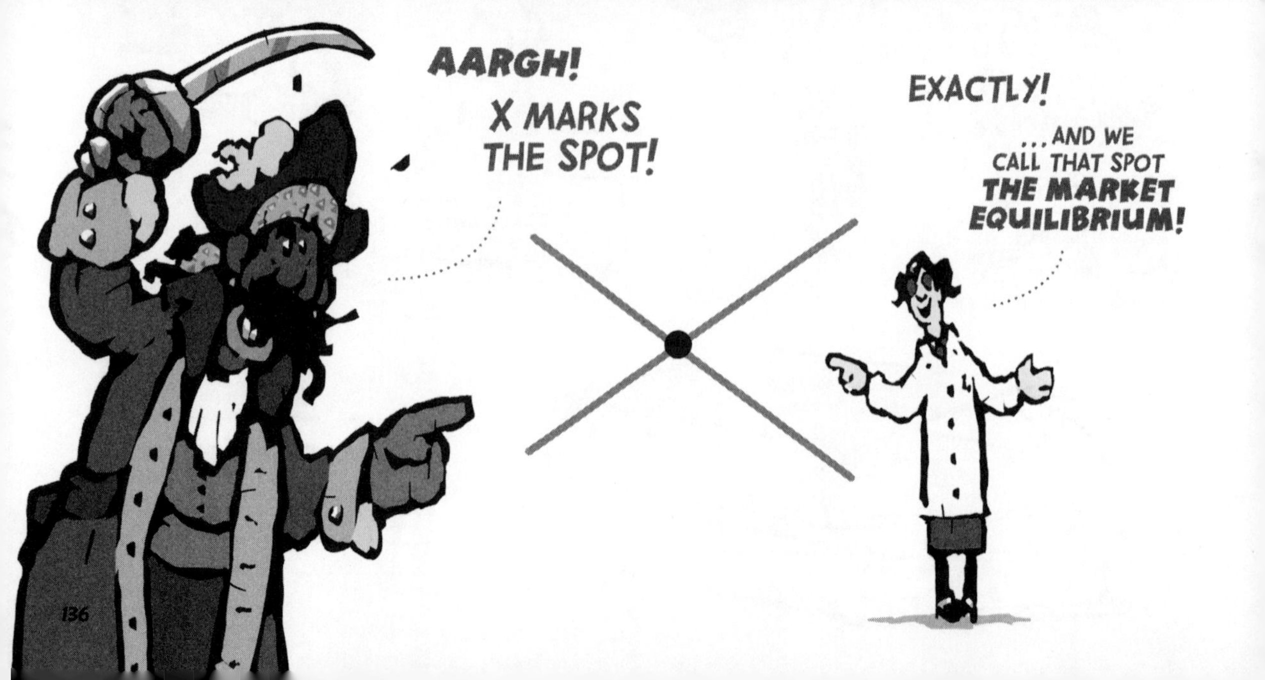
AARGH!
X MARKS THE SPOT!
EXACTLY!
. . . AND WE CALL THAT SPOT **THE MARKET EQUILIBRIUM!**

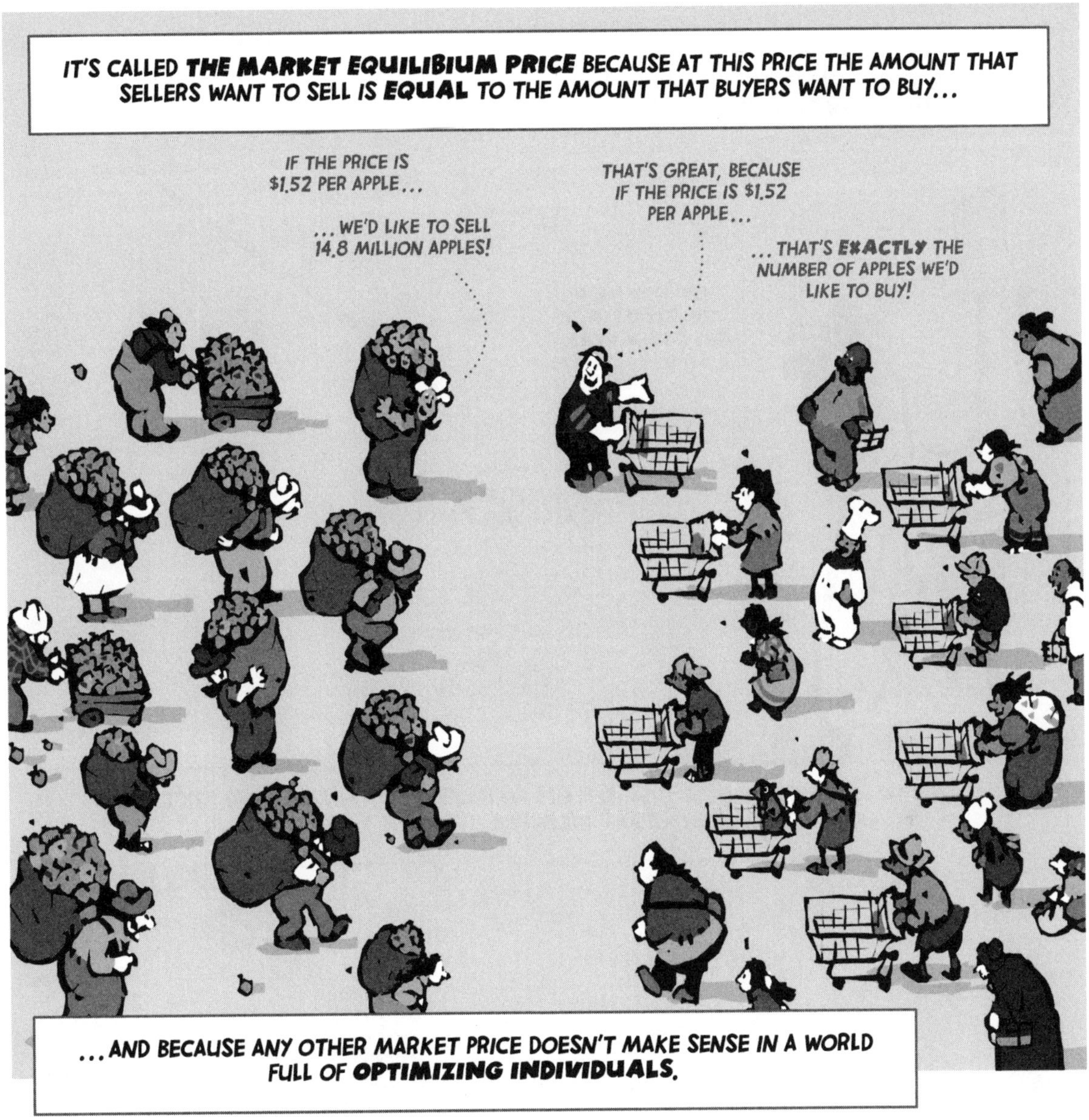
IT'S CALLED **THE MARKET EQUILIBIUM PRICE** BECAUSE AT THIS PRICE THE AMOUNT THAT SELLERS WANT TO SELL IS **EQUAL** TO THE AMOUNT THAT BUYERS WANT TO BUY...
IF THE PRICE IS $1.52 PER APPLE...
...WE'D LIKE TO SELL 14.8 MILLION APPLES!
THAT'S GREAT, BECAUSE IF THE PRICE IS $1.52 PER APPLE...
...THAT'S **EXACTLY** THE NUMBER OF APPLES WE'D LIKE TO BUY!
...AND BECAUSE ANY OTHER MARKET PRICE DOESN'T MAKE SENSE IN A WORLD FULL OF **OPTIMIZING INDIVIDUALS.**

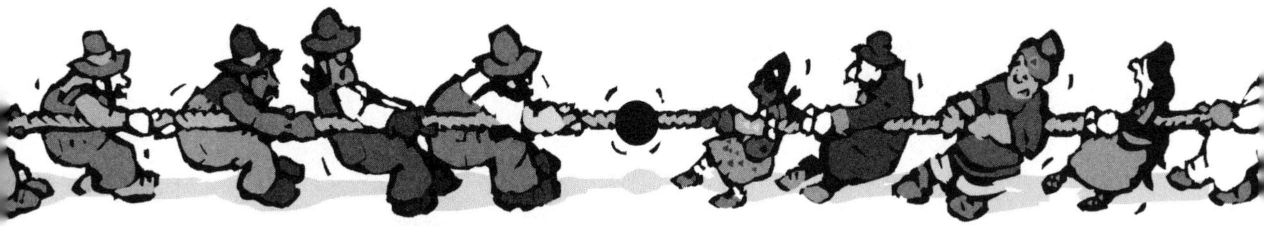

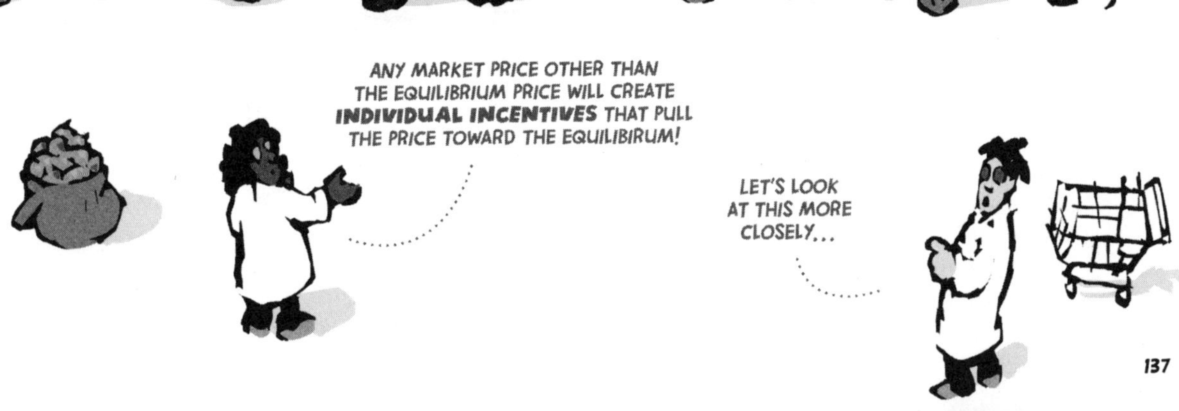
ANY MARKET PRICE OTHER THAN THE EQUILIBRIUM PRICE WILL CREATE **INDIVIDUAL INCENTIVES** THAT PULL THE PRICE TOWARD THE EQUILIBIRUM!
LET'S LOOK AT THIS MORE CLOSELY...

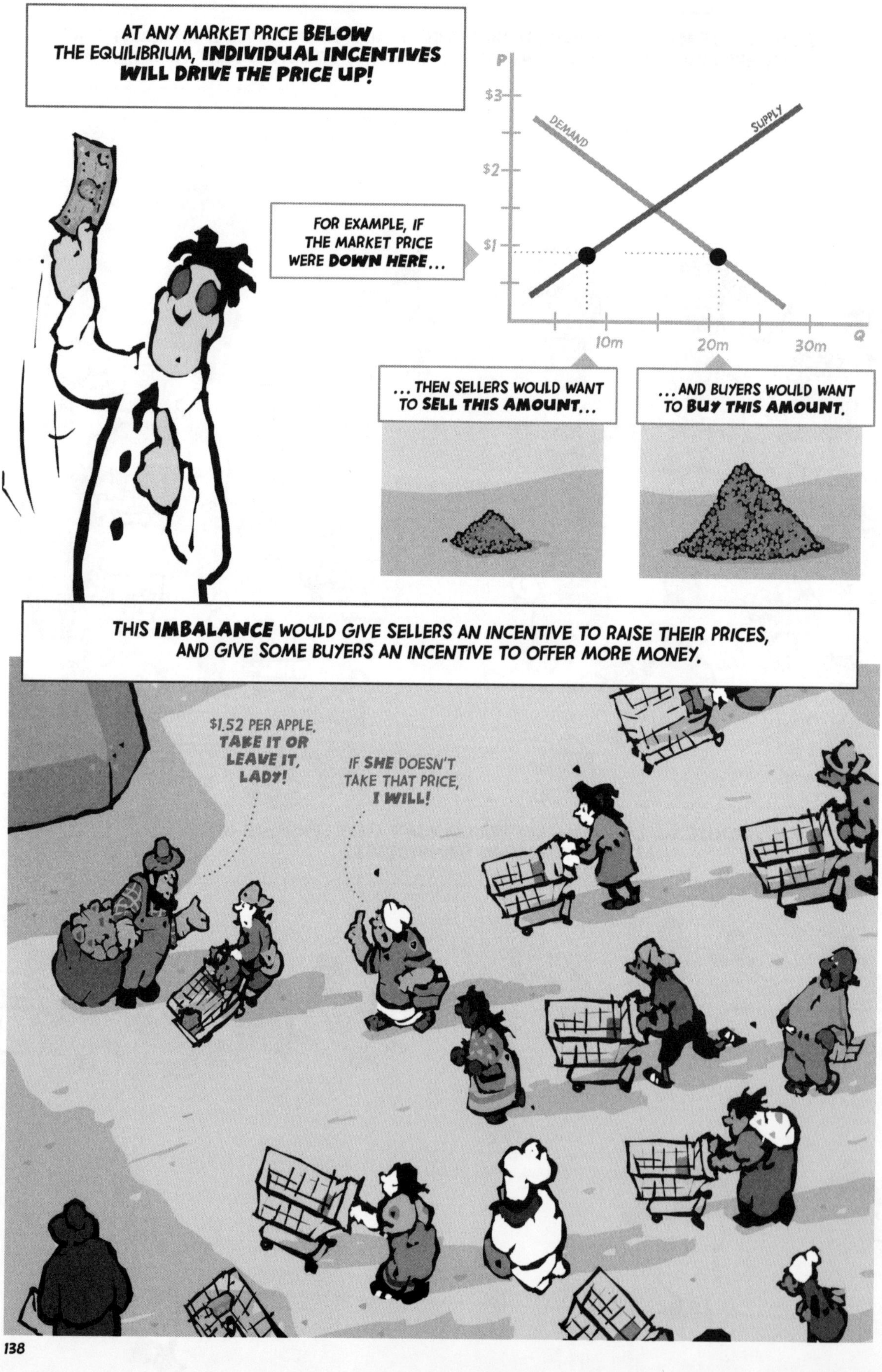

AT ANY MARKET PRICE **BELOW** THE EQUILIBRIUM, **INDIVIDUAL INCENTIVES WILL DRIVE THE PRICE UP!**
P
$3
$2
$1
DEMAND
SUPPLY
10m
20m
30m
Q
FOR EXAMPLE, IF THE MARKET PRICE WERE **DOWN HERE**...
...THEN SELLERS WOULD WANT TO **SELL THIS AMOUNT**...
...AND BUYERS WOULD WANT TO **BUY THIS AMOUNT.**
THIS **IMBALANCE** WOULD GIVE SELLERS AN INCENTIVE TO RAISE THEIR PRICES, AND GIVE SOME BUYERS AN INCENTIVE TO OFFER MORE MONEY.
$1.52 PER APPLE, **TAKE IT OR LEAVE IT, LADY!**
IF **SHE** DOESN'T TAKE THAT PRICE, **I WILL!**

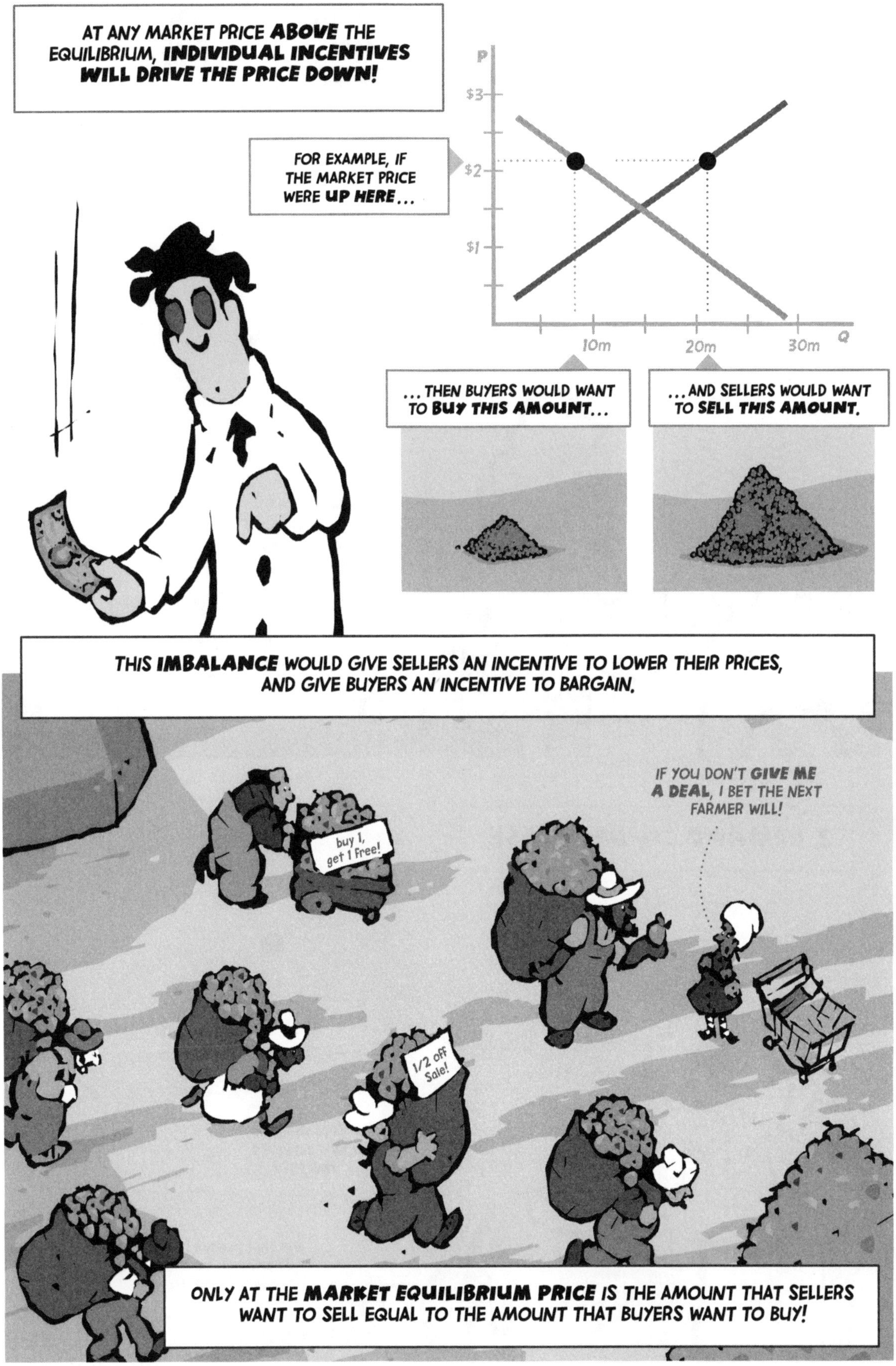

AT ANY MARKET PRICE **ABOVE** THE EQUILIBRIUM, **INDIVIDUAL INCENTIVES WILL DRIVE THE PRICE DOWN!**
FOR EXAMPLE, IF THE MARKET PRICE WERE **UP HERE**...
P
$3
$2
$1
10m
20m
30m
Q
...THEN BUYERS WOULD WANT TO **BUY THIS AMOUNT**...
...AND SELLERS WOULD WANT TO **SELL THIS AMOUNT.**
THIS **IMBALANCE** WOULD GIVE SELLERS AN INCENTIVE TO LOWER THEIR PRICES, AND GIVE BUYERS AN INCENTIVE TO BARGAIN.
buy 1, get 1 Free!
IF YOU DON'T **GIVE ME A DEAL**, I BET THE NEXT FARMER WILL!
1/2 off Sale!
ONLY AT THE **MARKET EQUILIBRIUM PRICE** IS THE AMOUNT THAT SELLERS WANT TO SELL EQUAL TO THE AMOUNT THAT BUYERS WANT TO BUY!

SINCE THE MARKET EQUILIBRIUM PRICE OCCURS AT THE INTERSECTION OF THE CURVES, ANY CHANGE IN THAT EQUILIBRIUM PRICE MUST COME FROM CHANGES IN THE CURVES!
THERE ARE FOUR BASIC SCENARIOS...
1. DEMAND CAN INCREASE.
THIS MIGHT HAPPEN IF LOTS OF BUYERS WANT TO TRY A NEW APPLE PIE RECIPE!
P
OLD DEMAND
NEW DEMAND
Q
This pushes the demand curve to the right...
...and that pushes the equilibrium price and quantity up.
P
Q
2. DEMAND CAN DECREASE.
APPLE PIE IS SO LAST YEAR...
...THIS IS THE YEAR OF THE PEAR TART!
P
NEW DEMAND
OLD DEMAND
Q
This pushes the demand curve to the left...
...and that pushes the equilibrium price and quantity down.
P
Q

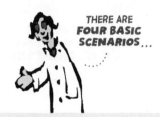

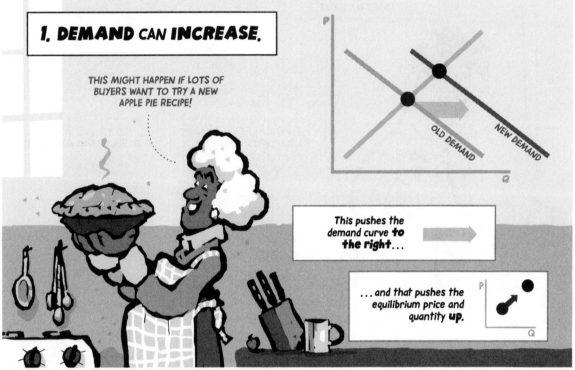

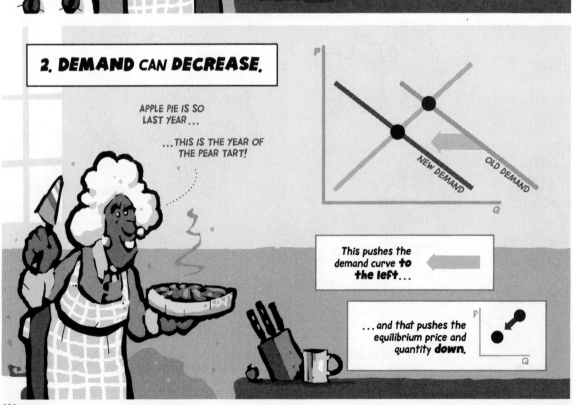

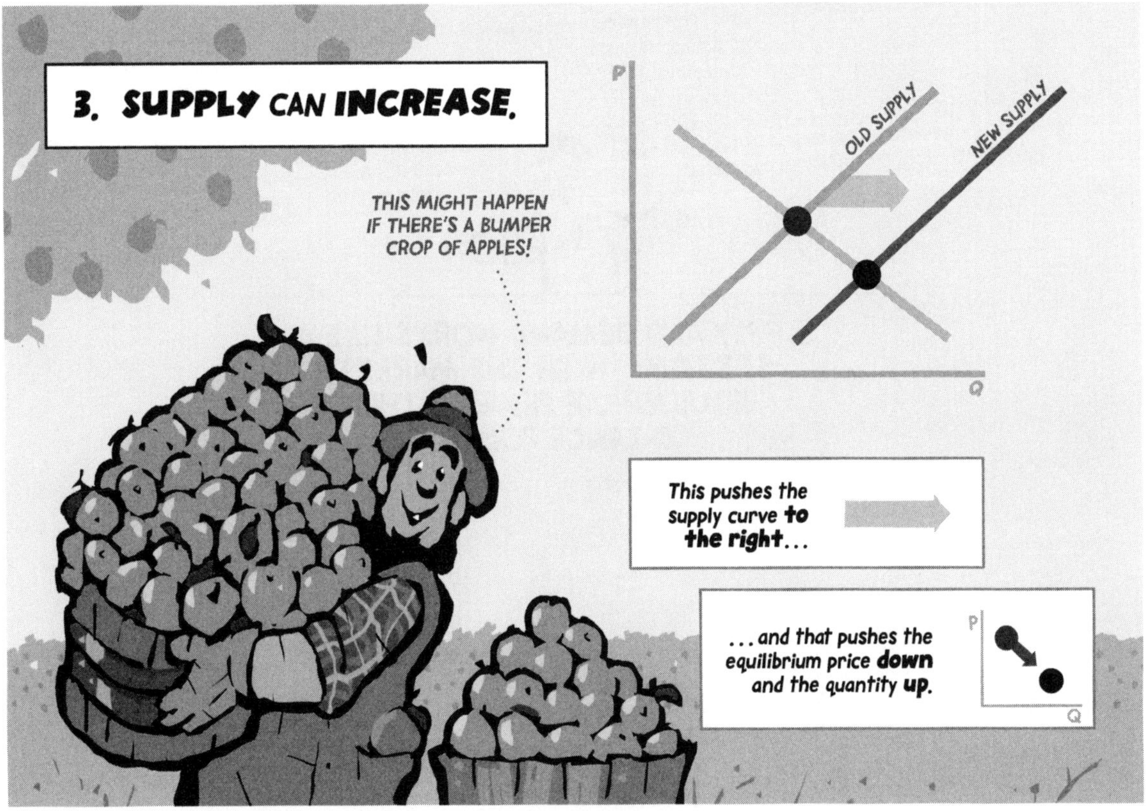
3. SUPPLY CAN INCREASE.
THIS MIGHT HAPPEN IF THERE'S A BUMPER CROP OF APPLES!
P
OLD SUPPLY
NEW SUPPLY
Q
This pushes the supply curve to the right...
...and that pushes the equilibrium price down and the quantity up.
P
Q

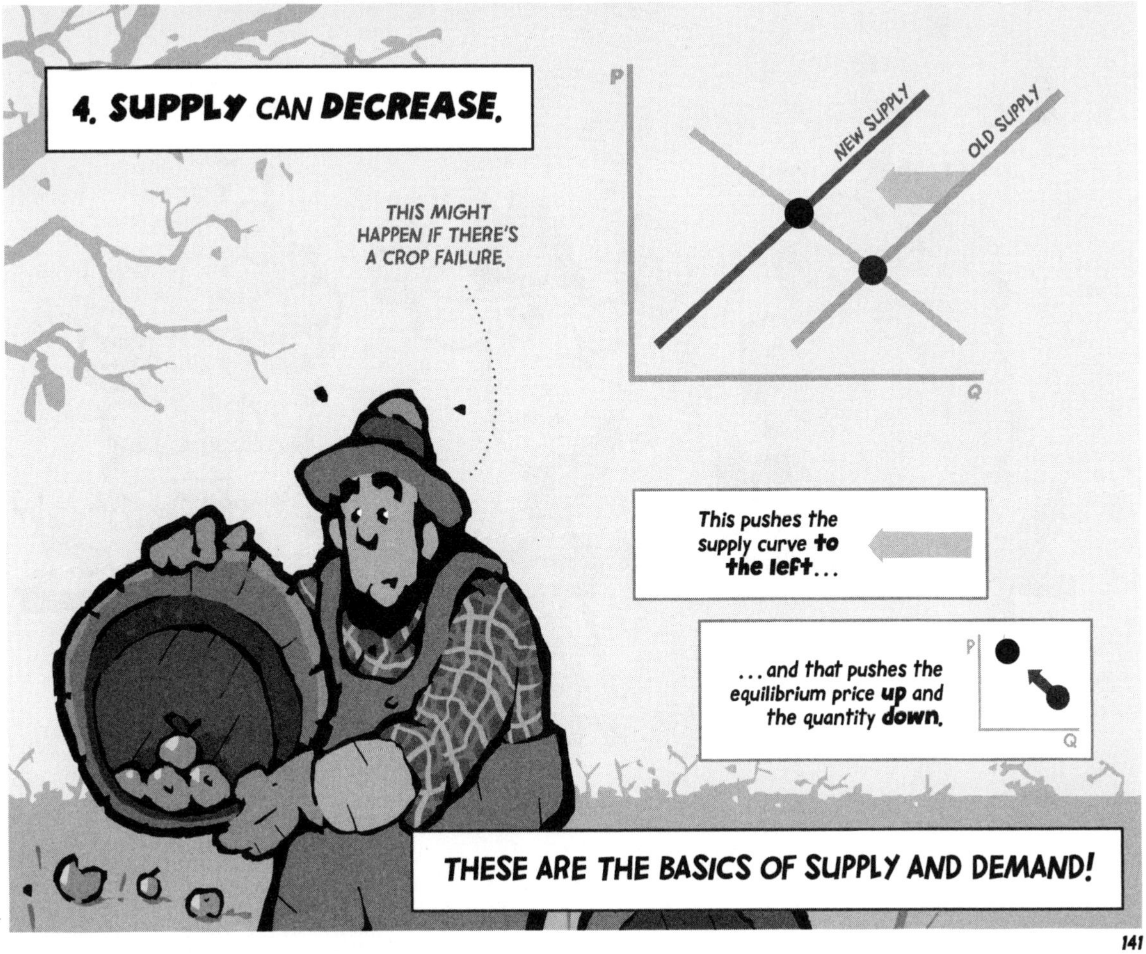
4. SUPPLY CAN DECREASE.
THIS MIGHT HAPPEN IF THERE'S A CROP FAILURE.
P
NEW SUPPLY
OLD SUPPLY
Q
This pushes the supply curve to the left...
...and that pushes the equilibrium price up and the quantity down.
P
Q
THESE ARE THE BASICS OF SUPPLY AND DEMAND!

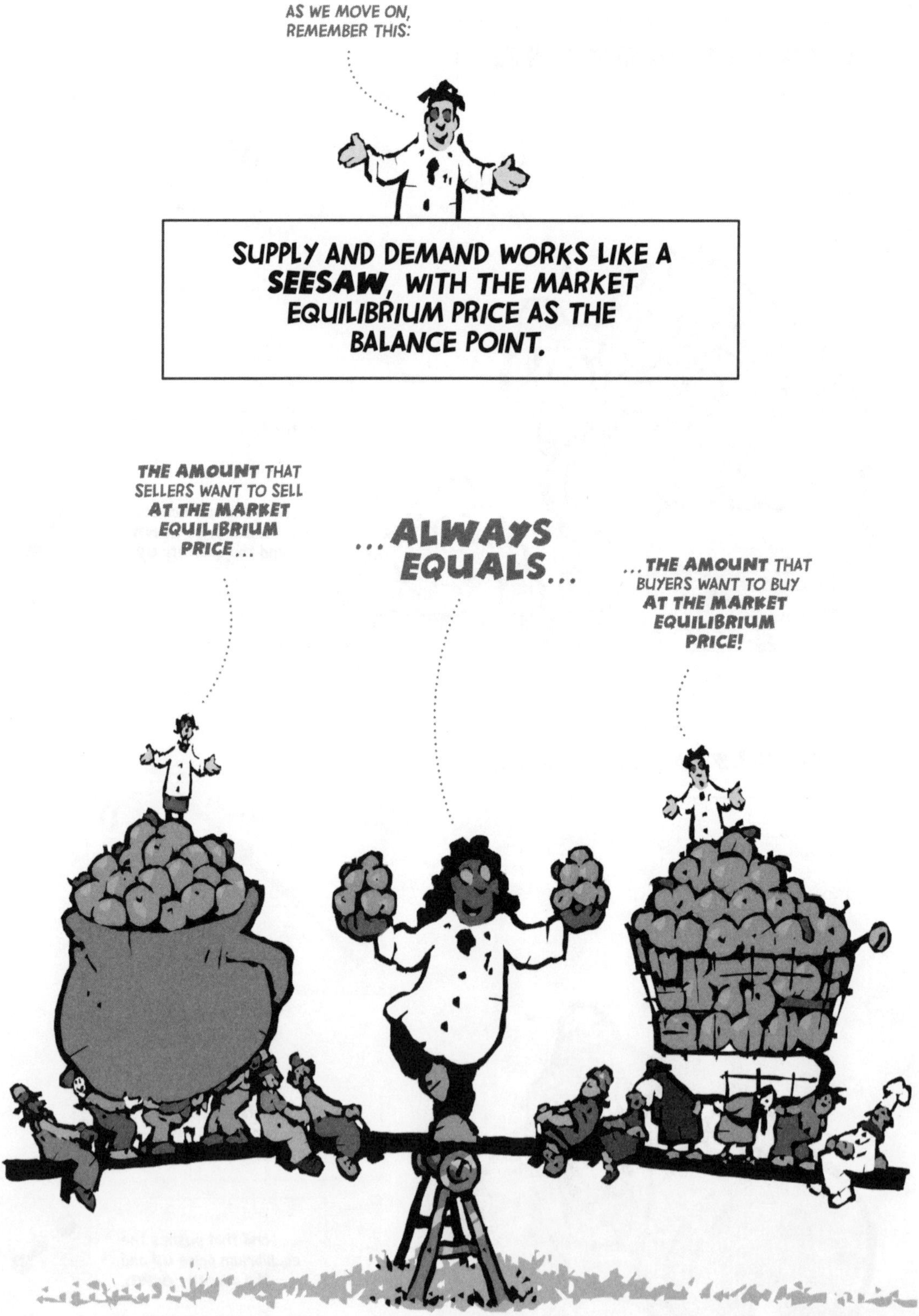
AS WE MOVE ON, REMEMBER THIS:
SUPPLY AND DEMAND WORKS LIKE A SEESAW, WITH THE MARKET EQUILIBRIUM PRICE AS THE BALANCE POINT.
THE AMOUNT THAT SELLERS WANT TO SELL AT THE MARKET EQUILIBRIUM PRICE...
...ALWAYS EQUALS...
...THE AMOUNT THAT BUYERS WANT TO BUY AT THE MARKET EQUILIBRIUM PRICE!

CHAPTER 12
TAXES

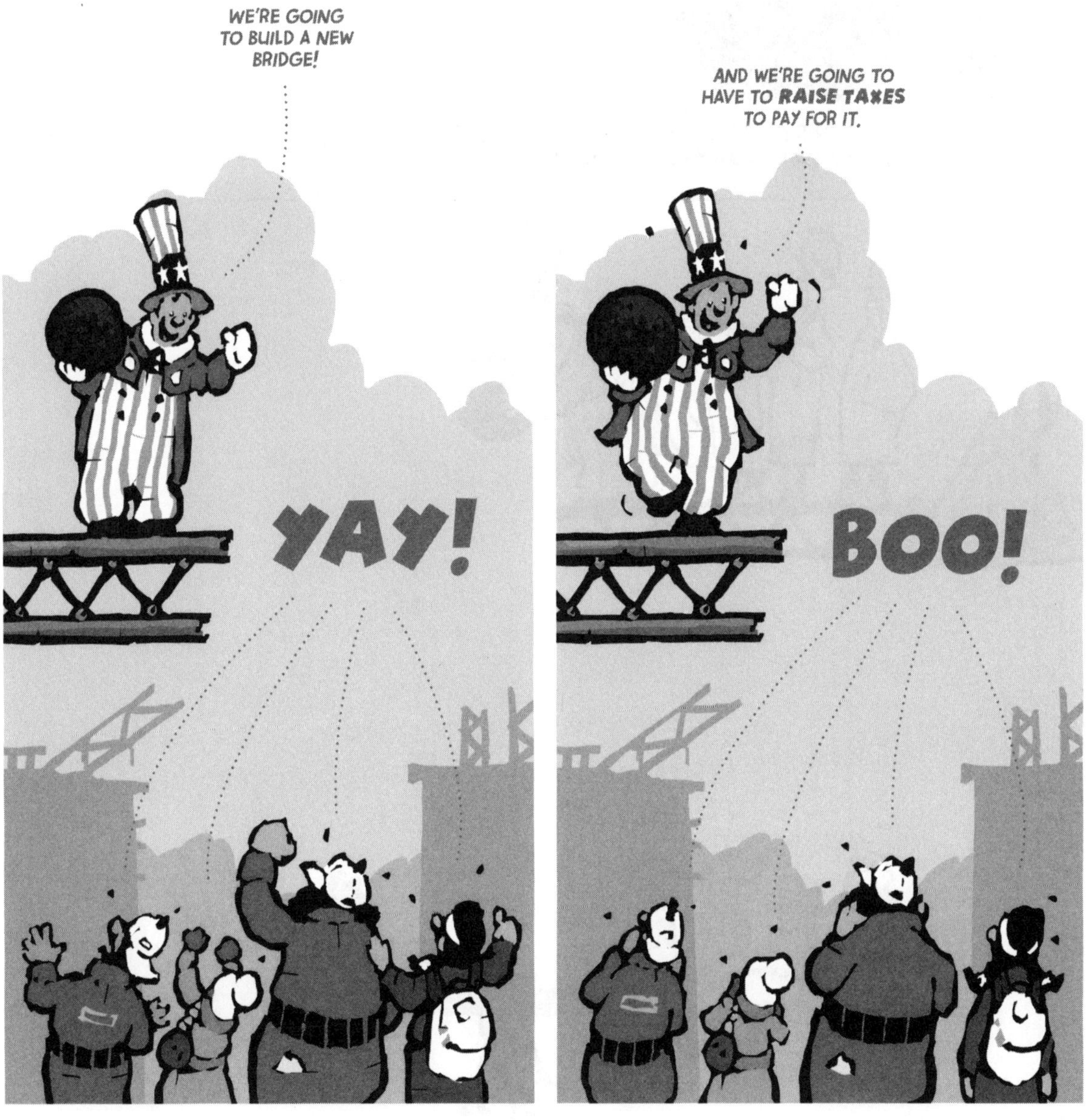
WE'RE GOING TO BUILD A NEW BRIDGE!
YAY!
AND WE'RE GOING TO HAVE TO **RAISE TAXES** TO PAY FOR IT.
BOO!

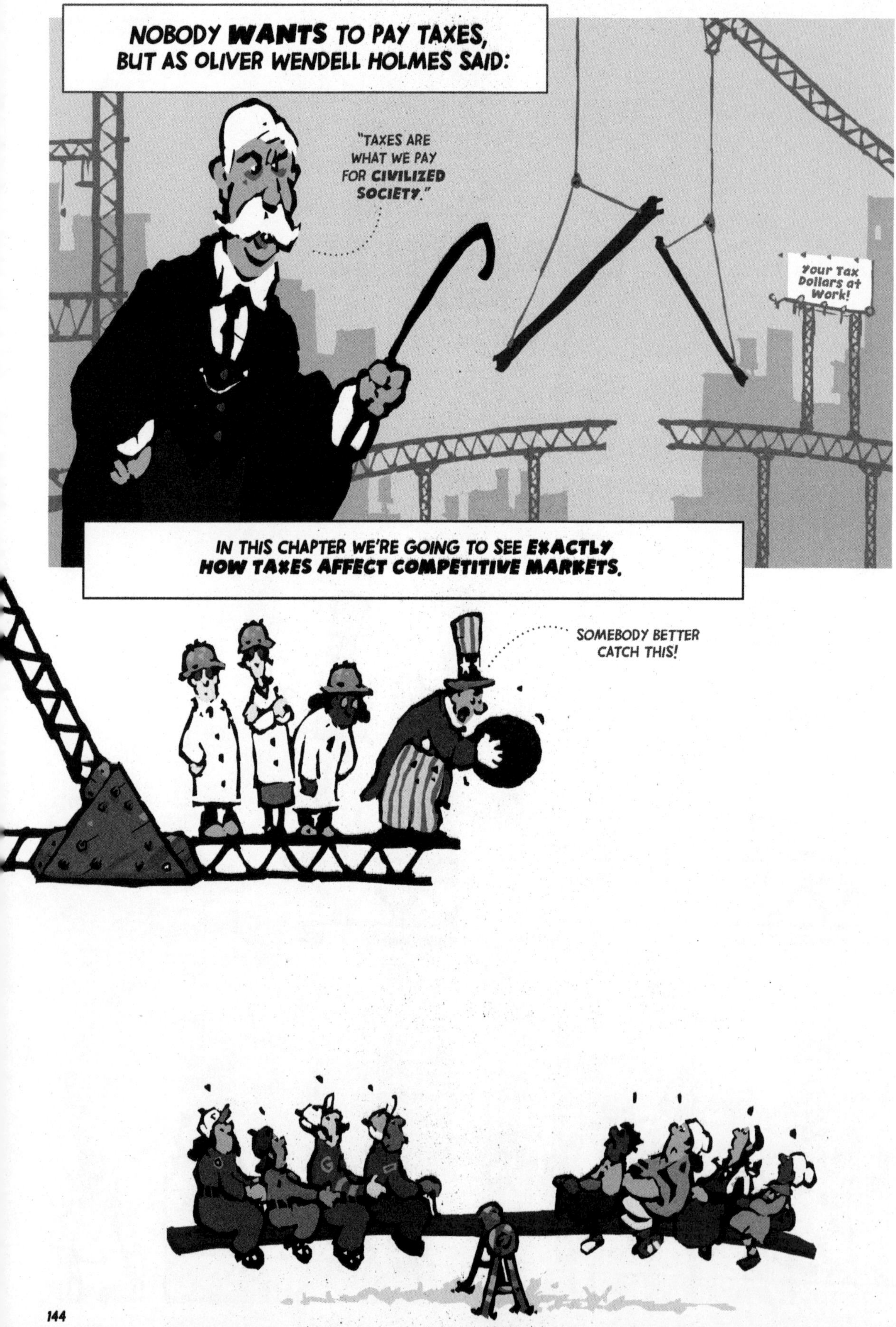
NOBODY **WANTS** TO PAY TAXES, BUT AS OLIVER WENDELL HOLMES SAID:
"TAXES ARE WHAT WE PAY FOR **CIVILIZED SOCIETY.**"
Your Tax Dollars at Work!
IN THIS CHAPTER WE'RE GOING TO SEE **EXACTLY HOW TAXES AFFECT COMPETITIVE MARKETS.**
SOMEBODY BETTER CATCH THIS!

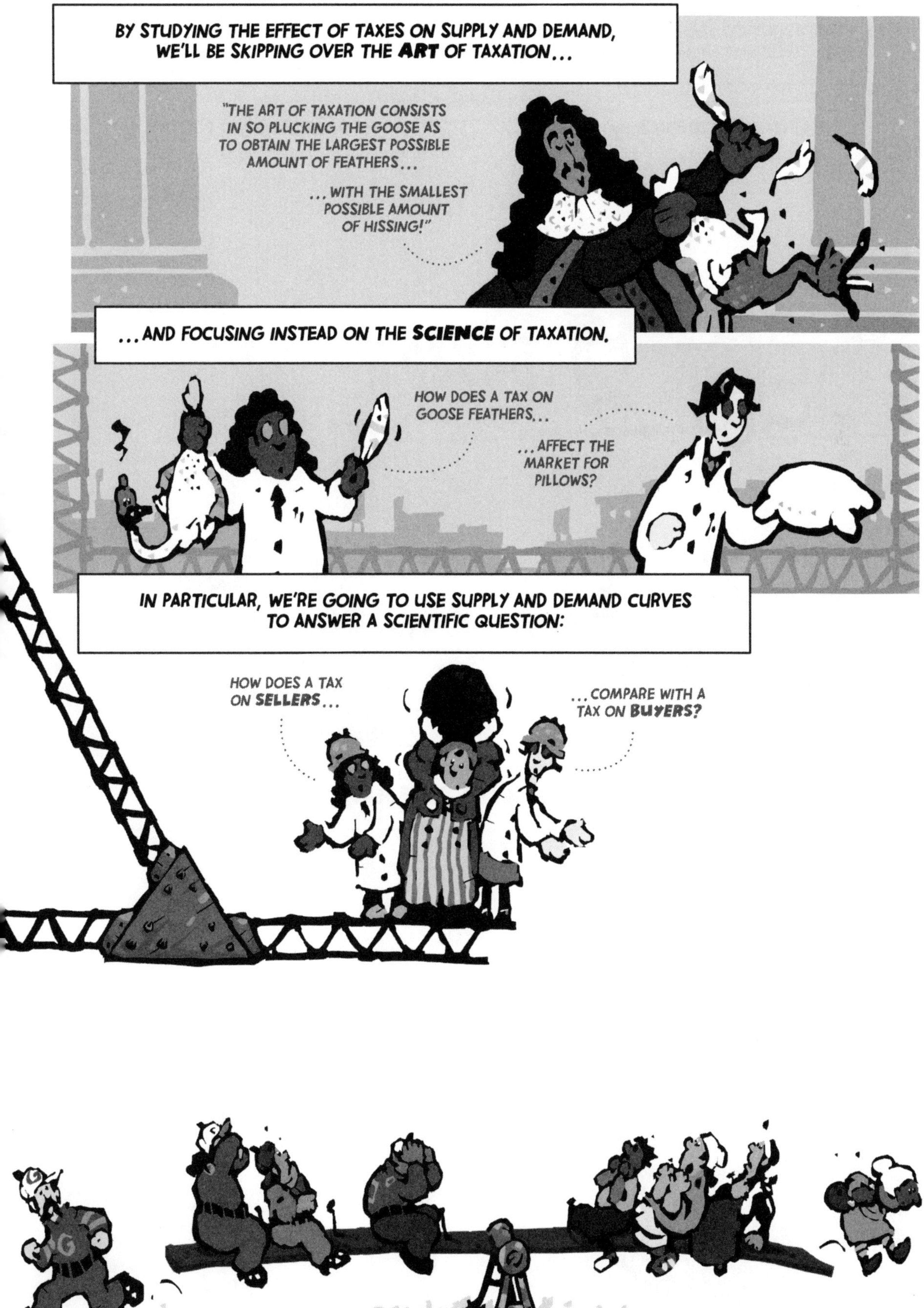
BY STUDYING THE EFFECT OF TAXES ON SUPPLY AND DEMAND, WE'LL BE SKIPPING OVER THE ART OF TAXATION...
"THE ART OF TAXATION CONSISTS IN SO PLUCKING THE GOOSE AS TO OBTAIN THE LARGEST POSSIBLE AMOUNT OF FEATHERS...
...WITH THE SMALLEST POSSIBLE AMOUNT OF HISSING!"
...AND FOCUSING INSTEAD ON THE SCIENCE OF TAXATION.
HOW DOES A TAX ON GOOSE FEATHERS...
...AFFECT THE MARKET FOR PILLOWS?
IN PARTICULAR, WE'RE GOING TO USE SUPPLY AND DEMAND CURVES TO ANSWER A SCIENTIFIC QUESTION:
HOW DOES A TAX ON SELLERS...
...COMPARE WITH A TAX ON BUYERS?

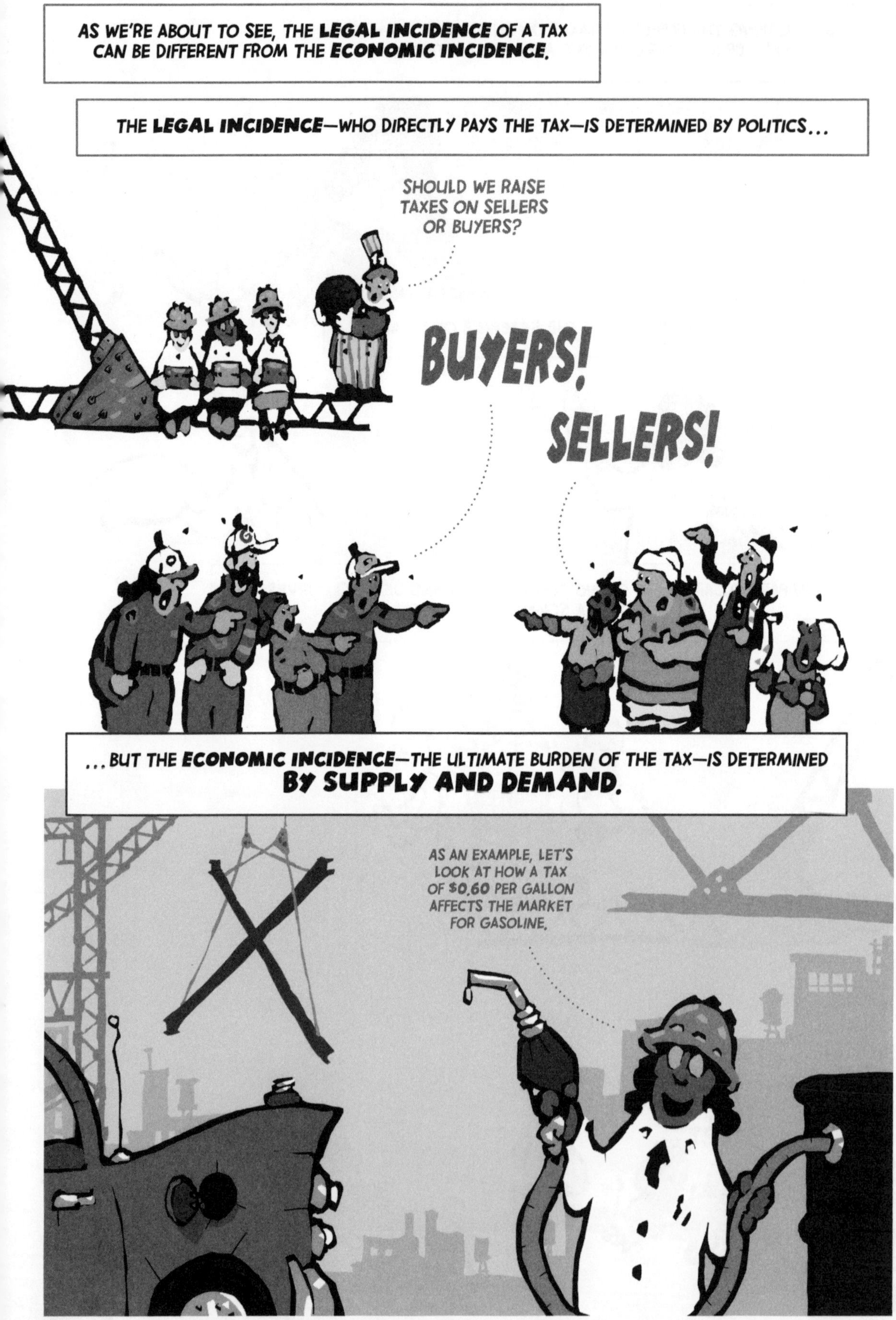
AS WE'RE ABOUT TO SEE, THE LEGAL INCIDENCE OF A TAX CAN BE DIFFERENT FROM THE ECONOMIC INCIDENCE.
THE LEGAL INCIDENCE—WHO DIRECTLY PAYS THE TAX—IS DETERMINED BY POLITICS...
SHOULD WE RAISE TAXES ON SELLERS OR BUYERS?
BUYERS!
SELLERS!
...BUT THE ECONOMIC INCIDENCE—THE ULTIMATE BURDEN OF THE TAX—IS DETERMINED BY SUPPLY AND DEMAND.
AS AN EXAMPLE, LET'S LOOK AT HOW A TAX OF $0.60 PER GALLON AFFECTS THE MARKET FOR GASOLINE.

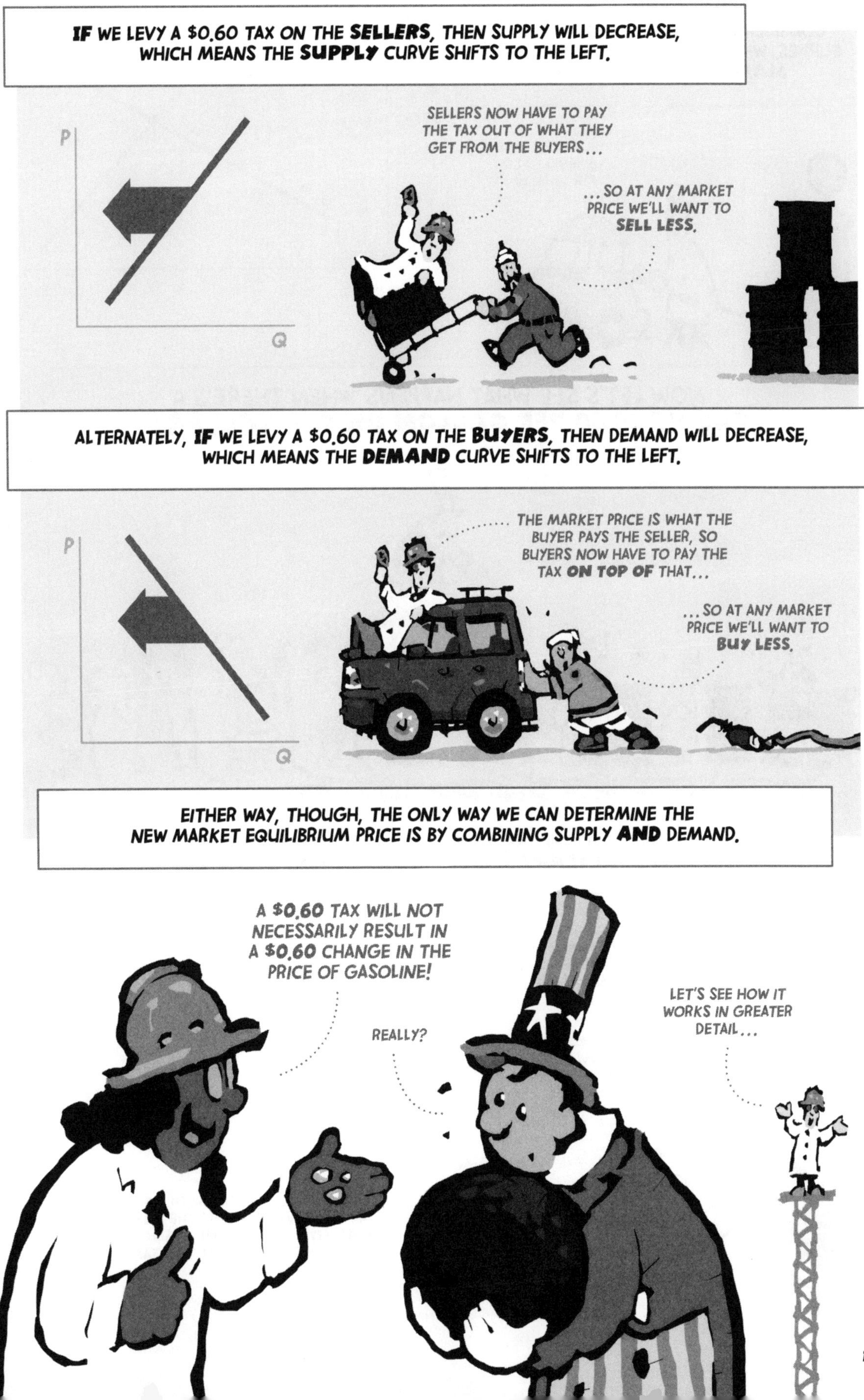
IF WE LEVY A $0.60 TAX ON THE SELLERS, THEN SUPPLY WILL DECREASE, WHICH MEANS THE SUPPLY CURVE SHIFTS TO THE LEFT.
P
Q
SELLERS NOW HAVE TO PAY THE TAX OUT OF WHAT THEY GET FROM THE BUYERS...
...SO AT ANY MARKET PRICE WE'LL WANT TO SELL LESS.
ALTERNATELY, IF WE LEVY A $0.60 TAX ON THE BUYERS, THEN DEMAND WILL DECREASE, WHICH MEANS THE DEMAND CURVE SHIFTS TO THE LEFT.
P
Q
THE MARKET PRICE IS WHAT THE BUYER PAYS THE SELLER, SO BUYERS NOW HAVE TO PAY THE TAX ON TOP OF THAT...
...SO AT ANY MARKET PRICE WE'LL WANT TO BUY LESS.
EITHER WAY, THOUGH, THE ONLY WAY WE CAN DETERMINE THE NEW MARKET EQUILIBRIUM PRICE IS BY COMBINING SUPPLY AND DEMAND.
A $0.60 TAX WILL NOT NECESSARILY RESULT IN A $0.60 CHANGE IN THE PRICE OF GASOLINE!
REALLY?
LET'S SEE HOW IT WORKS IN GREATER DETAIL...

CONSIDER THESE SUPPLY AND DEMAND CURVES, WHICH DESCRIBE A HYPOTHETICAL **MARKET FOR GASOLINE.**

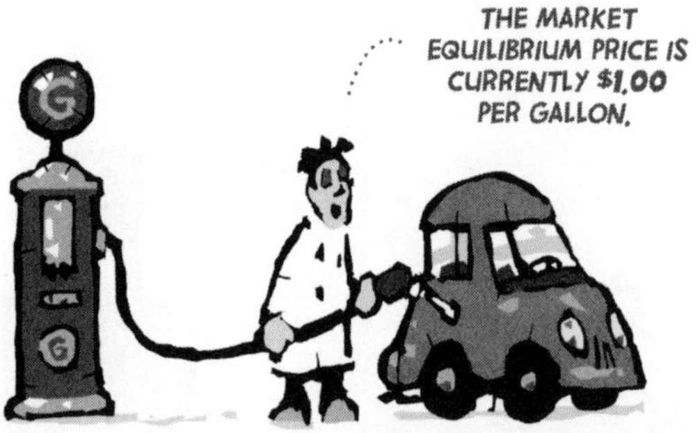
THE MARKET EQUILIBRIUM PRICE IS CURRENTLY $1.00 PER GALLON.

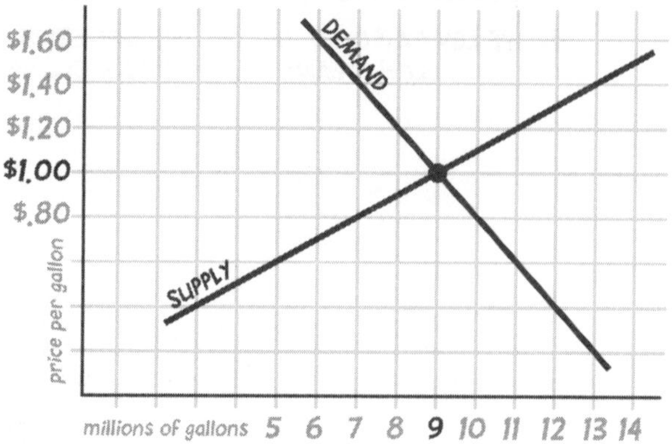
$1.60
$1.40
$1.20
$1.00
$.80
DEMAND
SUPPLY
price per gallon
millions of gallons 5 6 7 8 9 10 11 12 13 14

NOW LET'S SEE WHAT HAPPENS WHEN THERE'S A **TAX OF $0.60 PER GALLON ON THE SELLERS.**

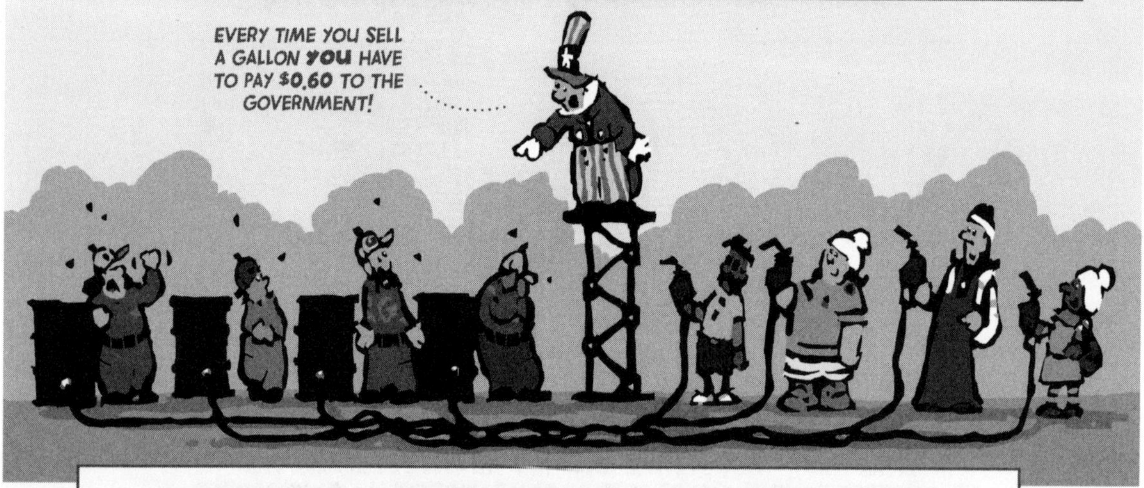
EVERY TIME YOU SELL A GALLON **YOU** HAVE TO PAY **$0.60** TO THE GOVERNMENT!

WHEN SELLERS ADJUST TO THE TAX, THEIR SUPPLY CURVES **SHIFT TO THE LEFT,** WHICH MEANS THAT AT **ANY** MARKET PRICE THEY'D WANT TO SELL LESS.

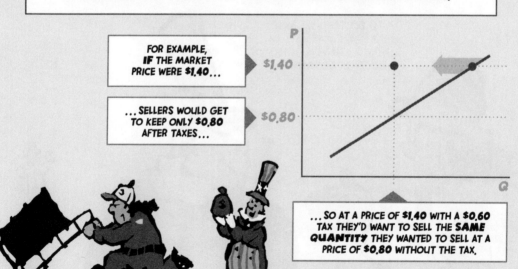

FOR EXAMPLE, **IF** THE MARKET PRICE WERE **$1.40...**

...SELLERS WOULD GET TO KEEP ONLY **$0.80** AFTER TAXES...

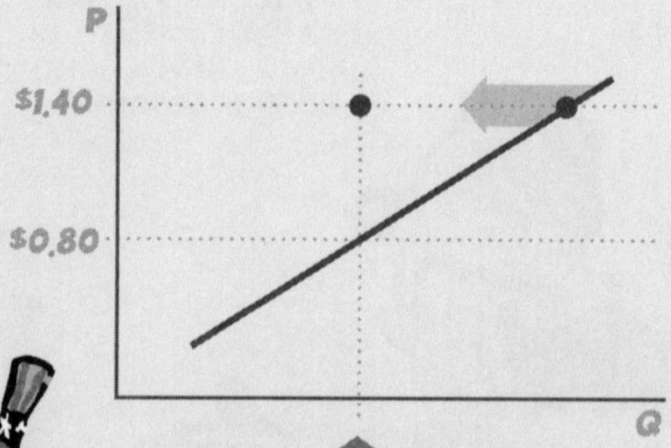
P
$1.40
$0.80
Q

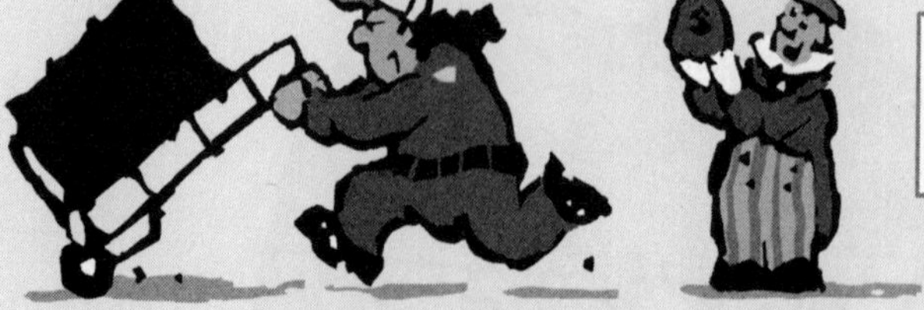

...SO AT A PRICE OF **$1.40** WITH A **$0.60** TAX THEY'D WANT TO SELL THE **SAME QUANTITY** THEY WANTED TO SELL AT A PRICE OF **$0.80** WITHOUT THE TAX.

SO WE CAN CALCULATE EXACTLY HOW THE MARKET SUPPLY CURVE SHIFTS.
HOWEVER MUCH THEY'D PREVIOUSLY WANTED TO SELL IF THE MARKET PRICE WERE $X PER GALLON...
...THEY WOULD NOW WANT TO SELL IF THE MARKET PRICE WERE $(X+0.60) PER GALLON...
...BECAUSE THEN AFTER THE TAX WE'D STILL GET TO KEEP $X PER GALLON!
P
$1.40
$1.20
$1.00
$.80
$.60
$.40
$.20
NEW SUPPLY
OLD SUPPLY
1 2 3 4 5 6 7 10 11 12 13 Q
AS FOR THE DEMAND CURVE, IT DOESN'T CHANGE BECAUSE THE TAX IS ON THE SELLERS.
BUT WHEN WE LOOK AT THE NEW MARKET EQUILIBRIUM PRICE, WE SEE THAT IT CHANGES BY LESS THAN THE AMOUNT OF THE TAX!
P
$1.40
$1.20
$1.00
$.80
$.60
$.40
$.20
1 2 3 4 5 6 7 8 9 10 11 12 13 Q
THE NEW MARKET EQUILIBRIUM PRICE IS $1.40.
SO A $0.60 TAX CAUSES THE MARKET EQUILIBRIUM PRICE TO INCREASE BY $0.40.
EVEN THOUGH THE TAX IS ON THE SELLERS, MARKET FORCES PUSH SOME OF THE TAX BURDEN ONTO THE BUYERS!

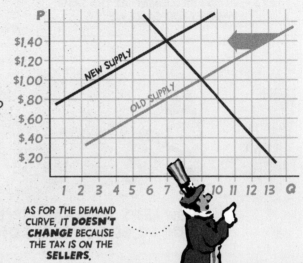

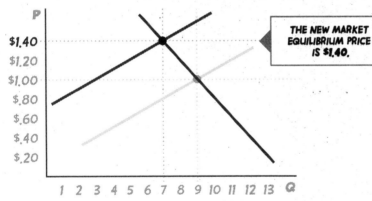

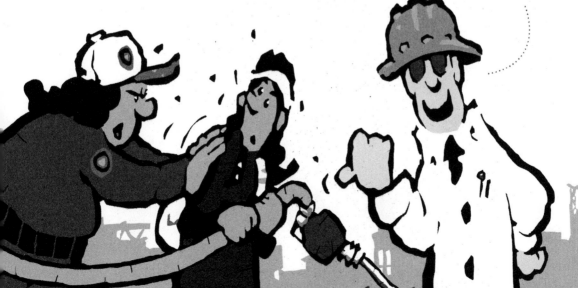

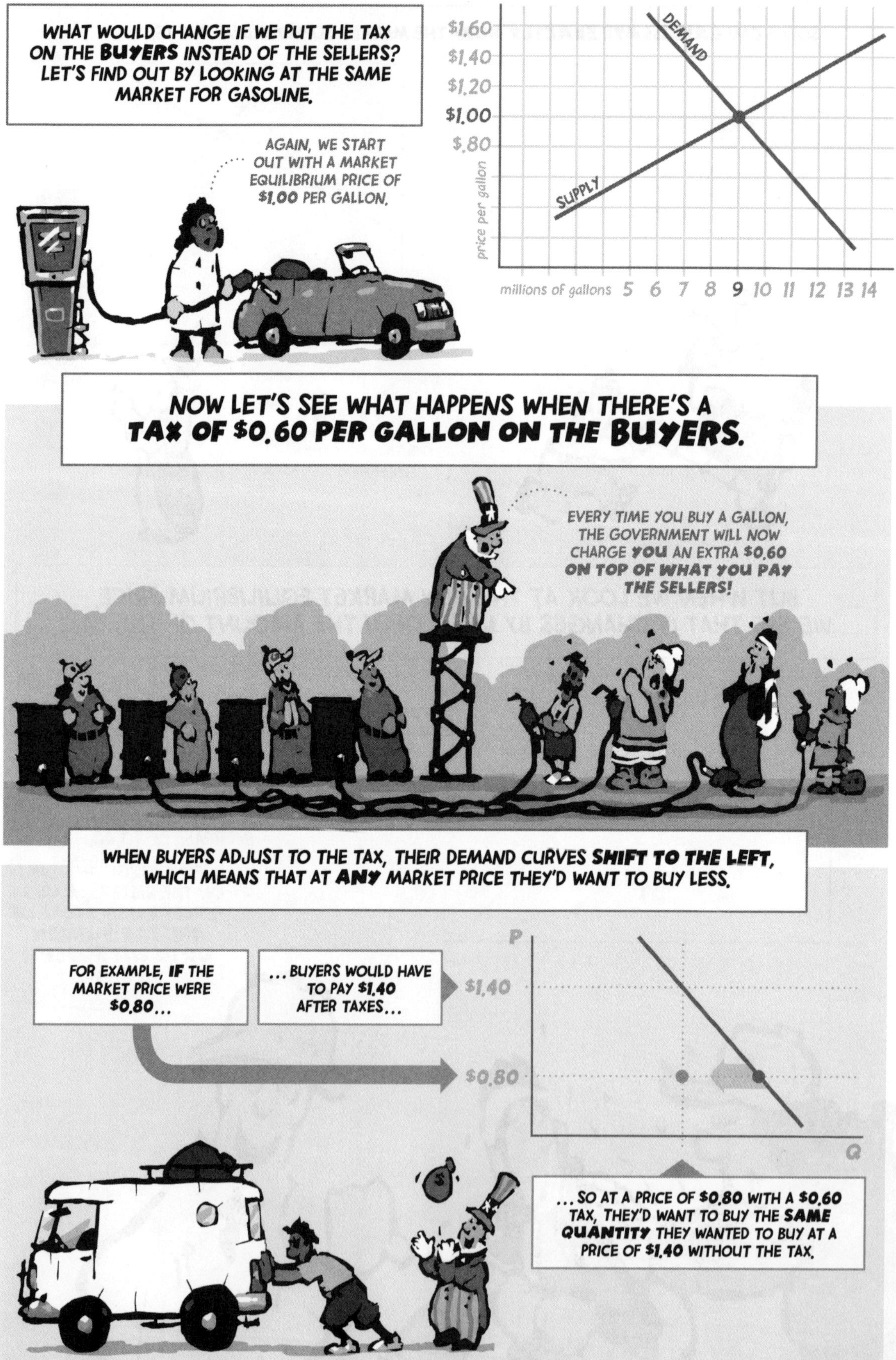
WHAT WOULD CHANGE IF WE PUT THE TAX ON THE BUYERS INSTEAD OF THE SELLERS? LET'S FIND OUT BY LOOKING AT THE SAME MARKET FOR GASOLINE.
AGAIN, WE START OUT WITH A MARKET EQUILIBRIUM PRICE OF $1.00 PER GALLON.
$1.60
$1.40
$1.20
$1.00
$.80
price per gallon
DEMAND
SUPPLY
millions of gallons 5 6 7 8 9 10 11 12 13 14
NOW LET'S SEE WHAT HAPPENS WHEN THERE'S A TAX OF $0.60 PER GALLON ON THE BUYERS.
EVERY TIME YOU BUY A GALLON, THE GOVERNMENT WILL NOW CHARGE YOU AN EXTRA $0.60 ON TOP OF WHAT YOU PAY THE SELLERS!
WHEN BUYERS ADJUST TO THE TAX, THEIR DEMAND CURVES SHIFT TO THE LEFT, WHICH MEANS THAT AT ANY MARKET PRICE THEY'D WANT TO BUY LESS.
FOR EXAMPLE, IF THE MARKET PRICE WERE $0.80...
...BUYERS WOULD HAVE TO PAY $1.40 AFTER TAXES...
P
$1.40
$0.80
Q
...SO AT A PRICE OF $0.80 WITH A $0.60 TAX, THEY'D WANT TO BUY THE SAME QUANTITY THEY WANTED TO BUY AT A PRICE OF $1.40 WITHOUT THE TAX.

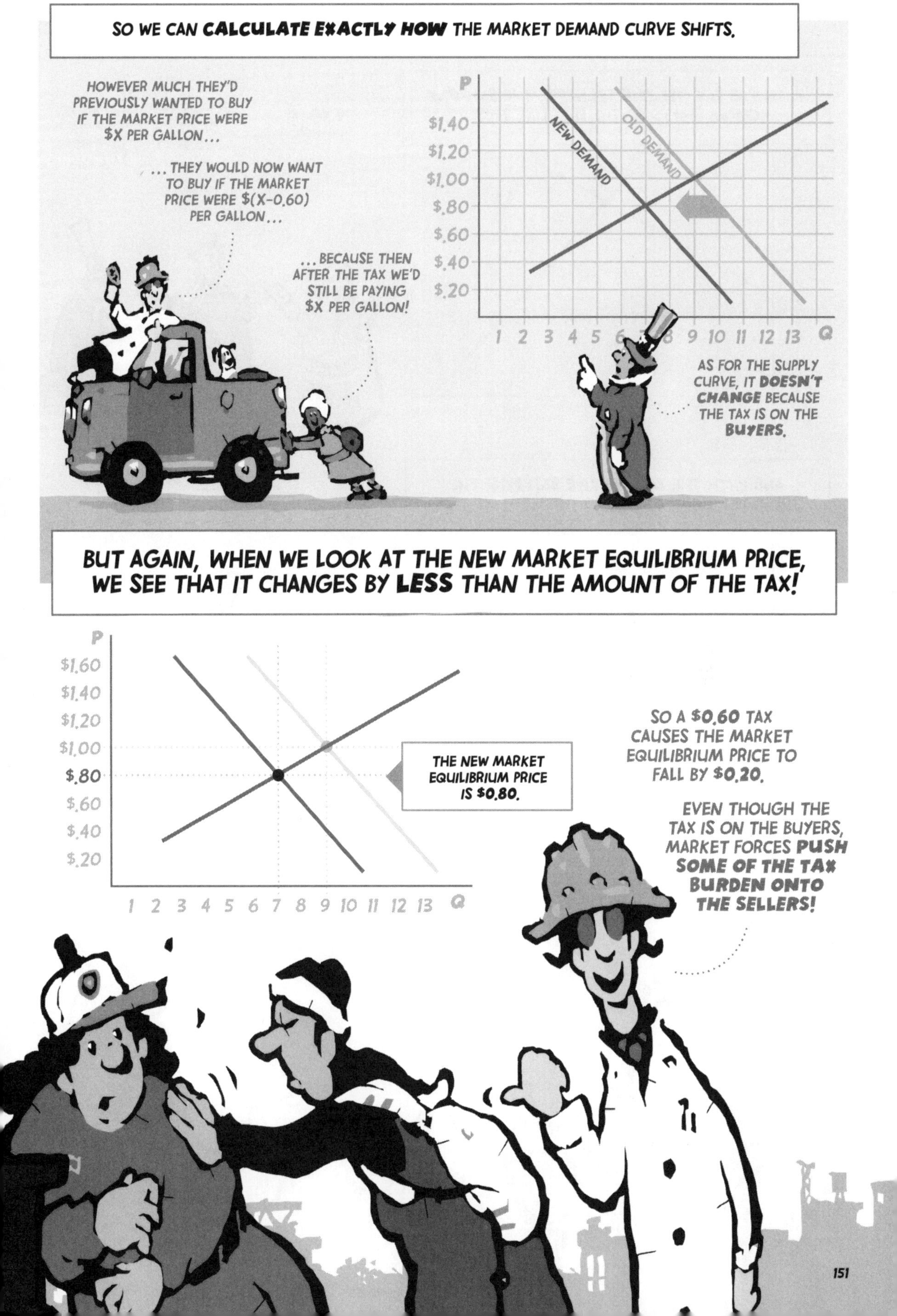

SO WE CAN CALCULATE EXACTLY HOW THE MARKET DEMAND CURVE SHIFTS.
HOWEVER MUCH THEY'D PREVIOUSLY WANTED TO BUY IF THE MARKET PRICE WERE $X PER GALLON...
...THEY WOULD NOW WANT TO BUY IF THE MARKET PRICE WERE $(X–0.60) PER GALLON...
...BECAUSE THEN AFTER THE TAX WE'D STILL BE PAYING $X PER GALLON!
P
$1.40
$1.20
$1.00
$.80
$.60
$.40
$.20
NEW DEMAND
OLD DEMAND
1 2 3 4 5 6 7 8 9 10 11 12 13 Q
AS FOR THE SUPPLY CURVE, IT DOESN'T CHANGE BECAUSE THE TAX IS ON THE BUYERS.
BUT AGAIN, WHEN WE LOOK AT THE NEW MARKET EQUILIBRIUM PRICE, WE SEE THAT IT CHANGES BY LESS THAN THE AMOUNT OF THE TAX!
P
$1.60
$1.40
$1.20
$1.00
$.80
$.60
$.40
$.20
1 2 3 4 5 6 7 8 9 10 11 12 13 Q
THE NEW MARKET EQUILIBRIUM PRICE IS $0.80.
SO A $0.60 TAX CAUSES THE MARKET EQUILIBRIUM PRICE TO FALL BY $0.20.
EVEN THOUGH THE TAX IS ON THE BUYERS, MARKET FORCES PUSH SOME OF THE TAX BURDEN ONTO THE SELLERS!

WITH THE TAX **ON THE SELLERS**, THE **SUPPLY** CURVE SHIFTS TO THE LEFT LIKE THIS:

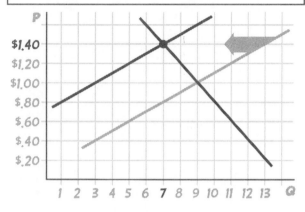

BUYERS PAY **$1.40** PER GALLON.

AND SELLERS GET $1.40 PER GALLON, BUT AFTER THE $0.60 TAX THEY TAKE HOME **$0.80** PER GALLON.

AND WITH THE TAX **ON THE BUYERS**, THE **DEMAND** CURVE SHIFTS TO THE LEFT LIKE THIS:

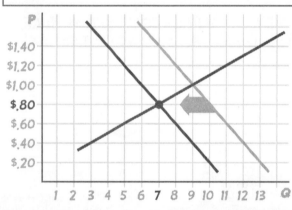

BUYERS PAY $0.80 TO THE SELLERS PLUS $0.60 TAX, FOR A TOTAL OF **$1.40** PER GALLON.

AND SELLERS TAKE HOME **$0.80** PER GALLON.

WAIT A MINUTE! **EITHER WAY, I PAY $1.40 PER GALLON!**

AND I TAKE HOME $0.80 PER GALLON!

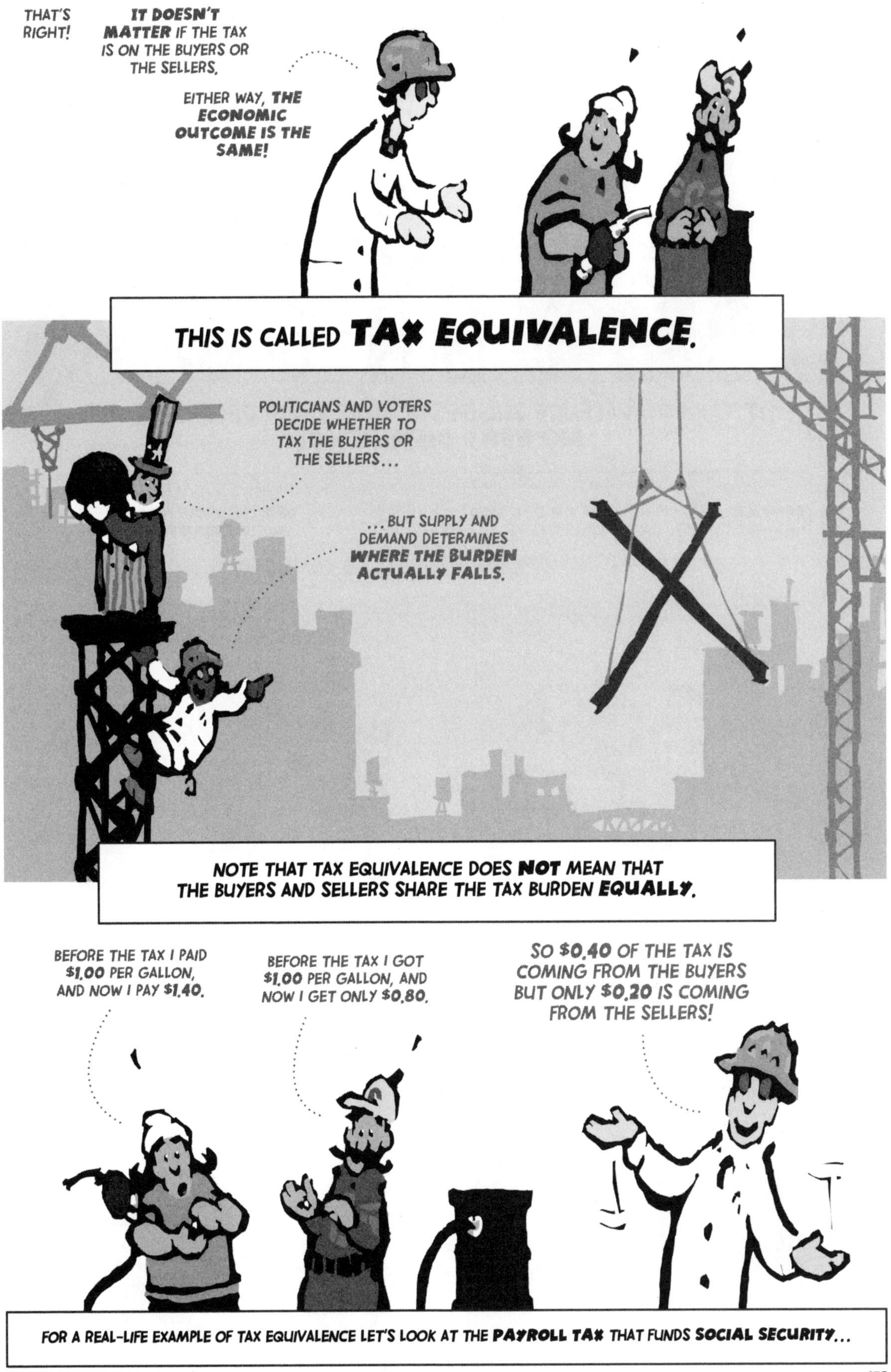
THAT'S RIGHT!
IT DOESN'T MATTER IF THE TAX IS ON THE BUYERS OR THE SELLERS.
EITHER WAY, THE ECONOMIC OUTCOME IS THE SAME!
THIS IS CALLED TAX EQUIVALENCE.
POLITICIANS AND VOTERS DECIDE WHETHER TO TAX THE BUYERS OR THE SELLERS...
...BUT SUPPLY AND DEMAND DETERMINES WHERE THE BURDEN ACTUALLY FALLS.
NOTE THAT TAX EQUIVALENCE DOES NOT MEAN THAT THE BUYERS AND SELLERS SHARE THE TAX BURDEN EQUALLY.
BEFORE THE TAX I PAID $1.00 PER GALLON, AND NOW I PAY $1.40.
BEFORE THE TAX I GOT $1.00 PER GALLON, AND NOW I GET ONLY $0.80.
SO $0.40 OF THE TAX IS COMING FROM THE BUYERS BUT ONLY $0.20 IS COMING FROM THE SELLERS!
FOR A REAL-LIFE EXAMPLE OF TAX EQUIVALENCE LET'S LOOK AT THE PAYROLL TAX THAT FUNDS SOCIAL SECURITY...

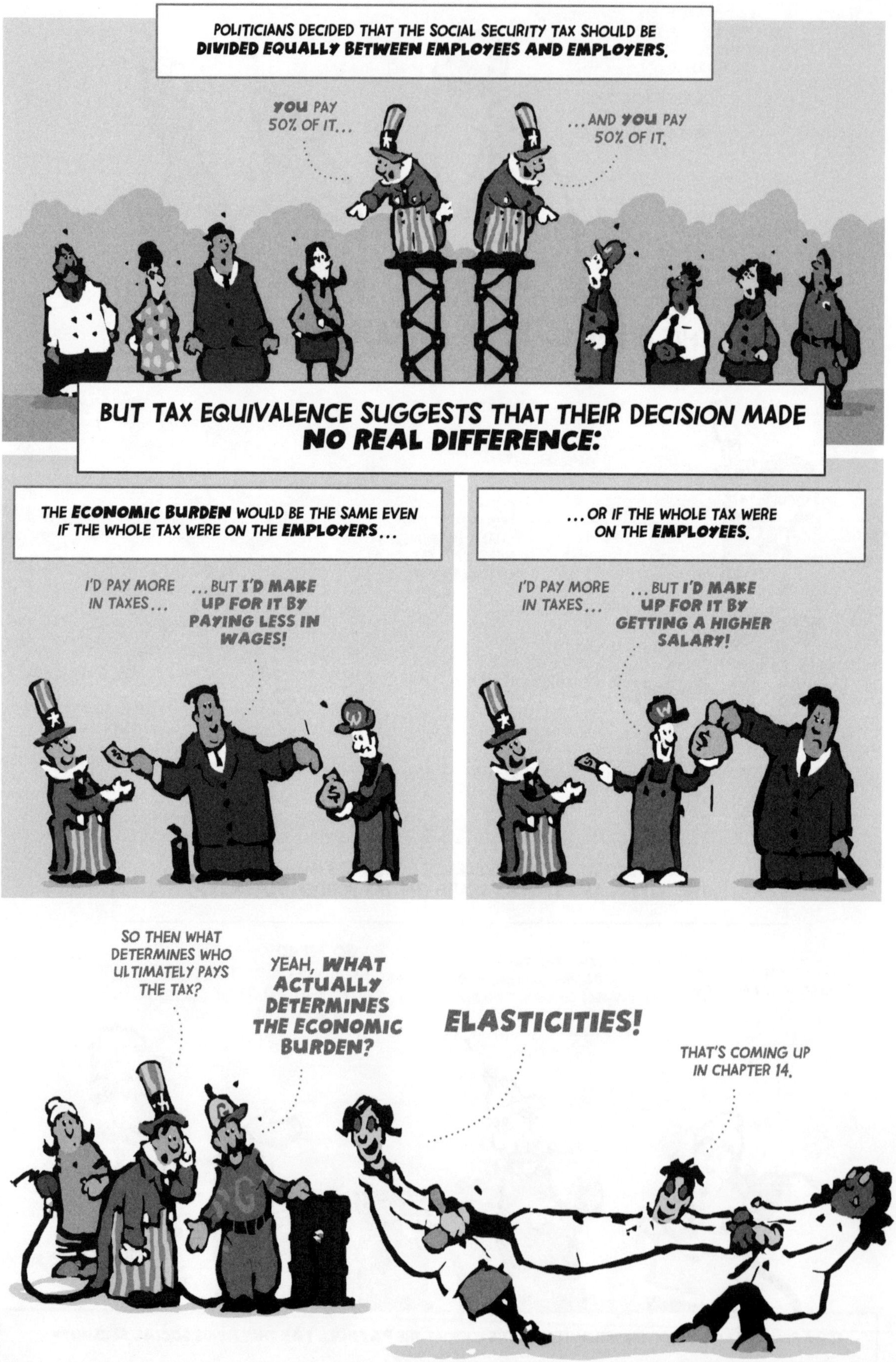
POLITICIANS DECIDED THAT THE SOCIAL SECURITY TAX SHOULD BE **DIVIDED EQUALLY BETWEEN EMPLOYEES AND EMPLOYERS.**
YOU PAY 50% OF IT...
...AND **YOU** PAY 50% OF IT.
BUT TAX EQUIVALENCE SUGGESTS THAT THEIR DECISION MADE **NO REAL DIFFERENCE:**
THE **ECONOMIC BURDEN** WOULD BE THE SAME EVEN IF THE WHOLE TAX WERE ON THE **EMPLOYERS**...
I'D PAY MORE IN TAXES...
...BUT **I'D MAKE UP FOR IT BY PAYING LESS IN WAGES!**
...OR IF THE WHOLE TAX WERE ON THE **EMPLOYEES.**
I'D PAY MORE IN TAXES...
...BUT **I'D MAKE UP FOR IT BY GETTING A HIGHER SALARY!**
SO THEN WHAT DETERMINES WHO ULTIMATELY PAYS THE TAX?
YEAH, **WHAT ACTUALLY DETERMINES THE ECONOMIC BURDEN?**
ELASTICITIES!
THAT'S COMING UP IN CHAPTER 14.

CHAPTER 13
MARGINS

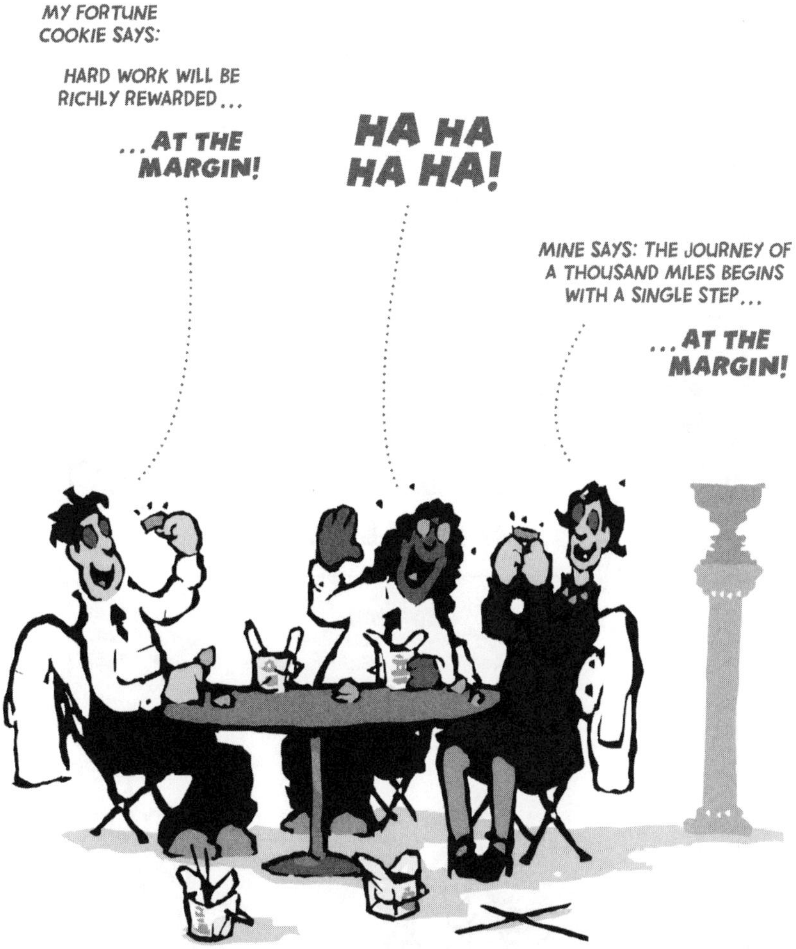

MY FORTUNE COOKIE SAYS:
HARD WORK WILL BE RICHLY REWARDED...
...AT THE MARGIN!
HA HA HA HA!
MINE SAYS: THE JOURNEY OF A THOUSAND MILES BEGINS WITH A SINGLE STEP...
...AT THE MARGIN!

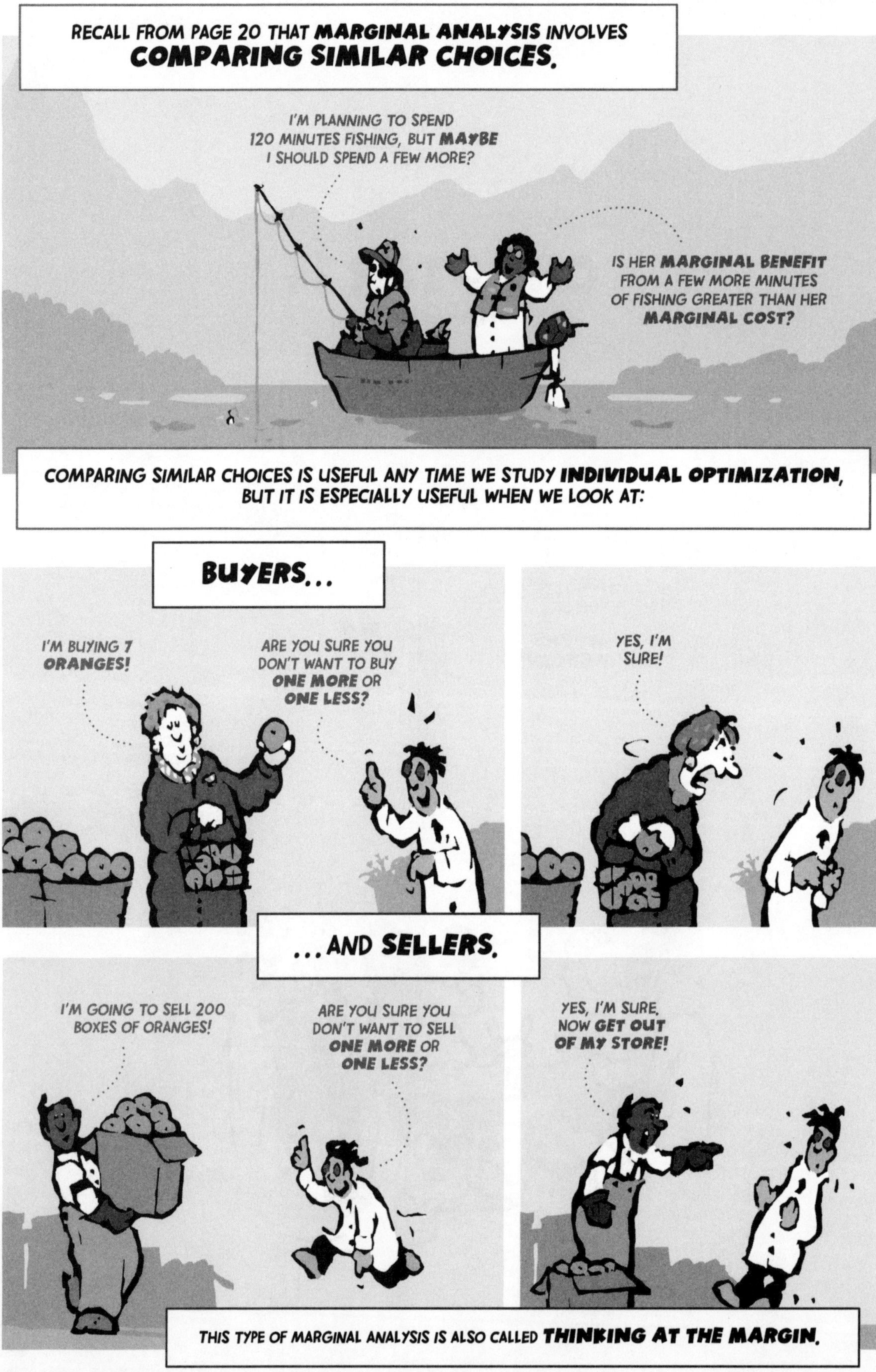
RECALL FROM PAGE 20 THAT MARGINAL ANALYSIS INVOLVES COMPARING SIMILAR CHOICES.
I'M PLANNING TO SPEND 120 MINUTES FISHING, BUT MAYBE I SHOULD SPEND A FEW MORE?
IS HER MARGINAL BENEFIT FROM A FEW MORE MINUTES OF FISHING GREATER THAN HER MARGINAL COST?
COMPARING SIMILAR CHOICES IS USEFUL ANY TIME WE STUDY INDIVIDUAL OPTIMIZATION, BUT IT IS ESPECIALLY USEFUL WHEN WE LOOK AT:
BUYERS...
I'M BUYING 7 ORANGES!
ARE YOU SURE YOU DON'T WANT TO BUY ONE MORE OR ONE LESS?
YES, I'M SURE!
...AND SELLERS.
I'M GOING TO SELL 200 BOXES OF ORANGES!
ARE YOU SURE YOU DON'T WANT TO SELL ONE MORE OR ONE LESS?
YES, I'M SURE. NOW GET OUT OF MY STORE!
THIS TYPE OF MARGINAL ANALYSIS IS ALSO CALLED THINKING AT THE MARGIN.

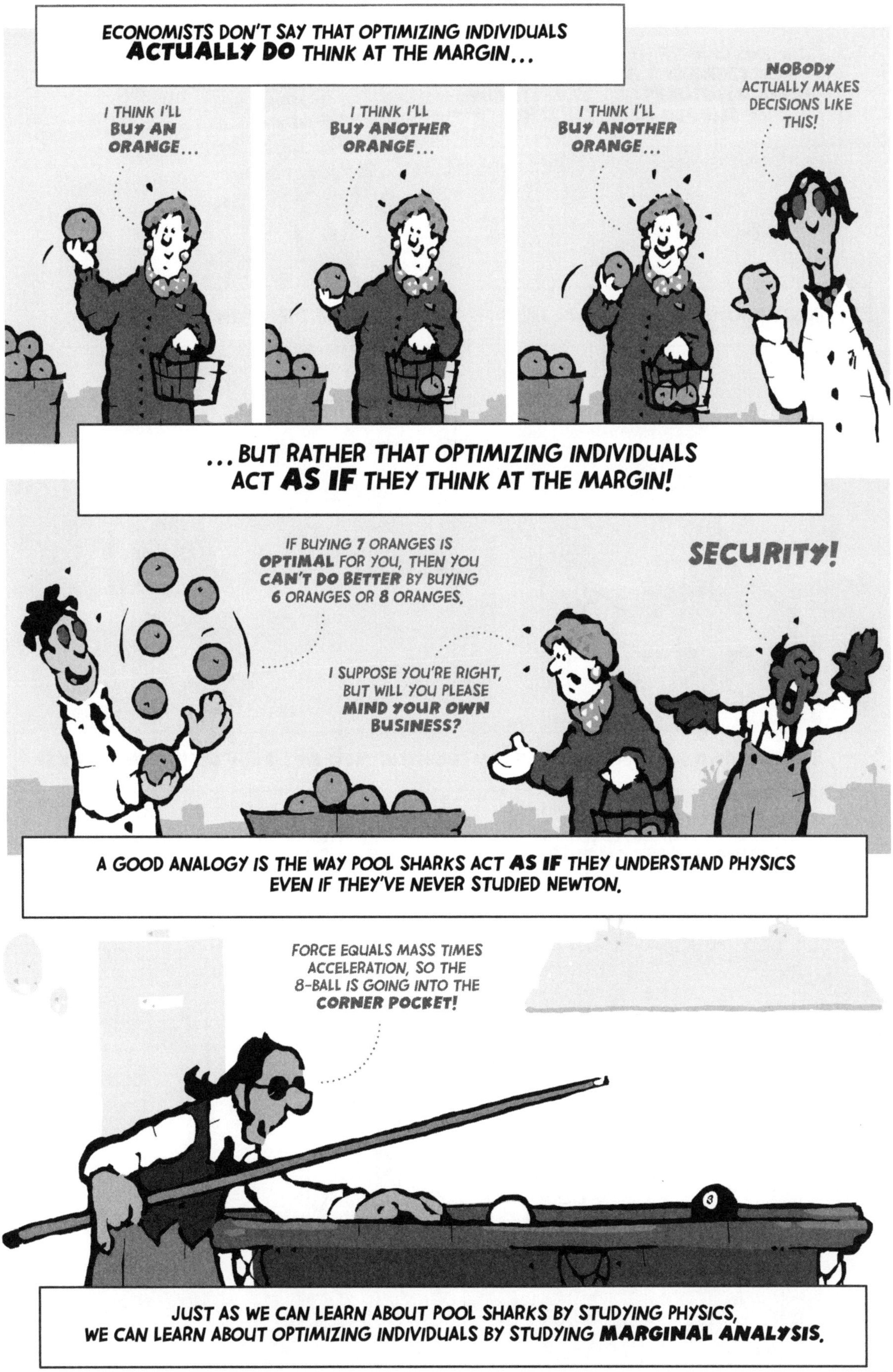

ECONOMISTS DON'T SAY THAT OPTIMIZING INDIVIDUALS ACTUALLY DO THINK AT THE MARGIN...
I THINK I'LL BUY AN ORANGE...
I THINK I'LL BUY ANOTHER ORANGE...
I THINK I'LL BUY ANOTHER ORANGE...
NOBODY ACTUALLY MAKES DECISIONS LIKE THIS!
...BUT RATHER THAT OPTIMIZING INDIVIDUALS ACT AS IF THEY THINK AT THE MARGIN!
IF BUYING 7 ORANGES IS OPTIMAL FOR YOU, THEN YOU CAN'T DO BETTER BY BUYING 6 ORANGES OR 8 ORANGES.
I SUPPOSE YOU'RE RIGHT, BUT WILL YOU PLEASE MIND YOUR OWN BUSINESS?
SECURITY!
A GOOD ANALOGY IS THE WAY POOL SHARKS ACT AS IF THEY UNDERSTAND PHYSICS EVEN IF THEY'VE NEVER STUDIED NEWTON.
FORCE EQUALS MASS TIMES ACCELERATION, SO THE 8-BALL IS GOING INTO THE CORNER POCKET!
JUST AS WE CAN LEARN ABOUT POOL SHARKS BY STUDYING PHYSICS, WE CAN LEARN ABOUT OPTIMIZING INDIVIDUALS BY STUDYING MARGINAL ANALYSIS.

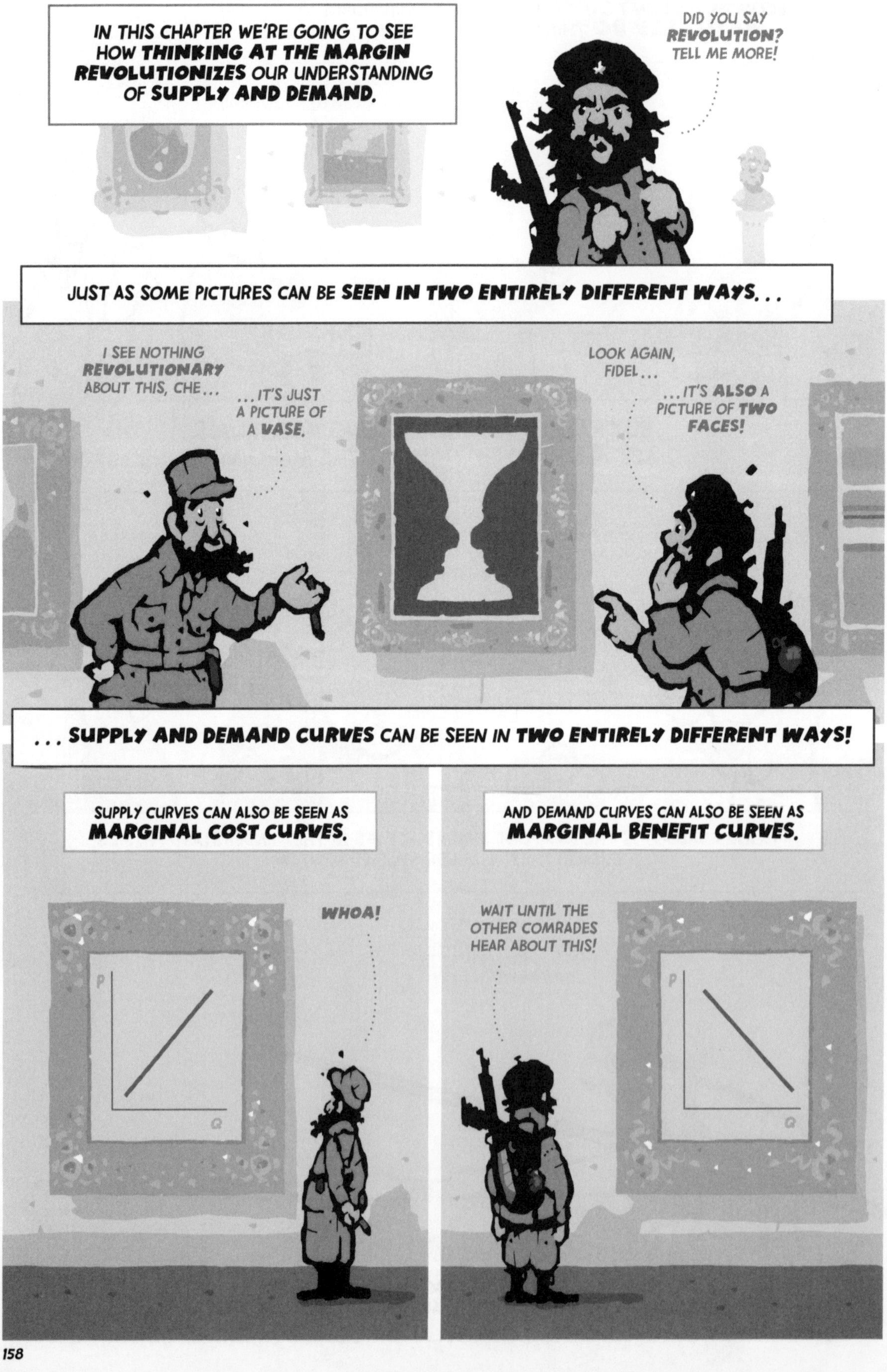
IN THIS CHAPTER WE'RE GOING TO SEE HOW **THINKING AT THE MARGIN REVOLUTIONIZES** OUR UNDERSTANDING OF **SUPPLY AND DEMAND.**
DID YOU SAY **REVOLUTION?** TELL ME MORE!
JUST AS SOME PICTURES CAN BE **SEEN IN TWO ENTIRELY DIFFERENT WAYS. . .**
I SEE NOTHING **REVOLUTIONARY** ABOUT THIS, CHE . . .
. . . IT'S JUST A PICTURE OF A **VASE.**
LOOK AGAIN, FIDEL . . .
. . . IT'S **ALSO** A PICTURE OF **TWO FACES!**
. . . **SUPPLY AND DEMAND CURVES** CAN BE SEEN IN **TWO ENTIRELY DIFFERENT WAYS!**
SUPPLY CURVES CAN ALSO BE SEEN AS **MARGINAL COST CURVES.**
P
Q
WHOA!
AND DEMAND CURVES CAN ALSO BE SEEN AS **MARGINAL BENEFIT CURVES.**
WAIT UNTIL THE OTHER COMRADES HEAR ABOUT THIS!
P
Q

AN INDIVIDUAL
MARGINAL COST CURVE
TELLS US THE *EXTRA COST*
FOR ONE PARTICULAR SELLER OF
PRODUCING **ONE MORE UNIT.**

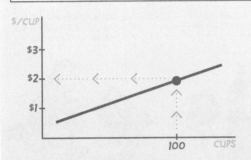

PRODUCING 99 CUPS OF COFFEE
PER HOUR COSTS $250 AND
PRODUCING 100 CUPS OF COFFEE
COSTS $252...

...SO MY
MARGINAL COST
FOR THE 100TH CUP
IS $2!

COMBINE ALL THE **SELLERS** AND YOU GET A
MARKET MARGINAL COST CURVE.

WHAT'S THE **MINIMUM**
AMOUNT IT WOULD COST
US TO PRODUCE ONE
MORE CUP OF COFFEE?

AN INDIVIDUAL
MARGINAL BENEFIT CURVE
TELLS US THE *EXTRA BENEFIT*
FOR ONE PARTICULAR BUYER OF
CONSUMING **ONE MORE UNIT.**

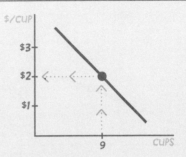

I'D BE WILLING TO PAY UP
TO $20 FOR 8 CUPS OF
COFFEE PER WEEK AND UP
TO $22 FOR 9 CUPS...

...SO MY **MARGINAL
BENEFIT** FROM THE
9TH CUP MUST BE $2!

COMBINE ALL THE **BUYERS** AND YOU GET A
MARKET MARGINAL BENEFIT CURVE.

WHAT'S THE **MAXIMUM**
AMOUNT WE'D BE WILLING
TO PAY FOR ONE MORE CUP
OF COFFEE?

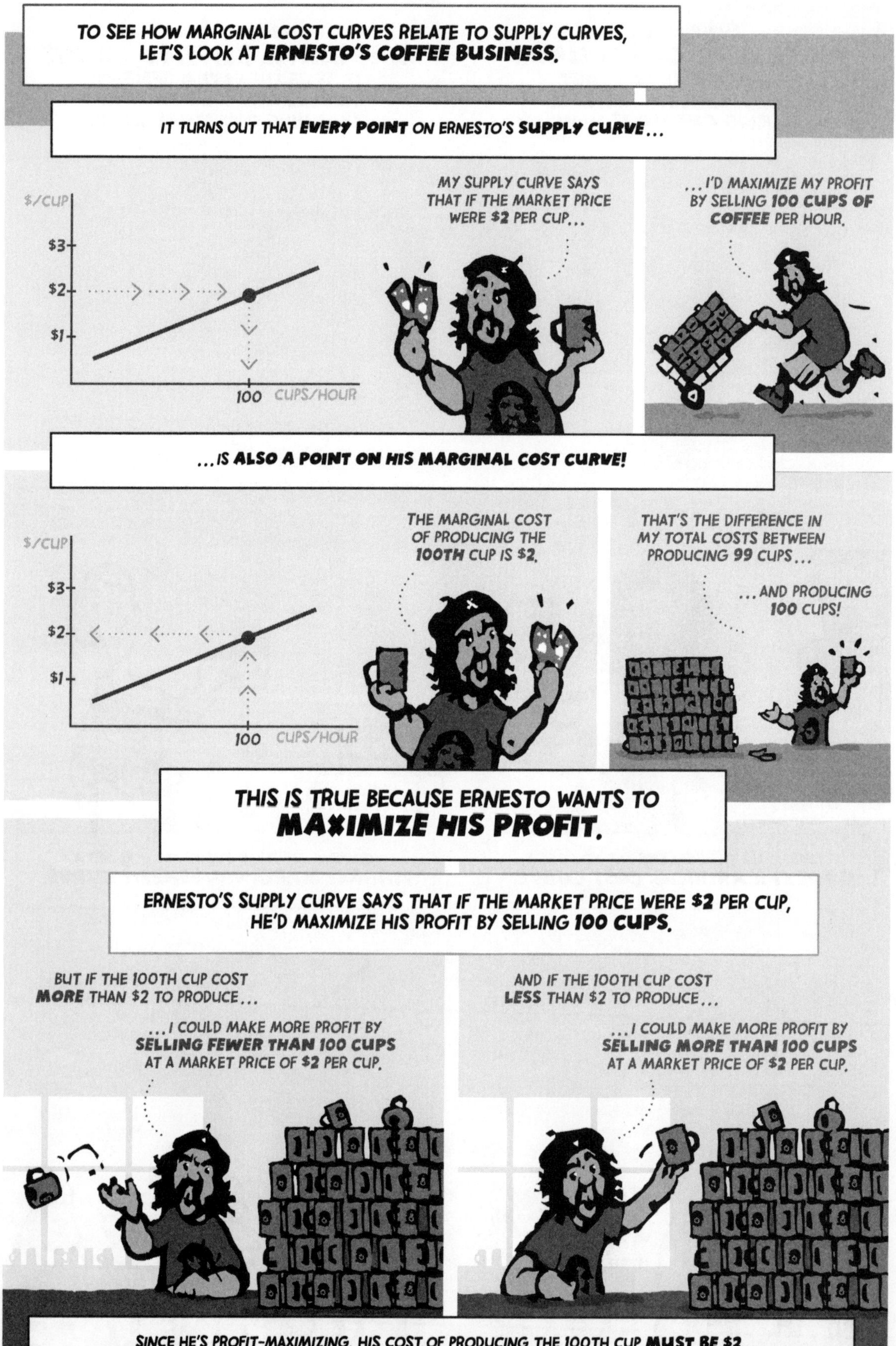
TO SEE HOW MARGINAL COST CURVES RELATE TO SUPPLY CURVES, LET'S LOOK AT ERNESTO'S COFFEE BUSINESS.
IT TURNS OUT THAT EVERY POINT ON ERNESTO'S SUPPLY CURVE...
$/CUP
$3
$2
$1
100
CUPS/HOUR
MY SUPPLY CURVE SAYS THAT IF THE MARKET PRICE WERE $2 PER CUP...
...I'D MAXIMIZE MY PROFIT BY SELLING 100 CUPS OF COFFEE PER HOUR.
...IS ALSO A POINT ON HIS MARGINAL COST CURVE!
$/CUP
$3
$2
$1
100
CUPS/HOUR
THE MARGINAL COST OF PRODUCING THE 100TH CUP IS $2.
THAT'S THE DIFFERENCE IN MY TOTAL COSTS BETWEEN PRODUCING 99 CUPS...
...AND PRODUCING 100 CUPS!
THIS IS TRUE BECAUSE ERNESTO WANTS TO MAXIMIZE HIS PROFIT.
ERNESTO'S SUPPLY CURVE SAYS THAT IF THE MARKET PRICE WERE $2 PER CUP, HE'D MAXIMIZE HIS PROFIT BY SELLING 100 CUPS.
BUT IF THE 100TH CUP COST MORE THAN $2 TO PRODUCE...
...I COULD MAKE MORE PROFIT BY SELLING FEWER THAN 100 CUPS AT A MARKET PRICE OF $2 PER CUP.
AND IF THE 100TH CUP COST LESS THAN $2 TO PRODUCE...
...I COULD MAKE MORE PROFIT BY SELLING MORE THAN 100 CUPS AT A MARKET PRICE OF $2 PER CUP.
SINCE HE'S PROFIT-MAXIMIZING, HIS COST OF PRODUCING THE 100TH CUP MUST BE $2.

IF WE LOOK AT ERNESTO AND ALL THE OTHER COFFEE SELLERS TOGETHER, WE CAN SEE THAT **EVERY POINT ON THE MARKET SUPPLY CURVE IS ALSO A POINT ON THE MARKET MARGINAL COST CURVE.**

IF THE MARKET SUPPLY CURVE SAYS THAT AT A PRICE OF $2 ALL THE SELLERS TOGETHER WANT TO SELL **20,000** CUPS OF COFFEE PER HOUR...

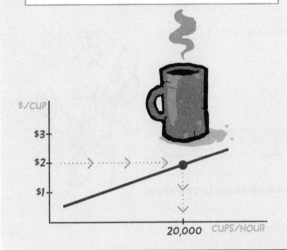

... THEN THE MARKET MARGINAL COST OF PRODUCING THE **20,000**TH CUP MUST BE $2.

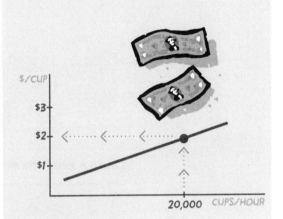

AGAIN, THE REASON IS **PROFIT MAXIMIZATION.**

IF THE 20,000TH CUP COST **MORE** THAN $2 TO PRODUCE...

...AT LEAST ONE OF US COULD MAKE MORE PROFIT BY **SELLING FEWER CUPS** AT A MARKET PRICE OF $2!

AND IF THE 20,000TH CUP COST **LESS** THAN $2 TO PRODUCE...

...AT LEAST ONE OF US COULD MAKE MORE PROFIT BY **SELLING MORE CUPS** AT A MARKET PRICE OF $2!

ALL THESE LOGICAL ARGUMENTS CAN BE BACKED UP WITH **ROCK-SOLID MATHEMATICS...**

...BUT WE'D NEED TO DO SOME **CALCULUS.**

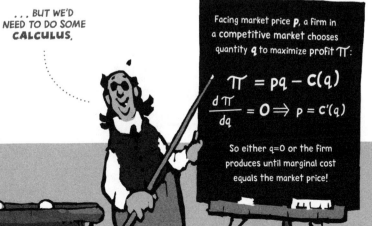

Facing market price **p**, a firm in a competitive market chooses quantity **q** to maximize profit π:

$$\pi = pq - C(q)$$

$$\frac{d\pi}{dq} = 0 \Rightarrow p = C'(q)$$

So either q=0 or the firm produces until marginal cost equals the market price!

BUYERS ARE OPTIMIZING INDIVIDUALS JUST LIKE SELLERS, SO FOR AN EXAMPLE ON THE DEMAND SIDE LET'S LOOK AT EVITA'S COFFEE-PURCHASING PREFERENCES.
IT TURNS OUT THAT EVERY POINT ON EVITA'S DEMAND CURVE...
$/CUP
$3
$2
$1
9
CUPS/WEEK
MY DEMAND CURVE SAYS THAT IF THE MARKET PRICE WERE $2 MY OPTIMAL CHOICE WOULD BE TO BUY 9 CUPS OF COFFEE PER WEEK.
1 2 3 4 5 6 7 8
...IS ALSO A POINT ON HER MARGINAL BENEFIT CURVE!
$/CUP
$3
$2
$1
9
CUPS/WEEK
MY MARGINAL BENEFIT CURVE SAYS THAT IF I'VE BOUGHT 8 CUPS OF COFFEE THIS WEEK...
...THEN MY MAXIMUM WILLINGNESS TO PAY FOR A 9TH CUP IS $2.
9
1 2 3 4 5 6 7 8
THE MATH HERE IS EVEN TRICKIER THAN ON THE SUPPLY SIDE. JOHN HICKS SHARED THE NOBEL PRIZE IN 1972 FOR FIGURING IT OUT.
IT'S ACTUALLY QUITE COMPLICATED.
CONGRATULATIONS, YOU WIN THE NOBEL PRIZE!

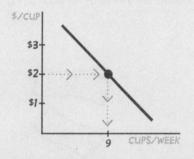

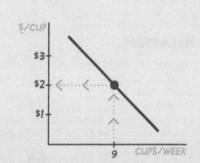

THE MATH MAY BE COMPLICATED, BUT THE INTUITIVE EXPLANATION IS PRETTY EASY: EVITA IS AN **OPTIMIZING INDIVIDUAL!**
MY DEMAND CURVE SAYS THAT IF THE MARKET PRICE WERE **ABOVE $2 PER CUP** I'D ONLY WANT TO BUY **8 CUPS**...
1 2 3 4 5 6 7 8
...BUT IF THE MARKET PRICE WERE **EXACTLY $2 PER CUP** I'D WANT TO BUY **9 CUPS**...
9
1 2 3 4 5 6 7 8
...SO MY **MAXIMUM WILLINGNESS TO PAY** FOR A 9TH CUP MUST BE ABOUT **$2!**
9
1 2 3 4 5 6 7 8
IF WE LOOK AT EVITA AND ALL THE OTHER COFFEE BUYERS TOGETHER, WE CAN SEE THAT **EVERY POINT ON THE MARKET DEMAND CURVE IS ALSO A POINT ON THE MARKET MARGINAL BENEFIT CURVE.**
IF THE MARKET DEMAND CURVE SAYS THAT AT A PRICE OF **$2** ALL THE BUYERS TOGETHER WANT TO BUY **20,000** CUPS PER WEEK...
$/CUP
$3
$2
$1
20,000
CUPS/WEEK
...THEN THE MARKET MARGINAL BENEFIT OF CONSUMING THE **20,000**TH CUP MUST BE **$2.**
$/CUP
$3
$2
$1
20,000
CUPS/WEEK
AGAIN, THE INTUITIVE REASON IS **INDIVIDUAL OPTIMIZATION.**
IF OUR MAXIMUM WILLINGNESS TO PAY FOR THE 20,000TH CUP IS **LESS** THAN $2...
...AT LEAST ONE OF US WOULD BE BETTER OFF **BUYING LESS** AT A MARKET PRICE OF **$2.**
AND IF OUR MAXIMUM WILLINGNESS TO PAY FOR THE 20,000TH CUP IS **MORE** THAN $2...
...AT LEAST ONE OF US WOULD BE BETTER OFF **BUYING MORE** AT A MARKET PRICE OF **$2.**

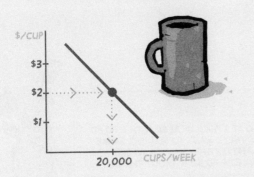

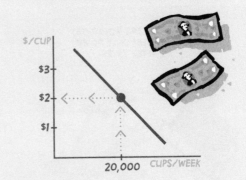

TO SEE HOW THIS **REVOLUTIONIZES** HOW WE THINK ABOUT SUPPLY AND DEMAND, LET'S LOOK AGAIN AT TAXES ON THE **SELLERS.**

SELLERS, EVERY TIME YOU SELL A GALLON **YOU** HAVE TO PAY **$0.60** TO THE GOVERNMENT!

TAXES AGAIN?!

WITH THESE ECONOMISTS IT'S ALWAYS ABOUT TAXES!

WE KNOW FROM THE PREVIOUS CHAPTER THAT A TAX OF $0.60 PER GALLON ON THE SELLERS **SHIFTS EACH SELLER'S SUPPLY CURVE TO THE LEFT...**

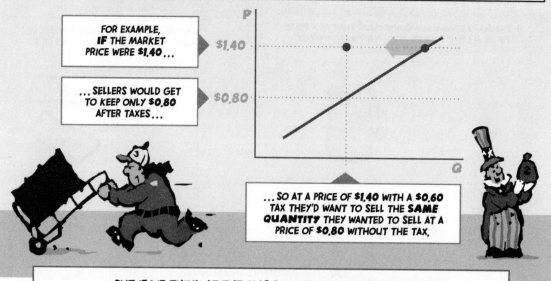

FOR EXAMPLE, **IF** THE MARKET PRICE WERE **$1.40**...

...SELLERS WOULD GET TO KEEP ONLY **$0.80** AFTER TAXES...

...SO AT A PRICE OF **$1.40** WITH A **$0.60** TAX THEY'D WANT TO SELL THE **SAME QUANTITY** THEY WANTED TO SELL AT A PRICE OF **$0.80** WITHOUT THE TAX.

...BUT IF WE THINK AT THE MARGIN, WE CAN INTERPRET THIS AS **EACH SELLER'S MARGINAL COST CURVE SHIFTING UP BY $0.60!**

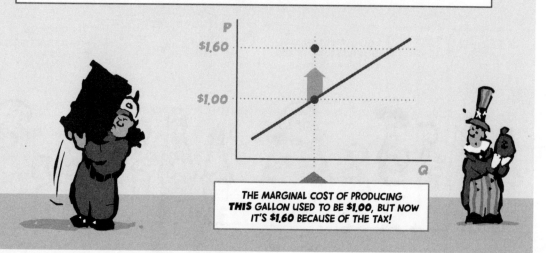

THE MARGINAL COST OF PRODUCING **THIS** GALLON USED TO BE **$1.00**, BUT NOW IT'S **$1.60** BECAUSE OF THE TAX!

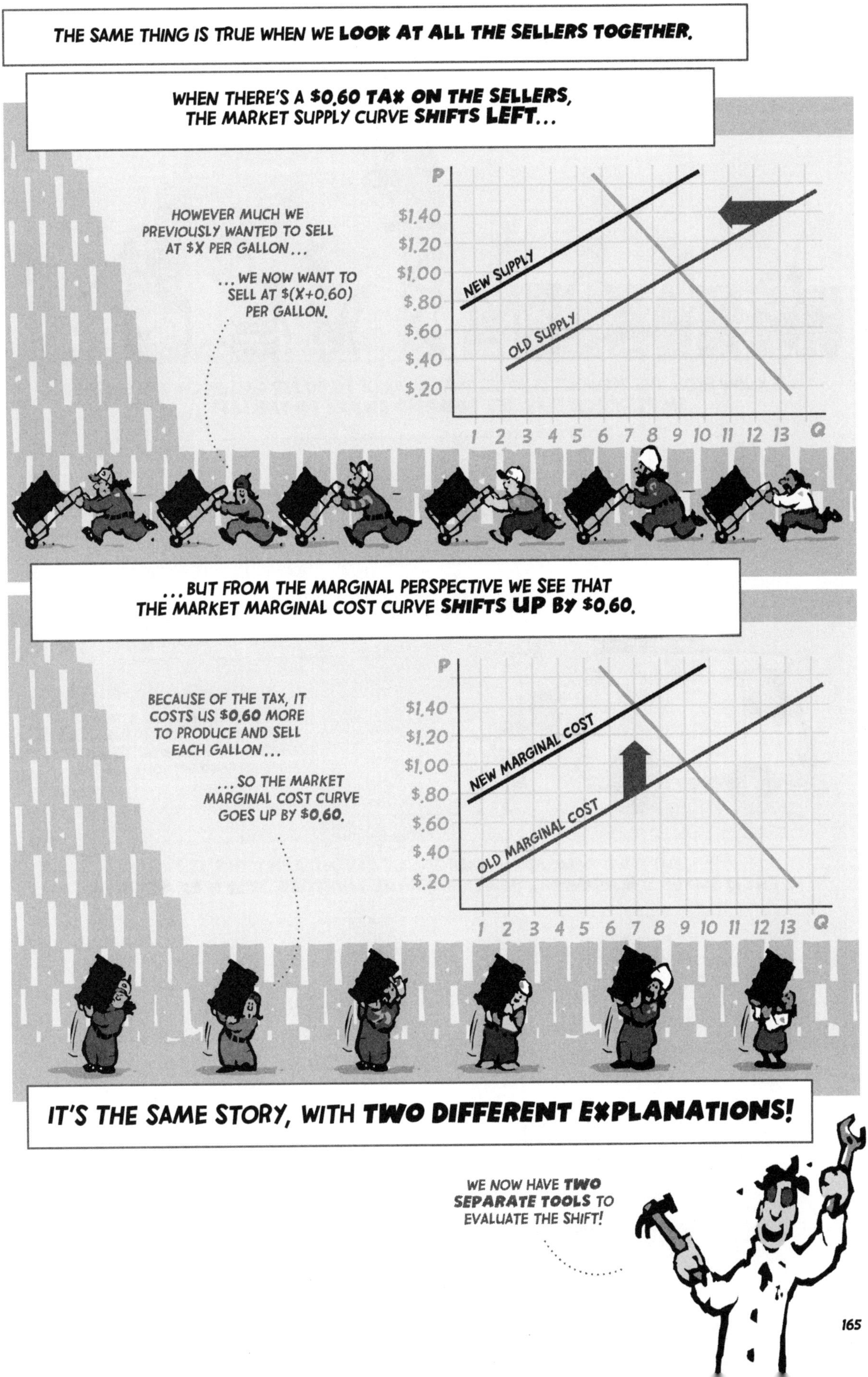

THE SAME THING IS TRUE WHEN WE **LOOK AT ALL THE SELLERS TOGETHER.**
WHEN THERE'S A **$0.60 TAX ON THE SELLERS,** THE MARKET SUPPLY CURVE **SHIFTS LEFT...**
HOWEVER MUCH WE PREVIOUSLY WANTED TO SELL AT $X PER GALLON...
...WE NOW WANT TO SELL AT $(X+0.60) PER GALLON.
P
$1.40
$1.20
$1.00
$.80
$.60
$.40
$.20
NEW SUPPLY
OLD SUPPLY
1 2 3 4 5 6 7 8 9 10 11 12 13 Q
...BUT FROM THE MARGINAL PERSPECTIVE WE SEE THAT THE MARKET MARGINAL COST CURVE **SHIFTS UP BY $0.60.**
BECAUSE OF THE TAX, IT COSTS US **$0.60** MORE TO PRODUCE AND SELL EACH GALLON...
...SO THE MARKET MARGINAL COST CURVE GOES UP BY **$0.60.**
P
$1.40
$1.20
$1.00
$.80
$.60
$.40
$.20
NEW MARGINAL COST
OLD MARGINAL COST
1 2 3 4 5 6 7 8 9 10 11 12 13 Q
IT'S THE SAME STORY, WITH **TWO DIFFERENT EXPLANATIONS!**
WE NOW HAVE **TWO SEPARATE TOOLS** TO EVALUATE THE SHIFT!

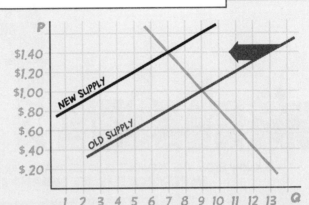

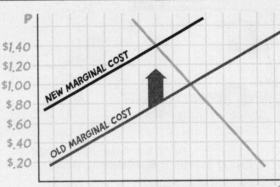

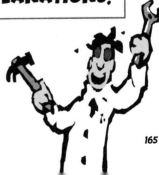

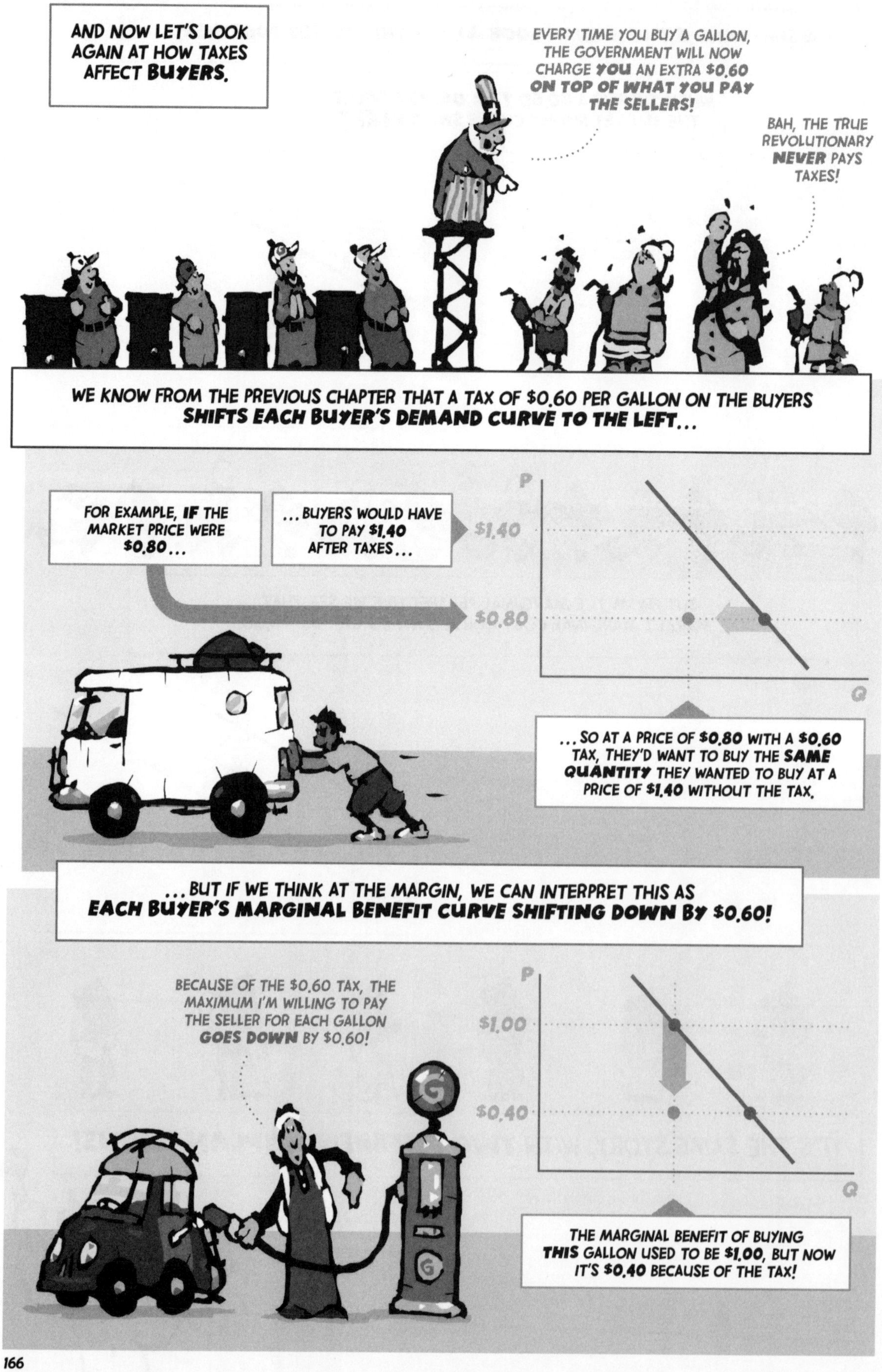
AND NOW LET'S LOOK AGAIN AT HOW TAXES AFFECT **BUYERS.**
EVERY TIME YOU BUY A GALLON, THE GOVERNMENT WILL NOW CHARGE **YOU** AN EXTRA $0.60 **ON TOP OF WHAT YOU PAY THE SELLERS!**
BAH, THE TRUE REVOLUTIONARY **NEVER** PAYS TAXES!
WE KNOW FROM THE PREVIOUS CHAPTER THAT A TAX OF $0.60 PER GALLON ON THE BUYERS **SHIFTS EACH BUYER'S DEMAND CURVE TO THE LEFT...**
FOR EXAMPLE, **IF** THE MARKET PRICE WERE **$0.80...**
...BUYERS WOULD HAVE TO PAY **$1.40** AFTER TAXES...
P
$1.40
$0.80
Q
...SO AT A PRICE OF **$0.80** WITH A **$0.60** TAX, THEY'D WANT TO BUY THE **SAME QUANTITY** THEY WANTED TO BUY AT A PRICE OF **$1.40** WITHOUT THE TAX.
...BUT IF WE THINK AT THE MARGIN, WE CAN INTERPRET THIS AS **EACH BUYER'S MARGINAL BENEFIT CURVE SHIFTING DOWN BY $0.60!**
BECAUSE OF THE $0.60 TAX, THE MAXIMUM I'M WILLING TO PAY THE SELLER FOR EACH GALLON **GOES DOWN** BY $0.60!
P
$1.00
$0.40
Q
THE MARGINAL BENEFIT OF BUYING **THIS** GALLON USED TO BE **$1.00**, BUT NOW IT'S **$0.40** BECAUSE OF THE TAX!

THE SAME THING IS TRUE WHEN WE **LOOK AT ALL THE BUYERS TOGETHER.**

WHEN THERE'S A **$0.60 TAX ON THE BUYERS,** THE MARKET DEMAND CURVE **SHIFTS LEFT...**

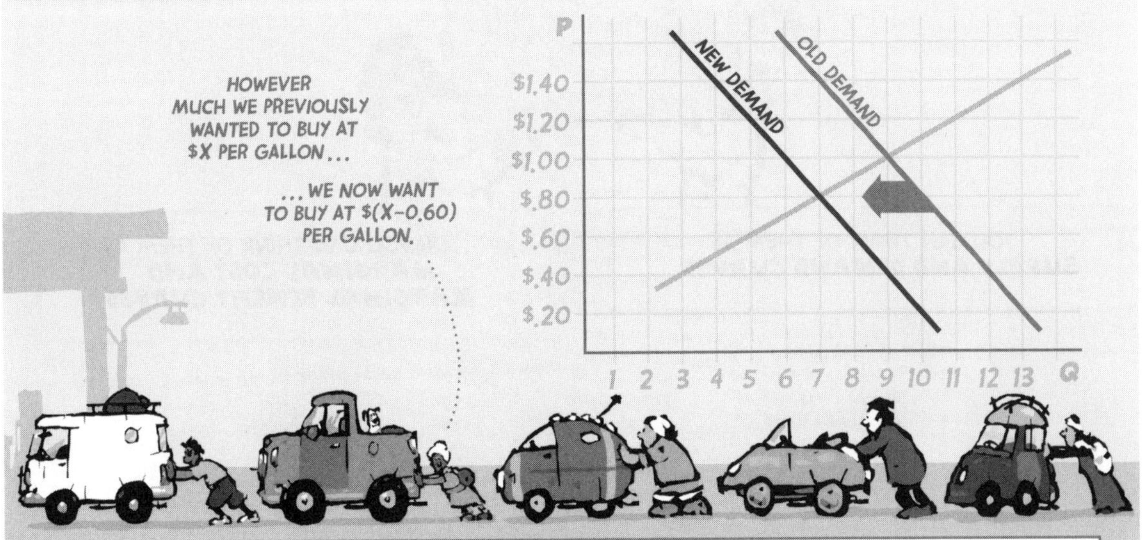

HOWEVER MUCH WE PREVIOUSLY WANTED TO BUY AT $X PER GALLON...
...WE NOW WANT TO BUY AT $(X–0.60) PER GALLON.
P
$1.40
$1.20
$1.00
$.80
$.60
$.40
$.20
NEW DEMAND
OLD DEMAND
1 2 3 4 5 6 7 8 9 10 11 12 13 Q

...BUT FROM THE MARGINAL PERSPECTIVE, WE SEE THAT THE MARKET MARGINAL BENEFIT CURVE **SHIFTS DOWN BY $0.60.**

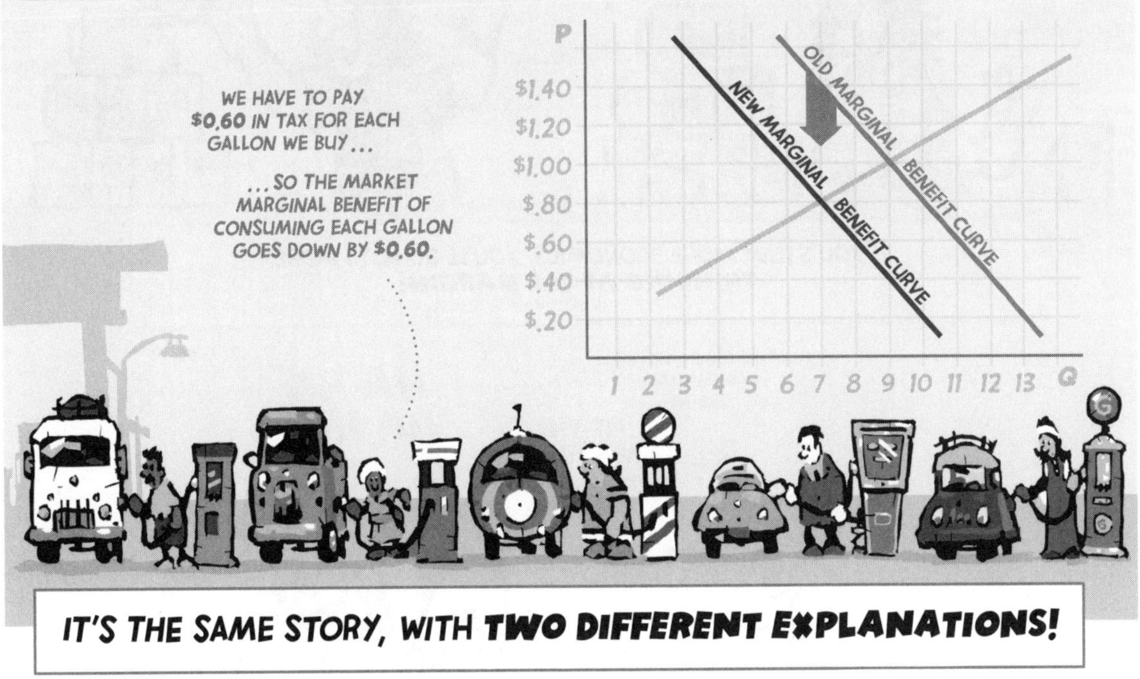

WE HAVE TO PAY $0.60 IN TAX FOR EACH GALLON WE BUY...
...SO THE MARKET MARGINAL BENEFIT OF CONSUMING EACH GALLON GOES DOWN BY $0.60.
P
$1.40
$1.20
$1.00
$.80
$.60
$.40
$.20
NEW MARGINAL BENEFIT CURVE
OLD MARGINAL BENEFIT CURVE
1 2 3 4 5 6 7 8 9 10 11 12 13 Q

IT'S THE SAME STORY, WITH **TWO DIFFERENT EXPLANATIONS!**

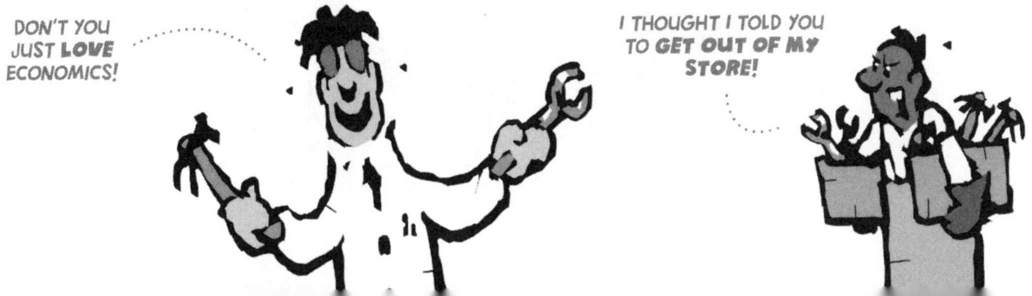

DON'T YOU JUST **LOVE** ECONOMICS!
I THOUGHT I TOLD YOU TO **GET OUT OF MY STORE!**

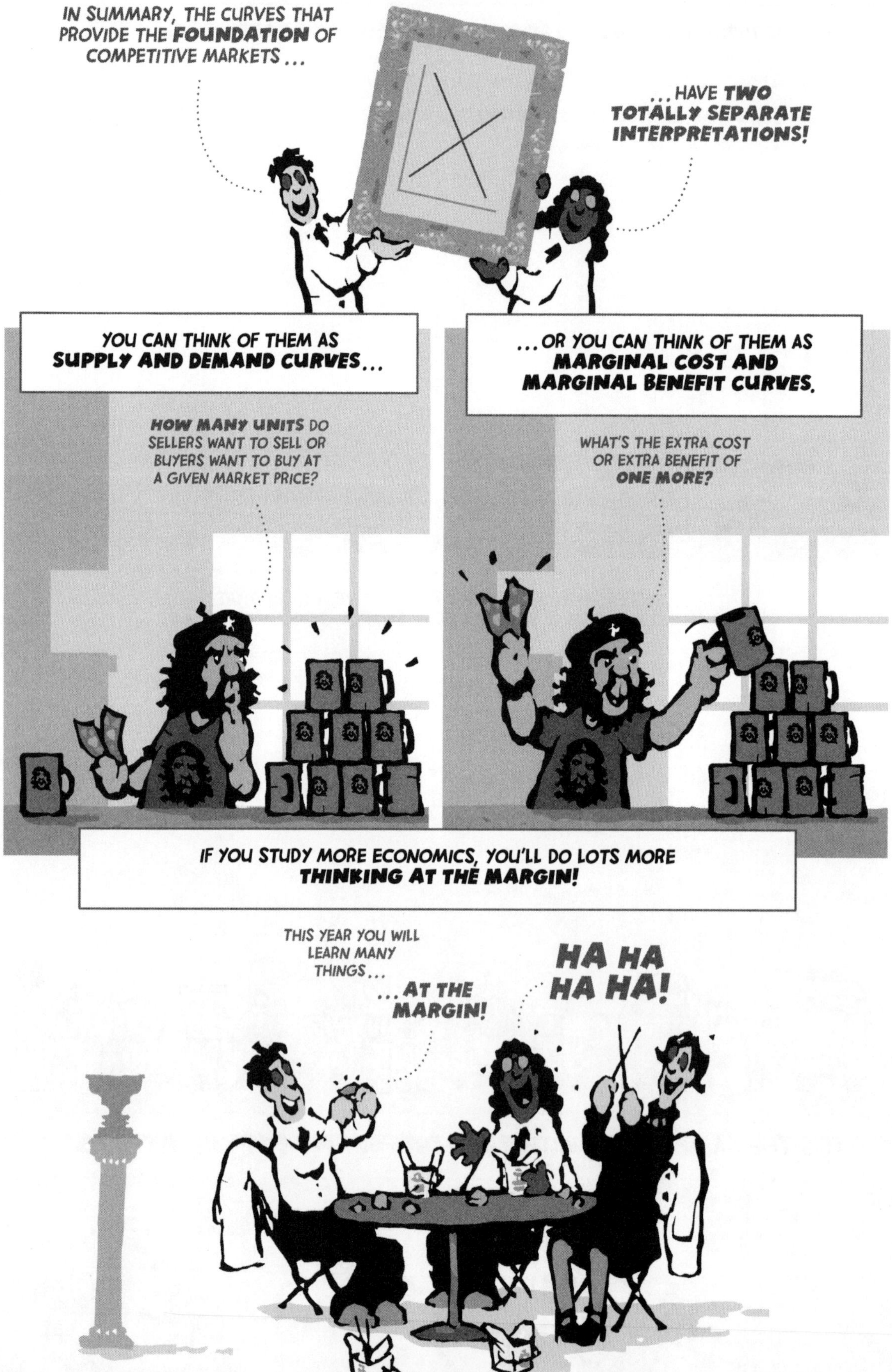
IN SUMMARY, THE CURVES THAT PROVIDE THE **FOUNDATION** OF COMPETITIVE MARKETS . . .
. . . HAVE **TWO TOTALLY SEPARATE INTERPRETATIONS!**
YOU CAN THINK OF THEM AS **SUPPLY AND DEMAND CURVES . . .**
HOW MANY UNITS DO SELLERS WANT TO SELL OR BUYERS WANT TO BUY AT A GIVEN MARKET PRICE?
. . . OR YOU CAN THINK OF THEM AS **MARGINAL COST AND MARGINAL BENEFIT CURVES.**
WHAT'S THE EXTRA COST OR EXTRA BENEFIT OF **ONE MORE?**
IF YOU STUDY MORE ECONOMICS, YOU'LL DO LOTS MORE **THINKING AT THE MARGIN!**
THIS YEAR YOU WILL LEARN MANY THINGS . . .
. . . AT THE MARGIN!
HA HA HA HA!

CHAPTER 14
ELASTICITY

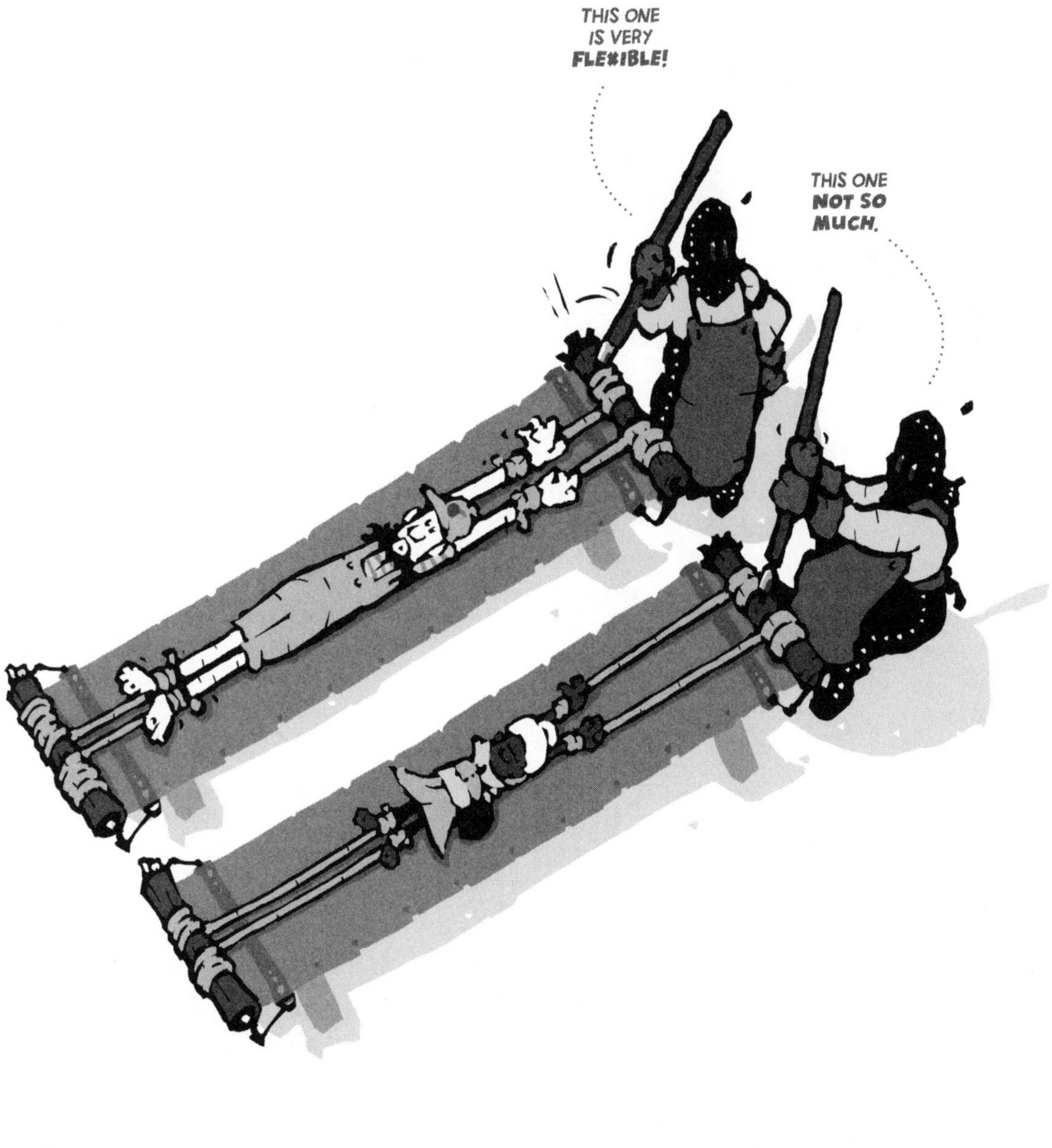

THIS ONE IS VERY FLEXIBLE!
THIS ONE NOT SO MUCH.

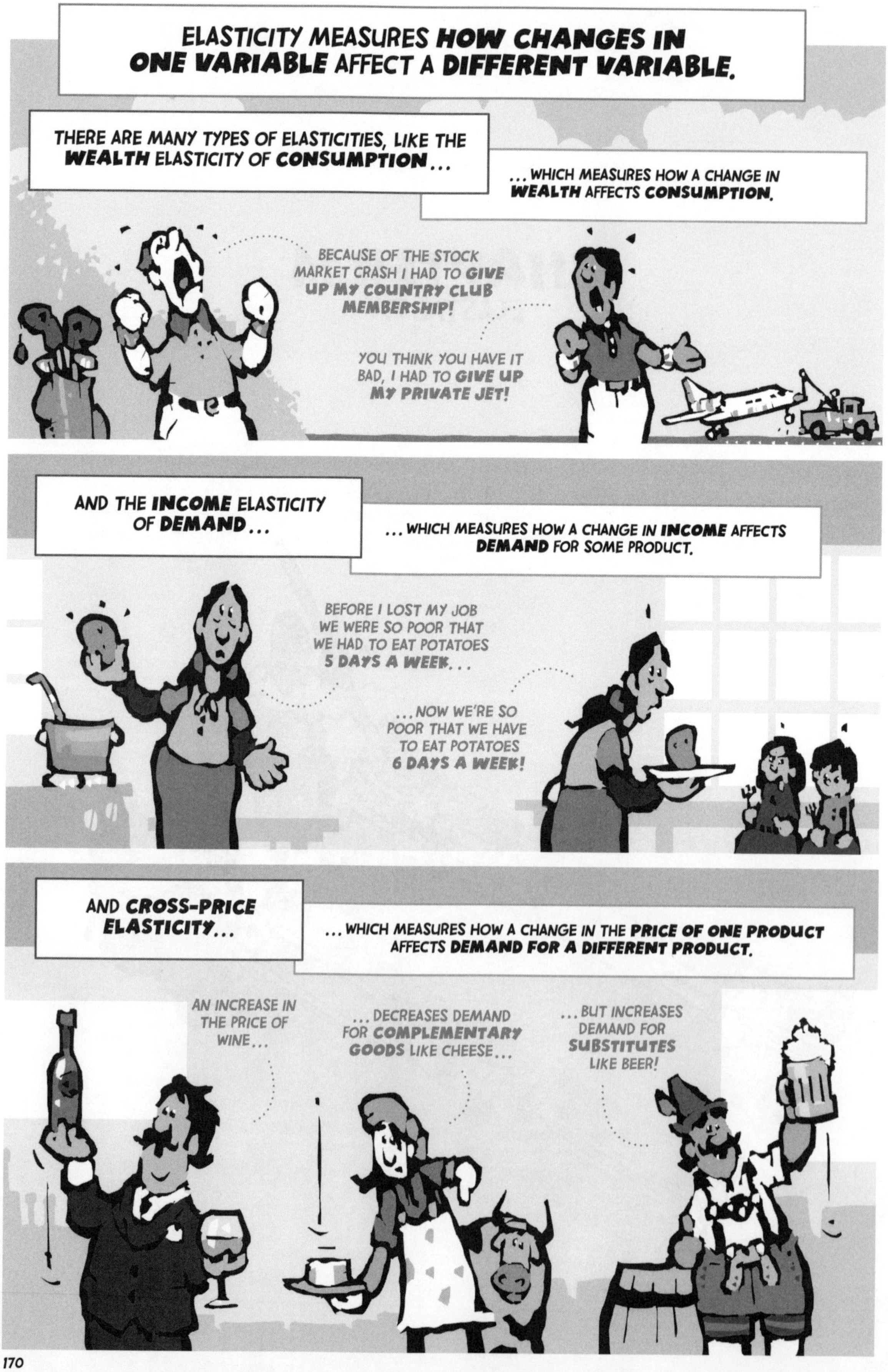
ELASTICITY MEASURES **HOW CHANGES IN ONE VARIABLE** AFFECT A **DIFFERENT VARIABLE.**
THERE ARE MANY TYPES OF ELASTICITIES, LIKE THE **WEALTH** ELASTICITY OF **CONSUMPTION**...
...WHICH MEASURES HOW A CHANGE IN **WEALTH** AFFECTS **CONSUMPTION.**
BECAUSE OF THE STOCK MARKET CRASH I HAD TO **GIVE UP MY COUNTRY CLUB MEMBERSHIP!**
YOU THINK YOU HAVE IT BAD, I HAD TO **GIVE UP MY PRIVATE JET!**
AND THE **INCOME** ELASTICITY OF **DEMAND**...
...WHICH MEASURES HOW A CHANGE IN **INCOME** AFFECTS **DEMAND** FOR SOME PRODUCT.
BEFORE I LOST MY JOB WE WERE SO POOR THAT WE HAD TO EAT POTATOES **5 DAYS A WEEK**...
...NOW WE'RE SO POOR THAT WE HAVE TO EAT POTATOES **6 DAYS A WEEK!**
AND **CROSS-PRICE ELASTICITY**...
...WHICH MEASURES HOW A CHANGE IN THE **PRICE OF ONE PRODUCT** AFFECTS **DEMAND FOR A DIFFERENT PRODUCT.**
AN INCREASE IN THE PRICE OF WINE...
...DECREASES DEMAND FOR **COMPLEMENTARY GOODS** LIKE CHEESE...
...BUT INCREASES DEMAND FOR **SUBSTITUTES** LIKE BEER!

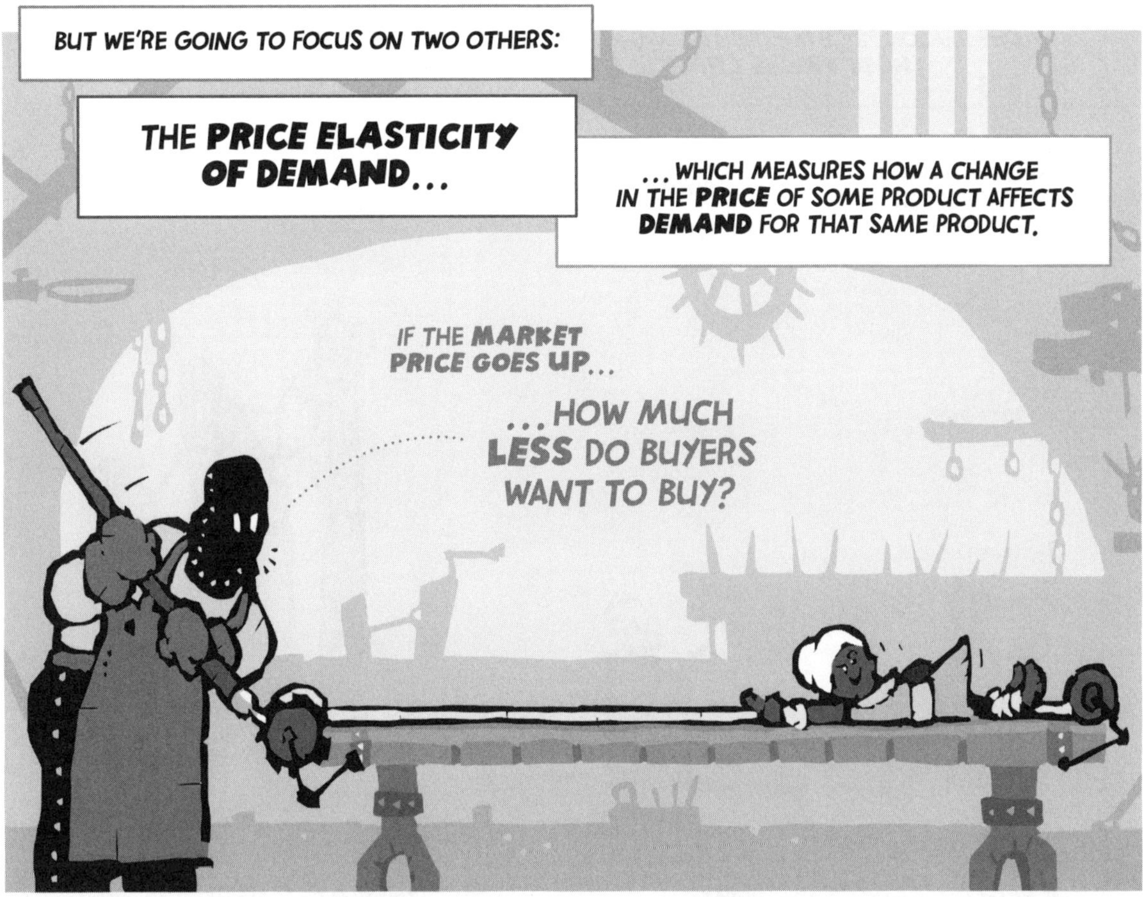

BUT WE'RE GOING TO FOCUS ON TWO OTHERS:
THE PRICE ELASTICITY OF DEMAND...
...WHICH MEASURES HOW A CHANGE IN THE PRICE OF SOME PRODUCT AFFECTS DEMAND FOR THAT SAME PRODUCT.
IF THE MARKET PRICE GOES UP...
...HOW MUCH LESS DO BUYERS WANT TO BUY?

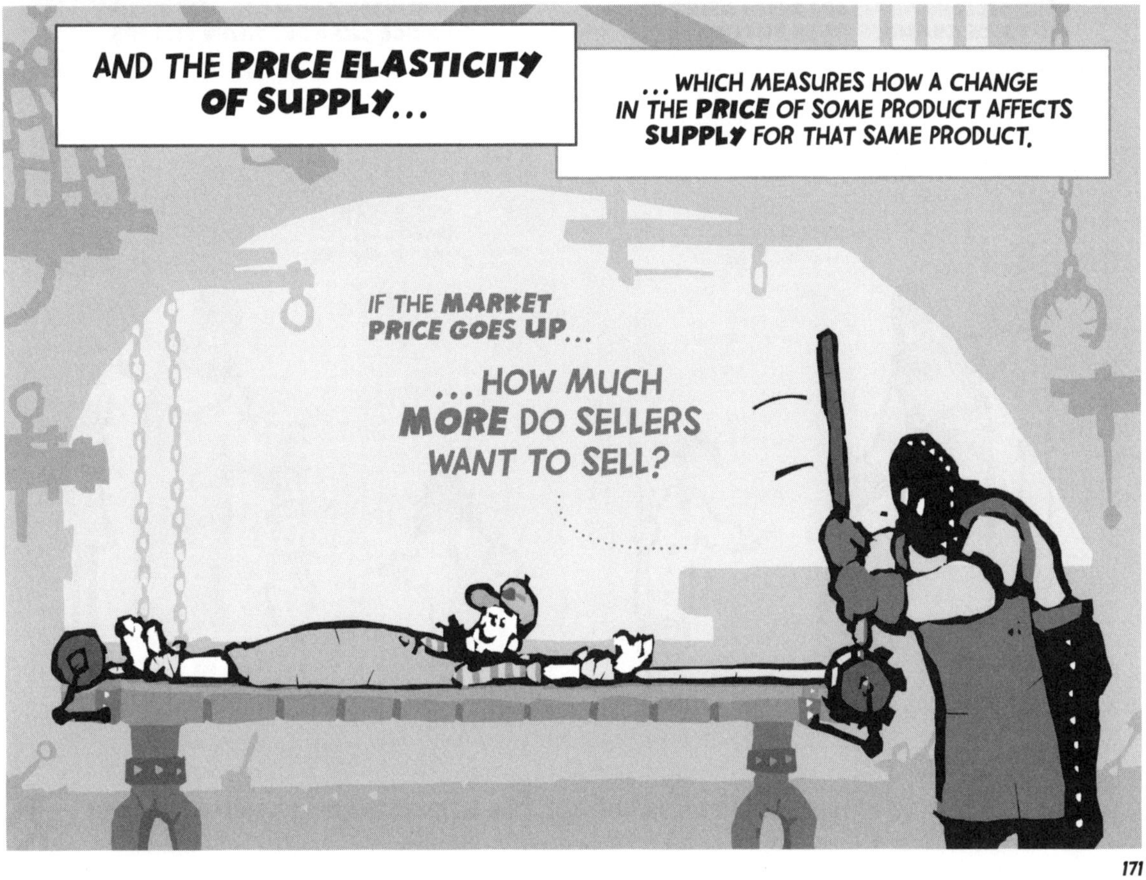

AND THE PRICE ELASTICITY OF SUPPLY...
...WHICH MEASURES HOW A CHANGE IN THE PRICE OF SOME PRODUCT AFFECTS SUPPLY FOR THAT SAME PRODUCT.
IF THE MARKET PRICE GOES UP...
...HOW MUCH MORE DO SELLERS WANT TO SELL?

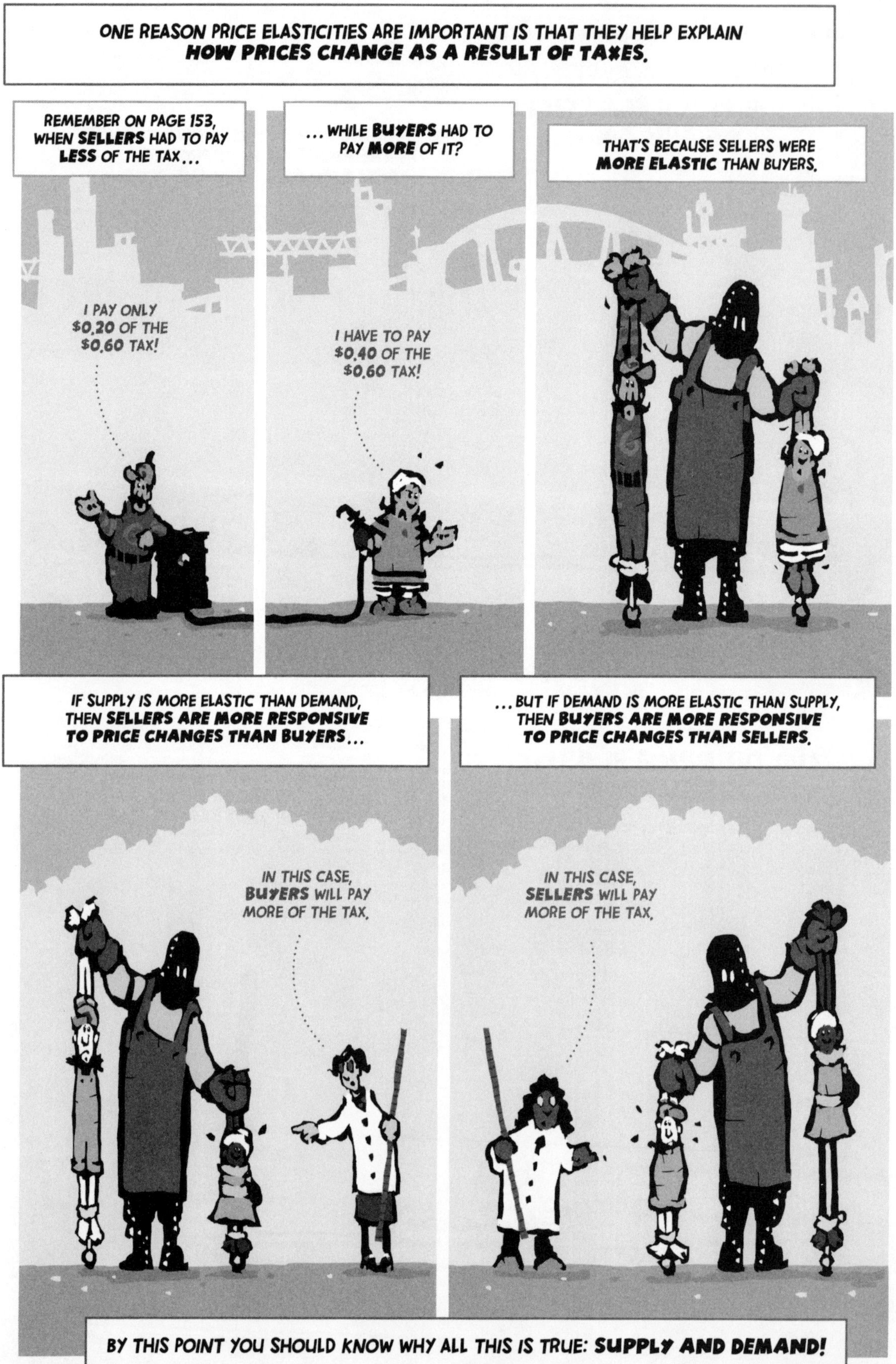
ONE REASON PRICE ELASTICITIES ARE IMPORTANT IS THAT THEY HELP EXPLAIN **HOW PRICES CHANGE AS A RESULT OF TAXES.**
REMEMBER ON PAGE 153, WHEN **SELLERS** HAD TO PAY **LESS** OF THE TAX...
I PAY ONLY $0.20 OF THE $0.60 TAX!
...WHILE **BUYERS** HAD TO PAY **MORE** OF IT?
I HAVE TO PAY $0.40 OF THE $0.60 TAX!
THAT'S BECAUSE SELLERS WERE **MORE ELASTIC** THAN BUYERS.
IF SUPPLY IS MORE ELASTIC THAN DEMAND, THEN **SELLERS ARE MORE RESPONSIVE TO PRICE CHANGES THAN BUYERS**...
IN THIS CASE, **BUYERS** WILL PAY MORE OF THE TAX.
...BUT IF DEMAND IS MORE ELASTIC THAN SUPPLY, THEN **BUYERS ARE MORE RESPONSIVE TO PRICE CHANGES THAN SELLERS.**
IN THIS CASE, **SELLERS** WILL PAY MORE OF THE TAX.
BY THIS POINT YOU SHOULD KNOW WHY ALL THIS IS TRUE: **SUPPLY AND DEMAND!**

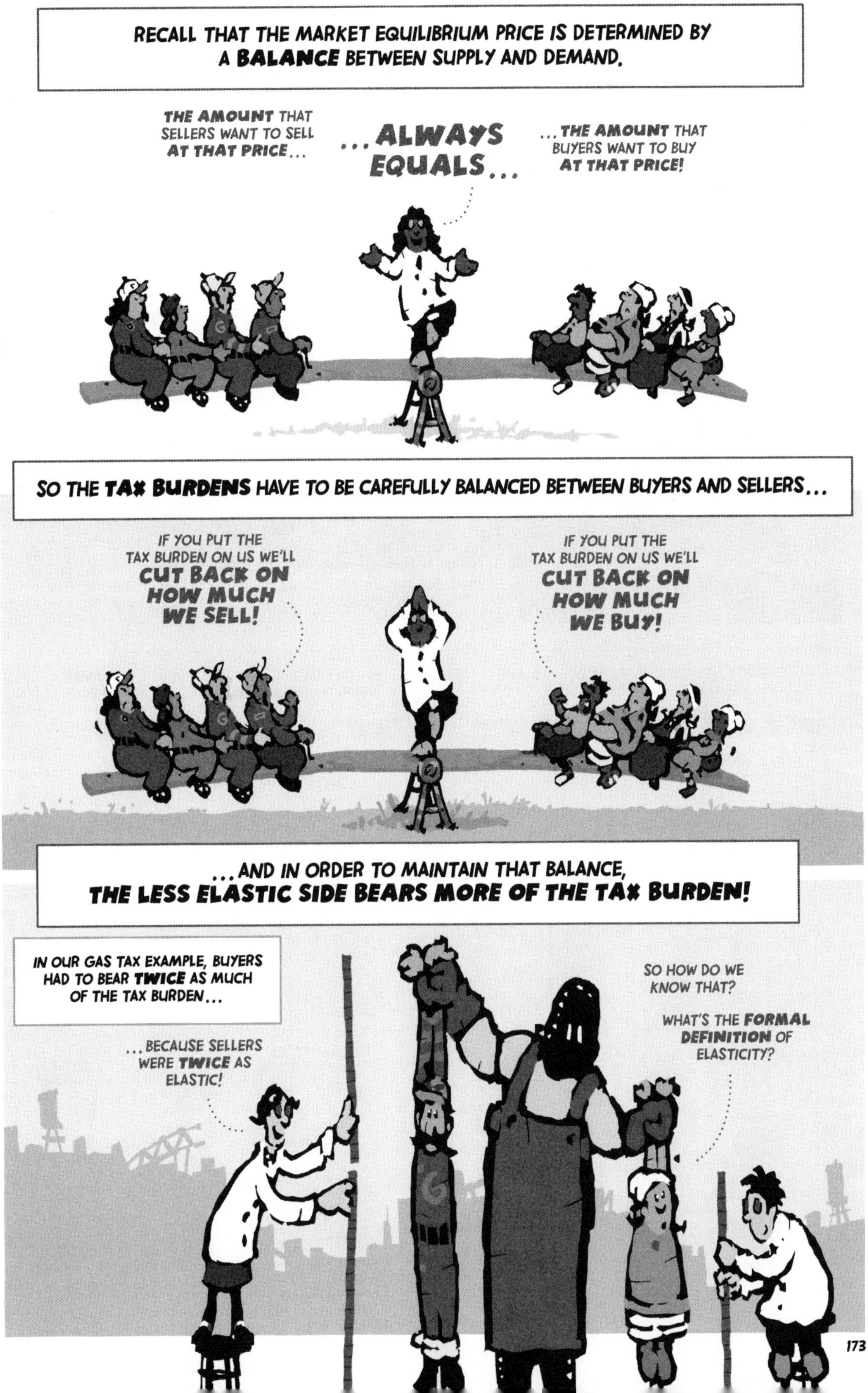
RECALL THAT THE MARKET EQUILIBRIUM PRICE IS DETERMINED BY A **BALANCE** BETWEEN SUPPLY AND DEMAND.
THE AMOUNT THAT SELLERS WANT TO SELL **AT THAT PRICE**...
...**ALWAYS EQUALS**...
...**THE AMOUNT** THAT BUYERS WANT TO BUY **AT THAT PRICE!**
SO THE **TAX BURDENS** HAVE TO BE CAREFULLY BALANCED BETWEEN BUYERS AND SELLERS...
IF YOU PUT THE TAX BURDEN ON US WE'LL **CUT BACK ON HOW MUCH WE SELL!**
IF YOU PUT THE TAX BURDEN ON US WE'LL **CUT BACK ON HOW MUCH WE BUY!**
...AND IN ORDER TO MAINTAIN THAT BALANCE, **THE LESS ELASTIC SIDE BEARS MORE OF THE TAX BURDEN!**
IN OUR GAS TAX EXAMPLE, BUYERS HAD TO BEAR **TWICE** AS MUCH OF THE TAX BURDEN...
...BECAUSE SELLERS WERE **TWICE** AS ELASTIC!
SO HOW DO WE KNOW THAT?
WHAT'S THE **FORMAL DEFINITION** OF ELASTICITY?

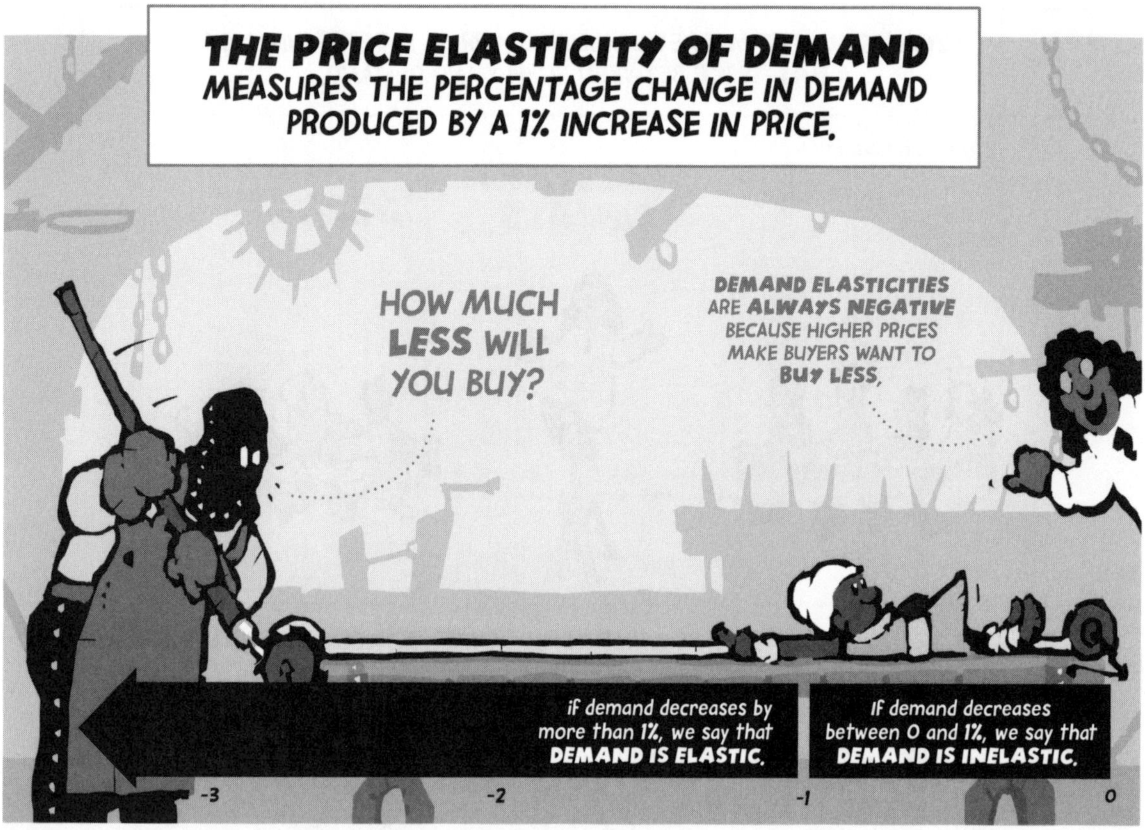
THE PRICE ELASTICITY OF DEMAND
MEASURES THE PERCENTAGE CHANGE IN DEMAND PRODUCED BY A 1% INCREASE IN PRICE.
HOW MUCH LESS WILL YOU BUY?
DEMAND ELASTICITIES ARE ALWAYS NEGATIVE BECAUSE HIGHER PRICES MAKE BUYERS WANT TO BUY LESS.
If demand decreases by more than 1%, we say that DEMAND IS ELASTIC.
If demand decreases between 0 and 1%, we say that DEMAND IS INELASTIC.
-3
-2
-1
0

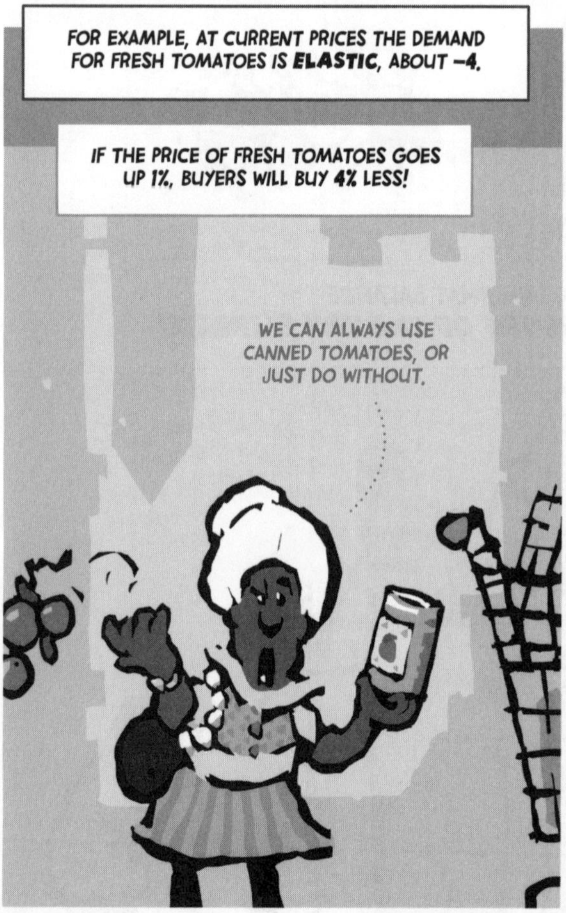
FOR EXAMPLE, AT CURRENT PRICES THE DEMAND FOR FRESH TOMATOES IS ELASTIC, ABOUT −4.
IF THE PRICE OF FRESH TOMATOES GOES UP 1%, BUYERS WILL BUY 4% LESS!
WE CAN ALWAYS USE CANNED TOMATOES, OR JUST DO WITHOUT.

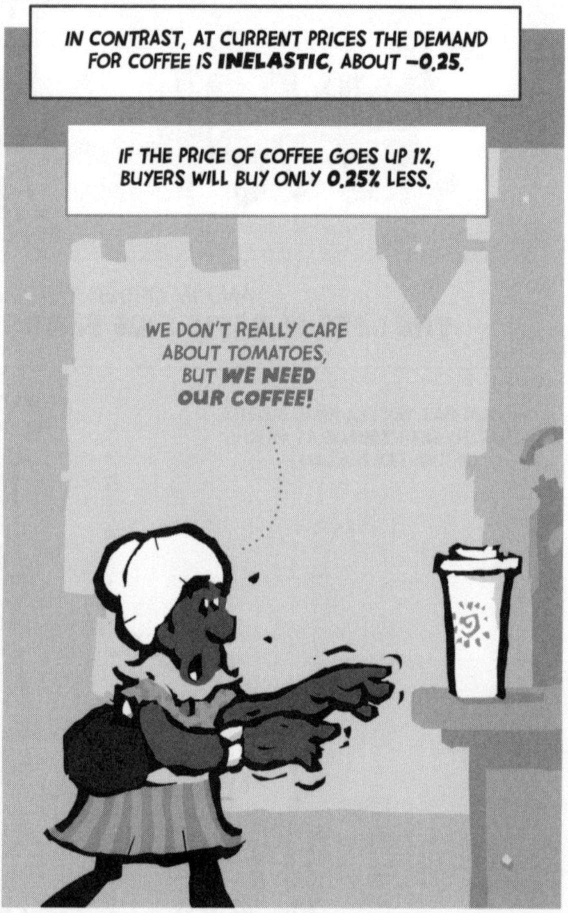
IN CONTRAST, AT CURRENT PRICES THE DEMAND FOR COFFEE IS INELASTIC, ABOUT −0.25.
IF THE PRICE OF COFFEE GOES UP 1%, BUYERS WILL BUY ONLY 0.25% LESS.
WE DON'T REALLY CARE ABOUT TOMATOES, BUT WE NEED OUR COFFEE!

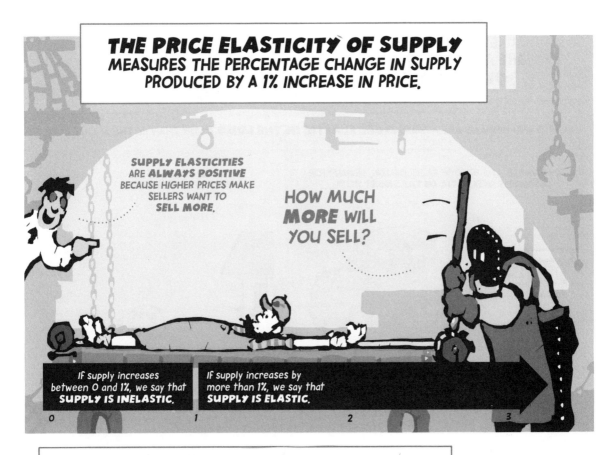

THE PRICE ELASTICITY OF SUPPLY
MEASURES THE PERCENTAGE CHANGE IN SUPPLY PRODUCED BY A 1% INCREASE IN PRICE.

SUPPLY ELASTICITIES ARE **ALWAYS POSITIVE** BECAUSE HIGHER PRICES MAKE SELLERS WANT TO **SELL MORE**.

HOW MUCH **MORE** WILL YOU SELL?

If supply increases between 0 and 1%, we say that **SUPPLY IS INELASTIC**.

If supply increases by more than 1%, we say that **SUPPLY IS ELASTIC**.

0   1   2   3

IT'S IMPORTANT TO NOTE THAT ELASTICITIES ARE **ALWAYS MEASURED AT A PARTICULAR POINT...**

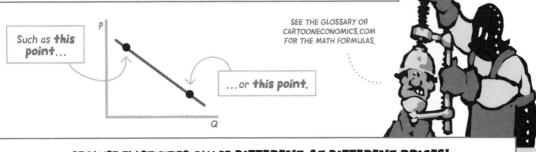

Such as **this point**...

...or **this point**.

SEE THE GLOSSARY OR CARTOONECONOMICS.COM FOR THE MATH FORMULAS.

... BECAUSE ELASTICITIES CAN BE **DIFFERENT AT DIFFERENT PRICES!**

MY PRICE SENSITIVITY IS A LOT **LESS** AT A MARKET PRICE OF $2 PER GALLON...

...THAN AT A MARKET PRICE OF $5 PER GALLON.

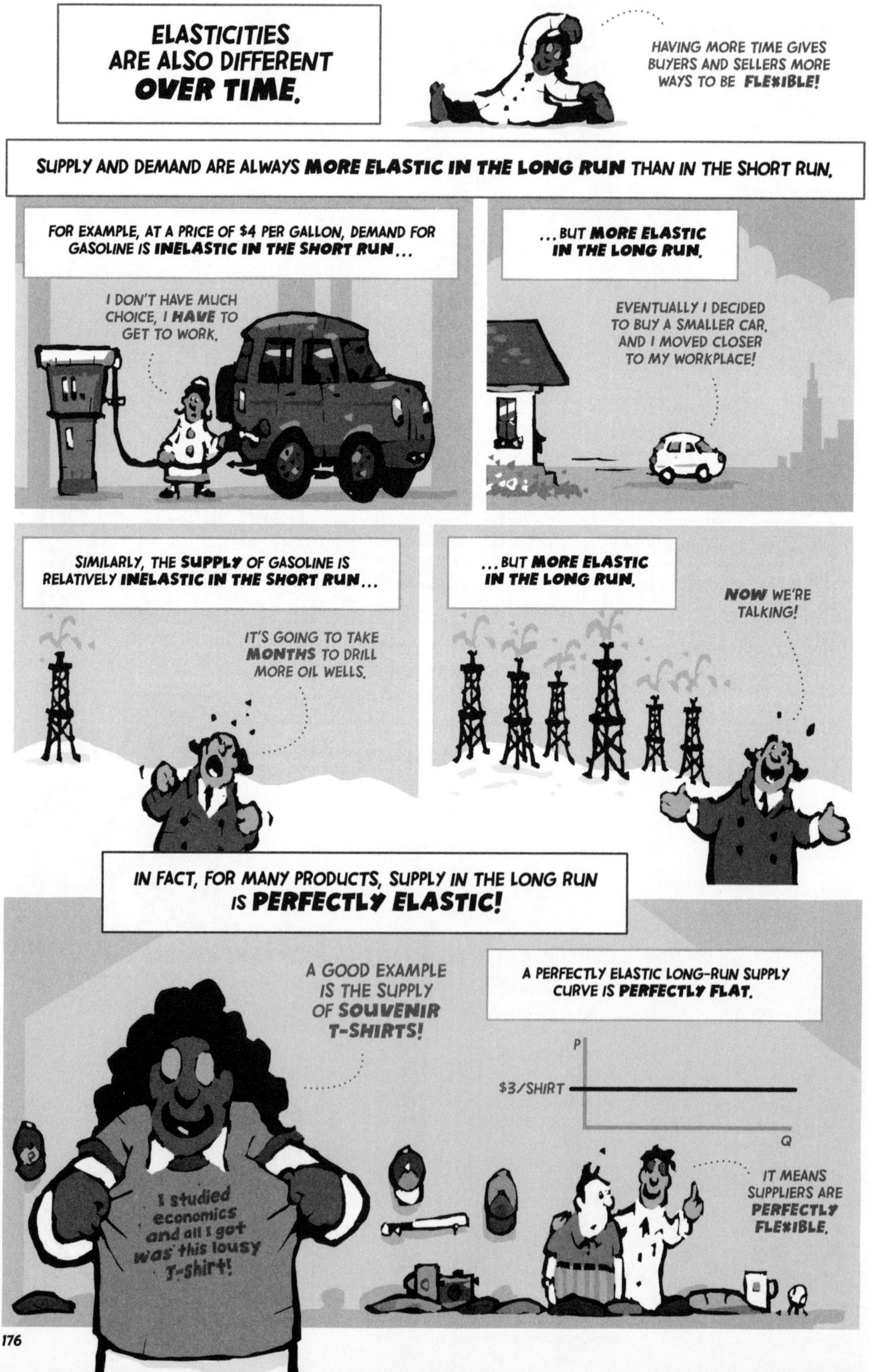
ELASTICITIES ARE ALSO DIFFERENT **OVER TIME.**
HAVING MORE TIME GIVES BUYERS AND SELLERS MORE WAYS TO BE **FLEXIBLE!**
SUPPLY AND DEMAND ARE ALWAYS **MORE ELASTIC IN THE LONG RUN** THAN IN THE SHORT RUN.
FOR EXAMPLE, AT A PRICE OF $4 PER GALLON, DEMAND FOR GASOLINE IS **INELASTIC IN THE SHORT RUN...**
I DON'T HAVE MUCH CHOICE, I **HAVE** TO GET TO WORK.
...BUT **MORE ELASTIC IN THE LONG RUN.**
EVENTUALLY I DECIDED TO BUY A SMALLER CAR, AND I MOVED CLOSER TO MY WORKPLACE!
SIMILARLY, THE **SUPPLY** OF GASOLINE IS RELATIVELY **INELASTIC IN THE SHORT RUN...**
IT'S GOING TO TAKE **MONTHS** TO DRILL MORE OIL WELLS.
...BUT **MORE ELASTIC IN THE LONG RUN.**
NOW WE'RE TALKING!
IN FACT, FOR MANY PRODUCTS, SUPPLY IN THE LONG RUN IS **PERFECTLY ELASTIC!**
A GOOD EXAMPLE IS THE SUPPLY OF **SOUVENIR T-SHIRTS!**
A PERFECTLY ELASTIC LONG-RUN SUPPLY CURVE IS **PERFECTLY FLAT.**
P
$3/SHIRT
Q
I studied economics and all I got was this lousy T-shirt!
IT MEANS SUPPLIERS ARE **PERFECTLY FLEXIBLE.**

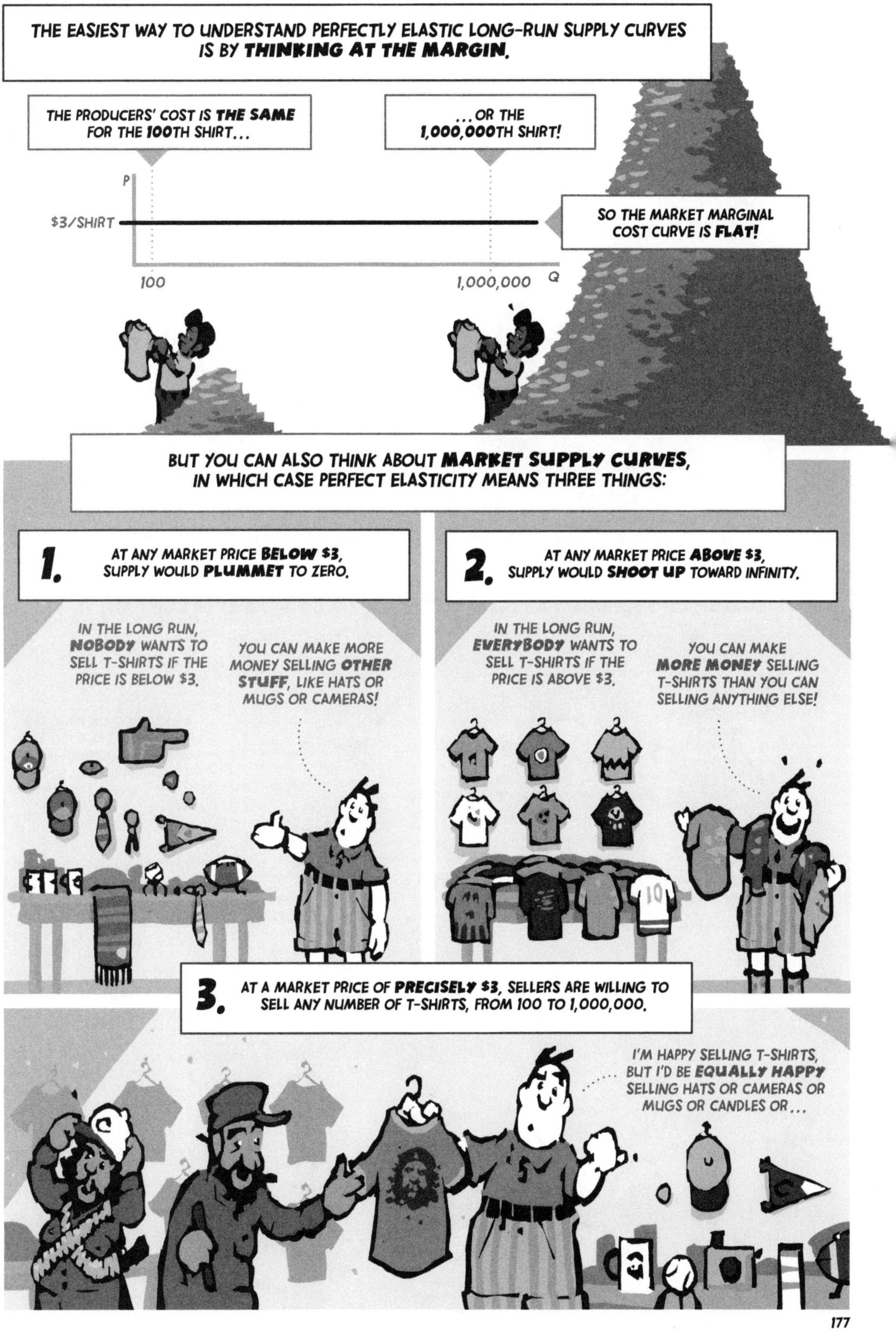
THE EASIEST WAY TO UNDERSTAND PERFECTLY ELASTIC LONG-RUN SUPPLY CURVES IS BY THINKING AT THE MARGIN.
THE PRODUCERS' COST IS THE SAME FOR THE 100TH SHIRT...
...OR THE 1,000,000TH SHIRT!
P
$3/SHIRT
100
1,000,000
Q
SO THE MARKET MARGINAL COST CURVE IS FLAT!
BUT YOU CAN ALSO THINK ABOUT MARKET SUPPLY CURVES, IN WHICH CASE PERFECT ELASTICITY MEANS THREE THINGS:
1. AT ANY MARKET PRICE BELOW $3, SUPPLY WOULD PLUMMET TO ZERO.
IN THE LONG RUN, NOBODY WANTS TO SELL T-SHIRTS IF THE PRICE IS BELOW $3.
YOU CAN MAKE MORE MONEY SELLING OTHER STUFF, LIKE HATS OR MUGS OR CAMERAS!
2. AT ANY MARKET PRICE ABOVE $3, SUPPLY WOULD SHOOT UP TOWARD INFINITY.
IN THE LONG RUN, EVERYBODY WANTS TO SELL T-SHIRTS IF THE PRICE IS ABOVE $3.
YOU CAN MAKE MORE MONEY SELLING T-SHIRTS THAN YOU CAN SELLING ANYTHING ELSE!
3. AT A MARKET PRICE OF PRECISELY $3, SELLERS ARE WILLING TO SELL ANY NUMBER OF T-SHIRTS, FROM 100 TO 1,000,000.
I'M HAPPY SELLING T-SHIRTS, BUT I'D BE EQUALLY HAPPY SELLING HATS OR CAMERAS OR MUGS OR CANDLES OR...

MANY GOODS AND SERVICES HAVE PERFECTLY ELASTIC LONG-RUN SUPPLY...

LIKE FLOUR AND GLASS BOTTLES AND HAMMERS...

...AND BUZZ CUTS...

...AND ANY OTHER GOOD OR SERVICE WHERE THE 100TH UNIT IS NO MORE AND NO LESS COSTLY TO PRODUCE THAN THE 1,000,000TH UNIT!

...SO IT'S IMPORTANT TO CONSIDER HOW TAXES AFFECT MARKETS WITH PERFECTLY ELASTIC LONG-RUN SUPPLY.

FOR AN EXAMPLE, LET'S SEE WHAT HAPPENS IF THERE'S A $1 TAX ON THE BUYERS OF T-SHIRTS.

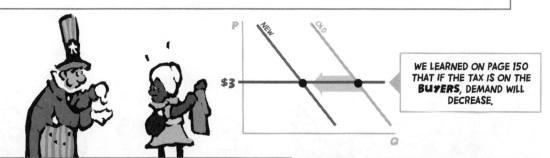

WE LEARNED ON PAGE 150 THAT IF THE TAX IS ON THE BUYERS, DEMAND WILL DECREASE.

AS THE GRAPH SHOWS, A TAX ON THE BUYERS DOESN'T CHANGE THE MARKET EQUILIBRIUM PRICE...

I PAY $3 TO THE SELLER, PLUS THE $1 TAX, FOR A TOTAL OF $4 PER SHIRT.

I STILL GET $3 PER SHIRT.

...WHICH MEANS THAT BUYERS BEAR THE ENTIRE TAX BURDEN!

SUPPLY IS SO ELASTIC THAT YOU CAN'T PUSH ANY OF THE TAX BURDEN ONTO HIM!

WE KNOW FROM **TAX EQUIVALENCE** THAT THE END RESULT WILL BE THE SAME IF THE TAX IS PLACED ON THE **SELLERS**.

BUT IT'S EASY TO SEE THIS BY JUST LOOKING AT THINGS FROM THE SELLERS' PERSPECTIVE IF THERE'S A $1 TAX ON THE **SELLERS** OF T-SHIRTS.

IN THE LONG RUN, SELLERS **WILL STOP SELLING T-SHIRTS** IF THEY END UP WITH LESS THAN $3 AFTER PAYING THE TAX...

IF I CAN'T MAKE A DECENT PROFIT SELLING T-SHIRTS...

...I'LL SELL OTHER STUFF, LIKE CAMERAS OR HATS.

... SO IN THE LONG RUN IT'S **IMPOSSIBLE** FOR THE SELLERS TO BEAR ANY OF THE TAX BURDEN!

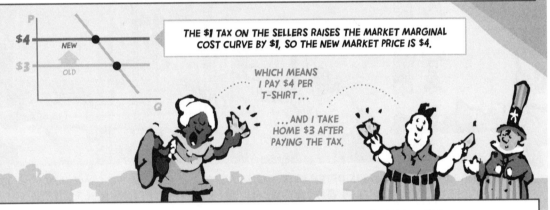

THE $1 TAX ON THE SELLERS RAISES THE MARKET MARGINAL COST CURVE BY $1, SO THE NEW MARKET PRICE IS $4.

WHICH MEANS I PAY $4 PER T-SHIRT...

...AND I TAKE HOME $3 AFTER PAYING THE TAX.

IN SUMMARY: WITH A PERFECTLY ELASTIC LONG-RUN SUPPLY CURVE, **THE BUYERS BEAR THE ENTIRE TAX BURDEN!**

THAT'S NOT FAIR, WHY DO **WE** ALWAYS HAVE TO PAY THE TAX?

WELL, WE DO HAVE **SOME** GOOD NEWS FOR YOU...

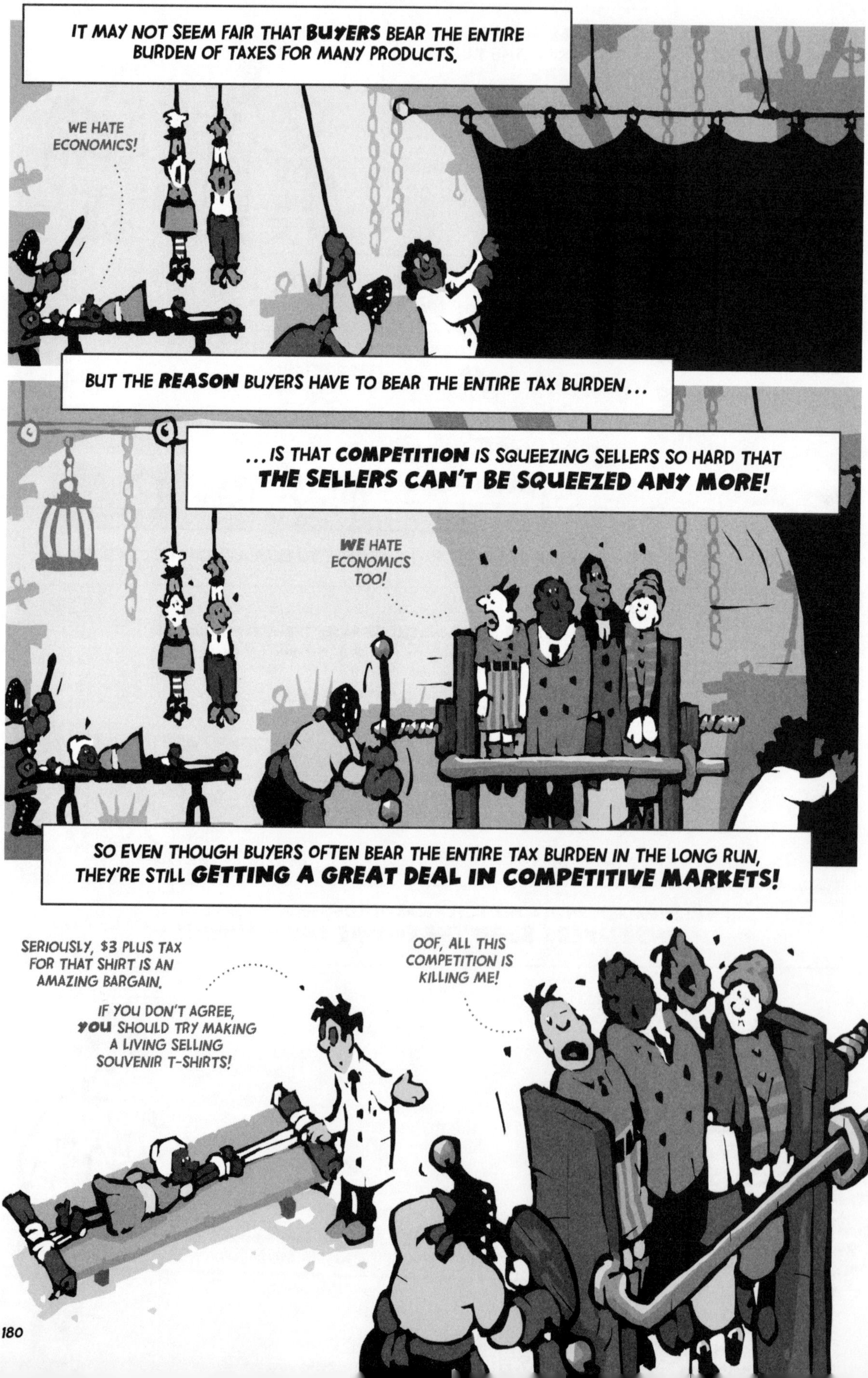
IT MAY NOT SEEM FAIR THAT BUYERS BEAR THE ENTIRE BURDEN OF TAXES FOR MANY PRODUCTS.
WE HATE ECONOMICS!
BUT THE REASON BUYERS HAVE TO BEAR THE ENTIRE TAX BURDEN...
...IS THAT COMPETITION IS SQUEEZING SELLERS SO HARD THAT THE SELLERS CAN'T BE SQUEEZED ANY MORE!
WE HATE ECONOMICS TOO!
SO EVEN THOUGH BUYERS OFTEN BEAR THE ENTIRE TAX BURDEN IN THE LONG RUN, THEY'RE STILL GETTING A GREAT DEAL IN COMPETITIVE MARKETS!
SERIOUSLY, $3 PLUS TAX FOR THAT SHIRT IS AN AMAZING BARGAIN.
IF YOU DON'T AGREE, YOU SHOULD TRY MAKING A LIVING SELLING SOUVENIR T-SHIRTS!
OOF, ALL THIS COMPETITION IS KILLING ME!

CHAPTER 15
THE BIG PICTURE

ECONOMISTS SEE THE WORLD **DIFFERENTLY.**

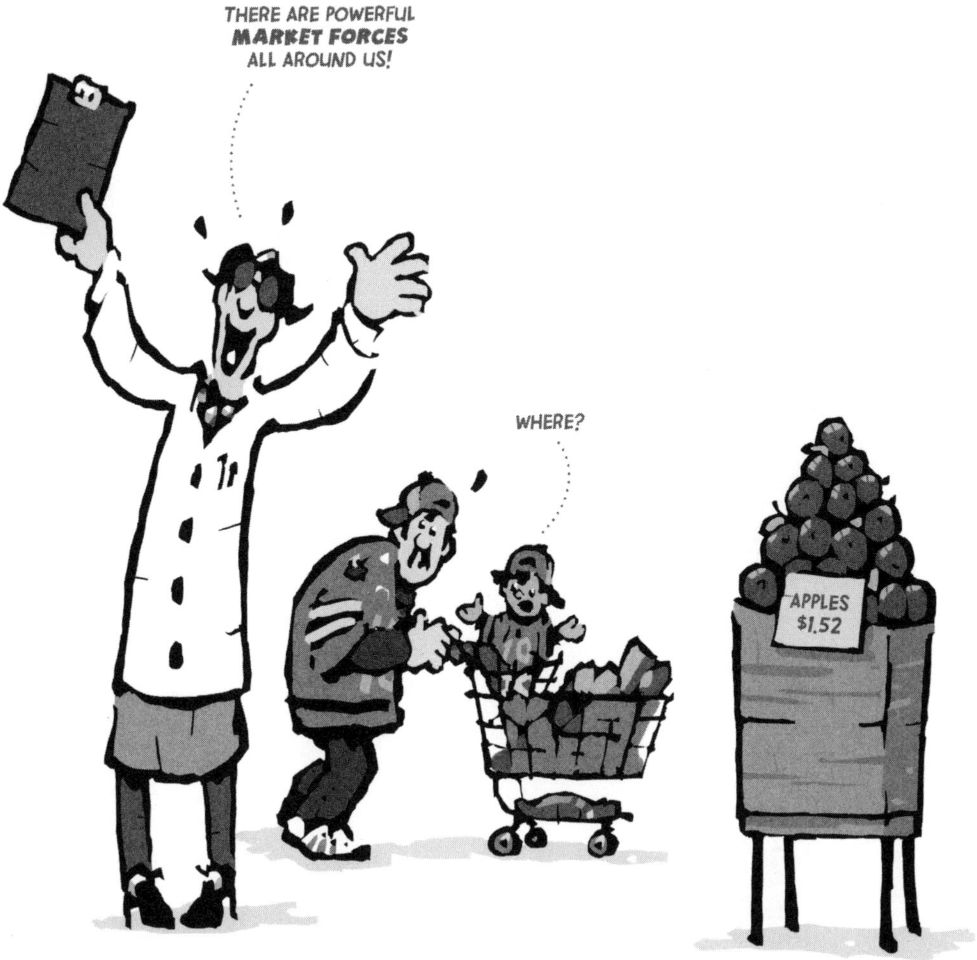
THERE ARE POWERFUL **MARKET FORCES** ALL AROUND US!
WHERE?
APPLES $1.52

THE ECONOMIC WORLDVIEW IS STRONGLY INFLUENCED BY ONE SIMPLE IDEA:
COMPETITIVE MARKETS ARE GREAT!

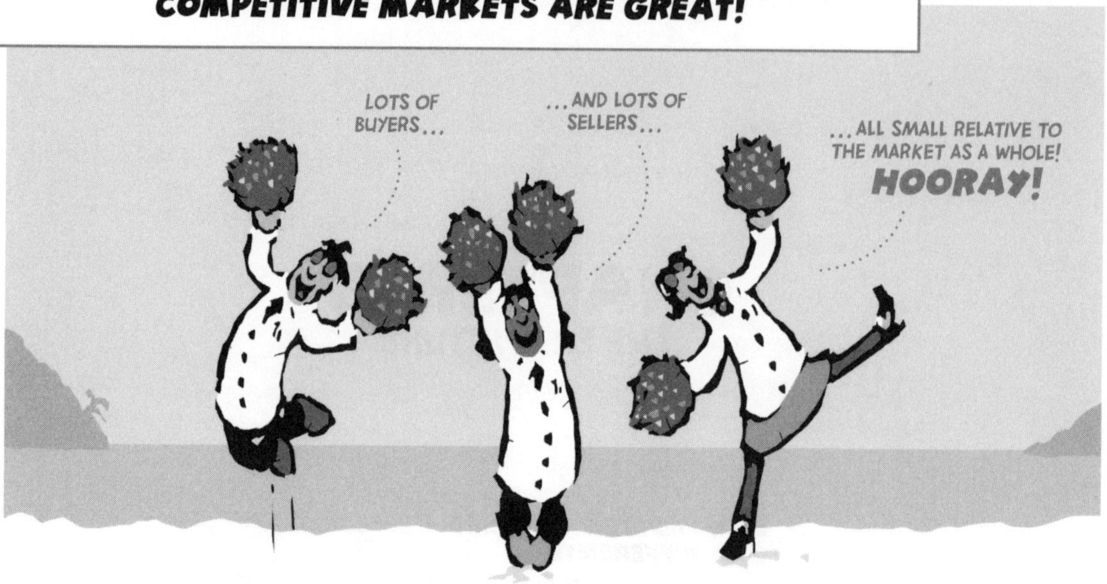
LOTS OF BUYERS...
...AND LOTS OF SELLERS...
...ALL SMALL RELATIVE TO THE MARKET AS A WHOLE!
HOORAY!

THE BENEFITS OF COMPETITIVE MARKETS CAN BE SEEN FROM THE **COASE THEOREM.**

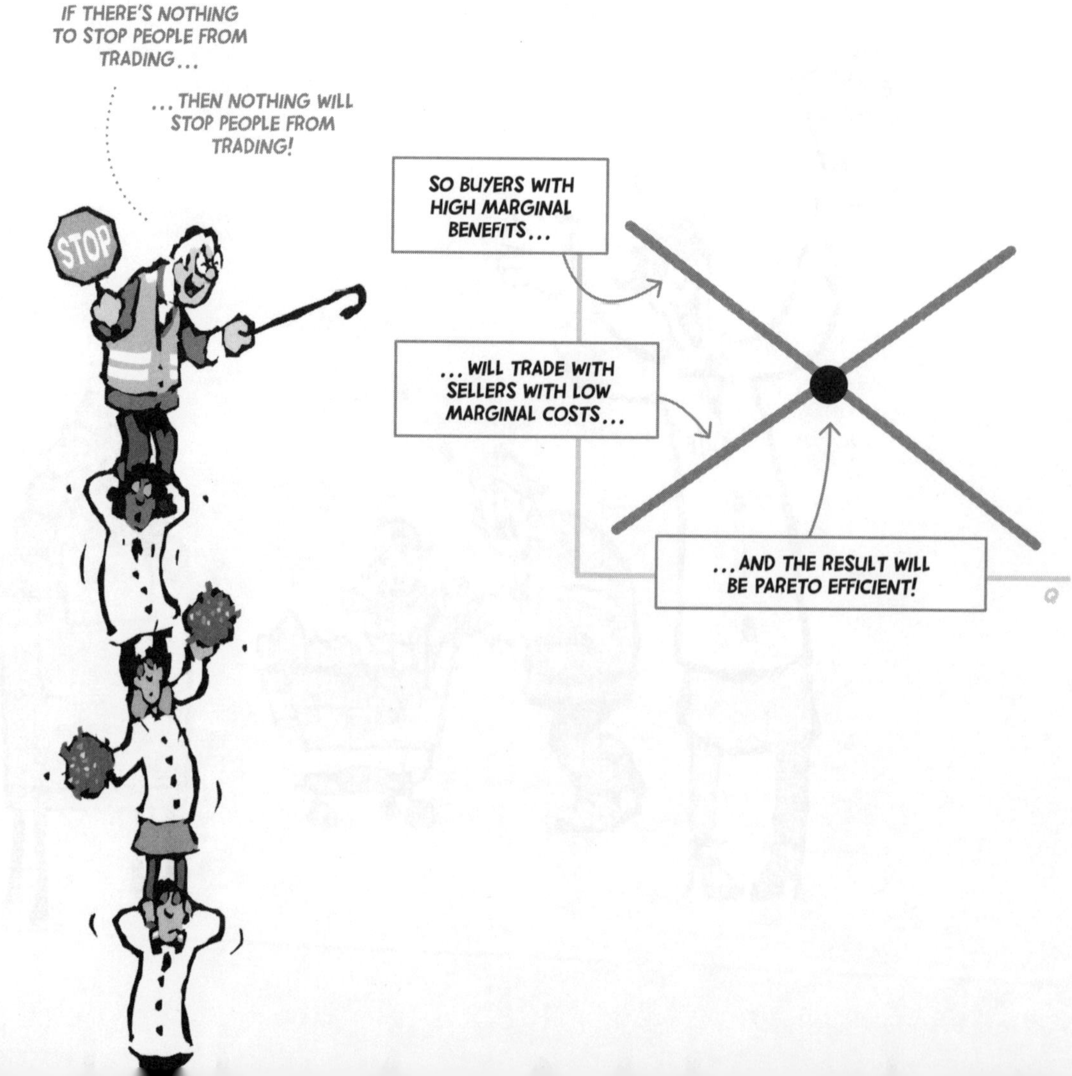
IF THERE'S NOTHING TO STOP PEOPLE FROM TRADING...
...THEN NOTHING WILL STOP PEOPLE FROM TRADING!
STOP
SO BUYERS WITH HIGH MARGINAL BENEFITS...
...WILL TRADE WITH SELLERS WITH LOW MARGINAL COSTS...
...AND THE RESULT WILL BE PARETO EFFICIENT!
Q

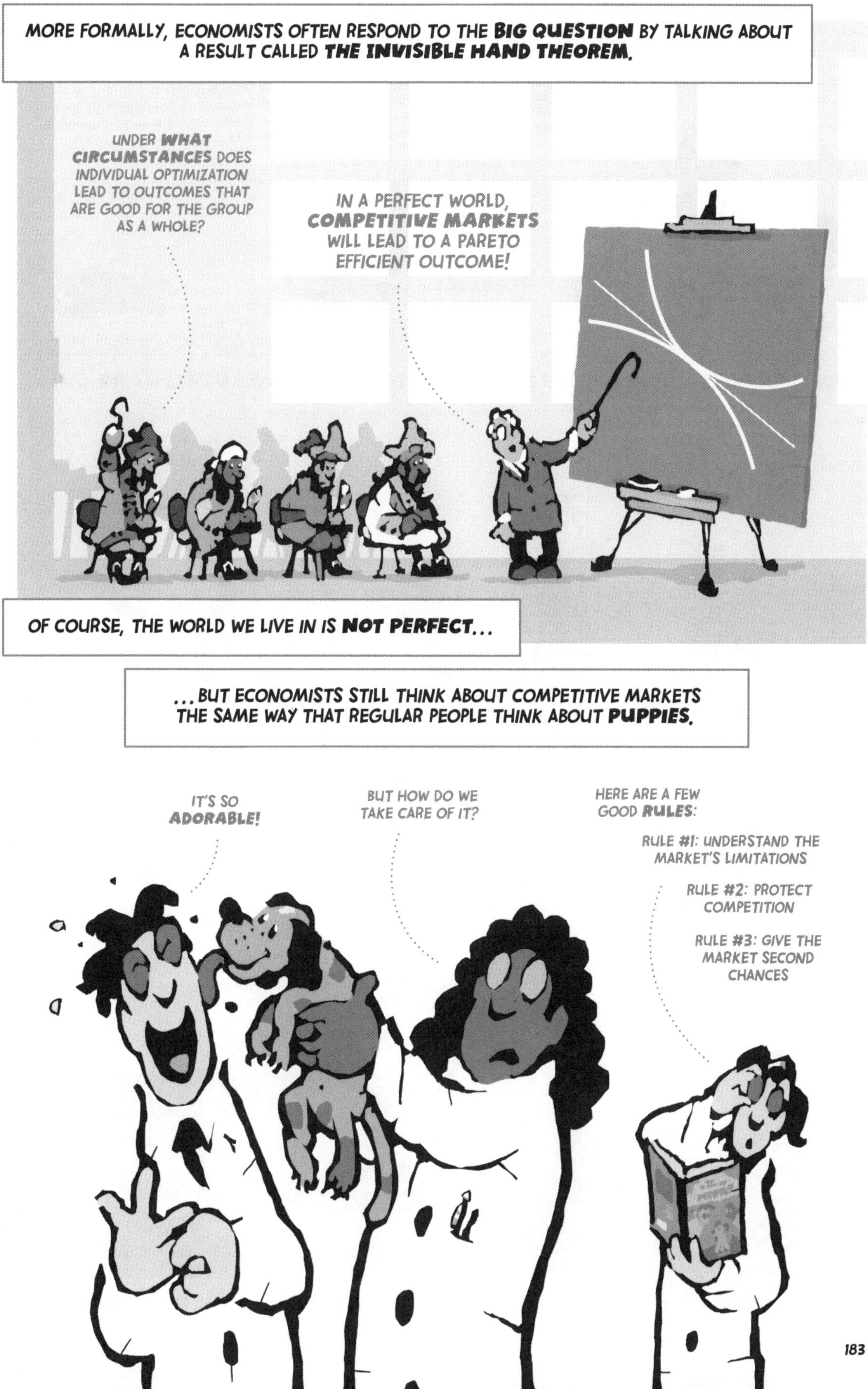
MORE FORMALLY, ECONOMISTS OFTEN RESPOND TO THE **BIG QUESTION** BY TALKING ABOUT A RESULT CALLED **THE INVISIBLE HAND THEOREM.**
UNDER **WHAT CIRCUMSTANCES** DOES INDIVIDUAL OPTIMIZATION LEAD TO OUTCOMES THAT ARE GOOD FOR THE GROUP AS A WHOLE?
IN A PERFECT WORLD, **COMPETITIVE MARKETS** WILL LEAD TO A PARETO EFFICIENT OUTCOME!
OF COURSE, THE WORLD WE LIVE IN IS **NOT PERFECT**...
...BUT ECONOMISTS STILL THINK ABOUT COMPETITIVE MARKETS THE SAME WAY THAT REGULAR PEOPLE THINK ABOUT **PUPPIES.**
IT'S SO **ADORABLE!**
BUT HOW DO WE TAKE CARE OF IT?
HERE ARE A FEW GOOD **RULES**:
RULE #1: UNDERSTAND THE MARKET'S LIMITATIONS
RULE #2: PROTECT COMPETITION
RULE #3: GIVE THE MARKET SECOND CHANCES

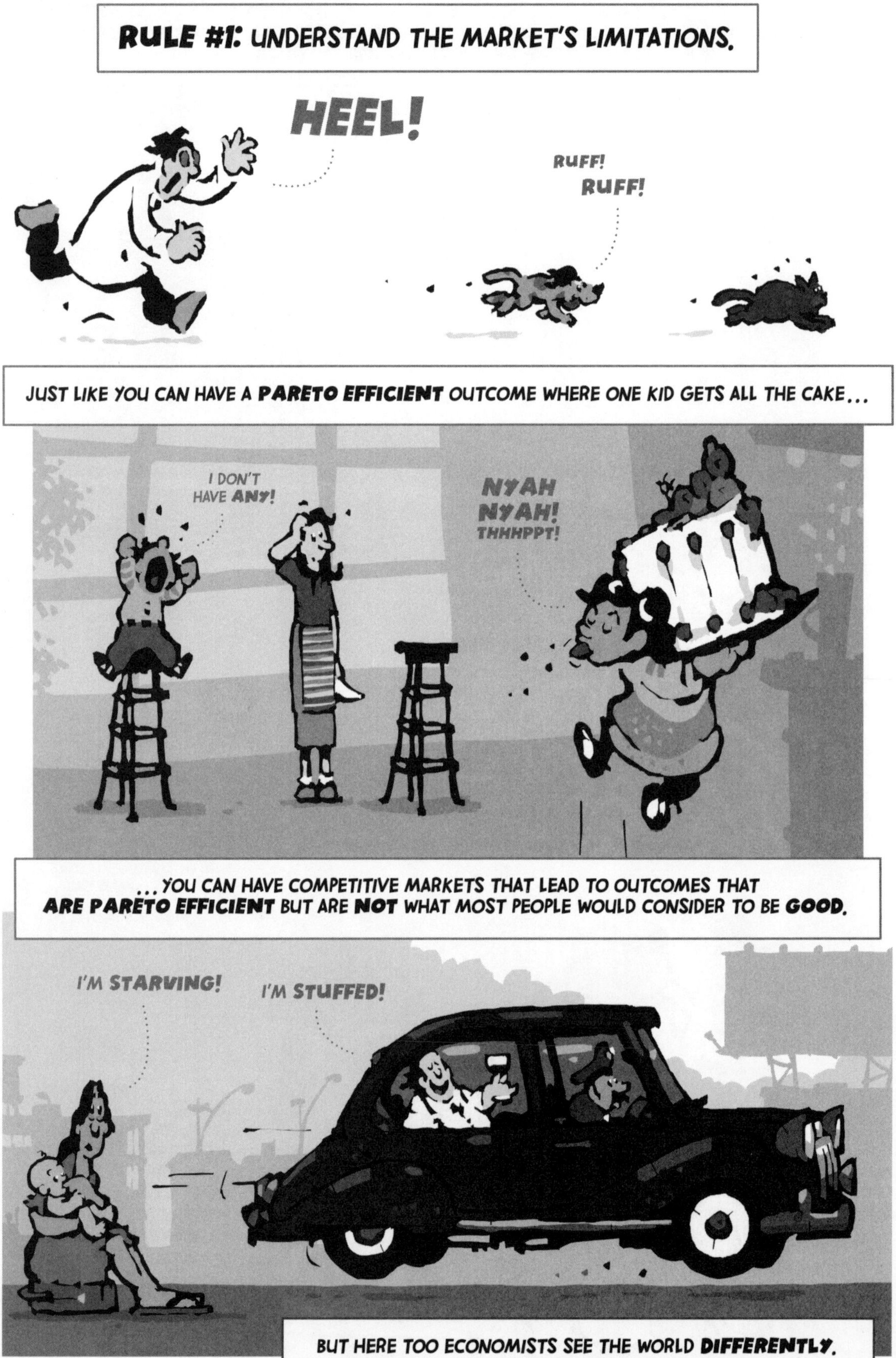
RULE #1: UNDERSTAND THE MARKET'S LIMITATIONS.
HEEL!
RUFF!
RUFF!
JUST LIKE YOU CAN HAVE A PARETO EFFICIENT OUTCOME WHERE ONE KID GETS ALL THE CAKE...
I DON'T HAVE ANY!
NYAH NYAH! THHHPPT!
...YOU CAN HAVE COMPETITIVE MARKETS THAT LEAD TO OUTCOMES THAT ARE PARETO EFFICIENT BUT ARE NOT WHAT MOST PEOPLE WOULD CONSIDER TO BE GOOD.
I'M STARVING!
I'M STUFFED!
BUT HERE TOO ECONOMISTS SEE THE WORLD DIFFERENTLY.

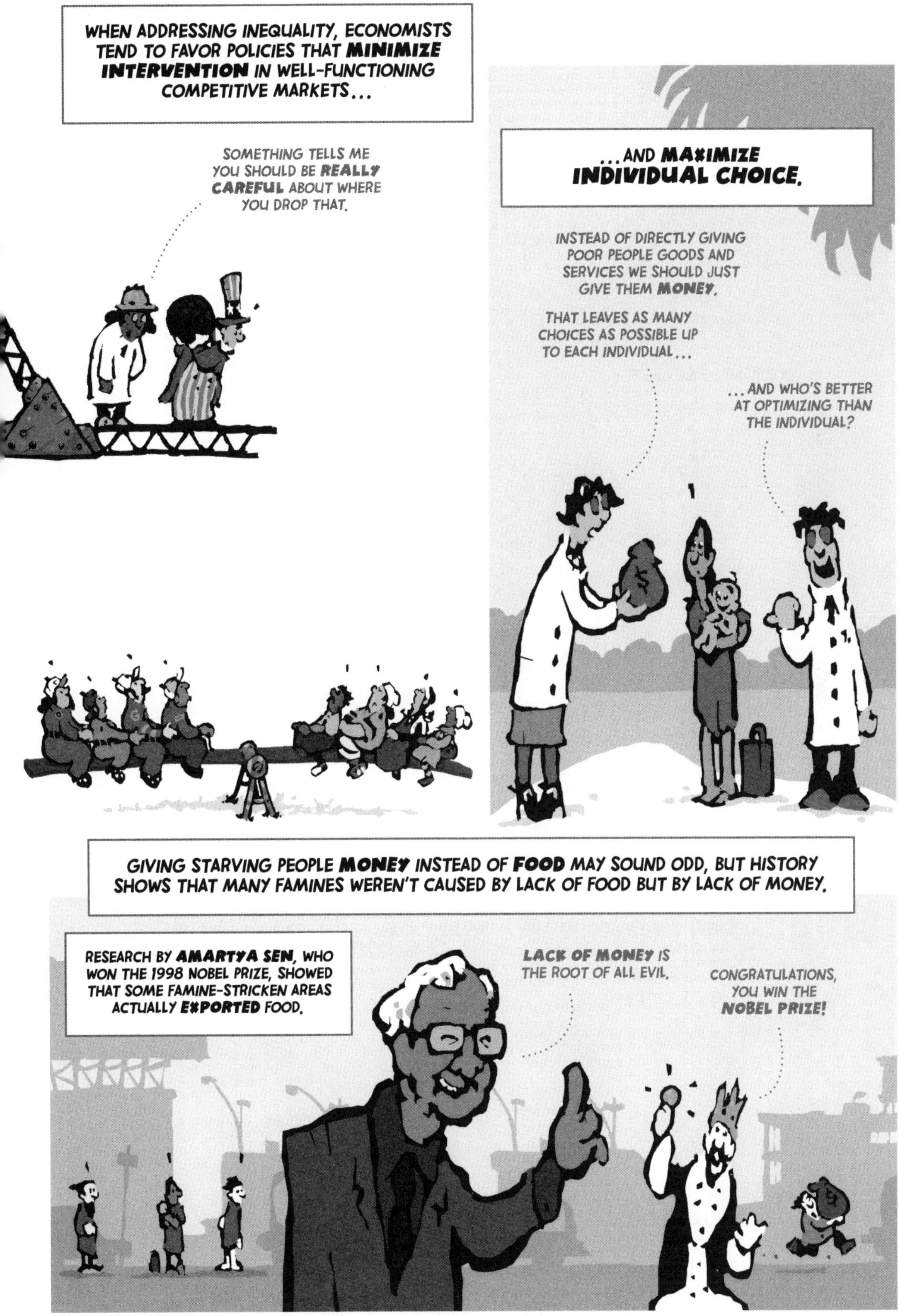
WHEN ADDRESSING INEQUALITY, ECONOMISTS TEND TO FAVOR POLICIES THAT MINIMIZE INTERVENTION IN WELL-FUNCTIONING COMPETITIVE MARKETS...
SOMETHING TELLS ME YOU SHOULD BE REALLY CAREFUL ABOUT WHERE YOU DROP THAT.
...AND MAXIMIZE INDIVIDUAL CHOICE.
INSTEAD OF DIRECTLY GIVING POOR PEOPLE GOODS AND SERVICES WE SHOULD JUST GIVE THEM MONEY.
THAT LEAVES AS MANY CHOICES AS POSSIBLE UP TO EACH INDIVIDUAL...
...AND WHO'S BETTER AT OPTIMIZING THAN THE INDIVIDUAL?
GIVING STARVING PEOPLE MONEY INSTEAD OF FOOD MAY SOUND ODD, BUT HISTORY SHOWS THAT MANY FAMINES WEREN'T CAUSED BY LACK OF FOOD BUT BY LACK OF MONEY.
RESEARCH BY AMARTYA SEN, WHO WON THE 1998 NOBEL PRIZE, SHOWED THAT SOME FAMINE-STRICKEN AREAS ACTUALLY EXPORTED FOOD.
LACK OF MONEY IS THE ROOT OF ALL EVIL.
CONGRATULATIONS, YOU WIN THE NOBEL PRIZE!

RULE #2: PROTECT COMPETITION.

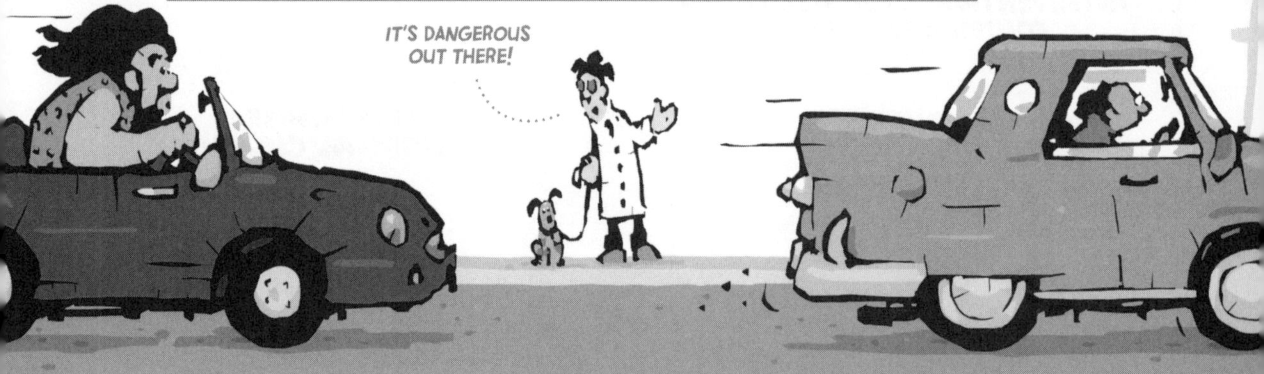
IT'S DANGEROUS OUT THERE!

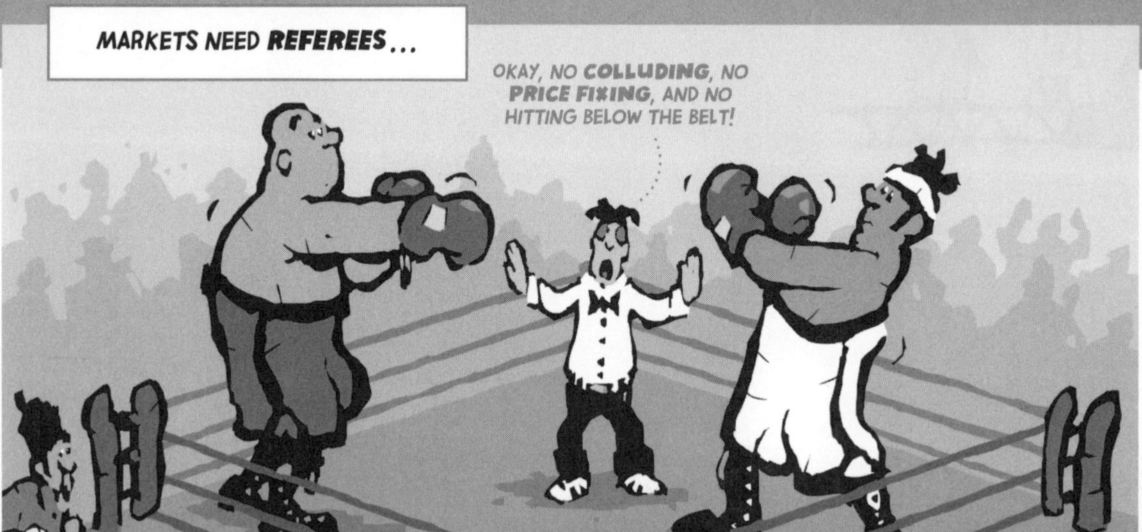
MARKETS NEED **REFEREES**...
OKAY, NO **COLLUDING**, NO **PRICE FIXING**, AND NO HITTING BELOW THE BELT!
... BECAUSE COMPANIES HAVE AN INCENTIVE TO FIX PRICES OR FORM CARTELS OR OTHERWISE ENGAGE IN **ANTI-COMPETITIVE BEHAVIOR**.

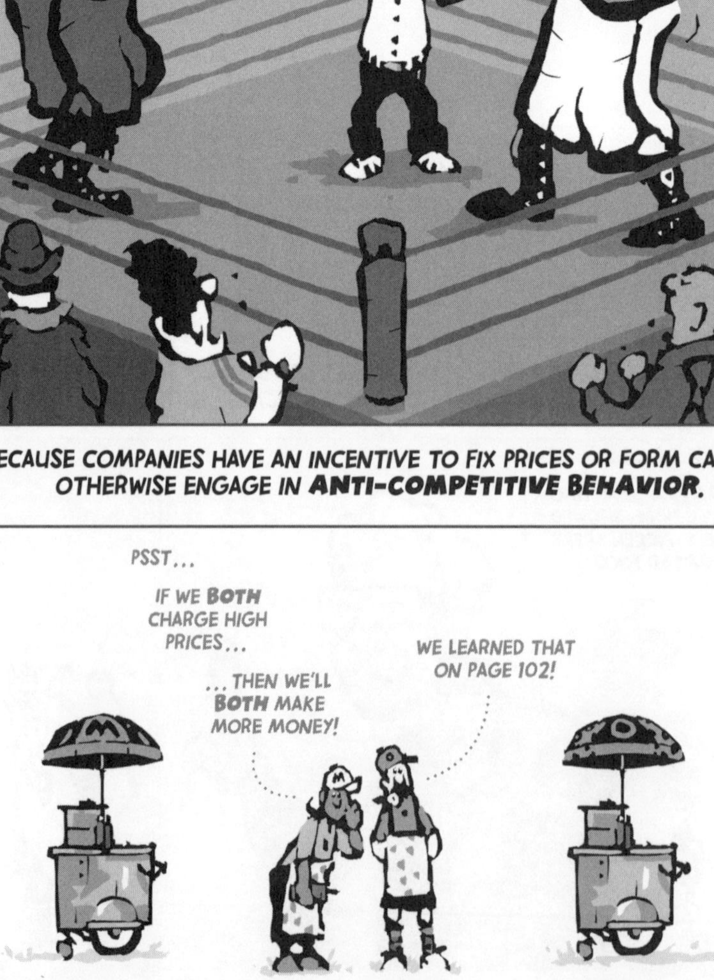
PSST...
IF WE **BOTH** CHARGE HIGH PRICES...
... THEN WE'LL **BOTH** MAKE MORE MONEY!
WE LEARNED THAT ON PAGE 102!

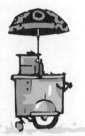

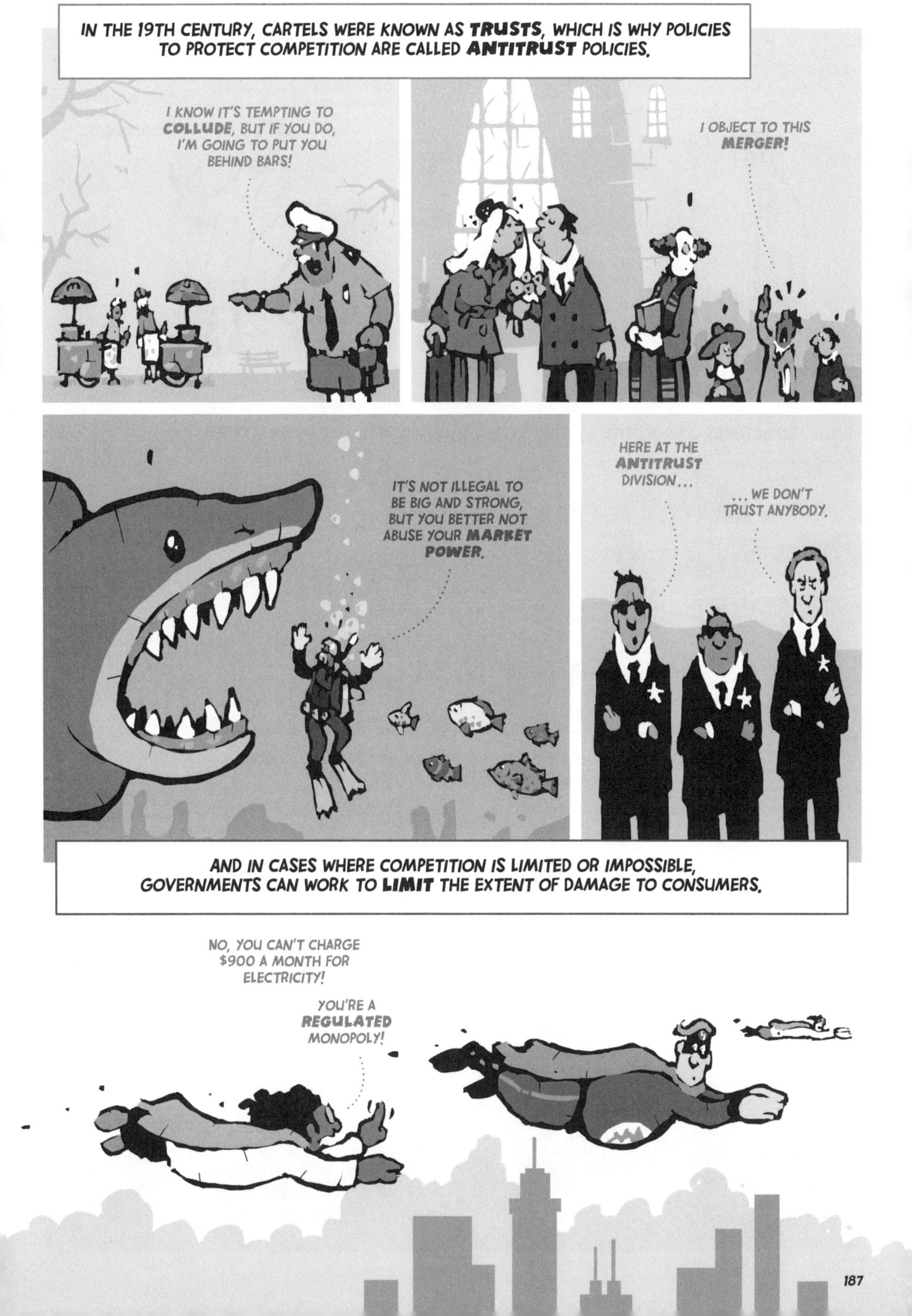
IN THE 19TH CENTURY, CARTELS WERE KNOWN AS TRUSTS, WHICH IS WHY POLICIES TO PROTECT COMPETITION ARE CALLED ANTITRUST POLICIES.
I KNOW IT'S TEMPTING TO COLLUDE, BUT IF YOU DO, I'M GOING TO PUT YOU BEHIND BARS!
I OBJECT TO THIS MERGER!
IT'S NOT ILLEGAL TO BE BIG AND STRONG, BUT YOU BETTER NOT ABUSE YOUR MARKET POWER.
HERE AT THE ANTITRUST DIVISION...
...WE DON'T TRUST ANYBODY.
AND IN CASES WHERE COMPETITION IS LIMITED OR IMPOSSIBLE, GOVERNMENTS CAN WORK TO LIMIT THE EXTENT OF DAMAGE TO CONSUMERS.
NO, YOU CAN'T CHARGE $900 A MONTH FOR ELECTRICITY!
YOU'RE A REGULATED MONOPOLY!

RULE #3: GIVE THE MARKET SECOND CHANCES.

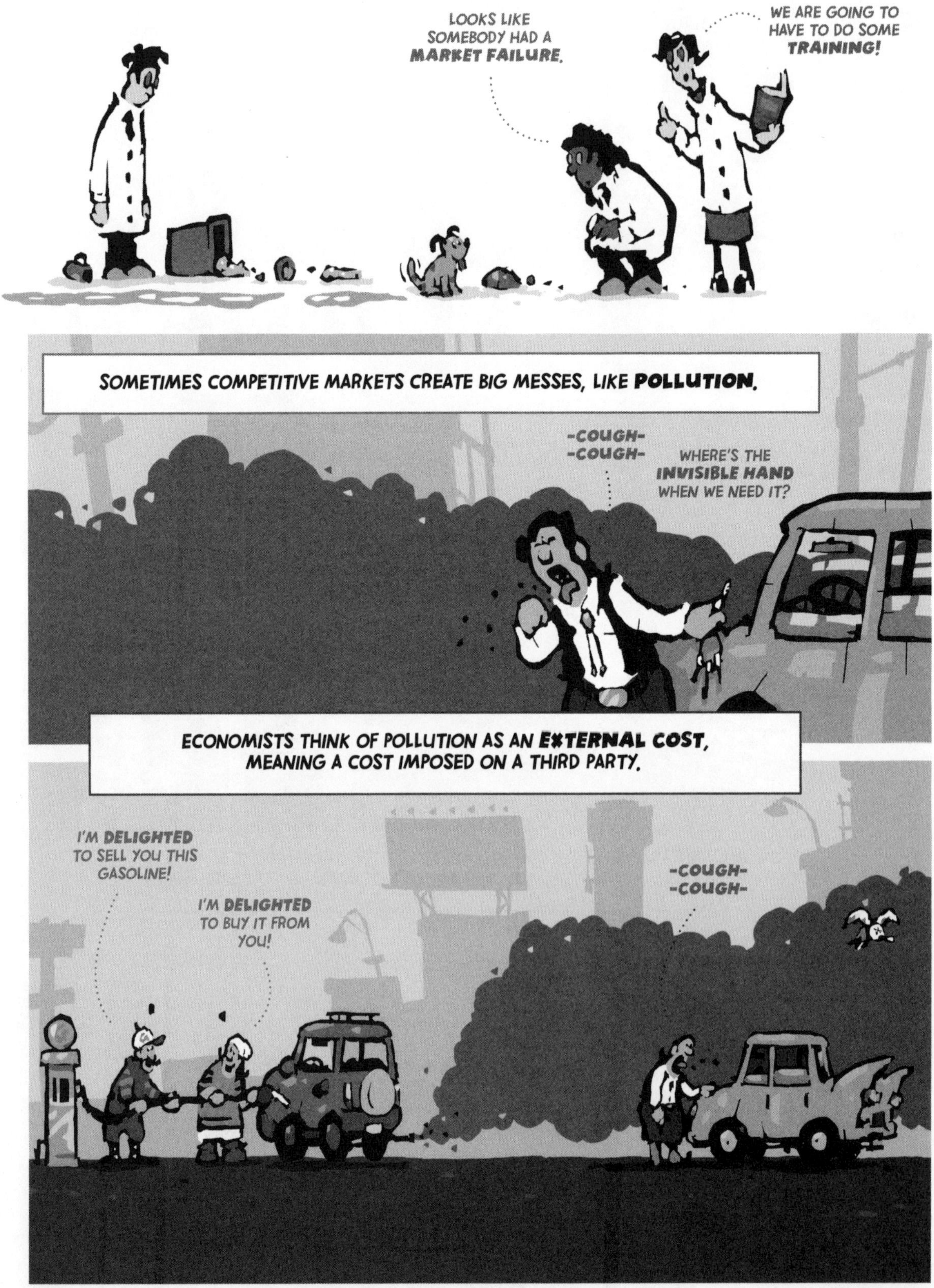

LOOKS LIKE SOMEBODY HAD A **MARKET FAILURE.**
WE ARE GOING TO HAVE TO DO SOME **TRAINING!**
SOMETIMES COMPETITIVE MARKETS CREATE BIG MESSES, LIKE **POLLUTION.**
-COUGH- -COUGH-
WHERE'S THE **INVISIBLE HAND** WHEN WE NEED IT?
ECONOMISTS THINK OF POLLUTION AS AN **EXTERNAL COST,** MEANING A COST IMPOSED ON A THIRD PARTY.
I'M **DELIGHTED** TO SELL YOU THIS GASOLINE!
I'M **DELIGHTED** TO BUY IT FROM YOU!
-COUGH- -COUGH-

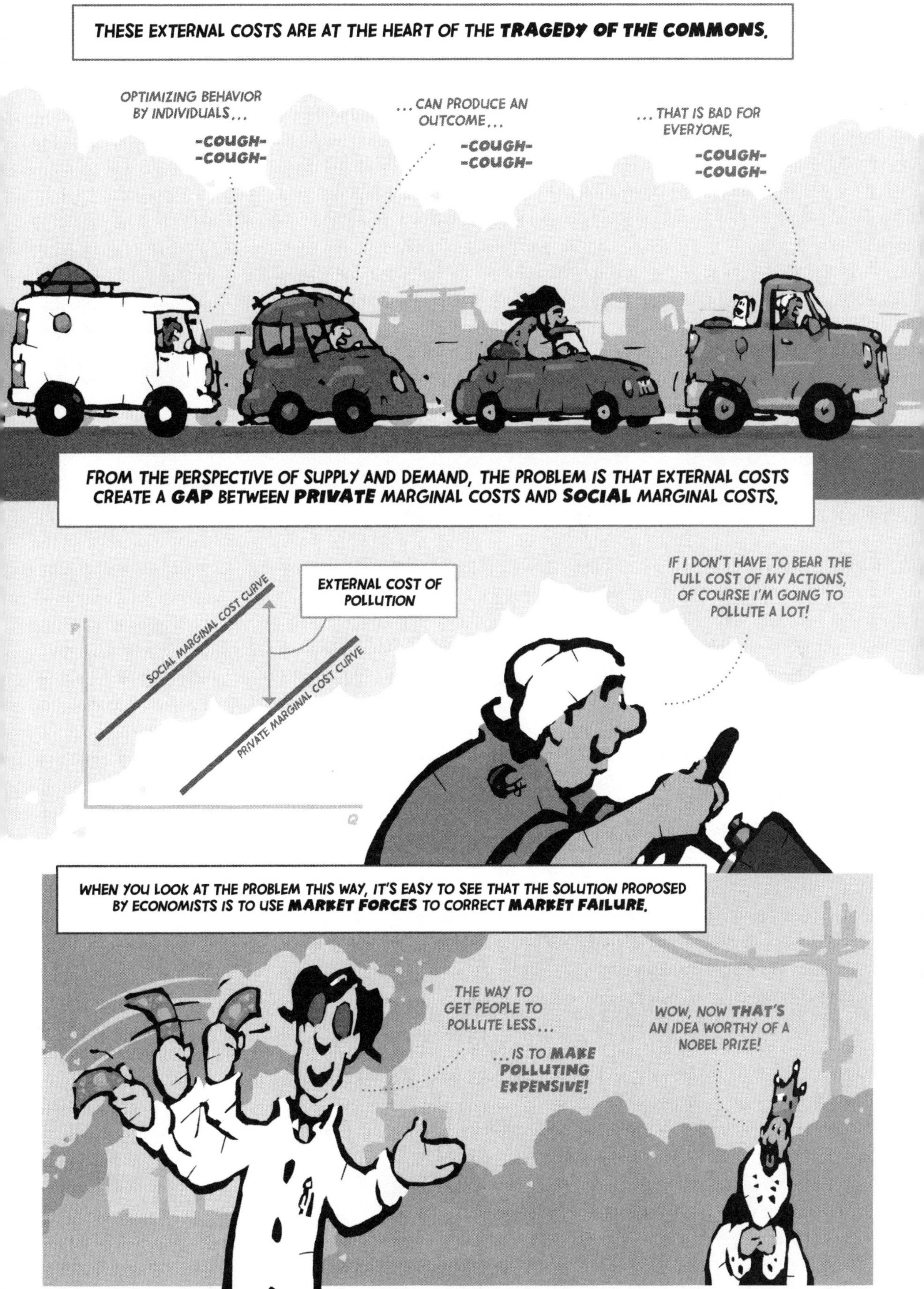
THESE EXTERNAL COSTS ARE AT THE HEART OF THE **TRAGEDY OF THE COMMONS.**
OPTIMIZING BEHAVIOR BY INDIVIDUALS...
-COUGH- -COUGH-
...CAN PRODUCE AN OUTCOME...
-COUGH- -COUGH-
...THAT IS BAD FOR EVERYONE.
-COUGH- -COUGH-
FROM THE PERSPECTIVE OF SUPPLY AND DEMAND, THE PROBLEM IS THAT EXTERNAL COSTS CREATE A **GAP** BETWEEN **PRIVATE** MARGINAL COSTS AND **SOCIAL** MARGINAL COSTS.
EXTERNAL COST OF POLLUTION
P
SOCIAL MARGINAL COST CURVE
PRIVATE MARGINAL COST CURVE
Q
IF I DON'T HAVE TO BEAR THE FULL COST OF MY ACTIONS, OF COURSE I'M GOING TO POLLUTE A LOT!
WHEN YOU LOOK AT THE PROBLEM THIS WAY, IT'S EASY TO SEE THAT THE SOLUTION PROPOSED BY ECONOMISTS IS TO USE **MARKET FORCES** TO CORRECT **MARKET FAILURE.**
THE WAY TO GET PEOPLE TO POLLUTE LESS...
...IS TO **MAKE POLLUTING EXPENSIVE!**
WOW, NOW **THAT'S** AN IDEA WORTHY OF A NOBEL PRIZE!

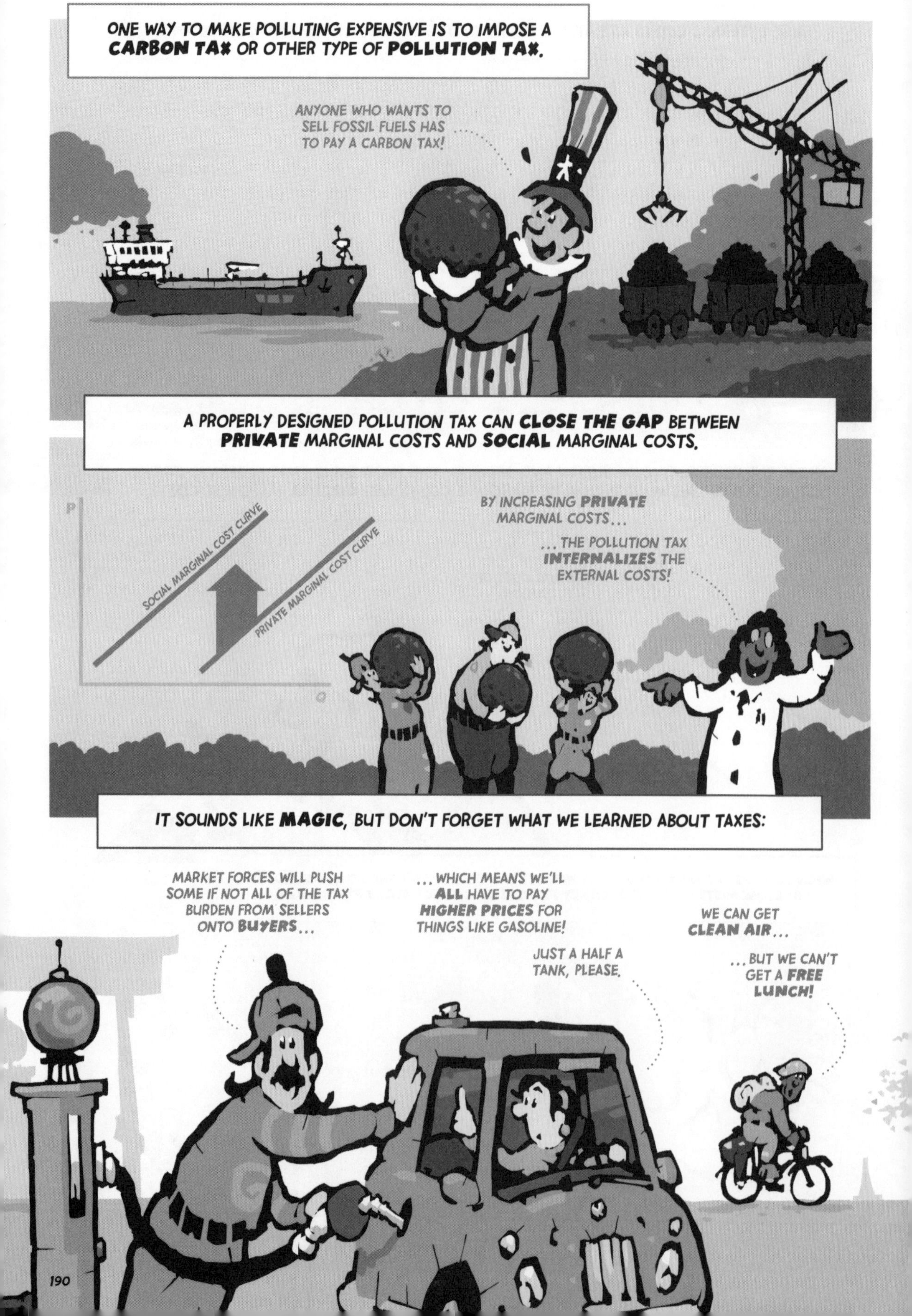
ONE WAY TO MAKE POLLUTING EXPENSIVE IS TO IMPOSE A CARBON TAX OR OTHER TYPE OF POLLUTION TAX.
ANYONE WHO WANTS TO SELL FOSSIL FUELS HAS TO PAY A CARBON TAX!
A PROPERLY DESIGNED POLLUTION TAX CAN CLOSE THE GAP BETWEEN PRIVATE MARGINAL COSTS AND SOCIAL MARGINAL COSTS.
P
SOCIAL MARGINAL COST CURVE
PRIVATE MARGINAL COST CURVE
Q
BY INCREASING PRIVATE MARGINAL COSTS...
...THE POLLUTION TAX INTERNALIZES THE EXTERNAL COSTS!
IT SOUNDS LIKE MAGIC, BUT DON'T FORGET WHAT WE LEARNED ABOUT TAXES:
MARKET FORCES WILL PUSH SOME IF NOT ALL OF THE TAX BURDEN FROM SELLERS ONTO BUYERS...
...WHICH MEANS WE'LL ALL HAVE TO PAY HIGHER PRICES FOR THINGS LIKE GASOLINE!
JUST A HALF A TANK, PLEASE.
WE CAN GET CLEAN AIR...
...BUT WE CAN'T GET A FREE LUNCH!

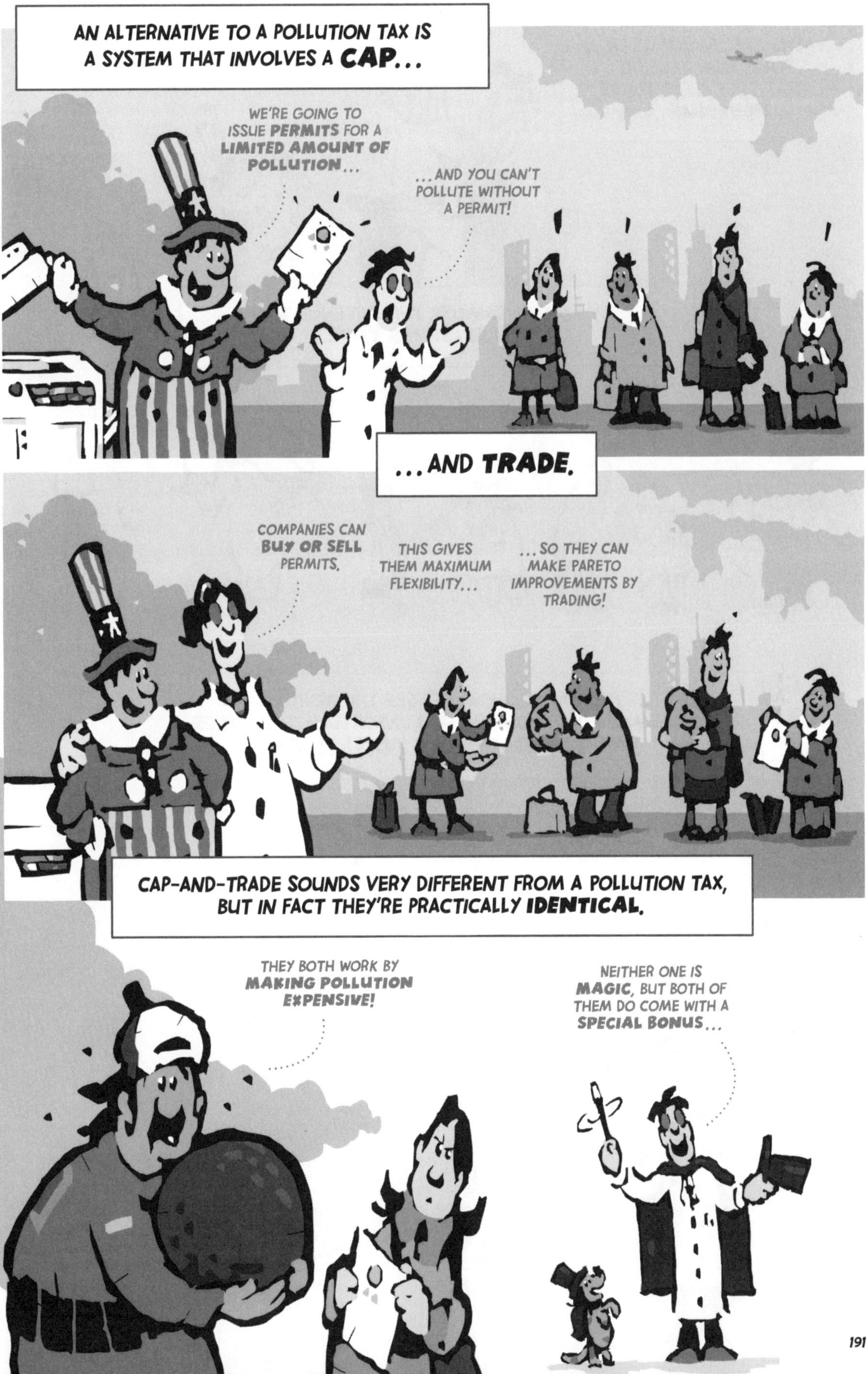
AN ALTERNATIVE TO A POLLUTION TAX IS A SYSTEM THAT INVOLVES A **CAP**...
WE'RE GOING TO ISSUE **PERMITS** FOR A **LIMITED AMOUNT OF POLLUTION**...
...AND YOU CAN'T POLLUTE WITHOUT A PERMIT!
...AND **TRADE**.
COMPANIES CAN **BUY OR SELL** PERMITS.
THIS GIVES THEM MAXIMUM FLEXIBILITY...
...SO THEY CAN MAKE PARETO IMPROVEMENTS BY TRADING!
CAP-AND-TRADE SOUNDS VERY DIFFERENT FROM A POLLUTION TAX, BUT IN FACT THEY'RE PRACTICALLY **IDENTICAL**.
THEY BOTH WORK BY **MAKING POLLUTION EXPENSIVE**!
NEITHER ONE IS **MAGIC**, BUT BOTH OF THEM DO COME WITH A **SPECIAL BONUS**...

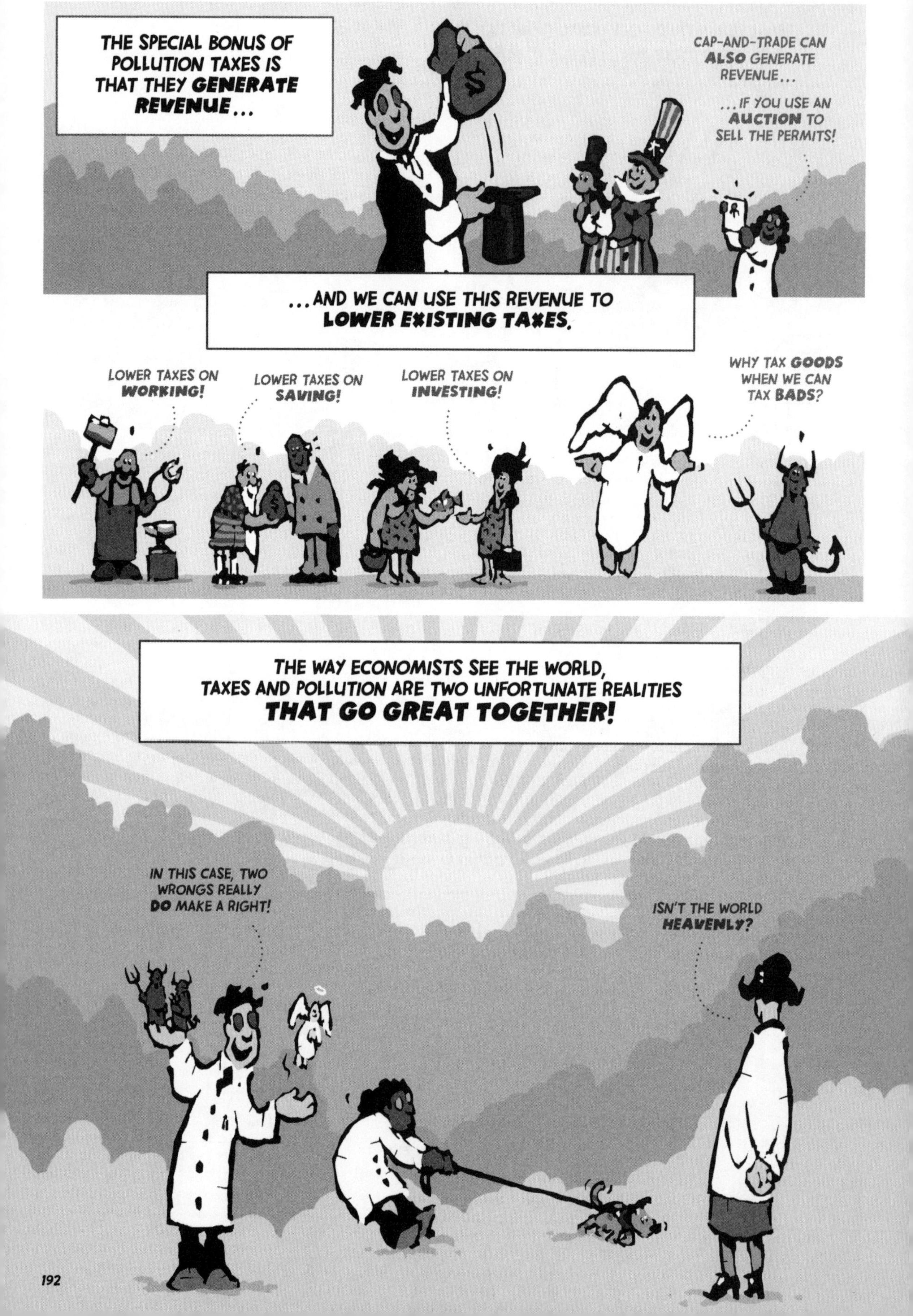
THE SPECIAL BONUS OF POLLUTION TAXES IS THAT THEY GENERATE REVENUE...
CAP-AND-TRADE CAN ALSO GENERATE REVENUE...
...IF YOU USE AN AUCTION TO SELL THE PERMITS!
...AND WE CAN USE THIS REVENUE TO LOWER EXISTING TAXES.
LOWER TAXES ON WORKING!
LOWER TAXES ON SAVING!
LOWER TAXES ON INVESTING!
WHY TAX GOODS WHEN WE CAN TAX BADS?
THE WAY ECONOMISTS SEE THE WORLD, TAXES AND POLLUTION ARE TWO UNFORTUNATE REALITIES THAT GO GREAT TOGETHER!
IN THIS CASE, TWO WRONGS REALLY DO MAKE A RIGHT!
ISN'T THE WORLD HEAVENLY?

CHAPTER 16
CONCLUSION

ECONOMETRICS

DEVELOPMENT
ECONOMICS

ENVIRONMENTAL
ECONOMICS

LABOR ECONOMICS

MACROECONOMICS

COST-BENEFIT
ANALYSIS

BEHAVIORAL
ECONOMICS

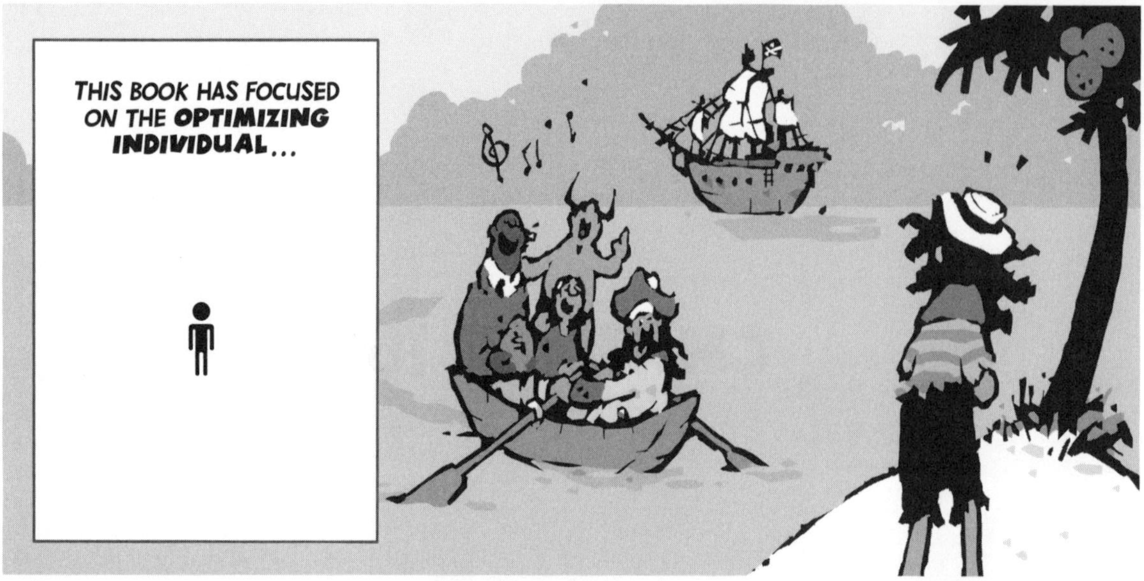
THIS BOOK HAS FOCUSED ON THE **OPTIMIZING INDIVIDUAL**...

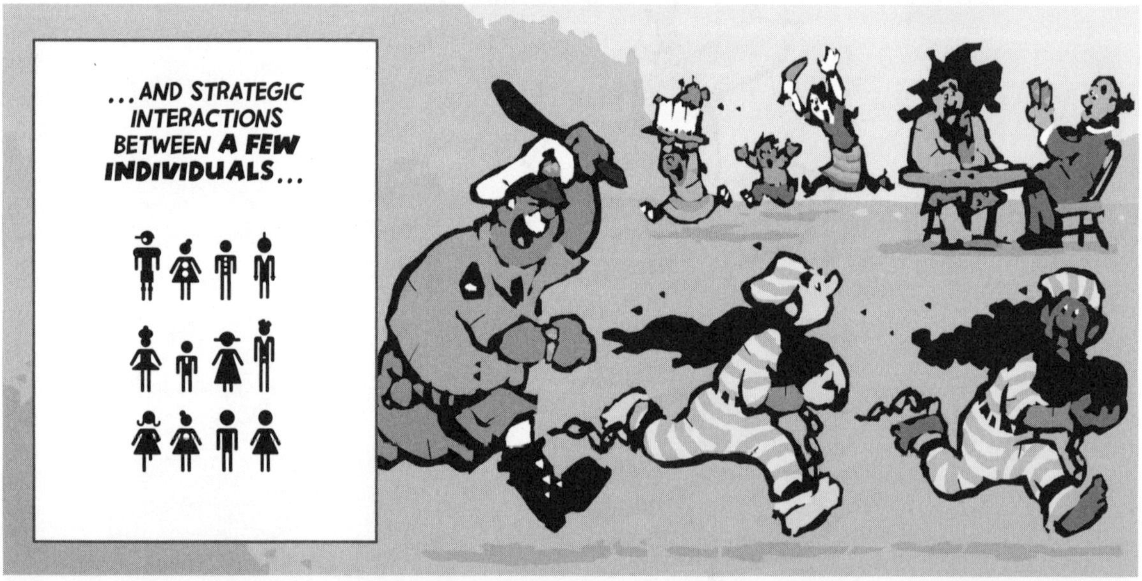
...AND STRATEGIC INTERACTIONS BETWEEN **A FEW INDIVIDUALS**...

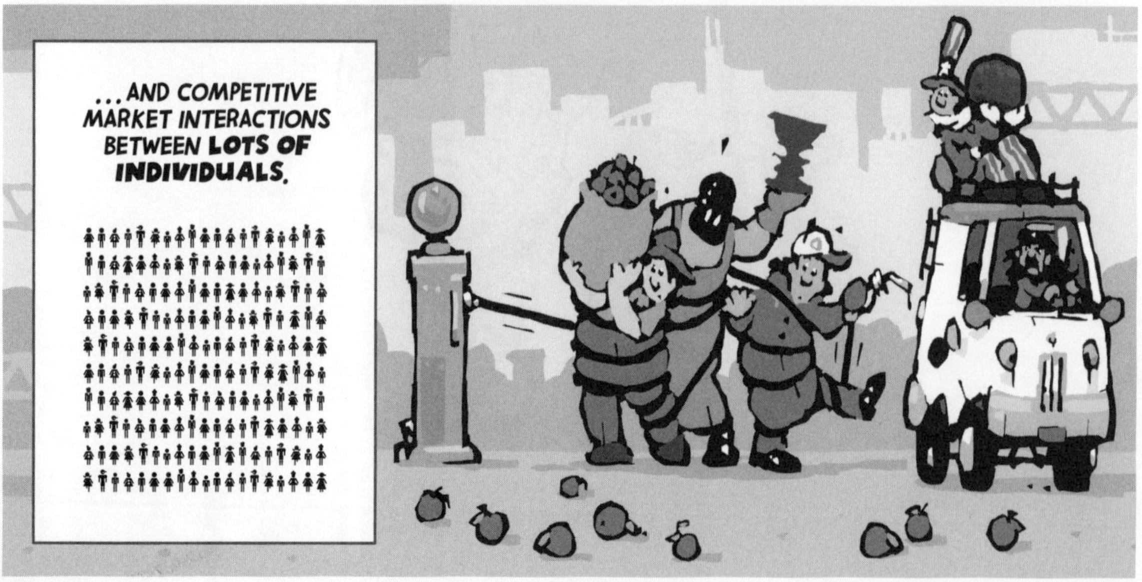
...AND COMPETITIVE MARKET INTERACTIONS BETWEEN **LOTS OF INDIVIDUALS.**

AND ALL ALONG WE'VE BEEN ASKING **ONE BIG QUESTION:**

UNDER WHAT CIRCUMSTANCES DOES **INDIVIDUAL** OPTIMIZATION LEAD TO OUTCOMES THAT ARE **GOOD FOR THE GROUP AS A WHOLE?**

IN OTHER WORDS:

WHEN I DO WHAT'S GOOD FOR **ME**...

...AND YOU DO WHAT'S GOOD FOR **YOU**...

...AND EVERYONE ELSE DOES WHAT'S GOOD FOR **THEMSELVES**...

...WHEN ARE THE RESULTS GOOD FOR **ALL OF US?**

WHEN ECONOMISTS SAY "GOOD," REMEMBER THAT THEY OFTEN FOCUS ON THE **PARETO EFFICIENT** PART OF GOOD.

HEY, MOM, HOW COME **I** DIDN'T GET ANY CAKE?

BUT WHERE DO WE **GO FROM HERE?**

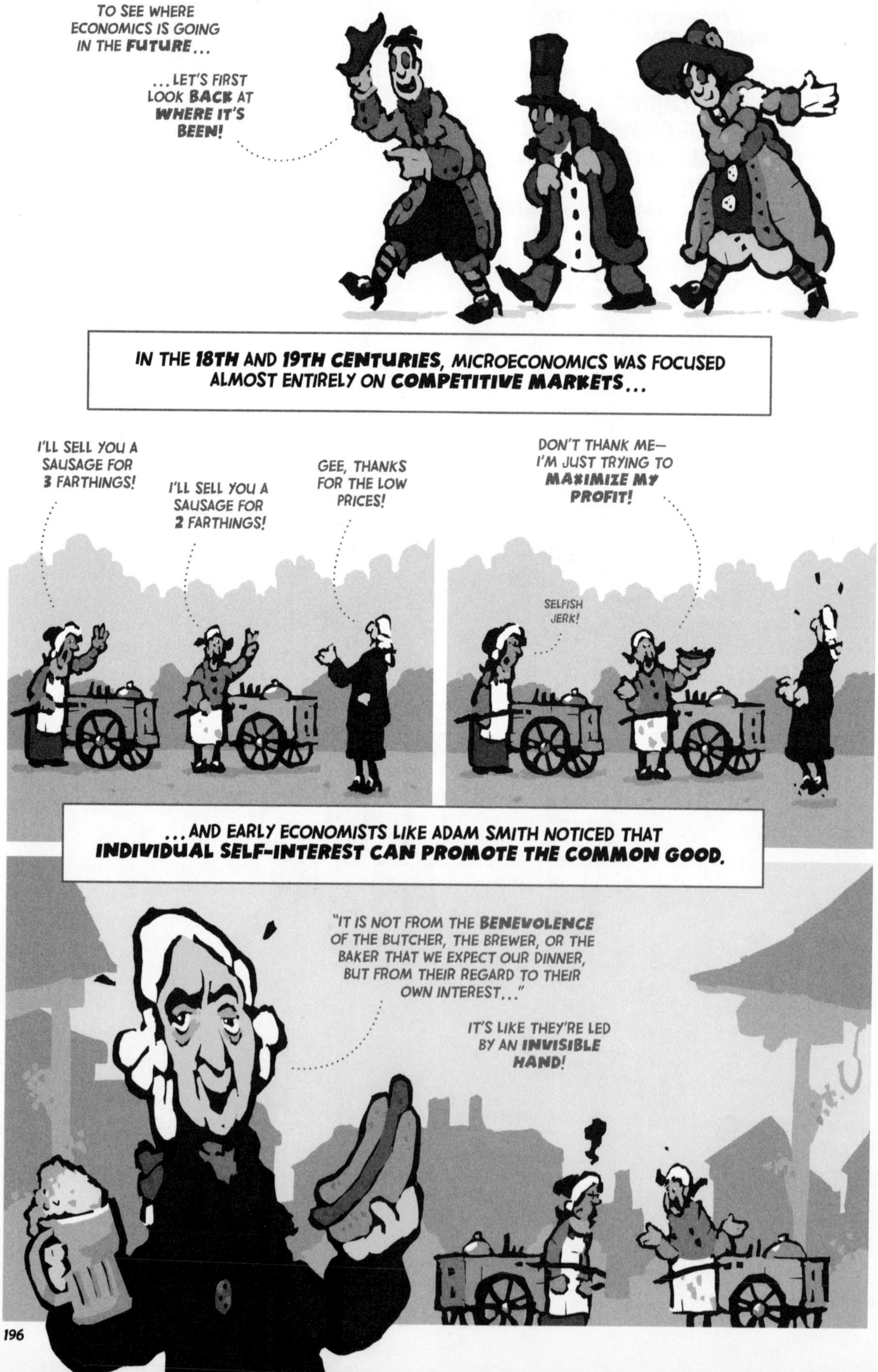
TO SEE WHERE ECONOMICS IS GOING IN THE FUTURE...
...LET'S FIRST LOOK BACK AT WHERE IT'S BEEN!
IN THE 18TH AND 19TH CENTURIES, MICROECONOMICS WAS FOCUSED ALMOST ENTIRELY ON COMPETITIVE MARKETS...
I'LL SELL YOU A SAUSAGE FOR 3 FARTHINGS!
I'LL SELL YOU A SAUSAGE FOR 2 FARTHINGS!
GEE, THANKS FOR THE LOW PRICES!
DON'T THANK ME— I'M JUST TRYING TO MAXIMIZE MY PROFIT!
SELFISH JERK!
...AND EARLY ECONOMISTS LIKE ADAM SMITH NOTICED THAT INDIVIDUAL SELF-INTEREST CAN PROMOTE THE COMMON GOOD.
"IT IS NOT FROM THE BENEVOLENCE OF THE BUTCHER, THE BREWER, OR THE BAKER THAT WE EXPECT OUR DINNER, BUT FROM THEIR REGARD TO THEIR OWN INTEREST..."
IT'S LIKE THEY'RE LED BY AN INVISIBLE HAND!

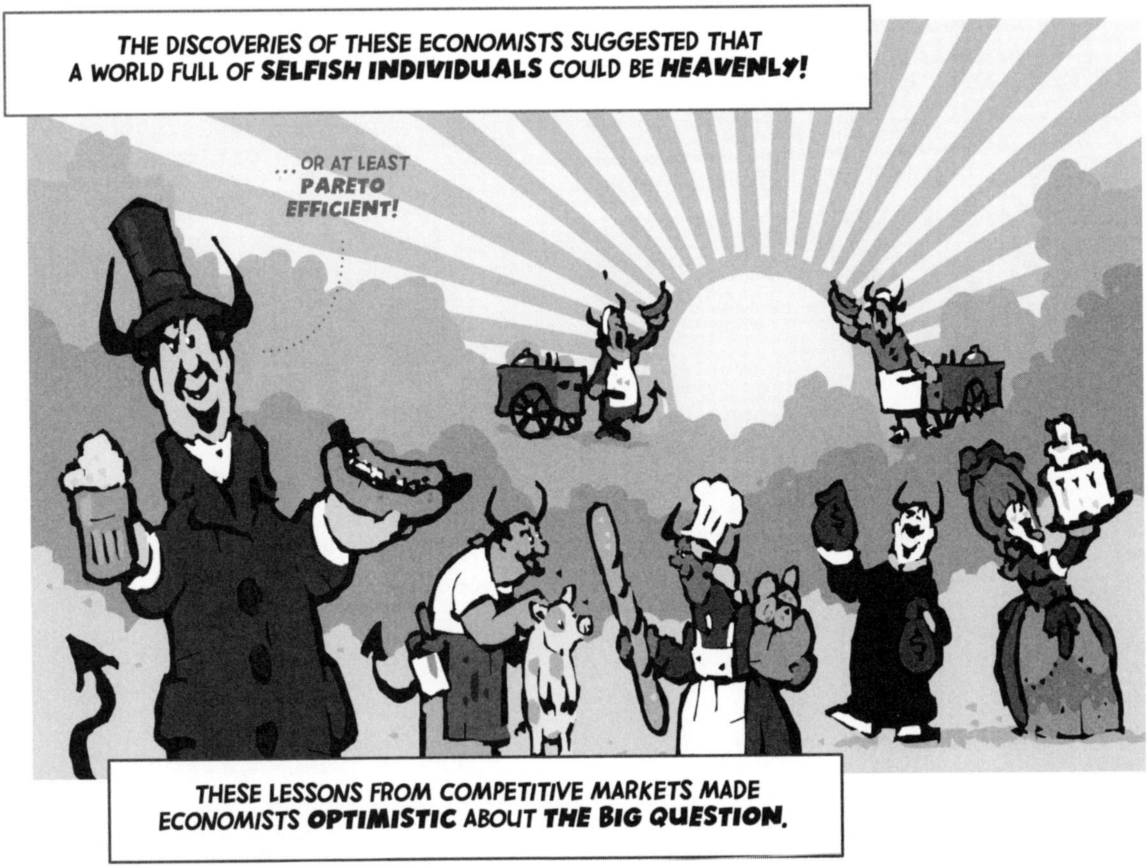
THE DISCOVERIES OF THESE ECONOMISTS SUGGESTED THAT A WORLD FULL OF **SELFISH INDIVIDUALS** COULD BE **HEAVENLY!**
... OR AT LEAST **PARETO EFFICIENT!**
THESE LESSONS FROM COMPETITIVE MARKETS MADE ECONOMISTS **OPTIMISTIC** ABOUT **THE BIG QUESTION.**

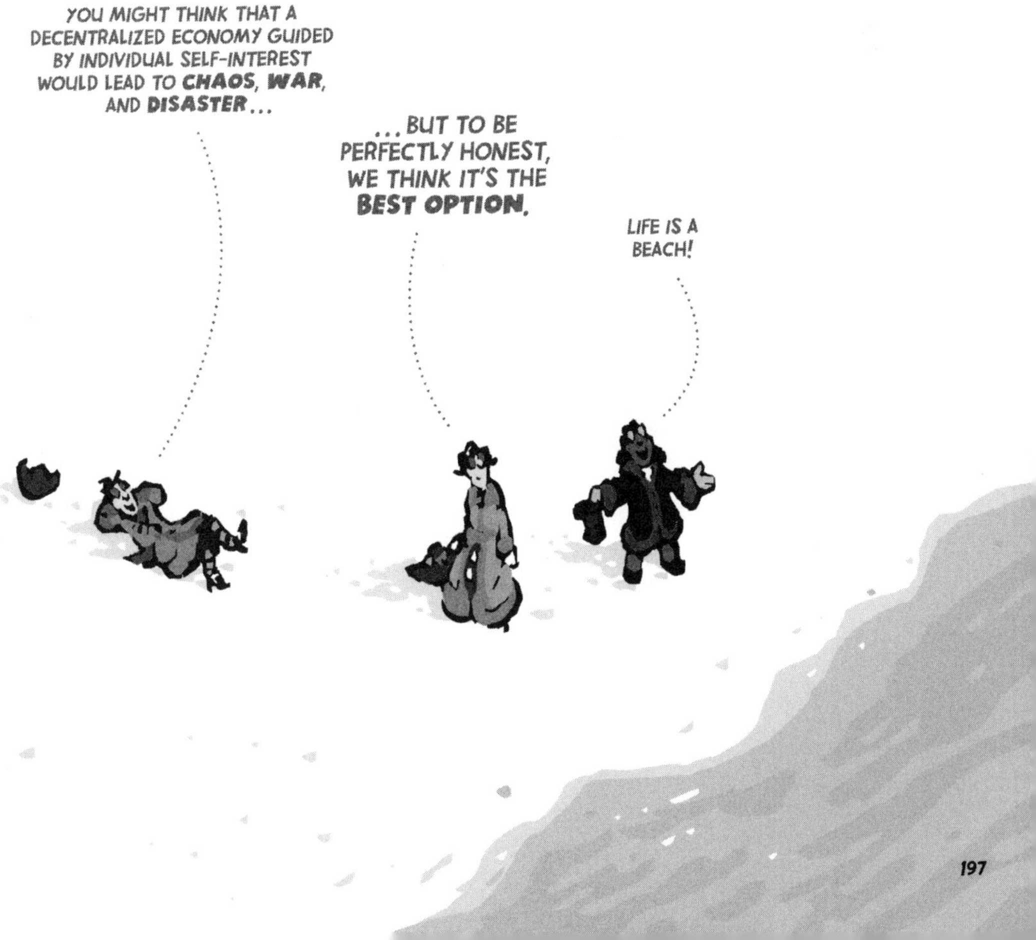
YOU MIGHT THINK THAT A DECENTRALIZED ECONOMY GUIDED BY INDIVIDUAL SELF-INTEREST WOULD LEAD TO **CHAOS, WAR,** AND **DISASTER**...
... BUT TO BE PERFECTLY HONEST, WE THINK IT'S THE **BEST OPTION.**
LIFE IS A BEACH!

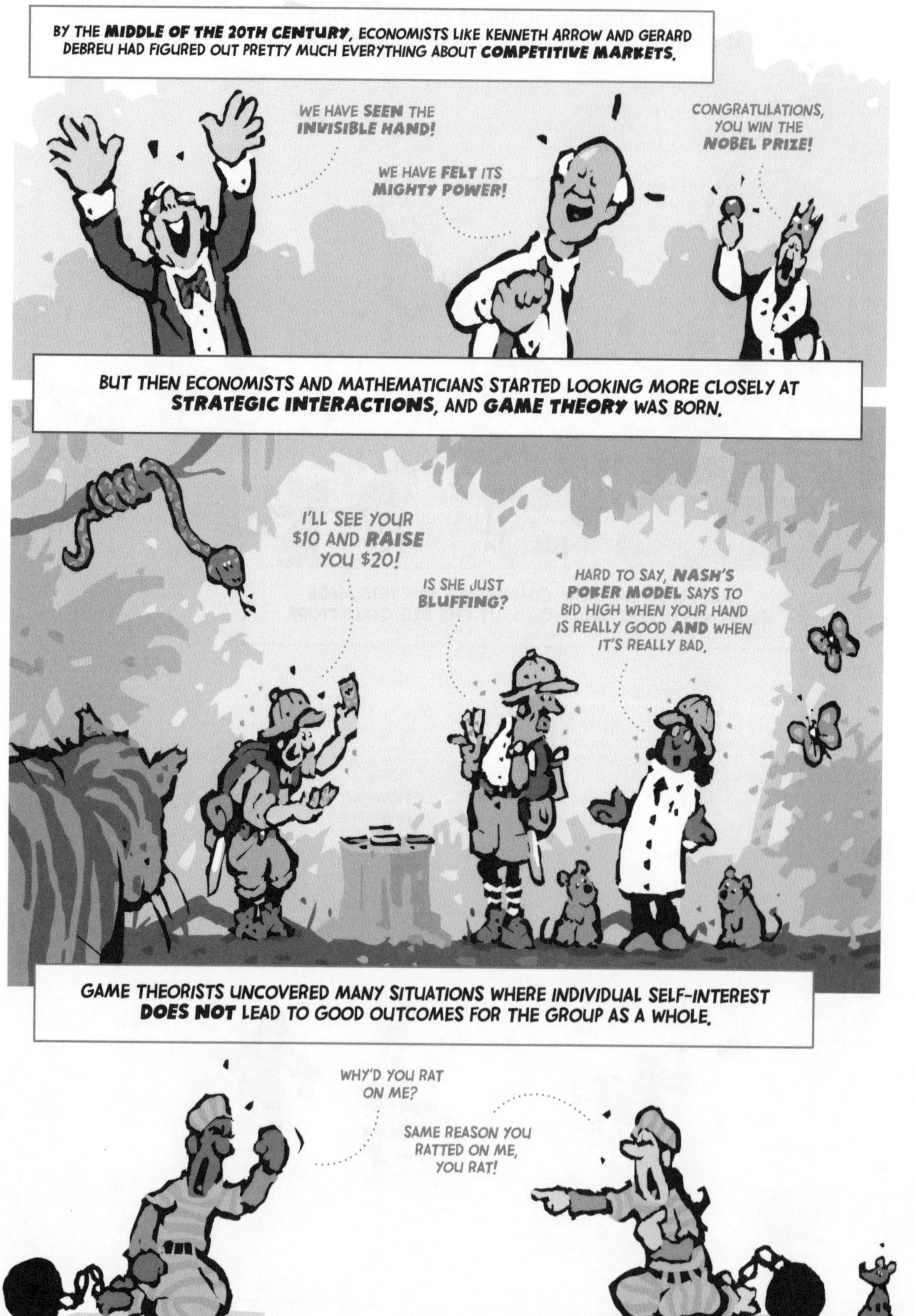
BY THE MIDDLE OF THE 20TH CENTURY, ECONOMISTS LIKE KENNETH ARROW AND GERARD DEBREU HAD FIGURED OUT PRETTY MUCH EVERYTHING ABOUT COMPETITIVE MARKETS.
WE HAVE SEEN THE INVISIBLE HAND!
WE HAVE FELT ITS MIGHTY POWER!
CONGRATULATIONS, YOU WIN THE NOBEL PRIZE!
BUT THEN ECONOMISTS AND MATHEMATICIANS STARTED LOOKING MORE CLOSELY AT STRATEGIC INTERACTIONS, AND GAME THEORY WAS BORN.
I'LL SEE YOUR $10 AND RAISE YOU $20!
IS SHE JUST BLUFFING?
HARD TO SAY, NASH'S POKER MODEL SAYS TO BID HIGH WHEN YOUR HAND IS REALLY GOOD AND WHEN IT'S REALLY BAD.
GAME THEORISTS UNCOVERED MANY SITUATIONS WHERE INDIVIDUAL SELF-INTEREST DOES NOT LEAD TO GOOD OUTCOMES FOR THE GROUP AS A WHOLE.
WHY'D YOU RAT ON ME?
SAME REASON YOU RATTED ON ME, YOU RAT!

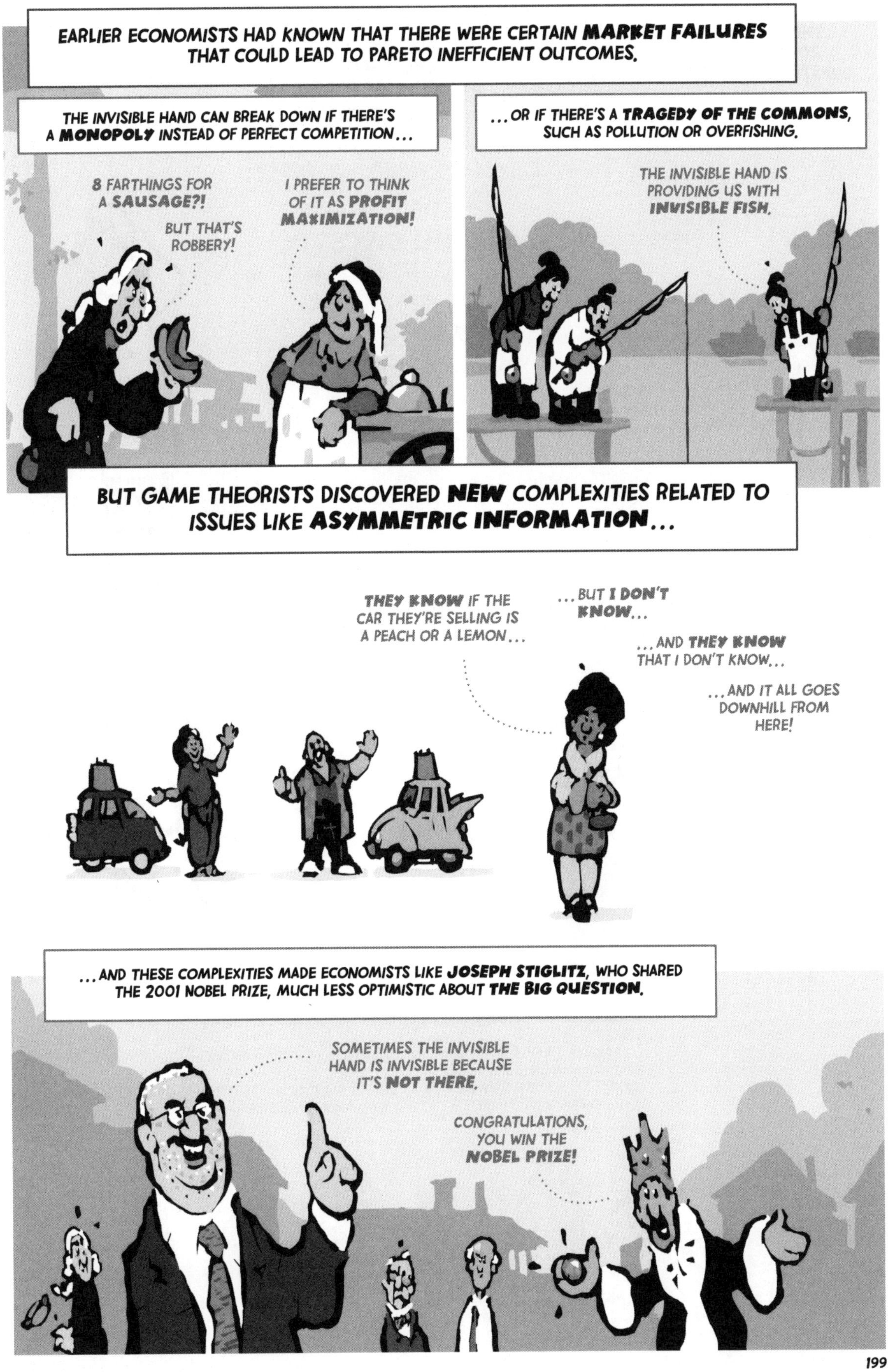
EARLIER ECONOMISTS HAD KNOWN THAT THERE WERE CERTAIN **MARKET FAILURES** THAT COULD LEAD TO PARETO INEFFICIENT OUTCOMES.
THE INVISIBLE HAND CAN BREAK DOWN IF THERE'S A **MONOPOLY** INSTEAD OF PERFECT COMPETITION...
8 FARTHINGS FOR A **SAUSAGE?!**
BUT THAT'S ROBBERY!
I PREFER TO THINK OF IT AS **PROFIT MAXIMIZATION!**
...OR IF THERE'S A **TRAGEDY OF THE COMMONS**, SUCH AS POLLUTION OR OVERFISHING.
THE INVISIBLE HAND IS PROVIDING US WITH **INVISIBLE FISH.**
BUT GAME THEORISTS DISCOVERED **NEW** COMPLEXITIES RELATED TO ISSUES LIKE **ASYMMETRIC INFORMATION**...
THEY KNOW IF THE CAR THEY'RE SELLING IS A PEACH OR A LEMON...
...BUT **I DON'T KNOW**...
...AND **THEY KNOW** THAT I DON'T KNOW...
...AND IT ALL GOES DOWNHILL FROM HERE!
...AND THESE COMPLEXITIES MADE ECONOMISTS LIKE **JOSEPH STIGLITZ**, WHO SHARED THE 2001 NOBEL PRIZE, MUCH LESS OPTIMISTIC ABOUT **THE BIG QUESTION.**
SOMETIMES THE INVISIBLE HAND IS INVISIBLE BECAUSE IT'S **NOT THERE.**
CONGRATULATIONS, YOU WIN THE **NOBEL PRIZE!**

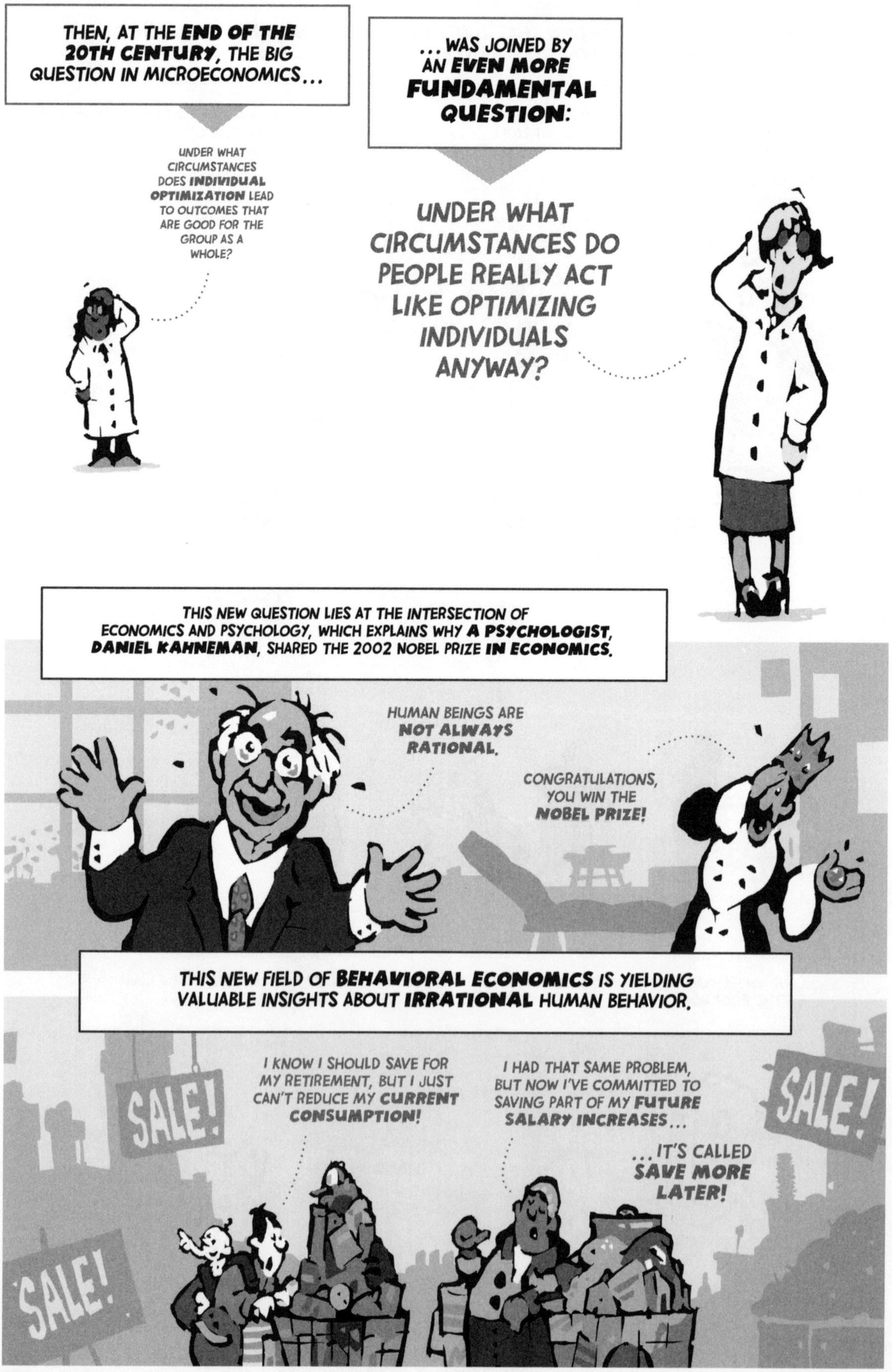
THEN, AT THE END OF THE 20TH CENTURY, THE BIG QUESTION IN MICROECONOMICS…
UNDER WHAT CIRCUMSTANCES DOES INDIVIDUAL OPTIMIZATION LEAD TO OUTCOMES THAT ARE GOOD FOR THE GROUP AS A WHOLE?
…WAS JOINED BY AN EVEN MORE FUNDAMENTAL QUESTION:
UNDER WHAT CIRCUMSTANCES DO PEOPLE REALLY ACT LIKE OPTIMIZING INDIVIDUALS ANYWAY?
THIS NEW QUESTION LIES AT THE INTERSECTION OF ECONOMICS AND PSYCHOLOGY, WHICH EXPLAINS WHY A PSYCHOLOGIST, DANIEL KAHNEMAN, SHARED THE 2002 NOBEL PRIZE IN ECONOMICS.
HUMAN BEINGS ARE NOT ALWAYS RATIONAL.
CONGRATULATIONS, YOU WIN THE NOBEL PRIZE!
THIS NEW FIELD OF BEHAVIORAL ECONOMICS IS YIELDING VALUABLE INSIGHTS ABOUT IRRATIONAL HUMAN BEHAVIOR.
SALE!
I KNOW I SHOULD SAVE FOR MY RETIREMENT, BUT I JUST CAN'T REDUCE MY CURRENT CONSUMPTION!
I HAD THAT SAME PROBLEM, BUT NOW I'VE COMMITTED TO SAVING PART OF MY FUTURE SALARY INCREASES…
…IT'S CALLED SAVE MORE LATER!
SALE!
SALE!

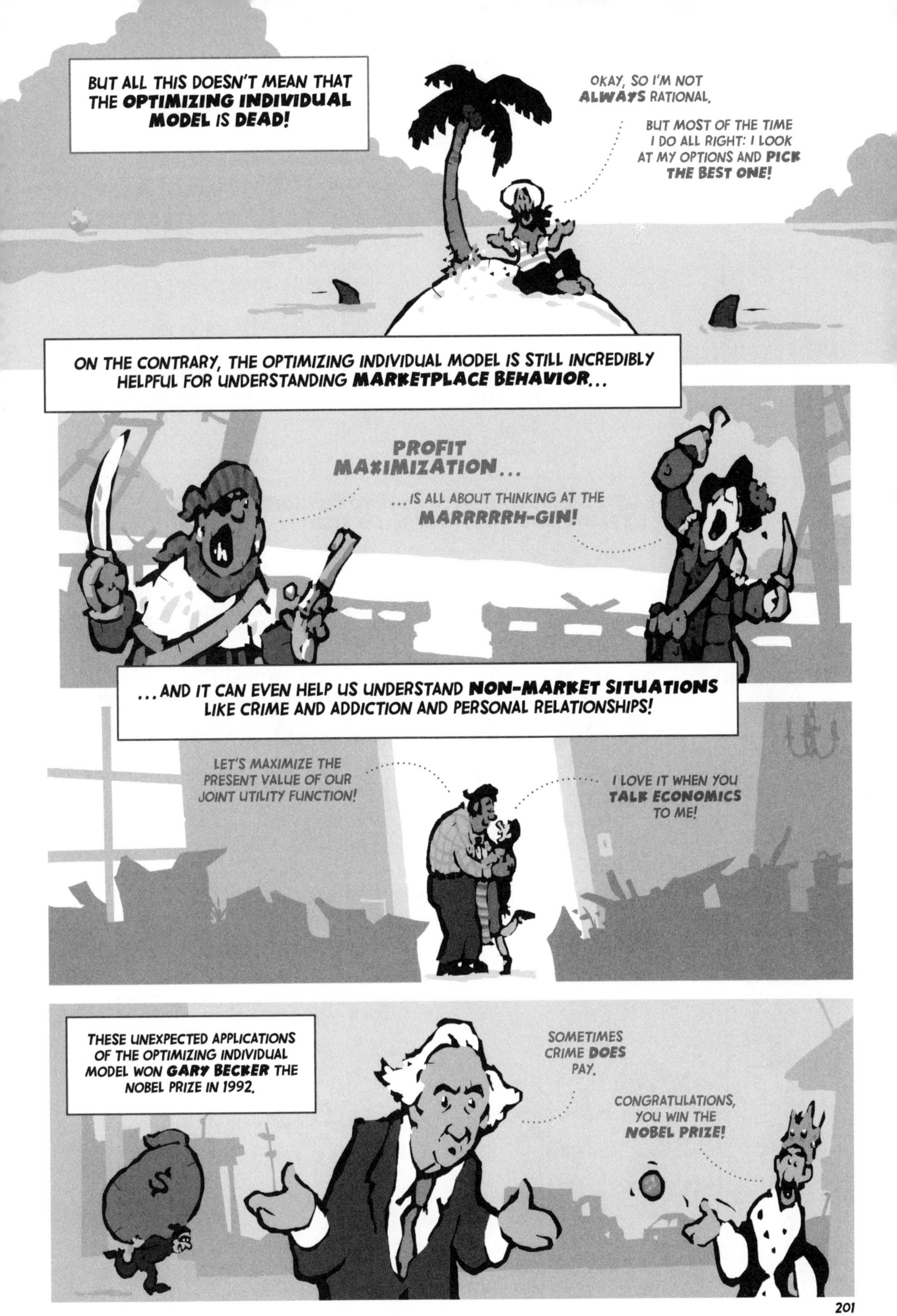
BUT ALL THIS DOESN'T MEAN THAT THE OPTIMIZING INDIVIDUAL MODEL IS DEAD!
OKAY, SO I'M NOT ALWAYS RATIONAL.
BUT MOST OF THE TIME I DO ALL RIGHT: I LOOK AT MY OPTIONS AND PICK THE BEST ONE!
ON THE CONTRARY, THE OPTIMIZING INDIVIDUAL MODEL IS STILL INCREDIBLY HELPFUL FOR UNDERSTANDING MARKETPLACE BEHAVIOR...
PROFIT MAXIMIZATION...
...IS ALL ABOUT THINKING AT THE MARRRRRH-GIN!
...AND IT CAN EVEN HELP US UNDERSTAND NON-MARKET SITUATIONS LIKE CRIME AND ADDICTION AND PERSONAL RELATIONSHIPS!
LET'S MAXIMIZE THE PRESENT VALUE OF OUR JOINT UTILITY FUNCTION!
I LOVE IT WHEN YOU TALK ECONOMICS TO ME!
THESE UNEXPECTED APPLICATIONS OF THE OPTIMIZING INDIVIDUAL MODEL WON GARY BECKER THE NOBEL PRIZE IN 1992.
SOMETIMES CRIME DOES PAY.
CONGRATULATIONS, YOU WIN THE NOBEL PRIZE!

AS WE CONTINUE INTO THE **21ST CENTURY**, THE BIG QUESTION IN MICROECONOMICS STILL LOOMS LARGE:

UNDER WHAT CIRCUMSTANCES DOES **INDIVIDUAL** OPTIMIZATION LEAD TO OUTCOMES THAT ARE **GOOD FOR THE GROUP AS A WHOLE?**

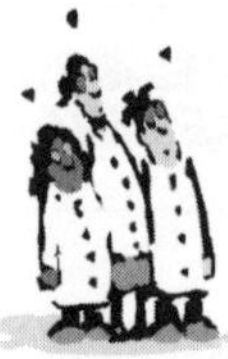

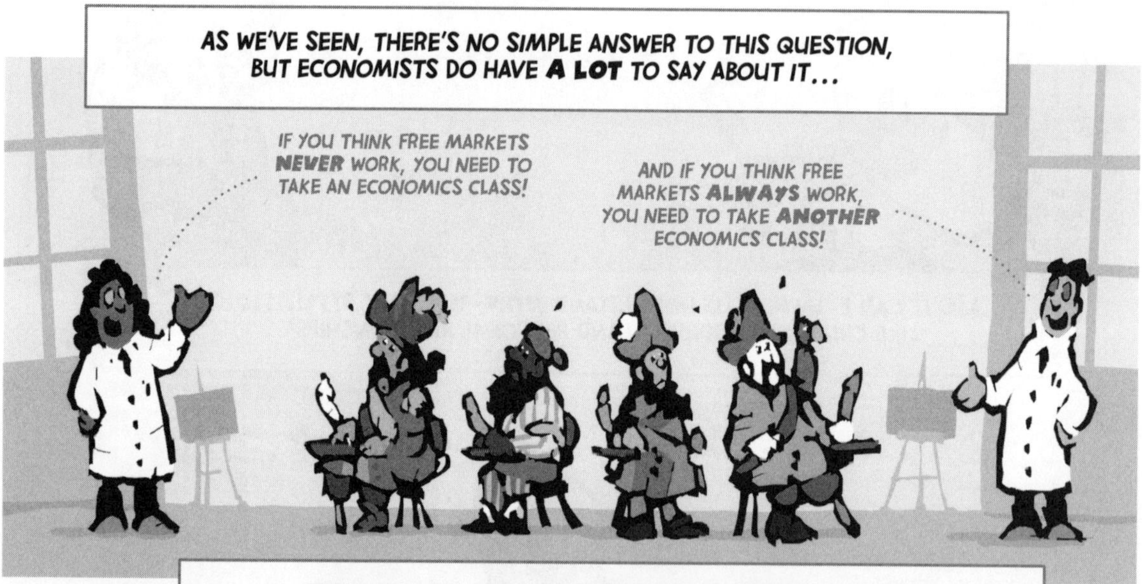
AS WE'VE SEEN, THERE'S NO SIMPLE ANSWER TO THIS QUESTION, BUT ECONOMISTS DO HAVE A LOT TO SAY ABOUT IT...
IF YOU THINK FREE MARKETS NEVER WORK, YOU NEED TO TAKE AN ECONOMICS CLASS!
AND IF YOU THINK FREE MARKETS ALWAYS WORK, YOU NEED TO TAKE ANOTHER ECONOMICS CLASS!

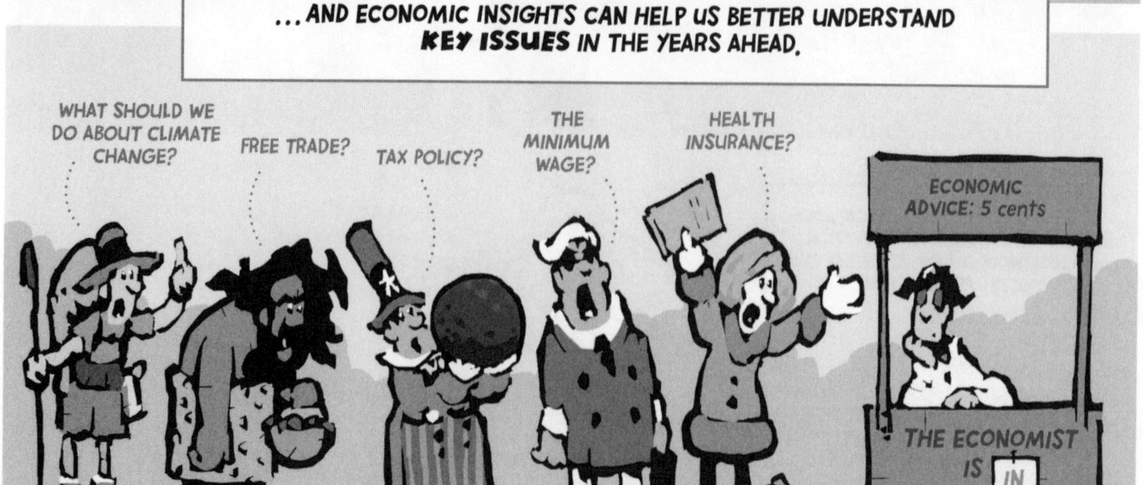
...AND ECONOMIC INSIGHTS CAN HELP US BETTER UNDERSTAND KEY ISSUES IN THE YEARS AHEAD.
WHAT SHOULD WE DO ABOUT CLIMATE CHANGE?
FREE TRADE?
TAX POLICY?
THE MINIMUM WAGE?
HEALTH INSURANCE?
ECONOMIC ADVICE: 5 cents
THE ECONOMIST IS IN.

AS WE CAN SEE FROM DISCUSSIONS ABOUT HEALTH CARE, ECONOMISTS **DON'T ALWAYS AGREE ABOUT EVERYTHING...**

ON THE ONE HAND, FREE MARKETS DON'T WORK PERFECTLY. PROBLEMS LIKE ADVERSE SELECTION MEAN THAT YOU'RE NOT GOING TO GET A PARETO EFFICIENT OUTCOME FROM FREE-MARKET COMPETITION. AND IN A SINGLE-PAYER SYSTEM THE GOVERNMENT COULD BRING DOWN DRUG PRICES BY USING ITS MONOPSONY POWER AS THE ONLY BUYER! THAT'S WHY ALMOST ALL DEVELOPED COUNTRIES HAVE ADOPTED

...ON THE OTHER HAND, GOVERNMENT PROGRAMS DON'T ALWAYS WORK PERFECTLY EITHER. THERE'S SOMETHING TO BE SAID FOR RELYING ON THE FISCAL DISCIPLINE THAT COMES FROM FREE-MARKET COMPETITION. AND DRUG COMPANIES WILL HAVE LESS INCENTIVE TO INVEST IN R&D IF THE GOVERNMENT IS GOING TO LIMIT THEIR POTENTIAL PROFITS. IS FOR INTERNATIONAL

DOES ANYONE KNOW WHERE I CAN FIND A **ONE-HANDED ECONOMIST?**

...BUT ECONOMISTS **HAVE** FIGURED OUT **CREATIVE AND POWERFUL SOLUTIONS** TO SOME OF OUR MOST DAUNTING PROBLEMS.

CLIMATE CHANGE IS A CLASSIC **TRAGEDY OF THE COMMONS** SITUATION.

BUT WE CAN HARNESS MARKET FORCES TO **SAVE THE ENVIRONMENT...**

...BY MAKING **POLLUTING EXPENSIVE!**

THERE'S PLENTY MORE **YOU** CAN LEARN ABOUT ALL THESE ISSUES! AND WHEN YOU'VE HAD ENOUGH OF **MICROECONOMICS,** THERE'S ALWAYS...

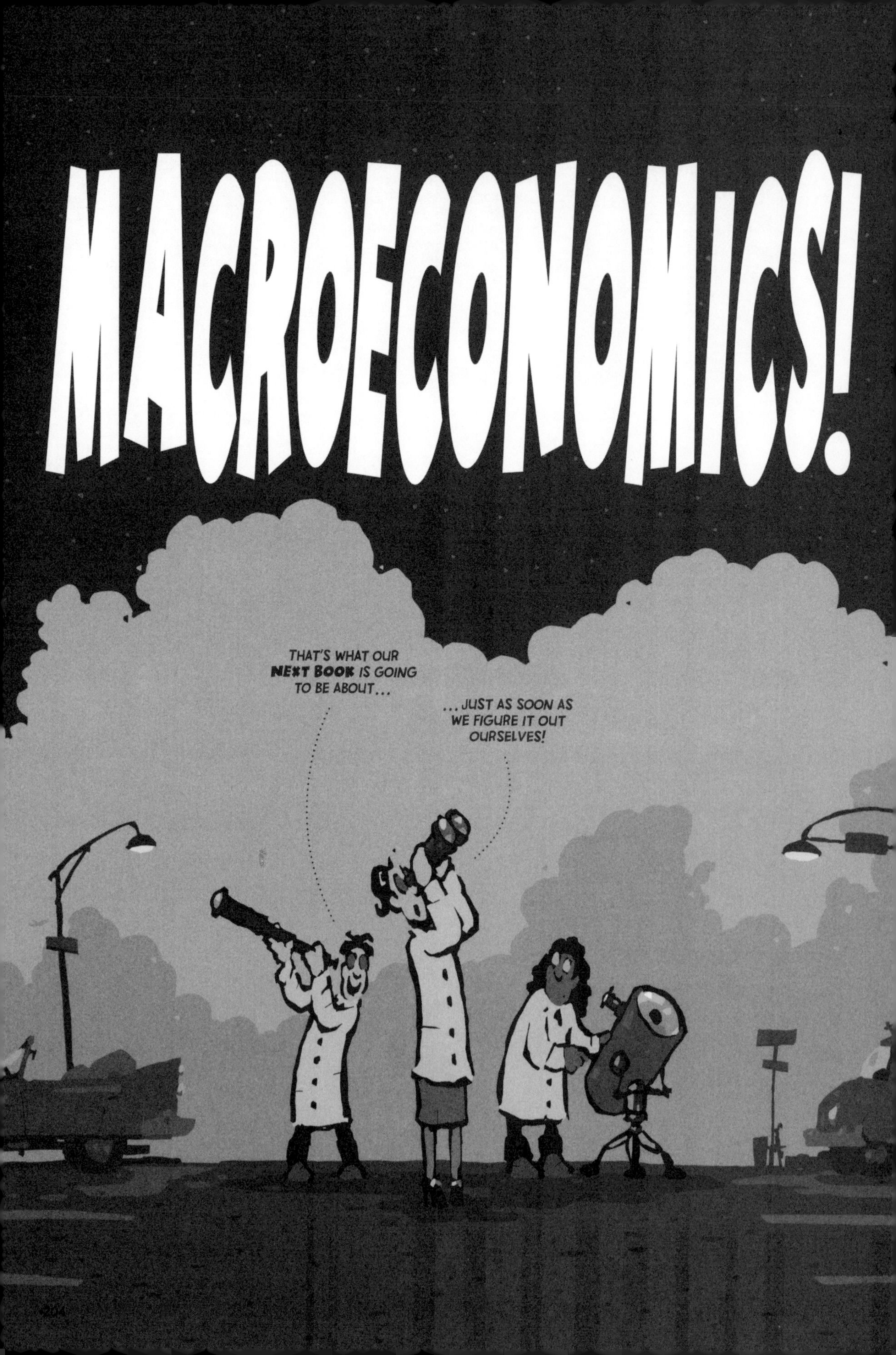
MACROECONOMICS!
THAT'S WHAT OUR NEXT BOOK IS GOING TO BE ABOUT...
...JUST AS SOON AS WE FIGURE IT OUT OURSELVES!

GLOSSARY

A

ADVERSE SELECTION
A SITUATION IN WHICH ASYMMETRIC INFORMATION (SELLERS KNOW SOMETHING BUYERS DON'T OR VICE-VERSA) CAUSES PROBLEMS WITH TRADE, AS IN THE USED CAR MARKET OR THE MARKET FOR HEALTH INSURANCE: 48–52

ANNUITY
A STREAM OF ANNUAL PAYMENTS FOR A CERTAIN NUMBER OF YEARS: 34

ASYMMETRIC INFORMATION
SEE ADVERSE SELECTION.

AUCTIONS
A TRADING METHOD THAT IS USED TO SELL EVERYTHING FROM ELECTRICITY TO EBAY COLLECTIBLES: 103–16

B

BEHAVIORAL ECONOMICS
A NEW FIELD THAT COMBINES ECONOMICS AND PSYCHOLOGY: 200

C

CAKE CUTTING
A FAIR-DIVISION GAME THAT GENERALIZES DIVORCE SETTLEMENTS, ALLOCATIONS OF FISHING PERMITS, AND MANY OTHER SITUATIONS: 67–78
AND PARETO EFFICIENCY: 85, 88

CAP-AND-TRADE AND CARBON TAXES
TWO TYPES OF ECONOMIC POLICIES THAT CAN BE USED TO REDUCE CARBON EMISSIONS BY MAKING POLLUTING EXPENSIVE; SIMILAR METHODS HAVE BEEN USED TO REDUCE OVERFISHING: 190–92
AND COASE THEOREM: 100

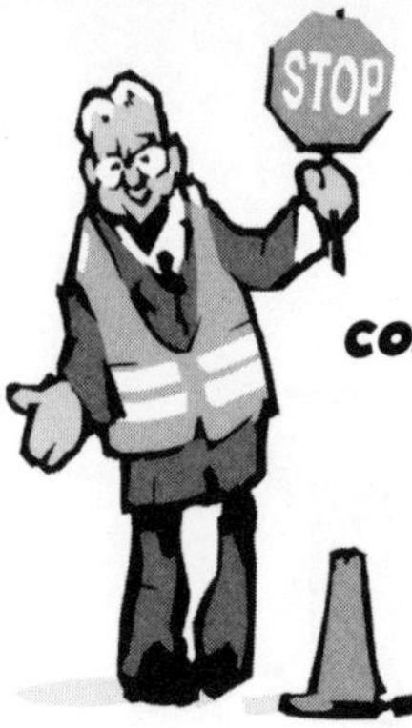
STOP

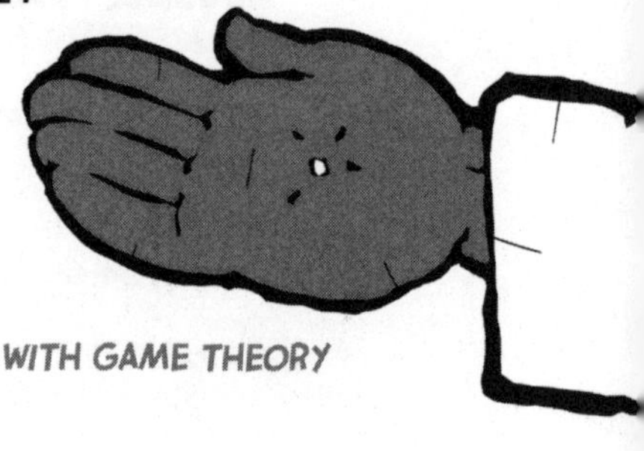

D

E

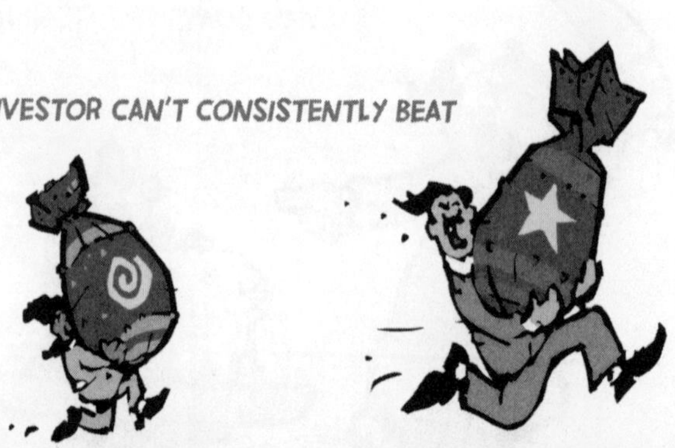

ELASTICITY

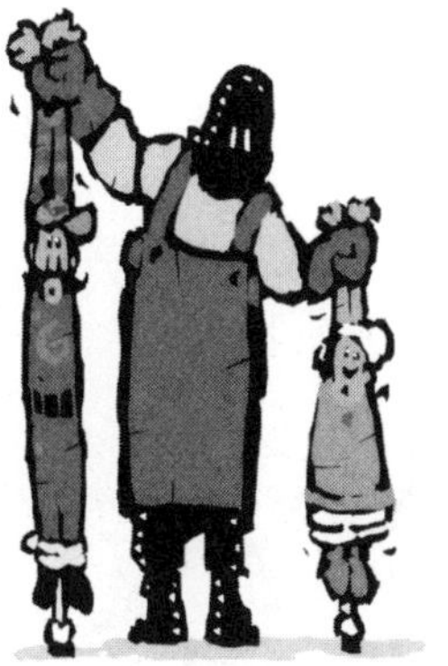

A FORMULA FOR MEASURING THE CHANGE IN ONE VARIABLE PRODUCED BY A CHANGE IN A DIFFERENT VARIABLE, THE X ELASTICITY OF Y MEASURES THE PERCENTAGE CHANGE IN Y PRODUCED BY A 1% INCREASE IN X: **169–80**

A **PERFECTLY ELASTIC LONG-RUN SUPPLY CURVE** MEANS THAT THE LONG-RUN COST OF PRODUCING THE 1 MILLIONTH UNIT IS THE SAME AS THE MARGINAL COST OF PRODUCING THE 100TH UNIT: **176–79**

THE **FORMULA** FOR ELASTICITY INVOLVES CALCULUS, BUT THERE ARE TWO ALGEBRAIC APPROXIMATIONS. ACCORDING TO ONE OF THESE APPROXIMATIONS, YOU CAN CALCULATE (SAY) THE PRICE ELASTICITY OF DEMAND AT POINT A (WITH PRICE P_A AND QUANTITY Q_A) BY PICKING A NEARBY POINT B ON THE DEMAND CURVE (WITH PRICE P_B AND QUANTITY Q_B) AND CALCULATING:

$$\text{ELASTICITY}_A = \frac{Q_B - Q_A}{P_B - P_A} \times \frac{P_A}{Q_A}$$

THE OTHER APPROXIMATION (CALLED THE MIDPOINT METHOD) SPECIFIES TWO POINTS (A AND B) AND CALCULATES THE ELASTICITY BETWEEN THEM AS:

$$\text{ELASTICITY}_{AB} = \frac{Q_B - Q_A}{P_B - P_A} \times \frac{P_A + P_B}{Q_A + Q_B}$$

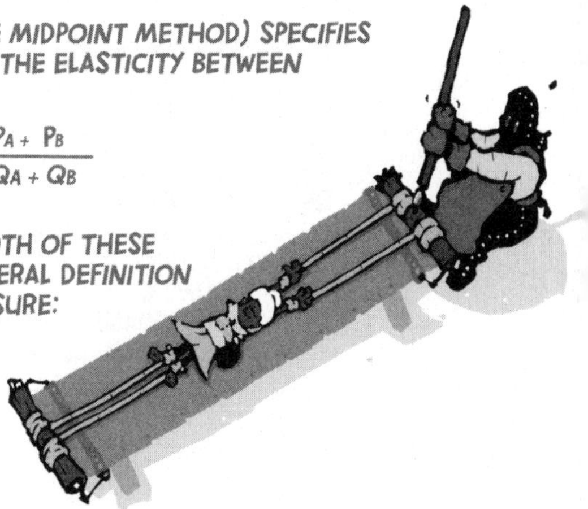

ALTHOUGH IT MAY NOT LOOK LIKE IT, BOTH OF THESE CALCULATIONS MATCH UP WITH THE GENERAL DEFINITION OF ELASTICITY BECAUSE THEY BOTH MEASURE:

$$\frac{\%\ \text{CHANGE IN Q}}{\%\ \text{CHANGE IN P}}$$

EVOLUTIONARY GAME THEORY

THE APPLICATION OF GAME THEORY TO EVOLUTION: **70**

EXPECTED VALUE

A MATHEMATICAL MEASURE OF THE "AVERAGE" OUTCOME OF A RISKY SITUATION: **42-43**

AND LAW OF LARGE NUMBERS: **46**

THE **FORMULA** IS:

$$\text{EXPECTED VALUE} = \sum_{\text{OUTCOMES } i} \text{PROBABILITY } (i) \times \text{VALUE } (i)$$

THE GREEK LETTER $\sum$ ("SIGMA") IS THE MATHEMATICAL NOTATION FOR SUMMATION, E.G.,

$$\sum_{Y=1,2,3} Y^2 = 1^2 + 2^2 + 3^2 = 14$$

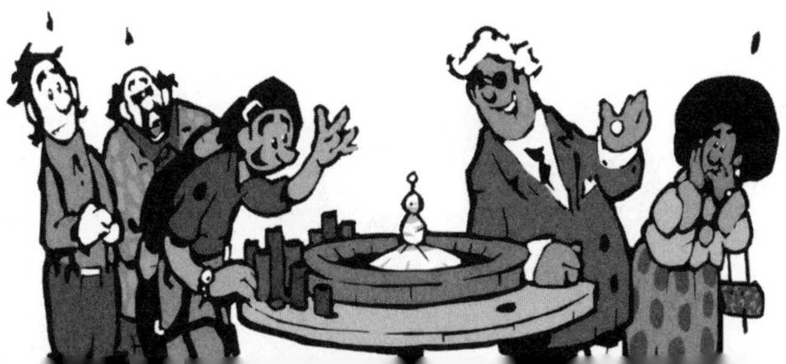

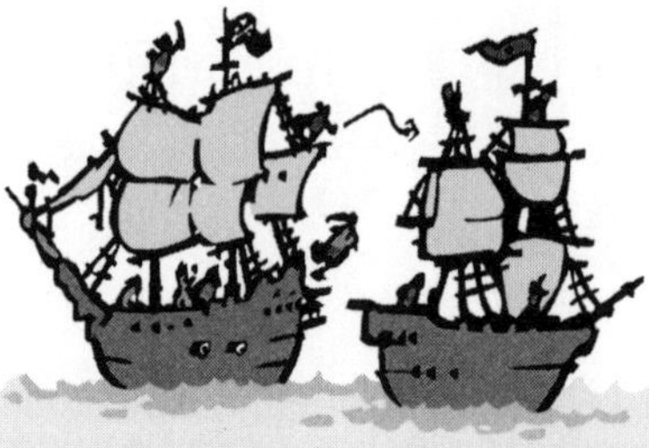

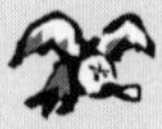

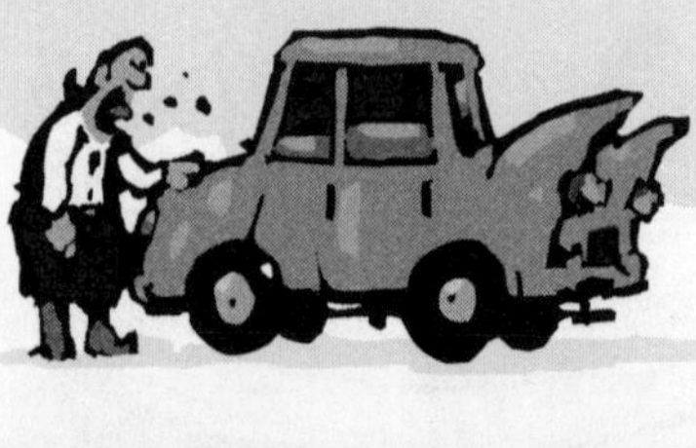

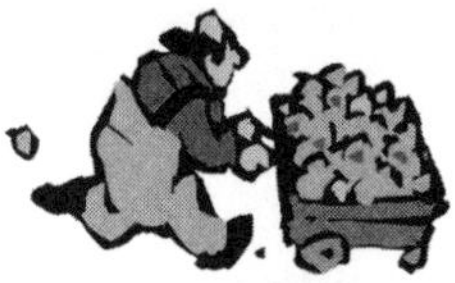

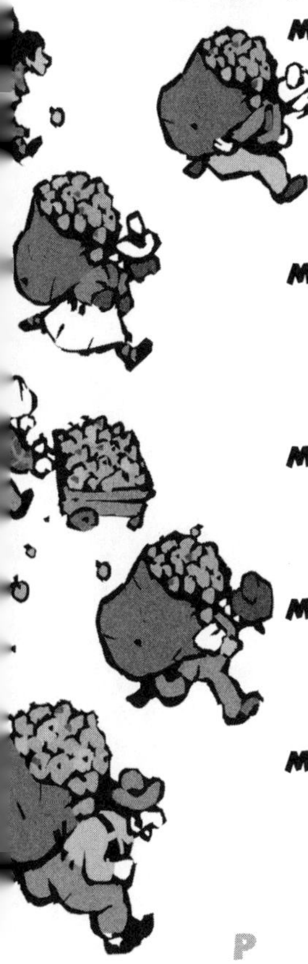

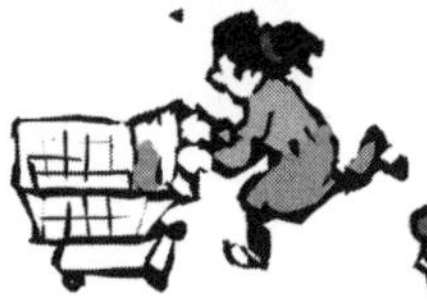

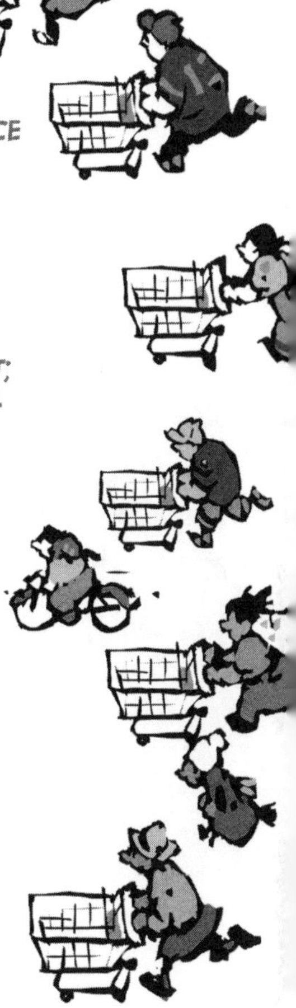

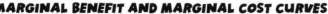

MARGINAL BENEFIT AND MARGINAL COST CURVES
CURVES THAT DESCRIBE THE EXTRA COST FOR SELLERS TO PRODUCE ONE MORE UNIT, OR THE MAXIMUM WILLINGNESS BY BUYERS TO PAY TO CONSUME ONE MORE UNIT: **158–68**
AND PERFECTLY ELASTIC LONG-RUN SUPPLY: **177**
AND THE COASE THEOREM: **182**
AND POLLUTION: **189–90**

MARKET EQUILIBRIUM PRICE
THE PRICE AT WHICH THE SUPPLY AND DEMAND CURVES INTERSECT; AT THIS PRICE, THE AMOUNT THAT BUYERS WANT TO BUY IS EQUAL TO THE AMOUNT THAT SELLERS WANT TO SELL: **136-39**
AND SEESAW: **142**

MARKET FAILURE
A SITUATION IN WHICH INDIVIDUAL OPTIMIZATION DOES NOT LEAD TO A PARETO EFFICIENT OUTCOME FOR THE GROUP AS A WHOLE, AS WITH POLLUTION OR OVERFISHING: **188-89, 199**

MARKET POWER
THE ABILITY OF A SINGLE BUYER OR SELLER TO AFFECT A MARKET BECAUSE OF ITS SIZE; CONTRAST WITH PRICE-TAKER: **120**
AND ANTITRUST POLICY: **187**

MONOPOLY AND MONOPSONY
A MARKET WITH ONLY ONE SELLER (**MONOPOLY**) OR ONLY ONE BUYER (**MONOPSONY**). THESE ARE THE MOST EXTREME FORMS OF MARKET POWER: **120**
MONOPOLY PRICING: **199**

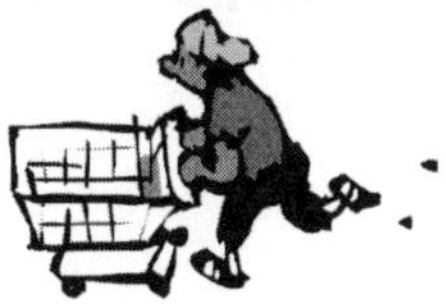

P

PARETO
THREE TERMS NAMED AFTER ITALIAN ECONOMIST VILFREDO PARETO. ONE OUTCOME IS A **PARETO IMPROVEMENT** OVER ANOTHER IF SWITCHING MAKES AT LEAST ONE PERSON BETTER OFF AND MAKES NOBODY WORSE OFF. ANY PARTICULAR OUTCOME IS EITHER **PARETO INEFFICIENT** OR **PARETO EFFICIENT** DEPENDING ON WHETHER THERE IS OR IS NOT ANY **PARETO IMPROVEMENT** OVER IT, I.E., ON WHETHER THERE IS OR IS NOT ANOTHER OUTCOME THAT MAKES AT LEAST ONE PERSON BETTER OFF WITHOUT MAKING ANYBODY WORSE OFF: **80–86**
AND COASE THEOREM: **87**
AND PRISONERS' DILEMMA: **95–96**
AND COMPETITIVE MARKETS: **183–84**

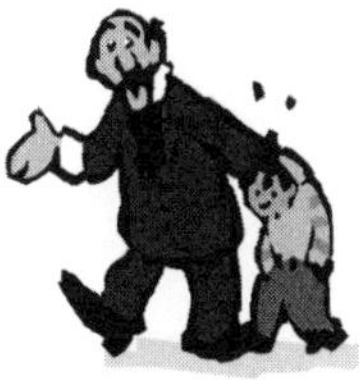

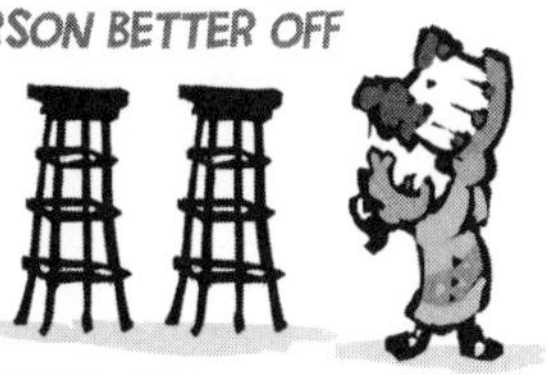

PAYOFF MATRIX
A VISUAL REPRESENTATION OF SIMULTANEOUS-MOVE GAMES: **90**

PRESENT VALUE
THE AMOUNT OF MONEY YOU NEED TO PUT IN THE BANK TODAY IN ORDER TO FINANCE ONE OR MORE FUTURE PAYMENTS: **32**

PRICE ELASTICITY
SEE ELASTICITY.

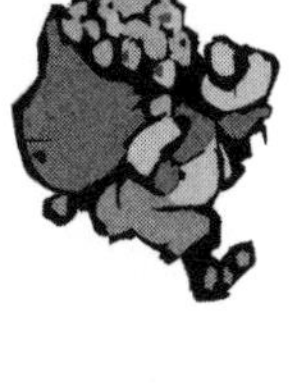

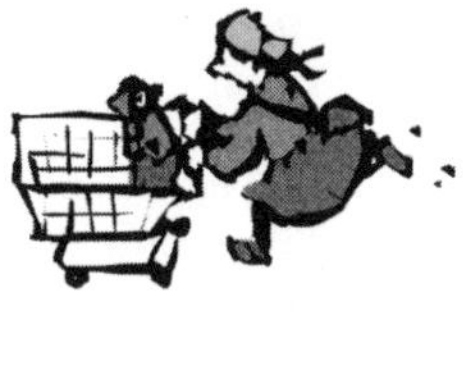

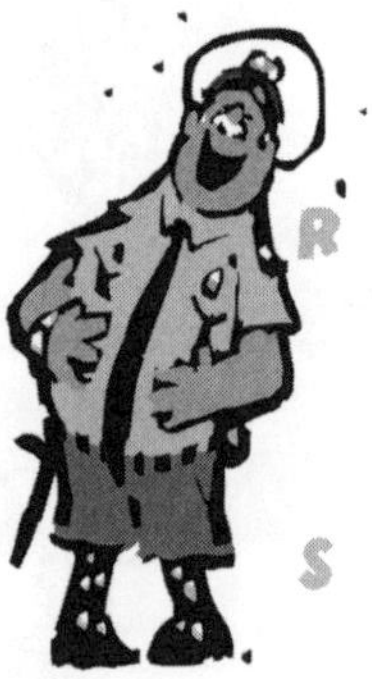

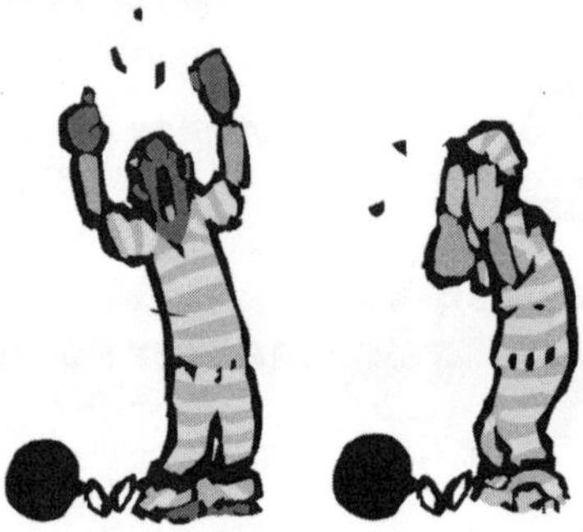

R

S

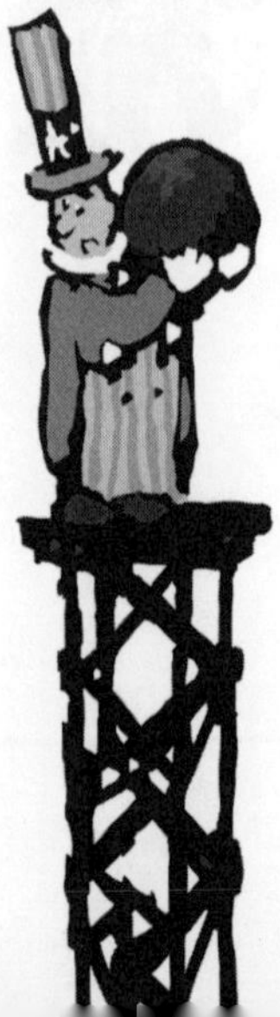

T

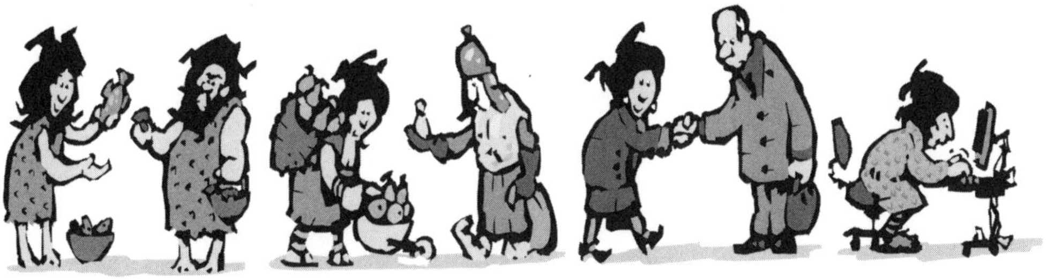

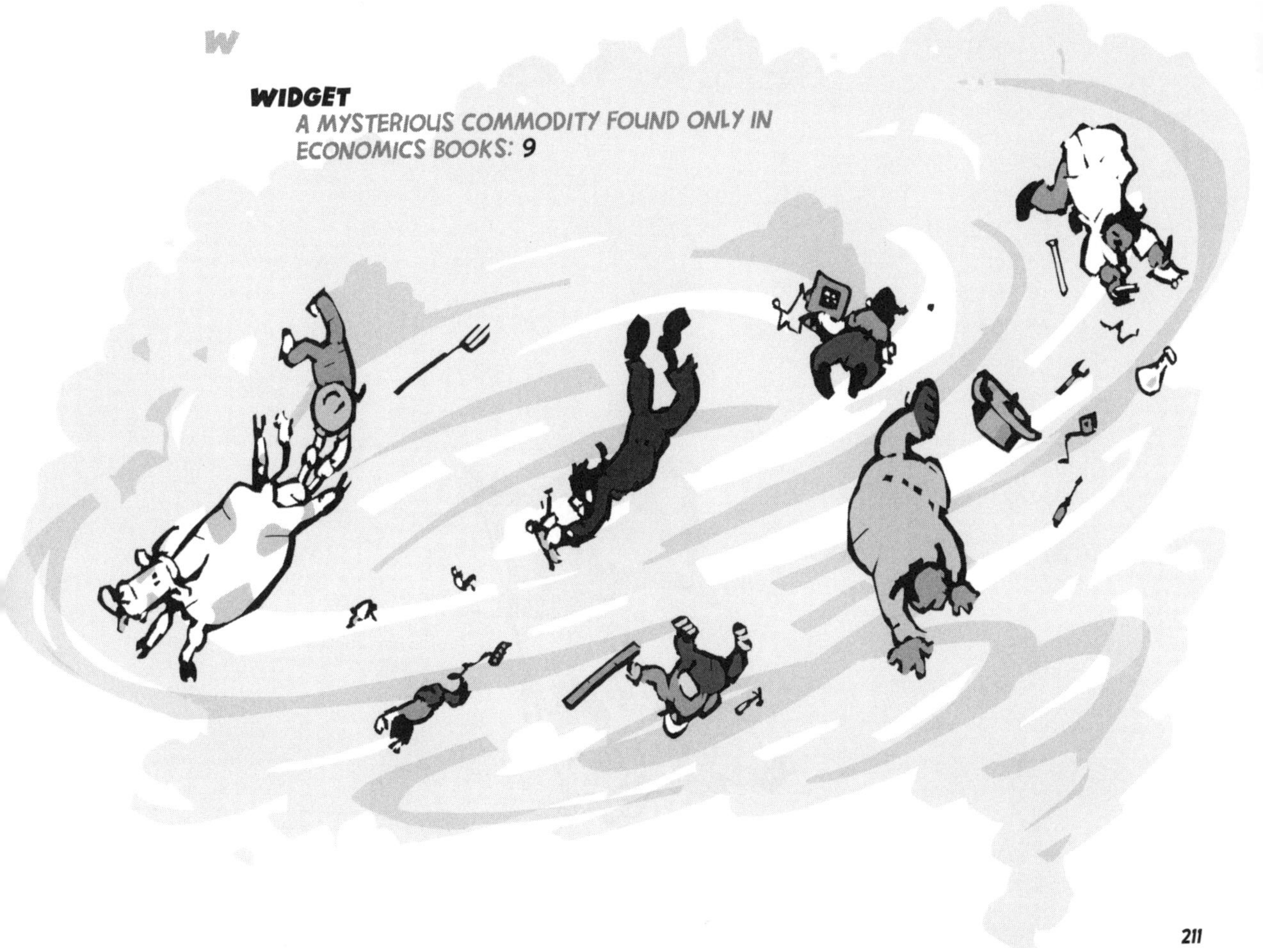

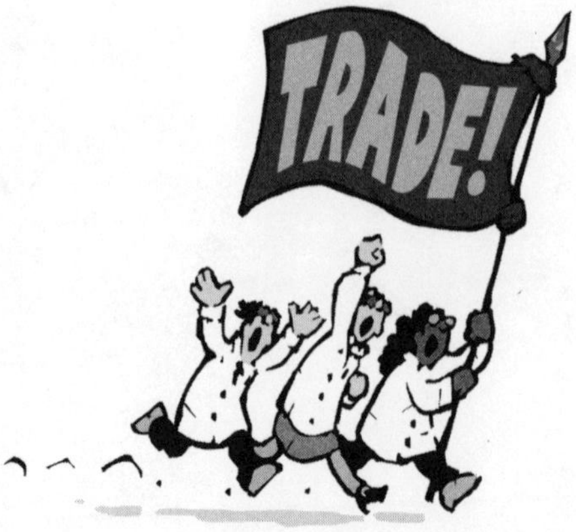
TRADE!